Waiting for Josiah

The Judges

Philippe Guillaume

T & T CLARK INTERNATIONAL
A Continuum imprint
LONDON • NEW YORK

Copyright © 2004 T&T Clark International
A Continuum imprint

Published by T&T Clark International
The Tower Building, 11 York Road, London SE1 7NX
15 East 26th Street, Suite 1703, New York, NY 10010

www.tandtclark.com

British Library Cataloguing-in-Publication Data
A catalogue record for this book is available from the British Library

Library of Congress Cataloging-in-Publication Data
A catalogue record for this book is available from the Library of Congress

Typeset by TMW Typesetting, Sheffield
Printed on acid-free paper in Great Britain by Cromwell Press, Trowbridge, Wiltshire

ISBN 0-8264-6988-4

JOURNAL FOR THE STUDY OF THE OLD TESTAMENT
SUPPLEMENT SERIES
385

CONTENTS

PREFACE

This study was presented at the Faculty of Theology of the University of Geneva as doctoral thesis. It was prepared under the supervision of Professor Albert de Pury. It also benefited from comments by Professors Françoise Smyth-Florentin, Ernst Axel Knauf (Bern), Konrad Schmid (Heidelberg and Zürich), and Hermann Michael Niemann (Rostock). I wish to express my thanks to all of them for their benevolence, their time and their stimulating guidance.

ABBREVIATIONS

AASF	Annales Academiae Scientarium Fennicae
AAT	Aegypten und Altes Testament
AB	Anchor Bible
ABD	D.N. Freedman (ed.), *The Anchor Bible Dictionary* (New York: Doubleday, 1992)
ABR	*Australian Biblical Review*
ABSA	*Annual of the British School at Athens*
AC	*Amsterdamse cahiers voor exegese en bijbelse theologie*
ACERB	*Annales du Centre d'Etudes des Religions de Bruxelles*
ADFU	Ausgrabungen der Deutschen Forschungsgemein-schaft in Uruk-Warka
ADPV	Abhandlungen des Deutschen Palästina-Vereins
AfO	*Archiv für Orientforschung*
AfR	*Archiv für Religionswissenschaft*
AJA	*American Journal of Archaeology*
AJSL	*American Journal of Semitic Languages and Literatures*
AnBib	*Analecta biblica*
ANET	J. Pritchard (ed.), *Ancient Near East in Pictures Relating to The Old Testament* (Princeton: Princeton University Press, 1950)
ANETS	Ancient Near Eastern Texts and Studies
AnOr	Analecta orientalia
AnSt	*Anatolian Studies*
AOAT	Alter Orient und Altes Testament
AOS	American Oriental Series
AOSup	Aula orientalis, Supplementa
AQ	*Anthropological Quaterly*
AS	*Acta Sumerologica*
ATANT	Abhandlungen zur Theologie des Alten und Neuen Testaments
ATD	Das Alte Testament Deutsch
ATSAT	Arbeiten zu Text und Sprache im Alten Testament
AVO	Altertumsurkunde des Vorderen Orients
BA	*Biblical Archaeologist*
BAe	*Bibliotheca Aegyptica*
BARev	*Biblical Archaeology Review*

BASOR	*Bulletin of the American Schools of Oriental Research*
BASORSup	*Bulletin of the American Schools of Oriental Research,* Supplements
BBB	Bonner Biblische Beiträge
BBVO	Berliner Beiträge zum Vorderen Orient
BCDA	*Bulletin du Centre d'Etude et de Documentation Archéologique de la Conservation de Carthage*
BCH	*Bulletin de Correspondance Hellénique*
BDB	F. Brown, S.R. Driver and C.A. Briggs, *A Hebrew and English Lexikon of the Old Testament* (Oxford: Clarendon Press, 1907)
BDBAT	Beihefte zur *Dielheimer Blätter zum Alten Testament*
BEAT	Beiträge zur Erforschung des Alten Testaments und des antiken Judentums
BETL	Bibliotheca ephemeridum theologicarum lovaniensium
BHK	R. Kittel (ed.), *Biblia hebraica* (Stuttgart: Württember-gische Bibelanstalt, 1937)
BF	Baghdader Forschungen
BHS	*Biblia hebraica stuttgartensia*
BibB	Biblische Beiträge
BibInt	*Biblical Interpretation: A Journal of Contemporary Approaches*
BIFAO	*Bulletin de l'Institut français d'archéologie orientale*
BInt	Biblical Interpretation Series
BK	Biblischer Kommentar
BK	*Bibel und Kirche*
BN	*Biblische Notizen*
BR	*Bible Review*
BibSem	Biblical Seminar
BSac	Bibliotheca sacra
BTB	*Biblical Theology Bulletin*
BWANT	Beiträge zur Wissenschaft vom Alten und Neuen Testament
BZ	*Biblische Zeitschrift*
BZAW	Beihefte zur *ZAW*
CAD	A.L. Oppenheim (ed.) *Dictionary of the Oriental Institute of the University of Chicago* (Chicago: Oriental Institute, 1964)
CBQ	*Catholic Biblical Quaterly*
CBQMS	*Catholic Biblical Quaterly,* Monograph Series
CE	*Chronique d'Egypte*
ConBOT	Coniectanea biblica, Old Testament
CoS	W.W. Hallo (ed.), *The Context of Scripture* (Leiden: E.J. Brill, 1997–2000)
CRINT	Compendia rerum Iudaicarum ad novum testamentum
DBAT	*Dielheimer Blätter zum Alten Testament*
DBSup	*Dictionaire de la Bible, Supplément*

DCPP	E. Lipinski (ed.), *Dictionnaire de la civilisation phénicienne et punique* (Turnhout: Brepols, 1992)
DDD	K. van der Torn, B. Becking and P.W. van der Horst (eds.), *Dictionary of Deities and Demons in the Bible* (Leiden: E.J. Brill, 1995)
DThR	Dissertationen Theologische Reihe
EA	W.L. Moran, *The Amarna Letters* (Baltimore / London: The Johns Hopkins University Press, 1992)
EB	Etudes Bibliques
EC	*Estudios Clásicos*
EF	Erlanger Forschungen
EPR	Etudes préliminaires aux religions orientales dans l'empire romain
EsE	*Ephemeris für semitische Epigraphik*
FAT	Forschungen zum AT
FO	*Folia Orientalia*
FRLANT	Forschungen zur Religion und Literatur des Alten und Neuen Testaments
FVCb	*Foi et Vie. Cahiers bibliques*
FzB	Forschung zur Bibel
GAAL	Göttinger Arbeitshefte zur Altorientalischen Literatur
GAT	Grundrisse zum Alten Testament
HAR	*Hebrew Annual Review*
HdO	Handbuch der Orientalistik
HKAT	Handkommentar zum AT
HR	*History of Religions*
HSAO	Heidelberger Studien zum alten Orient
HSAT	Die Heilige Schrift des Alten Testamentes
HSM	Harvard Semitic Monographs
HTR	*Harvard Theological Review*
HTS	*Hervormde Teologiese Studies*
HUCA	*Hebrew Union College Annual*
IEJ	*Israel Exploration Journal*
Int	*Interpretation*
IOS	*Israel Oriental Studies*
JAOS	*Journal of the American Oriental Society*
JARCE	*Journal of the American Research Centre in Egyptology*
JBL	*Journal of Biblical Literature*
JCS	*Journal of Cuneiform Studies*
JEA	*Journal of Egyptian Archaeology*
JHebS	*Journal of Hebrew Scriptures*
JHS	*Journal of Hellenic Studies*
JJS	*Journal of Jewish Studies*
JNES	*Journal of Near Eastern Studies*
JNSL	*Journal of Northwest Semitic Languages*

JQR	*Jewish Quaterly Review*
JRAI	*Journal of the Royal Anthropological Institute*
JSHRZ	*Jüdische Schriften aus hellenistisch-römischer Zeit*
JSNTSup	*Journal for the Study of the New Testament,* Supplement Series
JSOT	*Journal for the Study of the Old Testament*
JSOTSup	*Journal for the Study of the Old Testament,* Supplement Series
JSS	*Journal of Semitic Studies*
JTS	*Journal of Theological Studies*
KB	L. Koehler and W. Baumgartner (eds.), *Lexicon in Veteris Testamenti libros* (Leiden: E.J. Brill, 1953).
KHAT	Kurzer Hand-Kommentar zum Alten Testament
LAPO	Littératures Anciennes du Proche Orient
LCL	Loeb Classical Library
LTK	*Lexikon für Theologie und Kirche*
NABU	*Nouvelles archéologiques brèves et utilitaires*
NBL	M. Görg and B. Lang (eds.), *Neues Bibel-Lexikon* (Zürich: Benzinger Verlag, 1992)
NEA	*Near Eastern Archeology*
NEAEHL	E. Stern (ed.), *New Encyclopedia of Archeological Excavations in the Holy Land* (Jerusalem: Israel Exploration Society & Carta, 1993)
NEB	Die neue echter Bibel
NSKAT	Neuer Stuttgarter Kommentar Altes Testament
OA	Orbis Academicus
OBO	Orbis biblicus et orientalis
OCD	*Oxford Classical Dictionary*
OIP	Oriental Institute Publications; Chicago, Il.
OLA	Orientalia Lovaniensia Analecta
OrAnt	*Oriens antiquus*
OTE	*Old Testament Essays*
OTG	Old Testament Guides
OTS	*Oudtestamentische Studiën*
OTSt	*Old Testament Studies*
PEQ	*Palestine Exploration Quaterly*
PW	A.F. von Pauly and G. Wissowa (eds.), *Real-Encyclopädie der classischen Altertumswissenchaft* (Stuttgart: Metzler, 1894–)
QD	Quaestiones Disputatae
RA	*Revue d'assyriologie et d'archéologie orientale*
RAI	*Rencontre Assyriologique Internationale*
RB	*Revue biblique*
RBPH	*Revue belge de philologie et d'histoire*
Rel	*Revue des études latines*
RGG	H.D. Betz (ed.), *Die Religion in Geschichte und Gegenwart,* 1 (Tübingen: J.C.B. Mohr, 1998)

RHPR	*Revue d'histoire et de philosophie religieuse*
RIMA	Royal Inscriptions of Mesopotamia, Assyrian Period
RQ	*Revue de Qumran*
RSF	*Revista di Storia della Filosofia*
SAA	State Archives of Assyria
SAAB	*State Archives of Assyria Bulletin*
SAACT	State Archives of Assyria, Cuneiform Texts
SAAS	State Archives of Assyria, Supplements
SAM	Sheffield Archaeological Monographs
SBib	Subsidia Biblica
SBFLA	*Studii Biblici Franciscani analecta*
SBL	Society of Biblical Literature
SBLDS	SBL Dissertation Series
SBLSBS	SBL Sources for Biblical Study
SBLSCS	SBL Septuagint and Cognate Studies
SBLSP	SBL Seminar Papers
SBLSS	SBL Semeia Studies
SBS	Stuttgarter Bibelstudien
SBT	Studien zu den Boghazköy Texten
SCS	Septuagint and Cognate Studies
SeB	*Sémiotique et Bible*
SFS	Studia Francisci Scholten memoriae dicata
SH	Scripta Hierosolymitana
SHANE	Studies in the History of the Ancient Near East
SHAP	Studies in the History and Archeology of Palestine
SHCANE	Studies in the History and Culture of the Ancient Near East
SJOT	*Scandinavian Journal of the Old Testament*
SoSR	*Social Science Research*
SOTSMS	Society for Old Testament Study Monograph Series
SP	Studia Phoenicia
SSR	*Studi Storico-Religiosi*
ST	*Studia Theologica*
STDJ	Studies on the Texts of the Desert of Judah
StPo	Studia Pohl
SWBA	Social World of Biblical Antiquity
TA	*Tel Aviv*
TBü	Theologische Bücherei
TCS	Texts from Cuneiform Sources
TeKon	*Texte und Kontexte*
THAT	E. Jenni and C. Westermann (eds.), *Theologisches Handwörterbuch zum Alten Testament* (Munich: Chr. Kaiser Verlag, 1971-76)
ThB	Theologische Beiträge
ThL	*Theologische Literaturzeitung*
ThR	*Theological Review*

TQ	*Theologische Quartalschrift*
TUAT	Texte aus der Umwelt des Alten Testaments
TuK	*Theologie und Kultus*
TynBul	*Tyndale Bulletin*
TZ	*Theologische Zeitschrift*
UF	*Ugarit-Forschungen*
ÜS	*Überlielieferungsgeschichtliche Studien*
VT	*Vetus Testamentum*
VTSup	*Vetus Testamentum*, Supplements
VWGT	*Veröffentlichungen der Wissenschaftlichen Gesellschaft für Theologie*
WMANT	Wissenschaftliche Monographien zum Alten und Neuen Testament
WS	*Wiener Studien*
WTJ	*Westminster Theological Journal*
WVDOG	Wissenschaftliche Veröffentlichungen der Deutschen Orient-Gesellschaft
ZA	*Zeitschrift für Assyriologie*
ZAH	*Zeitschrift für Althebraistik*
ZAW	*Zeitschrift für die alttestamentliche Wissenschaft*
ZÄSA	*Zeitschrift für Ägyptische Sprache und Altertumskunde*
ZDPV	*Zeitschrift des deutschen Palästina-Vereins*

INTRODUCTION

Why another monograph on the book of Judges, while the last decade has produced a rich harvest of important studies on this book? Uwe Becker's *Richterzeit und Königtum* (1990)[1] is the most quoted reference with Barnabas Lindars' *Judges 1–5* (1995).[2] But both are incomplete: Becker skips over the Samson cycle and Lindars only reached Judges 5. Moreover, these two masterly studies are set within the framework of the theory of Martin Noth's Deuteronomistic History. The aim of the present work is precisely the opposite, to read the book of Judges outside the mental framework of Noth's Deuteronomistic History.

A New Starting Point

The original intention of this work was to read *Judges* as much as possible as an independent work, without reference to other Biblical books, specially Joshua and Samuel, in order to test the possibility of reading one of the books of the Former Prophets without referring to the Deuteronomistic History. Halfway through the process, Konrad Schmid provided a most unexpected support for this attempt.[3] The most important result of his work pertaining to the book of Judges is that *Judges* was inserted between *Joshua* and *1 Samuel* during the early Persian period rather than during the exile as Noth's partisans are still claiming. In light of Schmid's conclusion, *Judges* appears as one of the weakest points of the Nothian fortress, and the most obvious point to attack in order to undermine the exilic Deuteronomistic History.

---

1. U. Becker, *Richterzeit und Königtum* (BZAW, 192; Berlin: W. de Gruyter, 1990).

2. B. Lindars, *Judges 1–5: A New Translation and Commentary* (Edinburgh: T. & T. Clark, 1995).

3. K. Schmid, *Erzväter und Exodus* (WMANT, 81; Neukirchen-Vluyn: Neukirchener Verlag, 1999). Also E.A. Knauf, 'Die Priesterschrift und die Geschichten der Deuteronomisten', in Th. Römer (ed.), *The Future of the Deuteronomistic History* (BETL, 147; Leuven: Peteers, 2000), pp. 101-118 (111).

From Sitz in der Literatur to Sitz im Leben

The last decade has been rich in important monographs coming from less Nothian circles, although most of them work, consciously or not, within the framework of an exilic historiography. Yairah Amit has been a pioneer in reading *Judges* in the light of polemics, even hidden polemics.[4] Jichan Kim concentrated on the Samson cycle (1993)[5] while Robert H. O'Connell has provided an extremely detailed rhetorical analysis of the entire book (1995).[6] The book of Judges being particularly rich in liberating and libe rated feminine figures (Achsah, Deborah, Jael, and Samson's mother), feminist exegesis has produced the Feminist companion to Judges (1993).[7] Theological commentaries have recently been published, one on the Gideon and Abimelech cycles by Wolfgang Bluedorn and another one on Judges 17–18 by Uwe Bauer.[8] Mark Zvi Brettler has just published a study that seems to cover the whole book of Judges.[9] According to the available summary, Brettler contends that *Judge*s is a political tract arguing for the legitimacy of Davidic kingship.

However, the present study is not attempting to offer another exegetical technique, it is neither feminist, nor rhetorical. It certainly owes a debt to Amit as the analysis of ideology plays an important role in it. But it does not agree with her concept of 'hidden' polemics.[10]

After the excesses of diachronic exegesis, and after the healthy reaction of synchronic exegetes who study the text as it now stands, the author believes that it is now possible to a steer a middle course. Looking for older forms of the text does not necessarily lead to disrespect of its final

    4.   Y. Amit, *The Book of Judges: The Art of Editing* (The Biblical Encyclopedia Library, 6; Jerusalem—Tel Aviv: Mosad Bialik & Chaim Rosenberg School of Jewish Studies, Tel Aviv University, 1992), in Hebrew, English review by M. Polliack, *VT* 45 (1995), pp. 392-98.
    5.   J. Kim, *The Structure of the Samson Cycle* (Kampen: Kok Pharos, 1993).
    6.   R.H. O'Connell, *The Rhetoric of the Book of Judges* (VTSup, 63; Leiden: E.J. Brill, 1995).
    7.   A. Brenner (ed.), *A Feminist Companion to Judges* (Sheffield: JSOT Press, 1993).
    8.   W. Bluedorn, *Yahweh versus Baalism: A Theological Reading of the Gideon-Abimelech Narrative* (JSOTSup, 320; Sheffield: Sheffield Academic Press, 2001); U.F.W. Bauer, *Warum nur uebertretet ihr SEIN Geheiss: Eine synchrone Exegese der Anti-Erzaehlung Ri 17-18* (BEAT, 45; Frankfurt: Lang, 1998).
    9.   M.Z. Brettler, *The Book of Judges* (London: Routledge, 2001).
    10.   Y. Amit, *Hidden Polemics in Biblical Narrative* (BInt, 25; Leiden: E.J. Brill, 2000).

form and function. On the contrary, refusing to take into account the tensions that the text presents to its reader may finally be another kind of disrespect or indirect support for fundamentalist approaches to the Bible. If God is no liar, his word must have been revealed through time and fierce controversies, or there is no way to account for the blatant contradictions that the Bible conveys. The editors transmitted a text that preserved the traces of the work of their predecessors, without subjecting it to any heavy-handed harmonization process. The text itself begs for diachronic operations.

The great strides taken by archaeology now allow exegesis to move from 'Biblical paraphrase'[11] to interaction with the fast growing corpus of extra-biblical texts and even venture outside the philologist realm to take into account the material sources revealed by archaeology. Although the Bible has been dethroned from its place of sole provider of information on the history of the ancient Near East, exegesis cannot ignore the new picture that is arising from excavations across the Levant. Exegesis has to be subjected to the external control provided by historical reconstruction in order to escape the tyranny of dogmatic systems. Because the Bible was produced in the midst of very concrete and often dramatic events, revelation has now got to be unearthed.[12] It has to be dug out of archaeological sites. For this reason, for each literary development of the text one should look for a precise historical context. Ideological intentions are more reliable than style differences when it comes to separating successive editions.

This study is based on a hypothetical reconstruction of the unfurling process of the text rather than a quest for the original one. It will therefore privilege the periods where a lot is known about the concrete situation in Israel and Judah. The Assyrian period is the most important one for this purpose, rather than Solomon's tenth century BCE or the 'exilic' period, two useful shady eras of predilection for non-historical fancies.[13]

11. G. Garbini, *History and Ideology in Ancient Israel* (New York: Crossroad, 1988), p. 7.

12. I. Finkelstein and N.A. Silberman, *The Bible Unearthed: Archaeology's New Vision of Ancient Israel and the Origin of its Sacred Texts* (New York: Free Press, 2001).

13. B. Halpern, 'Sociological Comparativism and the Theological Imagination', in M. Fishbane (ed.), *Sha'arei Talmon: Studies in the Bible, Qumran and the Ancient Near East* (Winona Lake: Eisenbrauns, 1992), pp. 53-68 (55).

Chapter 1

THE BOOK OF SAVIOURS REDISCOVERED: JUDGES 3–9

State of Research

Before Martin Noth, the bulk of critical exegesis on Judges was mainly devoted to revealing the literary sources of the Pentateuch as if the book of Judges could be read and understood only in continuation of the Pentateuch.[1] Noth freed research on this book from the yoke imposed by this theoretical model in order to turn its quest for the genesis of Judges towards a new horizon. Considering the first drafts of Deuteronomy, Joshua, Judges, Samuel and Kings as a single work, the Deuteronomistic Historiography (DH), and showing that this ensemble was the very first literary presentation of the history of Israel from Moses to the last king of Judah, Noth put an end to the quest of direct literary links with Genesis, Exodus, Leviticus and Numbers.[2] According to him, Deuteronomy alone remained connected to the historiography he thought to have discovered, as this book provided the vocabulary and the ideology for the historiography. Arguing that his historiography was born in the wake of the fall of Jerusalem in 586, Noth offered a firm *terminus a quo* for this ambitious work, during the exile and not before. Of course, Noth did not deny that DH gathered many old traditions, some of those already organized into small literary units.[3] But Noth reckoned that the author (DtrH) was creative in organizing the old heterogeneous traditions along an unbroken chronological framework. According to Noth, DtrH inserted a historical

1. See the synoptic tables produced by W. Nowack, *Richter-Ruth* (HKAT 1.4; Göttingen: 1900), pp. XXIV-XXVIII (J, E, J$_2$, E$_2$, P, R$_{je}$, Rd, Pp) and O. Eissfeldt, *Die Quellen des Richterbuches* (Leipzig: J.C. Hinrichs, 1925), pp. 1*-58* (Laienschrift, J, E).

2. M. Noth, *Überlieferungsgeschichtliche Studien: Die sammelnden und bearbeitenden Geschichtswerke im Alten Testament* (Darmstadt: Max Niemeyer, 3rd edn, 1943), pp. 3-5.

3. Othniel, 'Barak, the Ark and the Saul Traditions: Noth', *ÜS*, pp. 50-51.

period of the Judges between the period of Joshua's conquest and the period of the monarchy. This way to organize Israel's traditions proved so compelling that most modern histories of Israel are still organized accordingly.[4] Compared to its predecessors, Noth's work was so forceful that it gained immediate acceptance and still dominates the field. Although this study resolutely abandons Noth's DH, its debt to Noth is real.

Once Noth had delineated the general structure of the historiography, his successors set out to identify and to analyze the material supposed to have been received by DtrH in more detail. It was thus necessary to identify the marks of the editorial work.[5] However, with closer scrutiny, that editorial material did not appear to be homogeneous. For instance, Smend was led to distinguish between two consecutive editorial stages in Joshua and at the beginning of Judges, because two opposite conceptions of the conquest appeared in those passages.[6] In Samuel and Kings, it is the attitude towards David and the monarchy that led F.M. Cross to discern two stages.[7] The date of those different editions effectively split exegetes into two camps: the American School of Cross and in Germany the Göttingen School around R. Smend. For Cross, the first edition of DH was to be dated under Josiah, while for Smend and his students, the editorial process, even at its earliest phase, did not start before 586 BCE.[8] New acronyms for the successive editions had to be found to account for the increasing complexity of the different theories.[9] This brief overview has to be curtailed in order to concentrate on the situation for Judges.

4.   G.W. Ahlström, *The History of Ancient Palestine from the Paleolithic Period to Alexander's Conquest* (JSOTSup, 146; Sheffield: JSOT Press, 1993), pp. 371-90; W.C. Kaiser Jr, *A History* [sic] *of Israel from the Bronze Age through the Jewish Wars* (Nashville: Broadman & Holman, 1998), pp. 175-202.

5.   M. Weinfeld, *Deuteronomy and Deuteronomistic School* (Oxford: Clarendon Press, 1972), established a catalogue of typical Dtr expressions.

6.   Accomplished against unaccomplished conquest: R. Smend, 'Das Gesetz und die Völker: Ein Beitrag zur deuteronomischen Redaktionsgeschichte', in H.W. Wolff (ed.), *Probleme biblischer Theologie* (München: Chr. Kaiser Verlag, 1971), pp. 494-509.

7.   F.M. Cross, 'The Themes of the Book of Kings and the Structure of the Deuteronomic History', in F.M. Cross (ed.), *Canaanite Myth and Hebrew Epic* (Cambridge, MA: Harvard University Press, 1973), pp. 274-89.

8.   Th. Römer and A. de Pury, 'Deuteronomistic Historiography (DH): History of Research and Related Issues', in A. de Pury and Th. Römer (eds.) *Israel Constructs its History* (JSOTSup, 306; Sheffield: Sheffield Academic Press, 2000), pp. 24-141 (67-68).

9.   See Römer and de Pury, 'Deuteronomistic Historiography', pp. 69-72.

Compositional History of Judges According to Noth

Noth affirmed that DtrH had combined two kinds of sources in Judges: heroic tales from various tribes and a list of 'minor' judges. Noth thought that the stories of heroes had already been assembled into a pre-Dtr source that included the stories of Ehud,[10] Deborah (prose and poem) and Gideon, plus the basis of the Jephthah story and part of the Samson cycle. To that source, DtrH would have just added the length of the foreign domination and substituted it to the original introduction of the heroic tales. The link between the two sources would have been Jephthah as this figure belonged both to the list of 'minor' judges (this problem will be discussed in Chapter 5) and to the autonomous heroic cycle. According to Noth, the insertion of the heroic tales into the list of judges broke its unity and turned it into a seemingly secondary element.[11]

Richter Discovers a Retterbuch

In 1962, Wolfgang Richter set out to analyze the collection of heroic tales outlined by Noth. With a formidable critique of literary genres (*Gattungskritik*), Richter isolated a *Retterbuch,* a book of Saviours within Judg. 3–9. This collection was made up of the narratives of Ehud, Barak, Gideon and Abimelech, although each story could, prior to its integration, go back to separate legends. Richter discerned in his *Retterbuch* an anti-monarchic bias pointing to a date of composition under the reign of Jehu (841–814 BCE). The wars of Yhwh, anti-monarchism and the various divine encounters inserted into the old legends were, in his eyes, best understood in this historical context. So was the enlargement of the geographical frame to all Israel.[12] According to Richter, only the tale of Ehud kept its original legendary thread, as the creator of the *Retterbuch* had just provided it with a narrative frame leading to the participation of all the children of Israel in the war of Yhwh (Judg. 3.27-30). The story of Barak (Judg. 4–5) was also received as an elaborate tradition. But Judg. 6–9 bears traces of a wider editorial activity. The main additions are placed in front of the traditional material (before Judg. 7.11b and 8.5) although in ch. 8 some are found in the middle of the story. Judges 7.9-11a replaces the tradition while Judg.

---

10. Names and quotations will follow the spelling of the Revised Standard Version of the Bible copyrighted 1971 and 1952 by the division on Christian Education of the National Council of the Churches of Christ in the USA.

11. Noth, *ÜS*, pp. 47-48.

12. W. Richter, *Traditionsgeschichtliche Untersuchungen zum Richterbuch* (BBB, 18; Bonn: Peter Hanstein, 1966), pp. 319-43.

8.10-13 transforms it. The insertion of Judg. 6.11b-17 led to the loss of the beginning of the old story concerning the Baal altar and, in ch. 9, some material was lost when Judg. 9.41-45 was added. Judges 9.1-6, 7, 21 and possibly Judg. 8.1-3 were reorganised along a clear geographical order:

- Benjamin in the South with Ehud (Judg. 3.15)
- Naphtali and Zebulun in the North with Barak (Judg. 4.6, 10; 5.18)
- Abiezer in the Centre with Gideon (Judg. 6.11) alongside Asher, Manasseh (Judg. 7.23) and Ephraim (Judg. 8.2).

In Judg. 7.15, the 'camp of Israel' replaces the various tribes found in Judg. 3.13; 6.2-4, 14-15. In this way the different legends are now serving an overall Israelite interpretation. The monarchy is understood to signal the end of the wars of Yhwh. A king has replaced saviour and *nagid*. Abimelech is the paradigm of the king who takes the place of the ideal saviour called to lead the war of Yhwh. Since Deborah the prophetess encourages the saviour, the author is close to the prophetic circles of Israel. Richter sees the murder of the 70 sons of Gideon (Judg. 9.5) as a reference to the assassination of the 70 sons of Ahab (2 Kgs 10.7) and dates the composition of the *Retterbuch* to the reign of Jehu. This date is confirmed by the absence of any saviour from Gilead (Richter did not include Jephthah in the *Retterbuch*) as it is under Jehu that Israel lost the Gilead to the kingdom of Damascus (2 Kgs 10.33).[13]

The lasting merit of Richter is to have identified a pre-Dtr collection of saviour narratives. Before him, a few authors had suggested the existence of such a work,[14] whose finality had deemed to range from a theology of history[15] to a war manual.[16] Richter, having studied the framing material of the saviour narratives,[17] found that the *Retterbuch* went through two additional editions (Rdt1 added the frame: Judg. 3.12-15, 30; 4.1-3, 24; 5.31; 6.1-10; 8.28 and Rdt2 added Othniel: 3.7-11) before being integrated into Noth's Deuteronomistic History shortly after the fall of Jerusalem in 586 BCE.

13. Richter, *Traditionsgeschichtliche Untersuchungen*, p. 340.

14. G.L. Studer, *Das Buch der Richter* (Bern: 1835).

15. H. Cazelles, 'Le livre des Juges', in H. Cazelles (ed.), *DBSup* (Paris: Letouzey & Ané, 1949), p. 1401.

16. F. Dornseiff, 'Das Buch der Richter. I. Die literarische Absicht' *AfO* 14 (1944), pp. 319-28.

17. W. Richter, *Die Bearbeitungen des 'Retterbuches', in der deuteronomischen Epoche* (BBB, 21; Bonn: Peter Hanstein, 1964).

Beyerlin on the Framework

While Richter was identifying the *Retterbuch,* Walter Beyerlin published an article on Judg. 6–8[18] and another on the editorial frame of the stories of judges.[19] Beyerlin pointed to the differences within the different material framing the narratives of Judges. He clearly separated the framework that structures the three narrative cycles (Judg. 3.12-15, 30; 4.1-3, 24; 5.31; 6.1-10; 8.28) from the introductory section in Judg. 2.11-19 (the 'schema'). He also showed that the account of Joshua's death in Judg. 2.6-10 could be reconciled neither with the schema nor with the two passages of condemnation, the *Rîb-Wörter* of Judg. 6.7-10 and 10.10-15. Like Richter, Beyerlin worked within the Nothian conceptual framework of DH and the pre-monarchical amphictyony; however, he concluded that these various editorial elements were not the work of DtrH but were to be attributed to many editorial stages over a large time spectrum.[20] He thus contested two widely accepted opinions, that the framework of Judges was produced in one stage (Noth) or in two stages (Budde, Eissfeldt, Cazelles) and that this framework is Deuteronomistic in style and provenience.

Beyerlin's demonstration shows that two antagonistic conceptions of the relation between God and Israel are at work in the schema (Judg. 2.11-19) and in the framework of the saviour stories (Judg. 3.12-15, 30; 4.1-3, 24; 5.31; 6.1-10; 8.28). In the framework, Yhwh sends a saviour in response to the cries of his people. These cries are significantly absent from the schema. Beyerlin rejects the usual explanation of this absence by a lacuna between Judg. 2.15 and 2.16. On the contrary, this absence of cries reveals a fundamental theological difference between the schema and the framework of the saviour stories. In the framework, God answers immediately and systematically by sending a saviour מושיע (Judg. 3.9, 15; 4.3; 6.6) while in the schema, God is moved by pity, not by cries, and sends judges שפטים instead of saviours. These theological differences, in Beyerlin's eyes, become self-evident when one notices that the recurrent formulas of the schema are nowhere to be found in the framework of the saviour stories: 'going after other gods' (Judg. 2.12, 19), 'bowing down in front of them' (Judg. 2.12, 17, 19). The schema ignores the cries and the saviours

---

18. W. Beyerlin, 'Geschichte und heilsgeschichtliche Traditionsbildung: Ein Beitrag zur Traditionsgeschichte von Richter VI-VIII', *VT* 13 (1963), pp. 1-25.

19. W. Beyerlin, 'Gattung und Herkunft des Rahmens im Richterbuch', in E. Würthwein and O. Kaiser (eds.), *Tradition und Situation, Studien zur alttestamentlichen Prophetie* (Göttingen: Vandenhoeck & Ruprecht, 1963), pp. 1-29.

20. Beyerlin, 'Gattung', pp. 28-29.

of the framework of the saviour stories because it is part of a later editorial stage bent on correcting the framework.

Within Judg. 2, the subject change between v. 10 (the generation who did not know Yhwh) and v. 11 (the people of Israel) shows that vv. 6-10 and 11-19 do not belong to the same hand. The introduction of the cries in v. 6b into v. 7a attests a secondary harmonizing stage. The opposition between the different editions is further illustrated by the additions of Judg. 6.7-10 and 10.10b-15.

Beyerlin then shows that five out of seven expressions of the framework ('to serve the Baals', 'to give into the hands of an enemy', 'to cry', 'to subdue the enemy' and the 'land in rest' formula) are related more closely to the old parts of Hosea, Jeremiah and Deuteronomy (Deut. 22; 26; 32) than to the parts that are attributed to the Dtr edition of these books.[21] The expressions 'to do evil in the sight of Yhwh' and 'the anger of Yhwh' do have parallels in Deuteronomy, but they were already in use at the beginning of the monarchy. Beyerlin understands the framework of the saviour stories as part of a liturgy used with Ps. 78, during a festival for the renewal of the amphictyonic covenant.

Beyerlin's dates were based as much on Wellhausen's Pentateuch sources as on Noth's amphictyony, two theoretical systems now obsolete. However, when Beyerlin bases his observations on the late Sumerian lamentation of Ibbisin and the Mesha stele, his argumentation has lost nothing of its validity. These texts can indeed be adduced to establish the archaic nature of the theology of the framework of the saviour stories.[22]

Although Beyerlin limited himself to the study of the editorial material and did not propose any overarching theory for the book of Judges as a whole, he concluded his article with an audacious proposal. It was not before the second century BCE that the traditions of Judges were connected with the Mosaic history through Judg. 2.11-19 and with the end of the Joshua narrative with Judg. 2.6-10.[23] This intuition went completely unheeded until the recent work of Konrad Schmid.[24] This proposal will be considered and its implications analyzed in Chapter 7 of this study.

In 1964, a year after Beyerlin's articles, Richter published a second study on Judges. Beyerlin's work is only quoted once, with a summary rejection of his attribution of the framework of the saviour stories and the

---

21. Beyerlin, 'Gattung', pp. 10-11.
22. Beyerlin, 'Gattung', p. 16.
23. Beyerlin, 'Gattung', p. 29.
24. Schmid, *Erzväter*, pp. 220, 235.

schema to different hands and of his use of the amphictyonic festival.[25] It is unfortunate that Richter did not discuss Beyerlin's proposals.

The two scholars managed, in spite of their differences, to open new horizons for the research on Judges. Whereas Beyerlin's long editorial history lacked well-defined stages, Richter's *Retterbuch* pointed to one such editorial stage, although his discovery was weakened by his adherence to Noth's DH. That presupposition indeed forced him to concentrate the bulk of the editorial work on his *Retterbuch* before 586 BCE. Therefore, the social and historical contexts of Richter's Rdt1 and Rdt2 remain theoretical, without any consistency.

The Crisis of the Pentateuch

The results of Beyerlin and Richter did not arouse much scholarly discussion, in spite of the initial favourable reception of the *Retterbuch* hypothesis. The main efforts of Old Testament exegesis were mobilized to face a more pressing challenge. As early as 1975, the Wellhausen system of the sources of the Pentateuch caved in under the assaults of John Van Seters, Rolf Rendorff, Hans Heinrich Schmid and Martin Rose.[26] The Nothian DH suddenly remained as the last standing pillar amidst the ruins of the interpretative system of the Pentateuch and the historical books. The survivors needed DH as a guideline, the time to subject it to the same devastating critique had not yet come. DH became the pivot that distinguished between exilic and postexilic material. Everything that had previously been considered as pre-exilic became suspect. The new trend was resolutely postexilic. So much so that Van Seters invented a Persian J to replace its Salomonic predecessor.[27] The narratives of Abraham, and even those of Jacob,[28] were propelled well after the exile, 586 BCE became the mirror behind which no one dared to venture.

25. Richter, *Bearbeitungen*, p. 2 n. 6.
26. J. Van Seters, *In Search of History: Historiography in the Ancient World and the Origins of Biblical History* (New Haven: Yale University Press, 1983); R. Rendtorff, *Das Überlieferungsgeschichtliche Problem des Pentateuch* (BZAW, 147; Berlin: W. de Gruyter, 1977); H.H. Schmid, *Der sogenannte Jahwist. Beobartungen und Fragen zur Pentateuchforschung* (Zürich: Theologischer Verlag, 1976); M. Rose, *Deuteronomist und Jahwist: Untersuchungen zu den Berührungspunkten beider Literaturwerke* (ATANT, 67; Zürich: Theologischer Verlag, 1981).
27. Van Seters, *In Search of History*.
28. B.J. Diebner and H. Schult, 'Thesen zu nachexilischen Entwürfen der frühen Geschichte Israels im Alten Testament', *DBAT* (1974), pp. 41-47; Rose, *Deuteronomist*.

Postexilic Pan-Deuteronomism
The diachronic studies on Judges followed suit. Becker rejects all possibilities to recover a pre-exilic collection of narratives in Judges. Becker
considers everything attributed by Richter to the author of his *Retterbuch*
as Dtr material written by DtrH. This conclusion rests on a literary analysis based on the results of the Göttingen School.[29] With so many options
predetermined, Becker could hardly reach conclusions very different from
Noth's. Predictably, Becker attributes to DtrH Judg. 2.11-19, the framework of the saviour stories and even Othniel and the other passages
attributed by Richter to the pre-exilic editions of the *Retterbuch* (Dtr1 and
Dtr2). Becker reckons that three editions between the time of Jehu and the
exile are far too many![30] Lindars follows Noth and Becker, but his
unfinished commentary does not permit to know whether he had any
precise arguments for the rejection of the *Retterbuch*.[31] This return to a
strict Nothian orthodoxy signals that a first cycle in the evolution of
exegetical hypotheses has been completed.[32] The debate is now limited to
the attribution of various parts of Judges to such sub-categories as DtrH,
DtrN and DtrP...with an unlimited number of variations, as each scholar
has his own understanding of the Dtr conglomeration. Dtr has become a
veil to cover the scholar's ignorance of the history of Israel. A recent
volume of the JSOT Supplement Series is even devoted to this rampant
pan-Deuteronomism.[33]

Some Problems with the Nothian Creed
In spite of this redoubtable rampart around 586 BCE, cracks in the wall
may indicate that change can be expected in the foreseeable future.
Diverse avenues of research have prepared the way. For instance, in spite
of the Göttingen creed, the Harvard school shows that it is possible to go
upstream, before the exile, and to date an important period of Dtr literary
production already under the reign of Josiah.[34] As for Yahwism, it is now
accepted that its exclusive character was no Dtr invention but went back,

29. See Römer and de Pury, 'Deuteronomistic Historiography', pp. 67-72.
30. Becker, *Richterzeit*, pp. 300-301.
31. Lindars, *Judges 1–5*, pp. viii, 91, 125.
32. Römer and de Pury, 'Deuteronomistic Historiography', p. 118.
33. N.F. Lohfink, 'Was there a Deuteronomistic Movement?', in L.S. Schearing
and S.L. McKenzie (eds.), *Those elusive Deuteronomists* (JSOTSup, 268; Sheffield:
Sheffield Academic Press, 1999), pp. 36-66 (37).
34. Römer and de Pury, 'Deuteronomistic Historiography', pp. 62-74.

well before Josiah, to reactionary groups during the time of Omri's dynasty.[35] Finally, the history of Israel has benefited from archaeological discoveries that provide an ever-richer historical context for the ancient Near East. Manasseh's and Josiah's seventh century BCE now appears as the peak of Judaean cultural development. Under the influence of the Assyrian Empire, Jerusalem became the undisputed centre of the kingdom of Judah.[36] In comparison, the population of Persian *Yehud* never reached a third of that of Assyrian Judah. As for Jerusalem, the numbers of its inhabitants in the Persian period never exceeded 20% of what it had been in the seventh century BCE.[37] The books of Ezra and Nehemiah illustrate the odds facing those who tried to revive Zion.

The aim is not to deny the literary activity of the Persian period, but to recover the significance of the late Assyrian period, potentially just as productive as the Persian one.[38] In fact, once the exilic straitjacket is removed from the DH landscape, the composition of the Former Prophets is freed to move upstream. On the opposite direction, the Maccabaean period also appears as another context for an intense editorial activity of prophetic literature, the last one to be sure, but not the least. The Maccabaean period becomes one of the cornerstones of the new approach to the formation of the Torah and the Prophets offered by K. Schmid which will be presented in detail in Chapter 7. Schmid believes that the book of Judges was not integrated within the DH before the second century BCE.[39] Time will tell how DH will survive the splits between the seventh and the second centuries BCE that it is increasingly subjected to.

---

35. F. Stolz, 'Monotheismus in Israel', in O. Keel (ed.), *Monotheismus im Alten Israel und seiner Umwelt* (BibB, 14; Freiburg: Schweizerisches katholisches Bibelwerk, 1980), pp. 143-84; B. Lang, *Monotheism and the Prophetic Minority* (SWBA, 1; Sheffield: Almond Press, 1983); M. Smith, *Palestinian Parties and Politics that Shaped the Old Testament* (London: SCM Press, 1987); A. de Pury, 'Erwägungen zu einem vorexilischen Stämmejahwismus', in W. Dietrich and M.A. Klopfenstein (eds.), *Ein Gott allein?* (OBO, 139; Freiburg: Universitätsverlag / Vandenhoeck & Ruprecht, 1994), pp. 413-39.

36. I. Finkelstein, 'The Archeology of the Days of Manasseh', in M.D. Coogan, J.C. Exum and L.E. Stager (eds.), *Scripture and Other Artifacts* (Louisville, KY: Westminster/John Knox Press, 1992), pp. 169-87 (177): the population of Jerusalem increased from 6 to 25 per cent of the total population of the kingdom.

37. C.E. Carter, *The Emergence of Yehud in the Persian Period: A Social and Demographic Study* (JSOTSup, 294; Sheffield: Sheffield Academic Press, 1999), p. 247.

38. Carter, *Yehud*, pp. 288, 309.

39. Schmid, *Erzväter*, p. 235.

Three Recent Voices in Favour of a Book of Saviours

The necessity of a reappraisal of the book of Saviours hypothesis was recognized during the doctoral level seminar organized by the Old Testament professors of the Universities of Fribourg, Lausanne and Geneva in 1995. The volume that followed the seminar contains the contributions of three authors arguing for the existence of an autonomous collection of saviour narratives. Römer and de Pury claim that, in spite of the work of Becker and Lindars, the hypothesis of a pre-Dtr collection is still valid because all the episodes of Judg. 3–12 are set within the geographic horizon of the Northern Kingdom: 'What Judaean Deuteronomist, whether Josianic or exilic, would have accomplished the amazing feat of ignoring so completely the familiar setting of the kingdom of Judah, if he was really the author of these accounts?'[40] Indeed, Judah appears only in the stories of Othniel (Judg. 3.7-11) and Samson (Judg. 13–16) both framing an Israelite core ranging from Ehud to Jephthah (Judg. 3–12). In an article published in the same book, Knauf offers an original date for the composition of this collection of saviour stories. Based on the same geographical observation, he affirms that this book 'which evidently seeks paradigms of deliverance from foreign oppression (without any king of Israel being involved), could definitely have been composed at Bethel after 720 BCE'.[41]

It is now clear that Becker and Lindars did not succeed in burying Richter's *Retterbuch*. Noth's hypothesis of an exilic DH may one day lose its popularity, like the pre-monarchical Israelite amphictyony, another famous Nothian hypothesis. In the mean time, a reconsideration of Beyerlin's and Richter's conclusions on this collection of deliverance stories is in order.

On the Trail of the Book of Saviours

If the quest for a pre-Judaean collection of saviour stories is to be renewed, we have first to go back to Richter's Israelite *Retterbuch* and to analyze its outline. The Othniel story will be examined in Chapter 2 as its geographical context clearly indicates a Judaean vantage point. The working hypothesis of the study will be Knauf's hypothesis of an Israelite book

---

40. Römer and de Pury, 'Deuteronomistic Historiography', pp. 118-19.

41. E.A. Knauf, 'Does "Deuteronomistic Historiography" Exist?', in A. de Pury and Th. Römer (eds.), *Israel Constructs its History* (JSOTSup, 306; Sheffield: Sheffield Academic Press, 2000), pp. 388-98 (396).

of Saviours composed in Bethel around 720 BCE. The tales of Ehud, Shamgar, Barak, Gideon and Abimelech are embraced in one glance, using 720 BCE as reference point. It will then be possible to evaluate the value of Knauf's hypothesis.

The originality and coherence of the collection are best revealed, as Beyerlin has shown, in the way it is re-interpreted and distorted by the introductory passage of Judg. 2.11-19 which will be referred to as the 'schema' from now on. This schema presents the stories of the Israelite saviours as an unbroken chain of transgression (Judg. 2.11) and desertion of Yhwh (Judg. 2.12-13) by Israel in order to follow other gods. Yhwh reacts by giving up his people into the hands of an external enemy who invades and oppresses the land. Yhwh's hand is then at work for Israel's misfortune (Judg. 2.15). Once the distress is extreme, Yhwh calls judges who deliver Israel from the oppressors (Judg. 2.16). This cycle of oppression and deliverance has nevertheless no lasting effect: the Israelites refuse to listen to the judges and continue to serve other gods (Judg. 2.17). The desertions are aggravated by ingratitude, salvation lasts as long as the judge is alive. Then, Israel hurries back to its unfaithfulness (Judg. 2.18-19).

In order to delineate the meaning of the book of Saviours (abbreviated BS), the schema has to be confronted with the notices that frame each saviour story. These very repetitive notices organize the saviour stories along a coherent narrative weft. These notes will be collectively designated as the 'frames', as opposed to the 'schema'.

All the elements of the frames do not appear systematically at the beginning or at the end of each saviour story, although most of these elements are also found in the schema. The picture presented by the frames always starts with the statement that the Israelites did what is evil in the sight of Yhwh. Yhwh then reacts by giving Israel into the hands of various oppressors. In consequence, Israel cries to Yhwh who calls a saviour to deliver his people. After each deliverance account, the frames close the narrative with the statement that the land was in peace for a given number of years. The next paragraph will show that the omissions by the schema of elements of the frames are significant. It is time to analyze the parallels and the oppositions between the schema and the frames.

Comparing the Schema with the Frames
To facilitate the comparison, Figure 1 presents the text of the schema in a synoptic table with the various elements of the frames. The perspective is

widened by integrating the narratives of Othniel and Jephthah. Samson is not presented as he holds only a few of the elements of the frames (evil: Judg. 13.1; spirit: Judg. 13.25; 14.6, 19; 15.14; judging: Judg. 15.20; 16.31).

The schema and the frames share the following elements: the evil committed by Israel, the enemy sent to punish this evil, the raising of a hero, the deliverance of Israel and the end of the oppression.

The differences are as follow: the schema clearly identifies the nature of the evil as desertion of Yhwh for other gods (Judg. 2.12-13, 19). This element is not found in the frames, apart from a passing mention in the story of Othniel (Judg. 3.7). But it reappears in the sermon of an anonymous prophet who disappears as quickly as he came (Judg. 6.7-10) and in two passages in the cycle of Jephthah: a list of foreign gods (Judg. 10.6) and a dialogue between Israel and Yhwh (Judg. 10.10-16). On the other hand, the stories of Ehud, Barak and Gideon offer no characterization of what constitutes the evil in the sight of Yhwh. The giving over into the hands of an enemy is present everywhere, in spite of variations in the verb used to express it: מכר 'to sell' in the story of Othniel (Judg. 3.8), חזק 'to strengthen the enemy' in the story of Ehud (Judg. 3.12) and נתן 'to give' in the stories of Gideon and Samson (Judg. 6.1; 13.1). The description of the oppression does not follow a pattern, but the cries of the oppressed people are always expressed with the verbs זעק or צעק (Judg. 3.9, 15; 4.3; 6.7; 10.10) while these cries are conspicuously absent from the schema.[42]

Within Judg. 3–16, the framing of the stories of Ehud, Barak and Gideon present strong similarities, whereas the framing of the Othniel, Jephthah and Samson stories show some significant discrepancies. *Samson* has preserved only a few elements of the frames, lost as they are in a cycle four chapters long. *Othniel* alone includes every element of the other frames. But *Jephthah* is the most complete, it contains most elements of the frames and of the schema. In fact, *Jephthah* shares with the schema, and with the anonymous prophet in Judg. 6.7-10, the characterization of the evil as the veneration of other gods. It is noteworthy that, outside of the schema, the two passages that deal with apostasy (Judg. 6.7-10; 10.10b-16) are situated strategically just after mentions of cries of Israel (Judg. 6.6; 10.10a) and that, at the same time, those cries are absent from the schema. Moreover, the schema qualifies the heroes as judges instead of saviours, insisting also on the transient nature of the relief from oppression

42. Beyerlin, 'Gattung', p. 4; Y. Amit, *History and Ideology* (BibSem, 60; Sheffield, Sheffield Academic Press, 1999), p. 36.

Schema	Othniel	Ehud	Barak	Gideon	Jephthah
2.11 The sons of Israel did the evil in Yhwh's eyes	3.7 They did the evil in Yhwh's...	3.12 they did again the evil in...	4.1 they did again the evil in...	6.1 they did again the evil in Yhwh's....	10.6 they did the evil in Yhwh's....
and served the Baals; 12 they forsook Yhwh, the god of their fathers, who had brought them out of the land of Egypt; they went after other gods, from the gods of the people around them and bowed down to them; they provoked Yhwh's anger. 13 They forsook Yhwh and served the Baals and the Ashtaroth.	forgetting Yhwh their god, serving the Baals and the Asherahs				they served the Baals and the Asherahs, the gods of Aram, Sidon, Moab, Ammon and the gods of the Philistines
14 Yhwh's anger was kindled against Israel,	8 Yhwh's anger was kindled...				7 Yhwh's anger was kindled...
he gave them to plunderers who plundered them;	he sold them to Cushān-rishathaim,		2 Yhwh sold them to Jabin	2 Yhwh gave them to Midian	8 he sold them to the Philistines and Ammonites
he sold them to their enemies around so they could no longer withstand their enemies.	they served Cushān-rishathaim	Yhwh strengthened Eglon		2 The hand of Midian prevailed over Israel	8 they crushed and oppressed Israel
15 Whenever they marched out, Yhwh was against them for evil as he said, and as he had sworn to them; they were in sore straits.		14 they served Eglon	3b he had 900 chariots of iron and oppressed the sons of Israel	6 Israel was brought low because of Midian	9 Israel was sorely distressed
for 8 years		for 18 years.	for 20 years.	17 years	8 18 years
	9 The sons of Israel cried to Yhwh	15 The sons of Israel cried to Yhwh	3a The sons of Israel cried to Yhwh	6 The sons of Israel cried to Yhwh. 7 Yhwh sent them a prophet...	10 The sons of Israel cried to Yhwh: 'we have sinned against you because we...

Schema	Othniel	Ehud	Barak	Gideon	Jephthah
Yhwh raised up a saviour	Yhwh raised up and he judged Israel	a Yhwh raised for them a saviour	14 Up, for this is the day in which 4 Deborah a prophetess, judged Israel.	7.15 Up for Yhwh has given Midian	12 Cry to them and let them deliver you! 12.7 Jephthah judged Israel.
16 Yhwh raised up judges who saved them from their plunders. 17 And yet, they did not listen to their judges for they played the harlot after other gods and bowed down to them; they soon turned aside from the way in which their fathers went to obey Yhwh's commandments;they did not do so.					
Yhwh's spirit came on him	Yhwh's spirit came on him			6.34 Yhwh's spirit clothed Gideon...	11.29 Yhwh's spirit was on...
18 When Yhwh raised up judges for them, Yhwh was with the judge	they served Cushân-rishathaim.	Cushân- 29 they killed 10.000 Moabites, not one escaped	15 Yhwh routed Sisera and his chariots	7.21 all the army ran, they fled	33 he smote them from Aroer
and he saved them from their enemies	he prevailed against Cushan	30 So Moab subdued	was 24 the hand of Israel bore harder	Israel Midian was subdued before	
all the days of the judge	11 land was at rest	land was at rest	5.31... was at rest	8.28...was at rest	
for Yhwh pitied their groaning before their oppressors. 19 But when the judge died, they turned and behaved worse than their fathers, going after other gods, serving them and bowing to them; they did not leave their practices or their stubborn ways.	40 years.	80 years.	40 years	40 years	40 the daughters of Israel went year by year to lament the daughter of Jephthah 4 days a year.

Figure 1. *Schema and Frames of the Book of Saviours*

by replacing the number of years of rest by the allegation of continued apostasy during the life and after the death of the judge (Judg. 2.17, 19). The deliverance account in *Jephthah* is closer to the schema than to the frames. Jephthah is not recognized as a saviour, although the root יש״ע is used four times (Judg. 10.13; 12.2-3 but every time in order to criticize it). The most devastating blow against the frames' conception of salvation comes from Judg. 10.14 where Yhwh suggests to his people to go and cry (זעק) to the other gods to be delivered (יש״ע) from their oppressors. At last, and contrarily to all the saviours, Jephthah's heroism does not inaugurate an era of peace and rest. His victory over the Ammonites leads to seasonal weeping in remembrance of the daughter he himself put to death (Judg. 12.40). A first set of conclusions can now be drawn from these remarks.

Judges and Saviours

Before proceeding any further, it is necessary to distinguish judges from saviours since they do not belong to the same literary levels.

The book of Judges derives its name from the judges (שׁפטים) that appear in the schema (Judg. 2.17-19) and from the other figures who are said to have 'judged' Israel (Judg. 3.10; 4.4; 10.2, 3; 12.7, 8, 11, 13; 15.20; 16.31). Among these, the five figures of Judg. 10.1-5 and 12.8-15, the so-called 'minor judges'[43] stand out as a particular case. Apart from the fact that 'they judged Israel', the short notices attributed to each one of them are devoted to family matters. These figures live in a peaceful context that requires no heroic deed of deliverance. One should also mention that Yhwh himself is once called 'Yhwh the judge' and that he 'judges today between Israel and Ammon' (Judg. 11.27). The situation gets more complicated when one notices that Othniel, who is explicitly designated as saviour (מושׁיע Judg. 3.9) is also said to have 'judged Israel' (Judg. 3.10). In Judg. 4.4-5, Deborah 'who judged Israel' seems to illustrate what 'judging' implies as she used to sit under a palm-tree 'and the sons of Israel came up to her for judgment'. However, the judge motive plays no role in the narrative of Judg. 4–5, no more than it does in the stories of the other heroes who also 'judged Israel' (Othniel, Jephthah and Samson Judg. 3.10; 12.7; 15.20; 16.31). A distinction between judges and 'minor' judges is often made in order to account for the striking differences among the

43. M. Noth, 'Das Amt des Richters Israels', in W. Baumgartner (ed.), *Festschrift Alfred Bertholet* (Tübingen: J.C.B. Mohr, 1950), pp. 389-412, reprint in *idem, Gesammelte Studien zum A.T.* 2 (ThB, 39; München: Chr. Kaiser Verlag, 1969), pp. 71-85.

various narratives of Judges.[44] This distinction is based on the length of the story.

However, a distinction between judges and saviours is also possible as the root ישׁע 'to save' is used in the schema for the judges who saved Israel (Judg. 2.16), or in the frames, for Othniel the saviour who saved Israel (Judg. 3.9) and for Ehud the saviour (Judg. 3.15). From ch. 4 on, the different heroes are not presented as saviours (מושׁיע), although ישׁע reappears in the mouth of Yhwh who sends Gideon to save Israel (Judg. 6.14). Joash suggests to the men of Ophrah who want to kill Gideon that it is not for them to save Baal (Judg. 6.31). The test of the fleece checks whether Yhwh really means to save Israel (Judg. 6.36-37) and Yhwh promises that he will save Israel with the 300 men that lapped water (Judg. 7.7). At the end of the cycle, the men of Israel ask Gideon to rule over them as he saved them (Judg. 8.22). The last two heroes, however, are not to be merged with the saviours: Yhwh flatly refuses to deliver Israel again at the beginning of *Jephthah* (Judg. 10.11-15) and Samson's mother is told that her son will only begin to save Israel (Judg. 13.5). On the basis of the use of the root ישׁע, Othniel, Ehud, Barak and Gideon form a homogeneous group of saviours, framed, on one side by the schema and on the other side by what could be considered as parodies of saviours (Jephthah and Samson).

The introduction of the terms 'judge' and 'judging' element in the analysis does not modify the overall picture. The schema with its saving judges is placed before the saviour narratives. Within the saviour narratives, only Othniel and Deborah are said to judge, and in both cases, this trait remains very peripheral to their mission. But when one comes to the judges (Judg. 10.1-5; 12.8-15), the picture changes: Tola, Jair, Ibzan, Elon and Abdon do little else apart from judging, although what is meant by judging remains completely unexplained. As for the last two cycles, the non-saviour Jephthah and the saviour-beginner Samson do judge Israel, although their judging is as superfluous as it is to the stories of Othniel, Ehud, Barak and Gideon.

It thus appears that we are not confronted with the categories of 'judges' and 'minor judges'. Instead, it is four well-defined categories that are emerging: the judges of the schema, the saviours proper (Othniel, Ehud, Barak and Gideon), the judges proper (Judg. 10.1-5; 12.8-15), and finally, Jephthah and Samson. These categories show that the simple distinction

44. See H.W. Hertzberg, 'Die kleinen Richter', *ThL* 79 (1954), pp. 285-90; Noth, 'Amt'.

between judges and 'minor' judges is not adequate to describe the complexity of the situation. Therefore, each of these four groups must be examined separately: the saviours here in Chapter 1, the schema and the judges in Chapter 3. Chapter 5 will be entirely devoted to the figures of Jephthah and Samson who will be labelled 'losers'.

Saved by Cries or by Obedience
What distinguishes the saviours from the judges of the schema, or from the judges of Judg. 10 and 12, or from the losers?

In the frames, the cries of Israel, צעק or זעק (Judg. 3.9, 15; 4.3; 6.6; 10.10) towards Yhwh are answered immediately by the calling of a saviour who delivers his people from its oppressor. Contrariwise, the schema avoids mentioning cries. Israel suffers under the hand of the enemy, but never cries out to Yhwh, even when in dire straits (Judg. 2.15). Verse 18 explains that Yhwh called judges to save Israel because he was moved to pity by Israel's groaning (נאק). This difference is no accident for the schema develops a consistent critique of the frames. Admittedly, Yhwh sends relief, but not in answer to cries, only out of pity for his suffering people. Logically, the Israel of the schema does not cry to Yhwh because the cycle of evil, punishment, cries and deliverance developed by the frames is transformed into an continuous scenario of apostasy, devoid of spells of apparent repentance and return to Yhwh. In the schema, Israel groans under the pain but cannot cry because crying would mean a return to the theology of the frames, implying Yhwh's immediate, unconditional answer through the sending of a saviour. Instead, the schema unfolds a spiral of rejection. Israel's guilt increases after each deliverance. The schema is clear, Israel is utterly bent on apostasy, forsaking Yhwh (Judg. 2.12-13), refusing to listen to the judges and to follow the way of their fathers who had obeyed the commandments of Yhwh (Judg. 2.17). The only change is that as soon as the judge dies they behave worse than their fathers did (Judg. 2.19). The foreign oppression is deprived of the pedagogical effects it has in the frames.

The radical critique of the frames by the schema appears in full light when two other passages are introduced into the discussion. Intervening directly after the Israelite cries in the Gideon narrative (Judg. 6.6), the anonymous prophet drives the first wedge between the well-established procedure of the frames. Instead of sending a saviour, Yhwh here sends a prophet who reveals the incoherence of the Israelites who cry towards Yhwh for help although they have not given heed to his voice ever since

Yhwh had delivered them from the hand of the Egyptians (Judg. 6.7-10). The point is finally driven home by Yhwh himself in the bargaining session of Judg. 10.14-16. Israel cries once more after being attacked by the Ammonites. This time, Yhwh tells his people to cry to the other gods for whom they deserted him: an explicit sarcasm aimed at the most favourable role the cries play in the saviour narratives. The pattern of automatic and unconditional salvation established by the frames is dismantled. The theologically homogeneous narrative bloc spanning from Othniel to Gideon is thus caught in a pincer movement between the schema and Yhwh's speech. The whole movement articulates around the sermon of the anonymous prophet, strategically placed halfway in between. This is no random juxtaposition of texts, but a powerful ideological machinery. The very place of the critical passages (chs. 2, 6 and 10) delineate the boundaries of the collection, a collection spanning roughly between Judg. 3 to 9. Beyerlin had rightly identified it against those who blindly followed Noth by placing the frames among Deuteronomistic texts.

'Doing Evil in the Sight of Yhwh': Not Deuteronomistic
Every single narrative from *Othniel* to *Samson* is introduced by the phrase 'The people of Israel did what was evil in the sight of Yhwh'. These words are widely considered as an unmistakable trait of Deuteronomistic theology, even by authors who are not particularly favourable to Noth's doctrine.[45] On the basis of this expression, the frames are attributed to a Deuteronomistic editor. The comparison between the frames and the schema has shown that the 'evil in the sight of Yhwh' is fundamental to the frames. It is the only cause supplied by the frames for the oppression of Israel by enemy hands. The evil in the sight of Yhwh is also present at the start of the schema, but it is treated differently; it is qualified as abandonment of Yhwh and veneration of other gods. We may conclude that the main purpose of the schema is to explain the nature of that unnamed evil: Israel's original sin in the eyes of the authors of the schema. That point is made also in the frame of *Othniel* (Judg. 3.7), in the sermon of the unnamed prophet and in Yhwh's tirade in Judg. 10. The explanation of Israel's military setbacks as consequence of the veneration of foreign gods is indisputably typically Deuteronomistic.[46] However, is this enough

---

45. Even E.A. Knauf, *Midian: Untersuchungen zur Geschichte Palästinas und Nordarabiens am Ende des 2. Jahrtausends v. Chr* (ADPV, Wiesbaden: Otto Harrassowitz, 1988), p. 35.

46. Weinfeld, *Deuteronomy*, pp. 346-49.

to attribute the mentions of an unqualified evil to the same milieu? Beyerlin is one of the few scholars to doubt it.[47] On the basis of the lamentation of Ibbisin, he shows that, already in the second millennium BCE, catastrophes were regularly attributed to divine wrath punishing human transgression. In Egypt, the reversal of fortune that was effected between the Syrian oppression and the reign of Setnakht (c. 1200 BCE) is also attributed to a change of attitude of the gods:

> ...a Syrian with them, made himself prince. He set the entire land as tributary before him. One joined his companion that their property might be plundered. They treated the gods like the people, and no offerings were presented in the temples. But when the gods reversed themselves to show mercy and to set the land right as was its normal state, they established their son, who had come forth from their body, to be Ruler–life, prosperity, health!–the son of Re: Set-Nakht...[48]

This understanding is still at work on the Mesha stele in the ninth century BCE.[49] Mesha uses it to explain the oppression of Moab by the Omrides: 'for Kemosh was angry against his land'. No details are given for the reasons of this anger, nor for the reversal that occurred under Mesha's reign when 'Kemosh restored his land'.[50] Mesha is not claiming to have pacified his god with exemplary behaviour, religious reform or choice sacrifices. He contents himself with saying, on the mode of an obvious finding, that Kemosh's anger, provoked by an unspecified evil, had come to an end for an unspecified reason. The similarity with the frames of the saviour narratives is striking. Defeat is explained by divine anger, as gods are responsible for the protection of their respective people from external aggression. No reasons for the anger are given for this is not the point of the matter. Unless one would claim that Mesha is a Deuteronomist, the theology of the frames is simply traditional, it can therefore predate the Josianic era. A good century and a half after the Mesha stele, an Egyptian text may be revealing that the traditional conception is becoming inadequate to explain military setbacks. Around 690 BCE, 20 years before

---

47. Beyerlin, 'Gattung', pp. 9-17.

48. Papyrus Harris I: *ANET*, p. 260.

49. Beyerlin, 'Gattung', p. 16.

50. K.A.D. Smelik, 'The Inscription of King Mesha', in W.W. Hallo (ed.), *CoS* 2, pp. 137-38 (137 lines 5-6). See discussion of this passage by B. Albrektson, *History and the Gods: An Essay on the Idea of Historical Events as Divine Manifestations in the Ancient Near East and in Israel* (ConBOT, 1; Lund: C.W.K. Gleerup, 1967), pp. 100-101.

Esarhaddon's victorious campaign in Egypt, Tirhakah is already pondering rather desperately on the causes of the routing of his army by the Assyrians. Contrarily to the frames of the saviour narratives, he refuses the idea that the evil that caused the defeat could come from his own god Amon because Amon is good. Someone must have committed some evil, but Amon must nevertheless give the victory.[51] In spite of his refusal to attribute the responsibility of the defeats to Amon, apparently because he fears that it would imply a flow in Amon's goodness, Tirhakah is still within the traditional theological framework. He does not yet inquire into the nature of the evil that prevents him to prevail over the Assyrians.

Deuteronomistic theology will go beyond this traditional view. But before turning to the Deuteronomistic solution to the problem of military defeat and divine wrath, the missing link between Tirhakah and the Deuteronomists has to be recovered. It has been missing due to the ignorance of the real nature of Assyrian propaganda. From Sennacherib on, an evolution is perceived in the traditional use of divine wrath to explain a defeat.[52] It is not any more the defeated king who is dealing with his (or his father's) misfortunes (Mesha), but the victorious Assyrian king who explains to the people he defeated that their own god called him, the Assyrian king, to punish them. The operations of the Assyrian army are justified since the local god has mandated the Assyrians to strike the rebels among his own people. For example, Sennacherib explains that he defeated the seven rebellious cities of the Qummuh border because 'their gods had abandoned them, rendering them powerless' (OIP 2.64.22-24). King Kirua, 'lord of Illubru', was 'a vassal whose gods had abandoned' (OIP 2.61.62-62).[53] The Assyrians displayed these divine desertions by ostensibly carrying away the images of the gods of the cities they defeated. They depicted the scenes of departure of the gods in their reception halls, not just as triumphal display of booty, but as vivid demonstration that these gods had given their people into Assyrian hands and were physically leaving them, abandoning them into enemy hands. Gods of a vanquished people are not necessarily vanquished gods! Vanquished people are

51. A. Spalinger, 'The Foreign Policy of Egypt', *CE* 105 (1978), pp. 22-47 (31 col. 5 and 21); P. Vernus, 'Inscriptions de la troisième période intermédiaire', *BIFAO* 75 (1975), pp. 1-73 (30-32).

52. M. Cogan, *Imperialism and Religion: Assyria, Judah and Israel in the Eighth and Seventh Centuries B.C.E.* (Missoula, MT: Scholars Press, 1974), p. 11 n. 12 discusses the emergence of this motive under Sargon.

53. See literature on these two texts in Cogan, *Imperialism*, p. 11.

vanquished because their gods wanted so. The Assyrians were therefore not carrying away the gods as booty in order to impose their own gods. Although the precious plating of some images was shared out between the soldiers (good for the morale of the troops), the images of the most significant god were treated with uttermost respect. Once the region had been pacified and the rebels killed or punished, the wrath of the local god came to an end, and the god was ready to bestow his grace anew which was good for the morale of the new vassals. This return to grace was duly signified when the Assyrians returned the image of the god, freshly cleaned and polished, welcomed by his people with great joy and relief.[54]

In that context, it is easily understood that the brunt of the Judaean Deuteronomists' anger bears on the media most privileged by Assyrian propaganda: divine statues. The Deuteronomists claimed that the return of the statue did not indicate renewed divine grace. On the contrary, it further provoked divine anger. Hence the Deuteronomistic condemnation of divine images. Anti-Assyrian cult had to avoid all aspects that had been manipulated by Assyrian propaganda. It had to replace them with a more specific definition of the causes of divine wrath, since divine wrath had become a powerful weapon in Assyrian hands. For this reason, Deuteronomism could not simply revert to the traditional theodicy. Reacting against Assyrian ideology, Deuteronomism systematically identified what constitutes the 'evil in the sight of Yhwh' as veneration of other gods, a specification hammered out throughout Deuteronomistic texts. What is implied, and what appears today so obvious that we lose the sheer force of the innovation, is the claim that veneration of other gods entails necessarily the abandonment of Yhwh, Israel's legitimate god.

The watershed between Judaean Deuteronomism and late Assyrian theology appears clearly in one of the last stages of evolution of the Assyrian concept of human guilt provoking military setbacks. It is found in a document attributed to Esarhaddon, the so-called Sennacherib's testament.[55] Sennacherib is fictitiously depicted as enquiring through extispicy about the sin committed by his father Sargon who died in battle in enemy country and was thus deprived of proper burial as his body was not recovered (Obverse 17). The answer is that such a fateful end befell Sargon because he had honoured his own gods at the expense of the gods of Babylon and therefore violated a divine covenant. The reader then

---

54. Cogan, *Imperialism*, pp. 22-41.

55. H. Tadmor, B. Landsberger and S. Parpola 'The Sin of Sargon and Sennacherib's Last Will' *SAAB* 3 (1989), pp. 3-51.

learns that Assyrian scribes prevented Sennacherib from making the statue of Marduk he had planed to produce, thus committing the same sin as his father. For this, Sennacherib paid also with his life (Reverse 21) and he was murdered. Esarhaddon is urged to get out of this vicious circle and to finally reconcile the gods of Babylon with those of Assyria.[56]

This document has obvious political implications for Esarhaddon's reign that saw the reversal of Sennacherib's harsh treatment of Babylon. Esarhaddon has to legitimize his policy of appeasement and reconstruction at Babylon. That the sins of the fathers are faced squarely, their origin carefully searched in order to amend them, seems to be a novelty compared to previous rhetoric. That the sin of Sargon consisted in forsaking some particular gods comes as no surprise to anyone familiar with Deuteronomistic theology, more so when one realizes that Josiah was crowned a mere 30 years after the death of Esarhaddon. But there is a fundamental difference in outlook. For the worldwide vantage point of the Assyrians, all and every god must be looked after. From the narrow perspective of Judaean mountains, one single god must be served and exclusively worshipped.

This presentation suggests that the evolution of propaganda from Mesha to Esarhaddon establishes the pre-Deuteronomistic character of the frames. By simply indicating an unspecified evil, the frames are closer to Mesha than they are to post-Sargonic ideology. On the other hand, the schema with its shameless blaming of the fathers is late Assyrian theology, or better, post-Assyrian.

Recapitulation

It now appears that Beyerlin's claim that the frames of the saviour narratives are not to be considered Deuteronomistic was right. The frames convey a theodicy irreconcilable with the one found in the schema (Judg. 2.11-19). The schema with the help of the two additional passages (Judg. 6.7-10 and 10.10-16) now appears as a secondary development that orchestrates a vast deconstruction of the theology of a BS presented by the frames. The systematic deliverance of Israel by the saviours is rejected. Yhwh did send judges to help Israel, but Israel has demonstrated its irremediable corruption and Yhwh now requires some stringent religious measures before delivering Israel from its enemies.

It is now time to go through this BS in order to check whether other

---

56. Tadmor, Landsberger and Parpola 'Sin of Sargon', pp. 9-10.

passages belonging to this secondary stage have been inserted into the primary collection. The Othniel narrative will be analyzed in Chapter 2, as its Judaean scope sets it apart from the others. The rest of Chapter 1 is therefore devoted to Judg. 3.12–9.57.

Judges 3.12-30: Ehud

Ehud is the most unbridled story of the whole collection. Eglon 'calf', Ehud's victim, is a fat guy (v. 17) who spends most of his time on the throne, in his closet (v. 20). He is struck[57] by Ehud, a Benjaminite 'son of the right', handicapped of the left hand,[58] but armed with a mighty *gomed*[59] between his thighs. The scatological humour[60] of this tale is peppered with sacrificial hints: Eglon, the recipient of the tribute becomes the sacrificial victim.[61] Beside the difficult readings of vv. 22-23 that barely covers up some saucy language closer to the one heard in army barracks than in the temple,[62] one finds some mythological allusions. Grottanelli discusses at great length the parallels with Ps. 68 in order to present Eglon as Yam the Ugaritic monster.[63] However, the 'cool roof chamber' in which Eglon retires offers a better mythological connection.

---

57. תקע favourite root of the book of Saviours: see 3.21; 4.21; 6.34; 7.18-22.

58. See J.A. Soggin, 'Ehud und Eglon: Bemerkungen zu Richter iii 11b-31', *VT* 39 (1989), pp. 95-100 (96-97). The left hand is reserved for the manipulation of excrements: U. Hübner, 'Mord auf dem Abort?', *BN* 40 (1987), pp. 130-40 (133 n. 14).

59. Arabic: 'to be hard!' Aram. גרמידא short cubit (or 'fist': T.A.G. Hartmann, 'גמד in Richter 3, 16 oder die Pygmäen im Dschungel der Längenmaße', *ZAH* 13 [2000], pp. 188-93) from Aram. גמר 'to be contracted' in Aphel 'to be reckless, shameless'!

60. Hübner, 'Mord' and L. K. Handy, 'Uneasy Laughter: Ehud and Eglon as Ethnic Humor', *SJOT* 6 (1992), pp. 233-46.

61. הקרב מנחה (vv. 15-16), always used in sacrificial contexts, never as gift.

62. The נחב (√חבל 'erected') of the *gomed* (v. 22) is only known to mean 'handle' in a rare Arabic expression. The 'vestibule' out of which Ehud escapes הפרשדנה is more likely to be an obscene glose composed from פרש 'dung, entrails', (Exod. 29.14, Lev. 4.11; 8.17) or פרש 'slit, anus' + שד 'devastation' + epenthetic נ + fem. suffix ה (male used as female): 'his shitty slit'. TM > LXXA: ויחא הפרשדנה LXXB translates καὶ ἐξῆλθεν Αωδ τὴν προστάδα found again in v. 23 LXXA. Ehud is added and הפרשדנה is translated 'vestibule'. See bibliography in O'Connell, *Rhetorics*, pp. 92-93.

63. C. Grottanelli, 'The Enemy King is a Monster', *SSR* 3 (1979), pp. 5-36, compares Ehud to other mythical left-handed heroes: the Roman Scaevola, the Persian Jamshid and the Scandinavian Tÿr.

This עלית המקרה is the lofty abode of the storm-god from which he waters the mountains (Ps. 104.3, 13).[64] Eglon's prolonged sojourns in his lonely throne room have therefore little to do with constipation.[65] Aping the storm-god, Eglon covers his feet (v. 24) and waters the land generously, so that his soldiers are all nice and fat (v. 29). Mythology is turned into a daring farce, the storm-god into a urinating calf, his lofty abode into a lowly chamber (from עליה to חדר 3.24) in Jericho.

The names and the plot of this colourful story are tailor-made by the compilers of the BS.[66] The acknowledgement of their fictitious character relieves the reader to postulate any old Benjaminite tradition reflecting historical events in pre-monarchic times.[67] In fact, the sheer idea of a Moabite annexation of a semi-independent tribe of Benjamin in pre-statehood times is ludicrous. Before Mesha, there was no Moabite entity. Mesha was, around 845 BCE,[68] the first Moabite king, the founder of the Moabite State.[69] His father was only a Dibonite and what was going to become Moab was controlled by Israel, already a full-fledged State that included Benjamin as well as Galaad and Gad. Before Mesha, there was no Moab that could have invaded Benjamin. After Mesha, there is no historical attestation of any Moabite extension across the Jordan.

Although there is no need to seek an old tradition, this fictitious creation of the BS does reveal some precious indications of the time of edition of the collection. The Benjaminite geographical horizon allows equating the city of Palms (v. 13) near Gilgal (v. 19) with Jericho. Since reinforcements are called from the hill country of Ephraim (v. 27) rather than from Judah, we can be sure that the text predates Josiah because until Josiah, Jericho was part of Israel.

64. P.E. Dion, 'Yhwh as Storm-God and Sun-God', *ZAW* 103 (1991), pp. 43-71 (50 n. 23).

65. Against Hübner, 'Mord', p. 135. Constipation is by large a modern ailment, characteristic of sedentary urban life: P. Fouet, *Gastro-entérologie* (Abrégés; Paris: Masson, 1983), pp. 244-46.

66. E.A. Knauf, 'Eglon and Ophrah', *JSOT* 51 (1991), pp. 25-44 (28).

67. Lindars, *Judges 1–5*, p. 126; Becker, *Richterzeit*, pp. 113-17.

68. E.A. Knauf, 'The Cultural Impact of Secondary State Formation: the Cases of the Edomites and Moabites', in P. Bienkowski (ed.), *Early Edom and Moab* (SAM, 7; Sheffield: J.R. Collis, 1992), pp. 47-54 (49-50).

69. Mesha turned Dibon into the capital of the State of Moab. Monumental architecture (palace, fortresses, roads and reservoirs) and writing (the Annals cited on the stele) laid the foundation of the new State. See N. Na'aman, 'King Mesha and the Foundation of the Moabite Monarchy', *IEJ* 47 (1997), pp. 83-92.

Conveniently placed between Mesha (840 BCE) and Josiah (640 BCE), the date suggested by Knauf for the composition of the BS (c. 720 BCE) is acceptable. At the time, Moab was a small State, created just a century before by Mesha. Mesha was able to expel the Israelite troops from Gadite territory without provoking any meaningful Israelite retaliation (2 Kgs 3) because, at the time, Israel was too involved on its northern border. Hazael, king of Aram, took over most of Israel (1 Kgs 20; 2 Kgs 5; 9–10) and Mesha profited from Israelite weakness to set himself up as king of Moab. A century later, Israelite memory could still be marked by these traumatic events. Some families had lost relatives in the fighting at Yahaz and in the *herem* of the entire population of Atarot perpetuated by Mesha to honour Ashtar Kemosh.[70] Others had a captured grandfather who spent the rest of his life digging the canals of *Qarho*.[71]

Memories were still sore, but Israel would not rule again over Moab until the Hasmonaean period. A story of victory over Moab had to be set on Israelite territory, at Jericho, for verisimilitude. The deliverance gained from Ehud's coup inaugurated a period of eighty peaceful years, while each of the other saviours managed to secure only 40 years of rest.

Judges 3.31: Shamgar

After Ehud, Judg. 3.31 mentions Shamgar who 'also saved Israel'. This נֹם־הוּא may indicate that *Shamgar* was added on later. This hypothesis is reinforced by the fact that some Greek manuscripts add the Shamgar notice after *Samson* (after Judg. 16.31) rather than after *Ehud.*

Shamgar ben Anath, also found in the Song of Deborah (Judg. 5.6), could be an imitation of Samson as the name Shamgar seems to derive from the Hurrite solar-god *Shimige,* attested in Ugarit and at the Phoenician city of Qatna (EA 55). Like Shamash, this god is the divine judge, the upholder of justice and the protector of the weak.[72] It will be seen that there is no valid reason to exclude him from Judg. 5, but here, the Shamgar notice is likely to have been added later, in order to reach the canonical number of twelve heroes alongside Othniel, Ehud, Barak, Gideon, Tola, Jair, Jephthah, Ibzan, Elon, Abdon and Samson. Since the

---

70. Smelik, 'Inscription', p. 137 lines 16-17.

71. Smelik, 'Inscription', p. 138 lines 25-26; D.J.A. Clines, 'Psalm 2 and the MLF (Moabite Liberation Front)', in D.J.A. Clines (ed.), *Interested Parties* (JSOTSup, 205; Sheffield: JSOT Press, 1995), pp. 244-75.

72. Judg. 15.15-17; K. van der Toorn, 'Shimige', *DDD,* pp. 1462-1464.

Shamgar notice lacks chronological indications, it is probable that it was introduced into the present context after the BS had been turned into a book of Judges: the edition could not afford the disruption of a time system that was already completed (see Chapter 5).

Judges 4–5: Deborah, Barak and Jael

Judges 4 and 5 present two versions of the same story, one in prose (ch. 4) and the other one as a victory song (ch. 5). The parallels between Judg. 4 and 5 are presented in Figure 2.

Judges 5	Judges 4
Kings v. 2, Kings of Canaan v. 19	King of Canaan at Hazor v. 2
Sisera	Sisera the commander vv. 2-3, 7
Storm theophany vv. 4-5	Military encounter v. 15
Mother in Israel v. 7	Prophetess, judge, wife vv. 4-5
Commerce discontinued vv. 6-7	Cyclical oppression vv. 1, 3
New gods v. 8	
Volunteers vv. 2, 9	Call up v. 10
Waters of Megiddo, Taanach v. 19,	From Ramah to Kedesh in Naphtali vv.
Kishon v. 21: Jezreel valley	5-6, Tabor vv. 6, 12, 14, Zaanannim v.
	11, Harosheth-hagoiim vv. 2, 13, 16.
10 tribes vv. 14-18	Zabulon and Naphtali v. 10
Stars and torrent vv. 20-21	Armies vv. 15-16
Curse on Meroz v. 23	
Jael, wife of Heber v. 24	Heber's origin v. 11, peace between
	Jabin and Heber v. 17
Sisera asks for water v. 25	Barak asks for Deborah's presence vv.
	8-9, flight by foot vv. 15, 17, invitation
	v. 18, thirst v. 19
Crushed skull v. 26	Pierced temple v. 21
Sisera sank v. 27	Sisera died asleep v. 21
Palace scene vv. 28-31	

Figure 2. *Parallels between Judges 4 and 5*

Order of Dependency

With such similar texts, the question of interdependency is crucial. In history of research, every possible combination has had its protagonists. We are confronted with three main options.

No direct link between Judges 4 and 5. The differences are stressed in order to consider the two texts as independent from each other. Budde refused the idea that Judg. 4 was first written as an introduction to the song because he believed that its author relied on a source that was too different from Judg. 5.[73] For Hertzberg, Judg. 4 cannot be a secondary elaboration from Judg. 5.[74]

The song depends on the prose. According to Bechmann, Judg. 5 depicts a reality far beyond that of the narrative, whose aim is restricted to the death of the enemy by the hand of a woman.[75] The function of the song is to be transposable in other situations. Judg. 5 seems therefore to have been introduced in Judges later than the narrative.[76] Although the core of the song is older than Judg. 4, the final text of the song is actually younger.[77] Apart from an old kernel, the bulk of the song would be a hymnal elaboration based on the information provided by Judg. 4.

The narrative depends on the song. This is at the moment the opinion of the majority. Many philological arguments plead in favour of the song's precedence and the prose does appear to be a literary development of the song. Judges 5 provides no detail about the circumstances of the meeting of Sisera with Jael. Jael is simply introduced by תברך 'blessed!' opposed to אורו the malediction of the previous verse. But Judg. 4 explains that Yhwh routed Sisera and all his chariots, and that Sisera alighted from his chariot and fled away on foot (Judg. 4.15). This detail provides a link between the battle narrative and the Jael episode. If the author had not known the song of Deborah, his narrative could have ended with the extermination of Sisera's army down to the last man in v. 16. However, his audience would have been very disappointed if the famous tent scene had been left out. Therefore, the story bounces back with the repetition of Sisera's flight on foot in v. 17. Logically, Judg. 4 supplies plenty of details that are missing in the elliptic poem: there was peace between Jabin and Heber (v. 17), Jael invites Sisera to come in (v. 18), she covers him with a rug (v. 19) and looks-out at the door (v. 20) so that Sisera can fall asleep. This detail explains why a woman could kill the mighty warrior. And yet,

---

73. K. Budde, *Das Buch der Richter* (KHAT, 7; Freiburg i. Br.: 1897).

74. H.W. Hertzberg, *Die Bücher Josua, Richter, Ruth* (ATD, 9; Göttingen: 1959).

75. U. Bechmann, *Das Deborahlied zwischen Geschichte und Fiktion: Eine exegetische Untersuchung zu Richter 5* (DThR, 33; St. Ottilien: EOS Verlag, 1989).

76. H.-P. Müller, 'Der Aufbau des Deboraliedes', *VT* 16 (1966), pp. 446-59.

77. H.-P. Mathys, *Dichter und Beter* (OBO, 132; Freiburg/Göttingen: Universitätsverlag/Vandenhoeck & Ruprecht, 1994), p. 176.

in spite of this wealth of details, the creator of Judg. 4 omits one that proves beyond doubt that he knew the song of Deborah in a version fairly close to the one we have in ch. 5. He does not indicate the reason for Sisera's flight on foot because he already knows, and he knows that his audience knows, that Yhwh had sent torrential rains in the Kishon that swept away the chariots, a fundamental element of the plot of Judg. 5 (vv. 4-5, 20-21), nowhere to be found in Judg. 4.[78] Judges 5 is therefore older than Judg. 4. The analysis of the language of the song will bring ample confirmation of it.

Philology of the Song of Deborah. The philology of the song attests a long history of transmission. Knauf considers its language as pre-classical Hebrew on the basis of the absence of *nota accusativi*,[79] the rarity of articles[80] and the systematic substantivisation of participles. An archaic text[81] received additions identifiable on phonologic,[82] orthographic[83] and vocabulary grounds.[84] Rather than Aramaisms,[85] these are dialectical

---

78. E.A. Knauf, 'Debora', unpublished.

79. First Millennium BCE innovation in Central Semitic.

80. The old textual witnesses indicate that the use of the article was even less frequent than in the present form: see v. 20: שמים but הכוכבים and n. 20a *BHS*.

81. Exemplified by the absence of wayyiqtol. It could go back to the end of the second millennium BCE: Knauf, 'Debora'.

82. ומחצה √מחץ pseudo-correction of the previous √: etymological ḍ => q and then => ץ. See J. Blau, *On Pseudo-Corrections in Some Semitic Languages* (Jerusalem: Israel Academy of Sciences and Humanities, 1976), p. 82.

83. Phoenicism חכמות 'wisest' (v. 29): short and long a become o when accentuated. At first, the a was prononced o to add a phoenician colouring, then around the fifth-fourth century BCE, a mater lectionis ו was added (see also Hos. 10.10): Knauf, 'Debora'.

84. Verse 14 ספר recruting 'officer' or 'bronze' (Akkadien *sipparu*). V. 16 המשפתים √שפת 'to level off', שפת 'tripod', or LXXB, διγομία 'packsaddle', Gen. 49.14 (Ps. 68.14*) (Ugar. *mtpdm*, Arab. *Maṭāfid*). V. 17 מפרציו 'slit, quay, bay, port' (Akk. *Parāṣum*, Arab. *Furḍa*).

85. V. 10 מדין plural דין. V. 11 יתנו forma mixta √תנא Aram. / √שנה Heb. piel 3 mpl. 'to repeat'. V. 7 קום √קומתי Shafel aff. 2 fsg. Aram.: 'Until you were called to stand up'. The Shafel is rejected by M. Waltisberg, 'Zum Alter der Sprache des Deboraliedes Ri 5*', *ZAH* 12 (1999), pp. 218-32 (219) on the disputable grounds that Amarna Aram. uses {h-} for causative forms. E.A. Knauf will argue in a forthcoming contribution that the Amarna evidence is not conclusive. In a very fragmented area like Palestine, 'modern' [h-] causative forms could used in the plains while the mountainous areas could be still be using the Shafel form. Note the persistence of such

elements from Gileadite, Moabite and proto-Arabic. Some 'Samarisms',[86] from the language of the court of the kings of Israel, show that the song was then transmitted and preserved in Samaria. These elements attest to the ancient character of the song, in spite of Waltisberg's claim of the contrary. He rejects Knauf's explanation of the irregular forms as Gilead-isms in order to maintain them as late Aramaisms to fit a date between the fifth and the third century BCE.[87] However, he admits that Gileadisms could be present if the song came from an old form of Northern Hebrew, which is exactly what Knauf suggests. But Waltisberg does not explain why he rejects such an eventuality.[88]

The precedence of the song is established. The effort will now be concentrated on identifying the use of the song by Judg. 4.

How Judges 4 Used the Song of Deborah

Avoiding Samarian involvement. At first, Judg. 4 seems to have a wider perspective than the song whose scene is limited to the plain of Jezreel (Sarid, Taanach, Megiddo, and Meroz). The scenario of the prose spreads from the South of the mountain of Ephraim (Ramah 60 km south of Taanach, where Deborah summons Barak) to the northern hill country of Naphtali (Kedesh, the home of Barak, 60 km north of Taanach) with special emphasis on the mountain. Barak's troops are assembled on Mount Tabor (north of the Jezreel plain) to attack Sisera's chariots at the Kishon and pursue them as far as Harosheth-hagoyim (location unknown). But, in spite of this larger horizon, Judg. 4 involves only two tribes in the fighting (Naphtali and Zebulun) while the song lists ten tribes, five of which actually take part of the battle. This difference could be explained in light of the Gideon story with its episode of voluntary reduction of the troops (Judg. 7). However, the sole mobilization of Naphtali and Zebulun may also reveal an important trait of the BS. From the point of view of editors writing in Bethel, the involvement of these two distant tribes, whose

---

differences in Arabia where Sabaean (from the first millennium BCE to c. 600 AD) used {h-} causative forms while modern South Arabian languages (Mehrī, Ǧibbālī) still use Shafel forms. The Shafel remains the best explanation for the form שׁמתי.

86. Verse 3 רעשׁה qal 3 fsg. 'tremble' (Ps. 68.9) West Semitic *r'sₐ* (arab. *ra'a/iša*). All other Biblical occurences come from Judg. 5.4. Syro-palestinian *r'š* is a Biblicism or Arabism. Arab. *ra'asa* is a Aramaism: Knauf, 'Debora'. V. 8 שׂערים reads שׂערים 'barleys', a for o and hesitation over the pronunciation of שׂ constitute a Samarism.

87. Waltisberg, 'Zum Alter', pp. 219, 229.

88. Waltisberg, 'Zum Alter', p. 223.

territories were part of the province of Megiddo since 732 BCE, could be a literary device to avoid the direct engagement of the populations of the province of Samaria, established around the time of the edition of the BS. This caution can mean either that the BS was issuing a call to arms in veiled terms to avoid censorship or that the aim of the collection was different. It is too early to decide, the question of the aim of the editors of the BS will clarify itself at the end, when Judg. 9 will be discussed.

Dropping the mythological elements of the song. As already seen, the mythological context in which the song is couched, is abandoned by Judg. 4. Yhwh is not giving the victory by liquefying the clouds and shaking the mountains (Judg. 5.4-5), nor are the stars fighting against Sisera (Judg. 5.20-21). Instead, Yhwh musters Barak's troops and sets up the Kishon trap through the agency of the prophetess Deborah (Judg. 4.6-7). Then, Yhwh routs Sisera's chariots through Barak's sword (Judg. 4.16) in a regular military encounter. The primaeval wadi נחל קדומים (Judg. 5.21) does not even overflow.[89] In Judg. 4, the mythical elements of Judg. 5 are turned into a human battle, where Yhwh alone intervenes to give victory, without the agency of stars, rivers or other gods.

Leaving aside some actors. The kings of Canaan, the stars (Judg. 5.19-20), Sisera's mother as much as the entire palace scene (vv. 28-30) all disappear from Judg. 4. The protagonists are organized in two neat pairs: Deborah and Barak work hand in hand despite initial tensions (Judg. 4.8-9), Jael and Sisera are locked up in a deadly conflict although they started off as allies (Judg. 4.11, 17). On the other hand, the heroines are given lawful husbands: Deborah is no more a 'mother in Israel' (Judg. 5.7)[90] but Mrs Lappidoth,[91] prophetess and judge (Judg. 4.4-5).

---

89. B. Halpern, 'Sybil, or the Two Nations? Archaism, Kinship, Alienation and the Elite Redefinition of Traditional Culture in Judah in the 8th-7th Centuries B.C.E.', in J.S. Cooper and G.M. Schwartz (eds.), *The Study of the Ancient Near East in the Twenty-First Century: The William Foxwell Albright Centennial Conference* (Winona Lake: Eisenbrauns, 1996), pp. 291-338 (310 n. 47), sees this demythologizing process at work already in the seventh centry BCE: 'Nature was depersonalised, in a development typical of Renaissance-type literate thinking, on the road to Reformation... Nature was alienated from the realm of the divine, which was thus less accessible to the individual.'

90. Compare Gen. 45.8.

91. Plur. fem. see Exod. 18.20! Smart allusion to Barak (lightning), Gideon (7.16, 20) and later also Samson (15.4, 5).

Enriching the murder scene. Judges 4.17-22 supplies a wealth of details to brush an extremely realistic scene: Sisera arrives at Jael's tent because he jumped off his chariot and left the battle scene on foot, leaving Barak to pursue his army. There is a peace agreement between Jabin and Heber, so Jael invites a thirsty and exhausted Sisera into the tent, gives him a drink, hides him under a blanket and stays on the look-out to calm Sisera until he falls asleep. The metaphoric parallel of Judg. 5.26 is read literally to mean two separate actions, with two different tools.[92] She takes a peg in one hand, a hammer in the other and approaches stealthily בלאט. The crushing blow on a standing Sisera (Judg. 5.26-27) becomes the delicate driving of the peg with the hammer through Sisera's temple into the ground. Barak then arrives conveniently at Jael's tent to witness Sisera's last convulsions.

According to the guiding hypothesis of this study, Judg. 4, the latter text, is likely to be the work of the editors of the BS around 720 BCE. The comparison between the song of Deborah and Judg. 4 permits a first evaluation of the characteristics of the BS: the Assyrian provincial geography seems to be presupposed as special care is taken to avoid any involvement of populations living within the province of Samaria in a battle that took place on the territory of the Megiddo province. The mythological traits of the Song are turned into a descriptive narrative focusing on the role of three heroes. The whole operation is masterminded by Deborah, somewhere in southern Benjamin, not too far from Bethel, but Deborah keeps her hands bloodless. Barak and Jael, who play the main roles are both coming from the periphery.

These observations should be kept in mind during the study of the other BS narratives, until Judg. 9 is reached. In the meantime, an objection concerning the date of the song of Deborah has to be faced.

In Defence of the Antiquity of Deborah's Song

Bernd Diebner has called in question the ancient date generally attributed to Deborah and Jael on the basis of some parallels with Greek mythology in Judg. 5, in particular with the birth legend of Zeus.[93] Callimachus provides the most detailed account of this episode:[94]

---

92. Reification and over-reading of the poetic language: B. Halpern, 'The Resourceful Israelite Historian', *HTR* 76 (1983), pp. 379-401 (396).

93. B.J. Diebner, 'Wann sang Debora ihr Lied?', *AC* 14 (1995), pp. 106-130.

94. Callimachus, *Hymns and Epigrams* (trans. A.W. Mair, LCL, London: Heinemann, 1960), pp. 41-43.

But thee, O Zeus, the companions of the Cyrbantes took to their arms, even the Dictaean Meliae, and Adrasteia laid thee to rest in a cradle of gold, and thou didst suck the rich teat of the she-goat Amaltheia, and thereto eat the sweet honey-comb. For suddenly on the hills of Ida, which men call Panacra, appeared the works of the Panacrian bee. And lustily round thee danced the Curetes a war-dance, beating their armour, that Cronus might hear with his ears the din of the shield, but not thine infant noise (45-53).

Judges 5 does contain the bee (Deborah), the goat (Jael) and Sisera, Σιούρα a Greek goat-hair blanket.[95] Judges 4 also seems to establish parallels with Zeus mythology. The hero Barak ברק 'lightning' and Deborah's husband Lappidoth לפידות, possibly deriving from Greek λαμπάδιον 'torch' are two attributes for the storm-god Zeus. Diebner also suggests that Mount Tabor was understood as the throne of Ζευς ʹΑταβύριος,[96] thus adding an extra parallel with Zeus.

Diebner then draws the conclusion that Judg. 5 presupposes the birth-legend of Zeus and thus requires a Hellenistic date, possibly not before the second half of the second century BCE.[97]

However, the therotrophy motive in the birth-legend of Zeus is already attested in Bronze Age Crete[98] and a Minoan seal from Knossos shows a naked child under a goat.[99] Diebner's Hellenistic evidence is therefore as old as the Late Bronze Age.

It may be doubted that Cretan mythology was then sufficiently known in Palestine in order to inspire Judg. 5. However, frescoes of clear Minoan inspiration were found as far as the Hyksos capital-city in Avaris (Tell el-Dabʾa, Egypt) going back to the period of the second Cretan palaces (1700-1450 BCE).[100] The techniques and the famous motive of the dancers

---

95. Diebner, 'Wann sang Debora', pp. 116-20.

96. Diebner, 'Wann sang Debora', p. 120; citing O. Eissfeldt, 'Der Gott des Tabor und seine Verbreitung' in R. Sellheim and F. Maass (eds.), *Kleine Schriften/Otto Eissfeldt* (Tübingen: J.C.B. Mohr, 1963), pp. 29-54.

97. Diebner, 'Wann sang Debora', pp. 126, 129-30.

98. H. Verbruggen, *Le Zeus crétois* (Paris: Belles Lettres, 1981), pp. 40-41.

99. H. Ransome, *The Sacred Bee* (London, 1937), pp. 92-94; M. Marconi, 'Melissa, dea cretese', *Athenaeum* 18 (1940), pp. 164-78.

100. M. Bietak, 'Une citadelle royale à Avaris de la première moitié de la XVIIIe dynastie et ses liens avec le monde minoen' in A. Caubet (ed.), *L'acrobate au taureau. Les découvertes de Tell el-Dabʾa (Egypte) et l'archéologie de la Méditerranée orientale (1800-1400 av. J.-C.)* (Louvre conférences et colloques; Paris: Documentation française, 1999), pp. 29-81 and J.-C. Poursat, 'Les découvertes de Tell el-Dabʾa et la Crète' in Caubet (ed.), *L'acrobate au taureau. Les découvertes de Tell el-Dabʾa*

with the bulls have led the specialists to infer the presence of Cretan artists in Avaris. These frescoes add up to other evidence to demonstrate the intensity of exchange within the first Eastern Mediterranean economic system during the Late Bronze Age. The situation in the Nile delta certainly applies also to Palestine at the same period. Very similar frescoes were found at Tel Kabri, then one of the largest cities of Palestine, a mere fifty kilometres north of the Jezreel valley, the backdrop of the events told in Judg. 5. Granted, the dancers with the bulls have no link with the birth-legend of Zeus, but they suffice to postulate that if they were known in Palestine, Zeus mythology could also have been known there and then.

We are therefore faced with the embarrassing choice to date the Zeus parallels found by Diebner in Judg. 4–5 between the Late Bronze Age and the Late Hellenistic period! Dating attempts must therefore be based on other criteria. Nothing prevents to imagine a first influence in the Bronze Age and a rediscovery and development of these parallels during Hellenistic times. Knauf's philological remarks provide a firmer basis for the antiquity of Judg. 5.

The Story of Jael and the History of the Kishon Valley

In consideration to the format of this study, rather than launching into a minute study of Judg. 4–5, the following will reconstruct the main editorial stages of both chapters, using the history of Israel as guideline. The literary development of Judg. 4 and 5 can be plotted, roughly of course, on the history of Israel and Judah.

An Iron I song of Deborah. Based on the philological grounds enumerated by Knauf, the earliest form of Deborah's song can be set in a group living in the periphery of the Jezreel valley in the post-Amarna period. The Amarna letters provide a vivid illustration of the constant fight between each city-state of the plain on one hand, and on the other hand the increasing threat of the mountain, exemplified by the troublesome Lab'ayu and his sons.[101] The situation got worse for the cities of the plains, and the song of Deborah could evoke a particularly memorable victory of the

---

(Egypte) et l'archéologie de la Méditerranée orientale (1800-1400 av. J.-C.) (Louvre conférences et colloques; Paris: Documentation française, 1999), pp. 181-94.

101. W.L. Moran, *The Tel Amarna Letters* (Baltimore: The Johns Hopkins University Press, 1992), see EA 244.246.249.253-54.280. I. Finkelstein, 'The Territorial-Political System of Canaan in the Late Bronze Age', *UF* 28 (1996), pp. 221-58 provides a comprehensive overview of the political configuration of the period.

inhabitants of the hill country of Zebulun (between the Jezreel plain and the Ephraimite mountains, around modern Jenin) over the dwellers of the plain. In fact, Zebulun is mentioned twice in the song, praised whole-heartedly and receiving a marshal's staff (Judg. 5.14, 18). This remarkable feature indicates that the song belonged to the Zebulunite folklore and entered Israelite traditions at the same time than Zebulun joined Israel.[102]

A first Israelite song of Deborah at the end of the tenth century BCE. The inhabitants of the mountain of Ephraim are organizing themselves into a complex chiefdom,[103] a process alluded to in 2 Sam. 2.9.[104] Ephraim is the driving force behind this process, since it has received several surrounding territories from the hands of pharaoh Shishak (c. 927 BCE) in an effort to consolidate indirect Egyptian rule over Palestine.[105] Manasseh is still called Machir, which confirms the antiquity of the song.[106] Ishbaal man-aged to extend his control across the Jordan over Gilead, and northwards over the Jezreel plain (2 Sam. 2.9). This latter move transformed the small hill-country Israelite principality into a major regional force. To celebrate the coming down of the people of Yhwh (Judg. 5.3, 5) to the doors of the mighty cities of the plain (v. 11), the bards at the courts of Tirzah and Shechem sang the song of the Zebulunites who were now part of Israel. These new Israelites were praised for their 'voluntary' enrolment (v. 9) and, hopefully, their willingness to remain within the new Israel.

Yahwistic elements at the beginning of the eighth century BCE. At the time of Jehu, or probably some time later,[107] Yahwism was used to sap the

---

102. Issachar, Asher and Naphtali were probably added later, thus blurring the stress on Zebulun: P. Guillaume, 'Deborah and the Seven Tribes', *BN* 101 (2000), pp. 18-21.

103. H.M. Niemann, *Herrschaft, Königtum und Staat* (FAT, 6; Tübingen: J.C.B. Mohr, 1993), pp. 7-8.

104. E.A. Knauf, *Die Umwelt des Alten Testaments* (NSKAT, 29; Stuttgart: Katholisches Bibelwerk, 1994), p. 188.

105. N. Na'aman, 'Israel, Edom and Egypt in the Tenth Century BCE', *TA* 19 (1992), pp. 71-79 (81), notices that in Shishak's topographical list, 'of the northern towns of the kingdom of Judah only Gibeon (No. 23) is mentioned; all other Benjaminite and Judean towns are conspicuously missing'. See also E.A. Knauf, 'The Low Chronology and How Not to Deal with It', *BN* 101 (2000), p. 62 n. 30.

106. Machir was then turned into a son of Manasseh and father of Gilead (Gen. 50.23): E.A. Knauf, 'Stämme Israels', *Evangelisches Kirchenlexikon* (Göttingen: 1994), 4, pp. 479-83 (481).

107. T. Schneider, 'Did Jehu Kill his Own Family?', *BARev* (1995), pp. 26-34.

foundation of Israelo-Tyrian entente (1 Kgs 19.15-17). The song of Deborah, praising Yhwh, the god of the dry mountains of Seir and Sinai (vv. 4-5) who had proved that he was capable to give victory even on the low-lands, became important again to affirm the control of the plain against the Canaanite merchants of the coast (Tyrians and Sidonians). The new gods of v. 8, if they are not due to a late gloss, could also reflect the rise of a radical Yahwism. In fact, these new gods could result from a slight modification of an older reading:

יבחר אלים חדשים אז להם צערים < יבחר אלהים חדשים אז לחם צערים

'New gods were chosen, then barleys bread' could have first read 'New leaders were chosen, then for them new princes'.

אלהים 'gods' would be a modernized reading of אלים 'rams, princes, leaders' (Exod. 15.15; 2 Kgs 24.15; Jer. 4.22; Ezek. 17.13; 30.13; 31.14; 32.20; 38.18; Pss. 2.5; 58.2) corresponding in the second part of the verse to צערים 'young rams'.[108]

The book of Saviours around 720 BCE. In the aftermath of the transformation of the kingdom of Israel into the Assyrian provinces of Megiddo and Samaria, the renowned Bethel 'Seminary' produced a collection of heroic deeds, the BS. After a short but virile episode with Ehud, the wisemen of Bethel set out to turn the song of Deborah into the story of Barak, a saviour who, like Ehud, was raised by Yhwh to save Israel as soon as his oppressed people cried to Yhwh (Judg. 4.3). The story of Barak is much more complicated than Ehud's because it is based on the well-known song of Deborah. The model forced constraints on the editors who had to work out a way to introduce the saviour Barak into the plot of the song. Deborah, whom the song is attributed to, becomes a prophetess (not yet a judge), who transmits Yhwh's orders to Barak. Barak complies and annihilates the army of the Canaanite king Jabin.[109] However, everyone

---

108. P.D. Miller, 'Animal Names as Designation in Ugaritic and Hebrew', *UF* 2 (1970), pp. 177-86.

109. The name of this king of Hazor has been connected with the Akkadian *Ibni-Adad* by H. Cazelles, 'Review of Jean-Robert Kupper, *Les nomades en Mésopotamie au temps des rois de Mari* (Paris: Belles Lettres, 1957)', *VT* 8 (1958), pp. 316-20 (230). The choice of an Akkadian name for the king of Hazor may be understood as a kind of antiquarian tribute to the Assyrians. The choice could also have been guided by one of the meaning of √יבן preserved in Arabic (N. Calder, 'The *sa'y* and *Jabîn*: some notes on Qur'ân 37.102-3', *JSS* 31 (1986), pp. 17-26): 'forehead / temple'. This would establish a playful parallel to Sisera's רקה into which Jael drove the peg.

knew that a woman, who was not Deborah, had murdered Sisera. Barak's unwillingness to go to war without Deborah allowed the introduction of a second woman who would rob Barak of his glory. Deborah goes with Barak (Judg. 4.9 repeated in v. 10) but then disappears from the narrative and Jael pops up in v. 17. Eventually, every actor plays his role and the conclusion records a forty-year period of rest (Judg. 5.31). It is not clear whether Barak was already present in the form of the song that the editors of the BS worked with, or whether Barak was added to Judg. 5.12, 15 later. But the plot of the song, even in its present form, does not require his presence. In v. 12, he is set in redundant parallel with Deborah and in v. 15 he is once again tagging on Deborah's heels in order to sustain the late insertion of Issachar. Barak could therefore be a creation of the BS.

The additions after 720 BCE. The Kenites (Judg. 4.11, 17; 5.24) are probably the signature of the next editorial stage, that will introduce a saviour from the South at the onset of the BS, Othniel son of Kenaz (see Chapter 2). Jael became then a Kenite.

At the end of the seventh century BCE, the derogatory Amalek gloss (Judg. 5.14) was probably meant to cut the secular link between Ephraim and Benjamin. Opprobrium was thrown on Ephraim, once Josiah annexed Benjamin to Judah. Some Greek manuscripts read ἐν κοιλάδι 'in the plain' instead of בעמלק 'in Amalek'. Except for the story of David's rise (1 Sam. 27.8-12; 30.1-20), Amalek is always an archaizing gloss.[110] Moreover, in the song, Ephraim is part of the tribes that did come to fight Sisera, there was therefore no reason to taint its honour until the Judaeans had good reasons to do so. But the reading בעמק 'in the plain' fits well with the first claims of the Israelites over the plain.

Deborah was turned into a judge when the schema, the list of Judges in Judg. 10 and 12 and the judge notices in 3.10; 12.7; 15.20; 16.31 were introduced into the BS (see Chapter 3).

---

110. E.A. Knauf, 'Amalekiter', *LTK,* 1.483. 1 Samuel 27 and 30 are the only passages to locate Amalek in a coherent geographical setting, namely among the various groups that shared the Negeb during Iron Age 1. Saul's campaign against Amalek (1 Sam. 15) is stereotyped, its sole aim is to legitimize the transfer of the crown from Saul to David. Its geographical data is useless: see the insolvable polemic over the 'city of Amalek' in 1 Sam. 15.5: I. Finkelstein, 'Arabian Trade in the Negev', *JNES* 47 (1988), pp. 241-52 (Tel Masos); D. Edelman, 'Saul's Battle against Amalek', *JSOT* 35 (1986), pp. 71-84 (Northern Samaria, south of Carmel). According to Knauf, *Midian,* 167, 1 Sam. 15 and Num. 31 reflect Edomite reality of the third to second centuries BCE.

Issachar, otherwise missing from the BS,[111] was added in Judg. 5.15 at the same time as Tola, grandson of a 'man from Issachar' (Judg. 10.1).

Barak was inserted into the song by someone who noticed that the hero of Judg. 4 was absent from the song of Deborah.

Finally, the staging of Deborah under her palm-tree, Jael's gripping the hammer מקבת (Judg. 4.21) and the Heber notice (Judg. 5.24 is a late gloss influenced by Judg. 4.11, 17 because it is now among the longest verses of the song) are likely to be the last details that were added into Judg. 4–5, around the Maccabaean period (see Chapter 7).

Judges 6–8: Gideon

Instead of having two parallel accounts like Deborah and Barak, Gideon is the spitting image of Jerubbaal. Their cycle now spreads over three chapters and the elements of the frame (see Figure 1) are now dispersed across these three chapters. The original saviour story appears to have swollen due to the addition of various developments.

In order not to be overwhelmed by the sheer amount of material, Judg. 6–8 are going to be read in the light of Judg. 3–4 to separate between the original saviour story and the subsequent developments. The sorting will be done according to a few simple criteria:

- Attitude towards Israel and the hero: a favourable attitude towards the hero and Israel will be taken as a mark of the BS. On the other hand, critical elements towards them will be considered as a secondary development, originating in all likelihood from Judah.
- Antimonarchical leanings: antimonarchical elements (implicit in Judg. 3–4 and explicit in Judg. 9) will be attributed to the BS.
- Idolatry: any mention of foreign gods will be understood as an extension of the accusation of the schema against the BS.
- Possible date around 720 BCE: elements that could not have been written in 720 BCE will be considered later than the BS.

The Gideon cycle will now be considered, section by section, following the order of the text.

---

111. Richter, *TU*, p. 333.

Judges 6.1-6: Frame

The story begins with the introductory elements of the frame of the BS. Israel did what was evil in the sight of Yhwh and is delivered into the hands of Midian for seven years (Judg. 6.1). But before Israel cries to Yhwh (v. 6), a vivid description of the oppression presents Israel hiding in caves in the mountain (v. 2) and the arrival of Midian who plunders Israel's fields and herds (vv. 3-5). The enemy is compared to locusts stripping the land thoroughly. Midian, who was alone in vv. 1-2, receives the help of Amalek and of the people of the East who come with their tents and their camels to waste the land as far as Gaza (vv. 3-5). These 'helpers' of Midian are clearly reflecting the raids of camel herders that appeared in Palestine in the aftermath of the Babylonian destruction in the sixth century BCE.[112] On the contrary, the Midianites correspond to the Proto-Arabs that were settled by Sargon II in Samaria after his campaign in Northern Arabia around 716 BCE.[113] Around 720 BCE, the BS could know these Midianites, recently settled in the area, but Amalek and the people of the East are secondary.

Judges 6.7-10: Anonymous Prophet

Instead of raising a saviour to answer the cries of the Israelites, Yhwh sends a prophet to accuse them of not listening to his voice. This is a frontal attack against the theology of the BS. The reference to the gods of the Amorites (v. 10) indicates that these verses are part of the critical reading of the BS inaugurated in the schema.[114]

Judges 6.11-24: Calling

The arrival of Yhwh's messenger introduces an intricate scene similar to a prophet's call. However, this oracle does not set Gideon on an equal footing with the prophets because Gideon's attitude is most peculiar. Everything is geared to turn Gideon into a farcical figure. Indeed, the regular elements of theophany and prophetic call are present. But from the very beginning, the dialogue between the heavenly messenger and Gideon goes off-track: the appearing of the מלאך־יהוה does not overwhelm

---

112. Knauf, *Midian,* p. 35; Becker, *Richterzeit,* p. 141.

113. A.G. Lie, *The Inscriptions of Sargon II* (Paris, 1929), pp. 20-23; Knauf, *Midian,* pp. 85-86.

114. LXXB, Syriac and Vulgate smoothened the sharp opposition between the cries of v. 6 and their critic in vv. 7-10 by removing v. 6b. The repetition of the cries, enhancing the opposition, thus disappears.

Gideon with godly terror. He is too busy hiding some grain from the
Midianites (v. 11) to enter a theological debate. Therefore the angel does
not introduce himself with the regular אל־תירא 'fear not!' (it will come in
v. 23, when it is clear that Gideon fears the Midianites rather than Yhwh's
messenger). Admittedly, the angel chooses the wrong time to sit under the
tree (v. 11), and his tongue in cheek יהוה עמך גבור החיל 'Yhwh is with
you strong hero' does not help. Therefore, Gideon clearly states his doubts
about the presence of Yhwh with his people: what was the point of pulling
us out of Egypt if it was to deliver us in the hands of Midian? (v. 13)
Yhwh has to face Gideon squarely (פנה) to force him to listen to his order
to save Israel (v. 14). Despite a wealth of assurances of divine support
(הלא שלחתיך 'Am I not sending you?' v. 14; אהיה עמך 'I am with you' v.
16),[115] despite the holocaust consumed in one stroke of a magical wand
(Judg. 6.21),[116] Gideon remains doubtful over anyone's ability to save
Israel (אם־ישך מושיע v. 36). Gideon merely sees (ראה) that it is Yhwh
who is speaking to him (v. 22), but he feels no fear of dying because he
has seen Yhwh (see Judg. 13.22).

If an old *Altarätiologie* is behind this text, one has to admit that it has
been seriously downgraded.[117] The Samaria ostraca support the localization of Ophrah and Abiezer (vv. 11, 24) in Manasseh (v. 15),[118] but
nothing indicates that Ophrah was a cultic centre.

Compared to Ehud and Barak, Gideon is turned into a coward by this
prevaricating. This passage is often read in a more positive light, as an
example of piety but it inevitably turns into a pale religiosity that has
nothing to do with the boldness of the saviours.[119] Moreover, the form

---

115. See Exod. 3 and A.G. Auld, 'Gideon: Hacking at the Heart of the Old Testament', *VT* 39 (1989), pp. 257-67 (257).

116. The meal turned into a holocaust is a very elaborate composition alluding to the
burning bush, Jacob at Peniel and Succoth (Gen. 32–33), Elijah at the Carmel (1 Kgs
18) and Manoah's offering (Judg. 13). The particle ש in v. 17 indicates a late editorial
note.

117. Becker, *Richterzeit*, pp. 148-51.

118. Ophra is Jinsāfūṭ, Fer'atah is in Abiezer, west of Shechem along wadi Qanah:
A. Lemaire, *Inscriptions hébraïques*. I *.Les ostraca* (LAPO, 9; Paris: Cerf, 1977), pp.
60-65; Knauf, 'Eglon and Ophrah', pp. 36-39. The date of the ostraca is discussed by
B. Becking, *The Fall of Samaria: An Historical and Archeological Study* (SHANE, 2;
Leiden: E.J. Brill, 1992), p. 5.

119. For instance B. Standaert, 'Adonaï Shalom (Judges 6-9)', in S.E. Porter and
T.H. Olbricht (eds.), *Rhetoric, Scripture and Theology* (JSOTSup, 131; Sheffield:
JSOT Press, 1996), pp. 195-202 (200): 'The double test is not just the repeated

שאתה (v. 17) has to be the particle־שׁ + the independent pronoun אתה a Late Hebrew form even if this is the only attestation of the vocalization:[120]

This linguistic element and the critique of the hero indicate that this scene has nothing to do with the BS. Its angel of Yhwh מלאך־יהוה mirrors the Bokim episode (Judg. 2.1-5) and belongs to the critical stage of the BS (see Chapter 3).

Judges 6.25-32: Demolishing an Altar

After the reproaches of the anonymous prophet, an altar dedicated to Baal is destroyed, at last. However, Gideon is not turning into a fearless Deuteronomist, for the destruction is done at night, with ten helpers (v. 27). The real hero is Joash, Gideon's father, to whom belonged the altar and the sacrificed animals. Surprisingly, Joash does not blame his son, he takes his defence against the men of the village who want to avenge Baal, Joash even manages to preserve the religious peace of the community with a cunning answer: 'let Baal himself contend against him who pulled his altar down!' (v. 31).[121]

In a very thorough study of this passage, de Pury attaches great importance to Joah's reply. According to him, the fact that Joash does not repent his Baalist past shows that this text is much older than the reign of Josiah and that it rests on an old Israelite tradition of the ninth century BCE. Gideon would be a Yahwist zealot, keen to demonstrate the irreducible character of his faithfulness to Yhwh by transgressing social taboos. Gideon breaks his father's altar just as Ehud lies in order to strike Eglon (Judg. 3.20) and as Jael murders the guest she has invited into her own tent. Joash, a distinguished member of the tribal elite, defuses a potential civil war by suggesting that humans should let the gods sort out their own problems.[122]

---

assurance of God's proximity: the sequence follows descriptively the culturally covered way from nomadism to consequent sedentarisation. Does our God accompany until the new cultural stage where we live now? It is interesting that Gideon never suggests a totalitarian answer: we never had everything dry or everything wet. You know God only in his elective proximity.'

120. P. Joüon and T. Muraoka, *A Grammar of Biblical Hebrew* (SBib, 14; Roma: Editrice Pontifico Istituto Biblico, 1996), §38.

121. A. de Pury, 'Le raid de Gédéon' (Jug 6, 25-32) et l'histoire de l'exclusivisme yahwiste', in Th. Römer (ed.), *Lectio Difficilior Probabilior? FS F. Smyth-Florentin* (DBAT, 12; Heidelberg: Esprint, 1991), pp. 173-205 (198).

122. de Pury, 'Raid', pp. 190-98.

If de Pury is correct, the BS is a collection of tales of Yahwist zealots and the Joash episode warns against religious violence. However, his argument can be altered and the subtle relationship between Gideon the Baal-basher and Joash the smart country aristocrat can be considered as a splendid advert for Josiah's rule addressed to the Israelite landowners at the end of the Assyrian period. With Judg. 6.7-32, Josiah and his advisers are inflicting on Gideon a moderate critique. The anonymous prophet reminds the Israelite landlords that crying to Yhwh as their BS suggests, without first purifying the cult of Yhwh of the traces of Assyrian rule it necessarily carries, falls short of Yhwh's requirements. The vocation under the tree plays down Gideon's boldness and suggests that the Israelites are less than perfect servants of Yhwh, which explains conveniently why Israel fell to Assyrian hands while Judah is still 'independent'. However, the aim of Jerusalem is to embroil Israel along Josiah's overthrow of Assyrian rule and to create Solomon's Great Israel from Dan to Beer-sheba. Hence the figure of Joash, unknown to the Gideon story of the BS, tailor-made by Josiah to appeal to the great men of the Israelite countryside who hold power over the rural population of the mountain. Joash is the opposite of his 'son' Gideon, not a critical word is uttered against him. Joash plays an impeccable part, he does not blame his son, thus showing that he agrees that Baalism has to be eradicated, he claims that Baal 'if he is a god' (v. 31) should deal with Gideon, thus suggesting that he is confident that no great risks threaten his son. And all the while, he is acting responsibly, for the best of the community at large.

It seems best therefore to consider Judg. 6.7-32, the anonymous prophet, the vocation at Ophrah and the Joash episode as a whole, a Josianic addition to the BS. The immediate and unconditional salvation of the BS, its hero Gideon and Baal are all criticized, and the way to real salvation is clearly marked out: it is not Baal that you should save אם־אתם תושיעון אותו (v. 31) but save your sons by getting rid of Baal and those who lord over you. Welcome to the Josianic club!

Judges 6.33-35: Arrival of the Enemy and Mobilization
Midian arrives in the Jezreel valley to plunder Israel. The spirit of Yhwh takes possession of Gideon who blows the *shofar* to call Abiezer behind him. In spite of Becker's affirmation, it is not clear whether the extension of the call to Manasseh, Asher and Zebulun in v. 35 is secondary, whether the first Gideon convoked only Abiezer,[123] this problem will be discussed

---

123. Becker, *Richterzeit*, p. 161 reckons that the calling up of Manasseh, Asher,

in the concluding section. Apart from the Amalekites, the people of the East and possibly Manasseh, Asher and Zebulun, these verses belong to the BS.

Judges 6.36-40: Fleece

Before attacking, Gideon submits Yhwh to the test and counter-test of the fleece. The method is excellent, as the clay of a threshing floor reveals moisture by changing colour.[124] However the aim is surprising, as Gideon is still wondering whether or not Yhwh means to save through him (vv. 36-37). In fact, these tests slow down the narrative: the act of deliverance is delayed and the saviour's courage is reduced once more. Compared to Ehud and Barak, Gideon appears as an outright sceptic, the hero of the BS has been downgraded by this passage.

Judges 7.1-3: Setting up Camps and Sending Home the Fearful

Jerubbaal and his followers camp near the spring of trembling הרד.[125] The fearful and the trembling are invited to go and chirp צפר at Gilead.[126] Israel must not think that the salvation came through its own hand (Judg. 7.2 and 8.22). This is no critique against Gideon, therefore this passage can belong to the BS. Only the numbers of v. 3b can be secondary as they prepare the second reduction of the task force in the following verses.

Judges 7.4-8: Selecting the Dogs

Yhwh requires a second reduction of the contingent because there is still too many courageous fighters, a compliment! The whole passage appears as a playful Midrash of the previous one: v. 4 transforms √צפר 'to chirp' (v. 3) into √צרף 'to test'. Verse 8b repeats the localization of the camp of

---

Zebulun and Naphtali in v. 35 contradicts the opposition between the small numbers of Gideon's followers and the countless plunderers in vv. 33-34. As for Abiezer 'my father is help', the name could be made up to fit the Joash episode where Gideon was helped by his father to the point of saving his life.

124. J.L. Kelso, *The Ceramic Vocabulary of the Old Testament* (BASORSup, 5-6; New Haven: ASOR, 1948), p. 42.

125. Near Beth-shean: H. Rösel, 'Studien zur Topographie der Kriege in den Büchern Josua und Richter 2', *ZDPV* 92 (1976), pp. 10-46 (22-23).

126. A possible hint at the song of Deborah where Gilead stays home (Judg. 5.17) like Reuben who prefers to listen to the shepherds pipe (Judg. 5.16). May the fearful Abiezerites please join the field orchestra of the disbanded Israel! In this case, Judg. 7.3 would be another argument in favour of the antiquity of the Song of Deborah.

Midian (v. 1), thus suggesting that this passage is secondary.[127] This is confirmed by the mode of selection. The selected men are precisely those who lapped water like dogs (v. 5), indeed a disparaging criterion for those who have the honour to be chosen! This is probably a mark of Judaean deriding of Israel, which sets this passage apart from vv. 1-3. Numbers were added in v. 3b in order to introduce this dogging episode, secondary to the BS.

Judges 7.9: Attack!

The fateful night arrives. Like the other saviours before him, Gideon receives orders to get up קום (see Judg. 3.9, 15; 4.14) and to go down to Midian's camp for Yhwh has given it in Gideon's hand. This is an essential element of the saviour narrative.

Judges 7.10-15: Rolling Loaf

Just when, at long last, the time has come to fight, it is now Yhwh himself who offers Gideon yet another way out. In case Gideon may still harbour the slightest doubt, he is invited to go, where else, if not down to the very camp that frightens him so terribly. Only his servant Purah[128] goes along with Gideon, to eavesdrop on a Midianite's account of a nightmare: a rolling צלול kneading basin[129] or, according to traditional translations, a cake of barley bread came down and flattened the tent. The interpretation is immediately supplied by the dreamer's tent-mate: the rolling object is no other than Gideon's sword to whom God has given Midian (v. 14)! Due

---

127. Becker, *Richterzeit*, p. 162.

128. פרה the vocalization is unsure as LXX reads Φαρα. Parah from √פרא 'wild ass' (Jer. 14.6) or 'mule' (Assyrian *parû*). From √פור, פורה is a wine-press or part of it (Isa. 63.3) a fitting name in light of the vocation of Gideon at the wine-press in Ophrah. Also possible is √פרר 'to break, to rend, to frustrate'.

129. חלול לחם שערים מתהפך from √חלל 'to shade', or Arabic *ṣalla* 'to dry up' (*KB*, 3.1025), or √חול *miṣwal* in Syria 'basin' (*BDB* p. 847). According to Rösel, 'Topographie 2', 14 n. 20, לחם could be a explanatory gloss. LXX translate μαγίς ἄρτου from μάσσω to knead. Rather than the kneaded paste, the unidentified rolling object could be the stone ustensil in which bread is kneaded, much more impressive than a loaf of bread (see illustrations in V. Fritz, *Kinneret: Ergebnisse der Ausgrabungen auf dem Tell el-'Orême am See Gennesaret 1982-1985* (ADPV, 15; Wiesbaden: Otto Harrassowitz, 1990), pp. 351, 353. √חלל provides the name of several cooking vessels: חלחה 'cooking pot' (2 Chron. 35.13), חלחת 'banquet bowl' (2 Kgs 21.13, Prov. 19.24; 26.15), חלחית 'bowl' (2 Kgs 2.20): Kelso, *Ceramic*, no. 59-60.

to the difficulty to understand the exact nature of the rolling object, it is not easy to decide whether the comparison with Gideon is ironic or not. But this ultimate check before the action is certainly serving the same purpose than the previous ones. They all slow the motion down to the point of exasperation, any leftover heroism has vanished for good. This passage is to be attributed to the secondary additions.

Judges 7.16-21: Victory without Fighting
The account of the deliverance at last! 300 disarmed men brandishing torches and blowing trumpets surround the camp. The words 'sword for Yhwh and for Gideon' (v. 20) throw the camp into a panic and they all flee while Gideon's men stand motionless (v. 21). The victory is complete, gained without striking a single blow. The Gideon story of the BS could end here.

Judges 7.22–8.3: Trouble at the Jordan and Beyond
Verse 22 repeats the sounding of the *shofar* from v. 20 in order to introduce a new development. Now the Midianites turn their sword against one another and run away towards the Jordan near Abel-Meholah.

Verse 23 introduces the men of Naphtali, Asher and Manasseh (// Judg. 6.35 Zebulun missing) called up (צעק) again to pursue Midian.

Then vv. 24-25 involve Ephraim to guard the Jordan fords. Ephraim strikes two Midianite princes who give their names to the rocks on which they were killed: Oreb 'Crow' and Zeeb 'Wolf'.

The men of Ephraim violently reproach Gideon for their belated mobilization (v. 1), and Gideon, like his father before him (6.31), manages to placate his opponents with a wise saying that supports the primacy of Ephraim over Abiezer. Ephraim comes through as full of vain-glory, his accusations mostly unjustified as Gideon seems to have gone out of his way to reserve the capture of the Midianite leaders to Ephraim. However, Ephraim's accusation ויריבון explain Gideon's other name, Jerubbaal (7.1), derived from √ריב 'to accuse'.

The polemic against Ephraim and the use of צעק in the sense of mobilizing an army rather than crying to Yhwh indicates that this passage is a secondary development to the BS Gideon narrative.[130]

---

130. Against Richter, *TU*, 173.238 who attributes it to the *Retterbuch*.

Judges 8.4-21: Gideon's Revenge

Surprisingly, the execution of the Midianite princes and Gideon's cunning answer to Ephraim do not mark the end of the war against Midian and the internal strife between Israelite groups. In v. 4, Gideon and his 300 'dogs' cross the Jordan and require food supplies from Succoth (v. 5) and Penuel (v. 8) as they are now pursuing two brand new Midianite kings, Zebah and Zalmunna. These, together with the people of the East (v. 10), the caravan route (v. 11) and the camel ornaments (v. 21) clearly reflect a late seventh century BCE reality at the earliest.[131] This new victory against Midian and the people of the East (v. 10) is dealt with in vv. 11-12 in general terms. The whole passage is interested in describing Gideon's personal vengeance: vv. 13-16 are devoted to the punishment of the 77 elders of Succoth who are taught a lesson with thorns (קוֹצִים) and thistles (ברקנים), a word that has defied attempts to explain it.[132] Then the tower of Penuel is overthrown נתץ (like the Baal altar Judg. 6.28) and its people killed (Judg. 8.17). It is not impossible that the Succoth and Penuel incident is meant as a reference to the Jacob cycle (Gen. 32.30-31;[133] 33.17), insisting once more on the strife between the descendants of the Patriarch. Finally, the execution of Zebah and Zalmunna is presented as avenging the murder of Gideon's brothers at Tabor, an incident unknown apart from this passage. King Zebah and king Zalmunna affirm that these brothers whom they slew resembled sons of the king (v. 18). They themselves are depicted with royal grandeur to the very end: as Gideon's eldest son Jether (Remain) is afraid to draw his sword, they demand that Gideon himself put them to death for 'as the man is, so is his strength'. This scene is clearly geared to establish the kingly nature of Gideon, thus legitimizing the crowning proposal of the next verse.

131. Knauf, *Midian*, pp. 39-40.

132. The meaning is always infered from the context of this passage. It could derive from √ברק like Barak! J. Servier, *Les portes de l'année: rites et symboles: l'Algérie dans la tradition méditerranéenne* (Les voies de l'homme; Paris: Lafont, 1962), pp. 243-44 reports a Kabyle legend that presents some similarities to Judg. 8.16: the students of a small Coranic school tried to gain control over the local population by asking for themselves the poor-man's share that every farmer is supposed to put aside from his harvest. In a nearby village, the farmers gave them hospitality, but during the night, the farmer fell on the sleeping students and forced them to thresh *tasenant* thistles bare footed before letting them go empty handed. Since then, the village is called Tasenant 'thistle'. Farmers remain eager to decide by themselves to whom they will give the compulsory pauper's tax.

133. According to 1 Kgs 12.25, it is Jeroboam who rebuilt Peniel.

This passage, like the previous one, is considered secondary to the BS: Judg. 7.22–8.4 go together with Judg. 8.4-21 because Judg. 8.4 cannot be the direct continuation of Judg. 7.21.[134]

Judges 8.22-23: Gideon Refuses the Crown
Hereditary rule משׁל is offered to Gideon as he saved Israel from the hand of Midian. But Gideon refuses the rule for him or for his son after him, for 'Yhwh rules'. There is no reason to reject these verses from the BS: they are both favourable to Gideon and antimonarchical.

Judges 8.24-27: Gideon Makes a Snare
After his impeccable refusal of the rule, Gideon requests instead the gold earrings that his men have plundered from the Ishmaelites. With these and all the gold trappings that were taken from the camels, Gideon makes an ephod and sets it up in Ophrah. All Israel prostitutes itself after it and it becomes a snare (מוקשׁ see Judg. 2.4).

These Ishmaelites belong to the late Persian period at the earliest.[135] The making of the ephod appears as a midrashic elaboration based on Aaron's and Jeroboam's golden calves (Exod. 32; 1 Kgs 12).[136] These verses interrupt the sequence between the refusal of rule and the concluding remarks (vv. 28-35).[137] Moreover, they put Gideon on an equal footing with the worst idol-makers, thus ruining his reputation just after he stepped down to let Yhwh rule over Israel. Here is a clear case of Deuteronomistic soiling of an Israelite hero, therefore secondary to the BS.

Judges 8.28: Frame
In regular BS fashion, the land enjoys a forty-year period of calm. This verse belongs to the frame of the BS, except for the last word 'in the days of Gideon' which, like the schema, limits the deliverance to the days of the judge (Judg. 2.18-19).

Judges 8.29-35: Transition
Jerubbaal goes home to look after his harem and his Shechemite con-

134. Becker, *Richterzeit*, p. 173 n. 116.
135. E.A. Knauf, *Ismael: Untersuchungen zur Geschichte Palästinas und Nordarabiens im 1. Jahrtausend v.Chr.* (ADPV; Wiesbaden, Otto Harrassowitz, 2nd edn, 1989), p. 14.
136. M. Garsiel, 'Name Derivations in Judges vi–viii', *VT* 43 (1993), pp. 302-317.
137. See Becker, *Richterzeit*, p. 182.

cubine and to produce a large offspring. Since the multitude of women is a Deuteronomistic favourite to explain idolatry (Solomon in 1 Kgs 11), and since the other BS heroes disappear from the scene as soon as the deliverance is accomplished, this passage is likely to be secondary. Furthermore, by naming Abimelech (v. 31), Gideon becomes directly embroiled in the disasters in ch. 9, while vv. 22-23 clearly exonerated him of any such responsibility. The last two verses are clearly based on the schema (Judg. 2.19) and on the mention of Baal-berith in Judg. 9.4.

Recapitulation

The end of Judg. 8 has been reached, and the full extent of the Gideon story of the BS is presented in Figure 3.

This reconstruction reveals a narrative of about twenty verses, comparable to the story of Ehud (fifteen verses) and Judg. 4 (thirty verses). In spite of the hypothetical nature of such a reconstruction, the characteristics of the saviour narratives as they have been seen in the stories of Ehud and Barak are easily recognizable. The elements of the frame are all present. The narrative itself presents the raising of a hero who, with the help of a band of men from his clan, gets rid of a large army simply by encircling its camp at night, shouting, smashing pottery and waving torches. Once again, a most unpromising individual obtains the victory through the use of a most unexpected device.

No attempt will be made to go upstream from the BS Gideon narrative to find an old Abiezerite tradition: such endeavour falls outside the scope of this inquiry and its validity is crippled by the lack of any literary framework that could offer the necessary historical background and criteria for such analysis. The lack of a clear literary unit does not permit to do to the Gideon story what was possible in the Barak cycle thanks to Judg. 5.

Although Gideon is never called 'saviour', √ישע is present twice in this reconstitution of the BS narrative: Yhwh fears that Israel will glorify itself against him, thinking 'my hand saved me' (7.2) and, at the end, where Gideon is offered a hereditary rule to reward him for saving Israel from the hand of Midian (8.22); a fitting conclusion for the third figure of the BS. The large amount of material which has been considered secondary (over 80 verses) is bent on questioning the validity of Gideon's saving act. The critical or at least derogatory setting of these five other attestations of √ישע (Judg. 6.14-15, 36-37; 7.7) is a good indicator of the prior existence of a BS which claimed that Yhwh saved Israel time and time again, through the agency of illustrious nobodies.

Book of Saviours Narrative	Additions
6.1-6 The people of Israel did what was evil in the sight of Yhwh and Yhwh gave them in the hands of Midian seven years. The hand of Midian prevailed over Israel and because of Midian, the people of Israel made for themselves dens in the mountains, caves and strongholds. Whenever Israel put in seed, Midian came and attacked them, they would encamp against them and destroy the produce of the land and leave no food in Israel, no sheep nor ox nor ass. They came up with their cattle and their tents, coming like locusts for numbers; they and their camels could not be counted, they entered the land and wasted it. Israel was brought very low because of Midian. The sons of Israel cried to Yhwh.	
	6.7-32 Anonymous prophet, calling, Baal altar
6.33-35 Midian crossed the Jordan and encamped in the Valley of Jezreel. But the spirit of Yhwh took possession of Gideon; he sounded the trumpet and the Abiezerites were called out to follow him	
	6.35-40 Manasseh, Asher, Zebulun and Naphtali? Fleece
7.1-3 Jerubbaal (he is Gideon) and all the people who were with him rose early and encamped at the spring of Harod; the camp of Midian was north of them, by the hill of Moreh, in the valley. Yhwh said to Gideon: 'The people with you are too many for me to give the Midianites in their hand, lest Israel vaunt itself against me saying 'my hand delivered me'. Now call in the ears of the people: 'Whoever is fearful and trembling may return and chirp at Gilead'.	
	7.4-8 Selecting the dogs
7.9 That night Yhwh said to him: 'Arise, go down against the camp for I have given it into your hand.'	
	7.10-15 Dream of the rolling loaf
7.16-21 He divided the men in three companies and put trumpets in all their hands and empty jars, with torches in the jars. He said to them: 'Look at me and do likewise; when I come to the outskirts of the camp, do as I do. When I blow the trumpet, I and all who are with me, then blow the trumpets around the camp and shout 'For Yhwh and for Gideon'. Gideon and the men who were with him came to the outskirts of the camp at the middle watch, when they had set the watch; they blew the trumpets and smashed the jars. The three companies blew the trumpets and broke the jars, holding in their left hands the torches and in their right hands the trumpets to blow. They cried: 'A sword for Yhwh and for Gideon!' They stood each man in his place round the camp. All the army ran, they screemed and fled.	
	7.22-8.21 Transjordan, Ephraim's anger, Gideon's revenge
8.22-23 The men of Israel said to Gideon: 'Rule over us, your son and your grandson also; for you saved us from the hand of Midian'. Gideon said: 'I will not rule over you; Yhwh will rule over you'.	
	8.24-27 Makind an Ephod
8.28 Midian was subdued before the sons of Israel and they did not lift their heads. The land had rest 40 years.	
	8.29-35 Gideon names Abimelech, Baal-Berith

Figure 3. *The Gideon Narrative and its Additions*

Whether or not Manasseh, Asher, Zebulun and Naphtali (Judg. 6.35) were present in the BS narrative is not so easy to determine. The story can function without them and without specific numbers, with the sole involvement of Abiezer or just with an unspecified group of followers because Abiezer can also be secondary.[138] Naphtali and Zebulun are the only Israelite groups mentioned in Judg. 4 and Barak is from Kedesh in Naphtali (Judg. 4.6, 10). If Naphtali and Zebulun are original in ch. 4, they probably are also in Judg. 6.35. But what about Manasseh? If the modern location of wadi Harod between Jezreel and Beth-shean corresponds to the one meant here, the mention of Manasseh would be normal as wadi Harod flows from the Manassite hills into the Jezreel valley. Manasseh, Asher, Zebulun and Naphtali have therefore a good probability to be original in the BS.

Gideon, Jerubbaal, Joash and Abimelech
In its present form, Judg. 6–9 is presenting itself like a saga of Gideon's family, with father Joash (Judg. 6.29; 8.13, 29), Gideon and his murdered brothers (Judg. 8.19), Jether, Gideon's first-born son (Judg. 8.20), and Abimelech his bastard son (Judg. 8.31 and throughout ch. 9). Gideon is nicknamed Jerubbaal after the destruction of the Baal altar (Judg. 6.32) although the rest of the narrative goes on to call him Gideon. Jerubbaal reappears thrice after the altar episode, in Judg. 7.1 and Judg. 8.35 (Jerubbaal, that is Gideon) and Judg. 8.29 (Jerubbaal ben Joash). In ch. 9, Abimelech is consistently called ben Jerubbaal, never ben Gideon in spite of Judg. 8.31 where Gideon names Abimelech.

The simplest way to explain this complex situation is to see it as the result of the linkage of two independent stories, Gideon the third hero of the BS and Abimelech the counter-hero of ch. 9. The family or dynastic elements are secondary to the original BS Gideon story, because the other saviours are free from such considerations. The logic of the saviour narratives is that a hero is raised by Yhwh and then disappears as quickly as he came once the deliverance has been accomplished. This is exactly why Gideon refuses to rule over Israel, he or his son and grandson after him (Judg. 8.23). The rule of Yhwh is preferable, and ch. 9 illustrates this very point by depicting the consequences of human rule and kingship. Judges 8 and 9 are connected by Gideon's refusal of the rule in order precisely to

---

138. Abi-ezer 'my father is help' fits the Joash episode too well not to be suspect. However, the argument can be reversed and it is Joash who could be secondary, illustrating the original name of the Abiezerites.

prevent any association between Gideon, the saviour beyond reproach, and Abimelech, the ruthless bandit who sets himself up as lord over Israel and ends up in disaster. Thus are opposed two different rules, the rule of Yhwh which consists in raising a saviour in times of need, and the rule of men who establish themselves as rulers solely because their father was king (Abimelech 'my father is king'). The preference of the text remains obvious in spite of the large additions made to the BS.

The material considered secondary to the BS establishes a link between Gideon and Jerubbaal, whereas the BS had set them apart. Gideon is given a father, a shrewd and influential member of the Ophrah aristocracy (Judg. 6.25-32) who manages to overshadow the saviour Gideon, although his own baalist past falls directly under the censure of the anonymous prophet (Judg. 6.7-10). Lengthy checks and procrastination (Judg. 6.36-40; 7.4; 8.10-15) then undermine Gideon's courage and faithfulness. Once Midian has finally been routed, the narrative develops into a campaign in Transjordan, true gangland killings (Judg. 8.4-21) where we learn that Gideon had brothers who looked like kings (Judg. 8.18). Gideon's refusal of the rule is tarnished by the melting of a golden ephod (Judg. 8.24-27), a feature that annihilates any credit Gideon could have gained by overturning the altar of Baal. Indeed, Israel now plays the harlot to the Baals and chooses Baal-berith as its god (Judg. 8.34 // 9.4, 46).

The naming of the child of the Shechem concubine (Judg. 8.31) stands in the most blatant contradiction to Gideon's refusal to rule: Gideon becomes the father of Abimelech, and as such, directly responsible for Abimelech's bloody rule by the very choice of such a name.

The function of Jerubbaal remains to be explained. In spite of his frequent mention in ch. 9 as father of Abimelech (vv. 1, 2, 5, 16, 19, 24, 28, 57), it is not sure that Jerubbaal belongs to the original Abimelech story, for the name Abimelech contains in itself the programme of ch. 9 and this name is obviously tailor-made to fit the story.[139] That Abimelech is ben Jerubbaal is a most dispensable element for the flow of ch. 9. However, it reinforces the connection between Gideon and Abimelech. Furthermore, Jerubbaal also introduces Joash into the Gideon story because it is after Joash's pythic answer that Gideon receives the name Jerubbaal (Judg. 6.32). And a second aetiology of Jerubbaal is provided in 8.1, where the men of Ephraim upbraid (וירבון) Gideon for not calling them earlier.[140] In

---

139. Against H. Haag, 'Gideon—Jerubbaal—Abimelek', *ZAW* 79 (1967), pp. 305-314 (311).

140. Obviously, the name Jerubbaal, like Jeribai (1 Chron. 11.46) and Assyrian Iribai,

Judg. 6–9, Jerubbaal is a narrative thread holding together Joash (Jerubbaal ben Joash), Gideon (Jerubbaal that is Gideon) and Abimelech (ben Jerubbaal). Because the BS only knew Gideon and Abimelech, radically opposing them, it was necessary to give Gideon a second name and two aetiologies of this name before Gideon could convincingly be Abimelech's father. Logically, the overall Deuteronomistic tradition which dominates the books of Samuel will have a clear preference for Jerubbaal (see 1 Sam. 12.11 and 2 Sam. 11.21),[141] favouring the Baal-basher rather than the saviour of the BS.

The BS hypothesis has thus provided a grid to chart the development of the Gideon and Abimelech stories in the light of those of Ehud and Barak. A clear case of circular reasoning, one might say, as the theory being tested is used at the same time to establish the scope of the corpus supposed to prove the theory! Most unscientific, and yet, is there any other way to proceed? This is a kind of equation with two unknown factors, a tricky operation but not an impossible one. In order to get an idea of the first unknown factor, the nature of the BS, its full hypothetical scope has to be considered and its last chapter (Judg. 9) scrutinized.

Judges 9: Abimelech

Compared to Judg. 6–8, ch. 9 is much more uniform. The situation is similar to the one in chs. 4–5 as the narrative is illustrated by a fable.[142] Both Judg. 9 and Judg. 4–5 unfold a ruthless critique of kingship and human rule, a critique often understood as the expression of the misgivings of a tribal society at the onset of the Israelite monarchy.[143] A date

---

finds its origin in the other meaning of √ריב 'to plead in favour of, to take one's side', rather than 'to accuse, to contend' which is used here. Whether or not an old Jerubbaal tradition was at work before the BS story is beyond the scope of the present enquiry.

141. Auld, 'Gideon', p. 264.

142. The literary genre of the fable is discussed by K.J. Cathcart, 'The Trees, the Beasts and the Birds: Fables, Parables and Allegories in the Old Testament', in J. Day, R.P. Gordon and H.G.M. Williamson (eds.), *Wisdom in Ancient Israel: Essays in Honour of J. A. Emerton* (Cambridge: Cambridge University Press, 1995), pp. 212-21 and A.M. Vater Solomon, 'Fable', in G.W. Coats (ed.), *Saga, Legend, Tale, Novella, Fable* (JSOTSup, 35; Sheffield: JSOT Press, 1985), pp. 114-25.

143. H. Reviv, 'The Governement of Shechem in the El-Amarna Period and in the Days of Abimelech', *IEJ* 16 (1966), pp. 252-57; E. Würthwein, 'Abimelech und der Untergang Sichems. Studien zu Jdc 9', in E. Würthwein (ed.), *Studien zum deuteronomistischen Geschichtswerk* (BZAW, 227; Berlin: W. de Gruyter, 1994), pp. 12-28.

after the collapse of the monarchy may be preferable, but Judg. 9 has to be examined before the question can be answered.

Judges 9.1-6: Introduction

Abimelech is the son of Jerubbaal, from a Shechemite concubine. Jerubbaal and his 70 sons, as seen previously, are latecomers in the Abimelech story, a secondary transition between Judg. 8 and 9. The 70 rulers of Shechem need not be Abimelech's half-brothers for Abimelech to suggest that the rule of one man is preferable to the rule of 70 (9.2). On the contrary, once the 70 members of the Shechem senate have become Gideon's sons, Abimelech has to go to Ophrah to slaughter them. How 70 men of Ophrah could become rulers of the city of Shechem and what they were doing in Ophrah is unaccounted for. Before the link between Gideon and Abimelech was established, Abimelech (whoever his parents were) simply offered to take the place of the 70 (whatever their number and whoever their father was) on the simple basis that one is better than many and obviously because his name qualified him for the office.

Abimelech received 70 pieces of silver to slaughter the 70 sons of Jerubbaal, 70 men upon one stone, but the youngest was able to hide, which makes only 69 on one stone.

Judges 9.7-15: Jotham's Parable

When Jotham is informed of the blood bath, he climbs Mount Garizim and shouts the story of foolish trees that set out to anoint a king for themselves. As the good trees, according to this story, cannot stop their essential production (olive oil, figs and wine) in order to sway over (נוע על) the other trees, they end up offering the throne to the most useless one among them. The bramble offers its ridiculous shade to its loyal subjects but also threatens to set fire to the whole forest, even the cedars of Lebanon, in case it was not anointed king in good faith (באמת).

The relation between the fable and the narrative has been debated.[144] As the fable is found in a very similar form in Aesop's fables,[145] a comparison

---

144. Bibliography in Becker, *Richterzeit*, pp. 190-93: the main issues discussed are whether the critique is aimed at kingship in general or Abimelech's in particular, and whether Abimelech is the sole culpritt or if the Shechemites are also responsible.

145. Text published by B.E. Perry, *Aesopica* (Urbana: University of Illinois Press, 1952), pp. 422-23 and E. Chambry, *Fables/Escope* (Budé; Paris: Belles Lettres, 5th edn, 1996), p. 414. Thanks owed to Françoise Smyth-Florentin for mentioning this parallel.

between Aesop and Judg. 9.8-15 is presented in Figure 4.

The closeness of the parallel between Aesop and the Bible is impressive. The main difference is the omission of the vine by Aesop.[146] LXX B is obviously correcting LXX A in order to follow MT.[147]

LXX A is very close to Aesop. Apart from a few insignificant details,[148] the differences are situated in the introduction (v. 8). Aesop opens with Ξύλα ποτὲ[149] but LXXA's πορευόμενα ἐπορεύθησαν is a Hebraism from הלוך הלכו.[150] The anointing is also different: χρῖσαι (A) corresponding to משׁח where Aesop has χειροτονῆσαι 'to elect, to vote by a show of hands'.[151] All these differences are influenced by MT excepted the amiguous formulation of v. 13: Ἀφεῖσα τὸν οἶνόν μου τὴν εὐφροσύνην τὴν παρὰ τοῦ θεοῦ τῶν ἀνθρώπων 'Shall I leave my wine, joy of humans from god' or '…joy coming for the god of humans'. The ambiguity of this formula covers up MT's anthropomorphism which carries on the same logic than v. 9: in the same way that oil is glorified by gods and humans alike, wine rejoices both gods and humans. This variant occurs precisely

---

146. This fable (Chambry no 252) is among those with the fewest variant readings, possibly due to its parallel transmission in the Bible.

147. In v. 8, B changes χρῖσαι ἑαυτοῖς (A) into χρῖσαι ἐφ' ἑαυτὰ closer to למשׁח עליהם . In v. 9, B translates the question החדלתי with Μὴ ἀπολείψασα whereas A and Ae have Ἀφεῖσα (equally in vv. 11 + ἐγω and 13). Again in v. 9, B is theologically more 'orthodox' when it changes the glorification of the olive-tree by men and god alike thanks for his oil ἣν ἐν ἐμοὶ ἐδόξασεν ὁ θεός καὶ ἄνθρωποι (A, Ae) into glorification of god by humans ἐν ᾗ δοξάσουσι τὸν θεὸν ἄνδρες, whereas MT is strictly parallel to Ae and A with a very complicated wording that could indicate that MT translated the Greek: אשׁר־בי יכבדו אלהים ואנשׁים. B changes ἄρχειν into κινεῖσθαι closer to לנוע see Arabic nâ'a 'to shake branches', nau'at 'freshly picked fruits'.

V. 14: B follows MT which adds כל. A and B have οὐ (= אתה) but in v. 10 neither A nor B translated אתה.

The rare deviations of B from its MT model are in v. 8: B keeps the participle of A πορευόμενα instead of MT's infinitive and has the next verb in singular ἐπορεύθη instead of plural (TM, A, Ae). In v. 15, fire comes out of me ἀπ' ἐμοῦ instead of out of the bramble (MT, A, Ae).

148. Verse 11 γένημά for γέννημά, v. 14 + οὐ, 15 πεποίθατε for ὑπόστητε.

149. The formula X (main character of the fable) + ποτὲ introduces 19 of the 358 fables collected by Chambry (nos 6.29.48.59.60.69.78.112.190.191.227.247.262.269. 288.297.303.357.358).

150. Participle neuter nominative + conjugated verb instead of an absolute genitive.

151. Chambry, *Fables,* 414 indicates a variant χρύσαι for χειροτονῆσαι.

Aesop	LXXA	MT	LXXB
Ξύλα ποτὲ ἐπορεύθη τοῦ χειροτονῆραι ἐφ᾽ ἑαυτῶν βασιλέα	8 πορευόμενα ἐπορεύθησαν τὰ ξύλα τοῦ χρῖσαι ἑαυτοῖς βασιλέα	הלכו העצים הלוך למשח עליהם מלך	8 πορευόμενα ἐπορεύθη τὰ ξύλα τοῦ χρῖσαι ἐφ᾽ ἑαυτὰ βασιλέα
καὶ εἶπαν τῇ ἐλαίᾳ βασίλευσον ἐφ᾽ ἡμῶν	καὶ εἶπον τῇ ἐλαίᾳ βασίλευσον ἐφ᾽ ἡμῶν	ויאמרו לזית מלוכה עלינו	καὶ εἶπον αὐτοῖς τῇ ἐλαίᾳ βασίλευσον ἐφ᾽ ἡμῶν
καὶ εἶπεν αὐτοῖς ἡ ἐλαία	9 καὶ εἶπεν αὐτοῖς ἡ ἐλαία	ויאמר להם הזית	9 καὶ εἶπεν αὐτοῖς ἡ ἐλαία
Ἀφεῖσα τὴν πιότητά μου,	Ἀφεῖσα τὴν πιότητά μου,	החדלתי את־דשני	Μὴ ἀπολείψασα τὴν πιότητά μου,
ἣν ἐδόξασεν ἐν ἐμοὶ ὁ θεὸς καὶ οἱ ἄνθρωποι,	ἣν ἐν ἐμοι ἐδόξασεν ὁ θεός καὶ ἄνθρωποι,	אשר־בי יכבדו אלהים ואנשים	ἐν ᾗ δοξάσουσιν τὸν θεὸν ἄνδρες,
πορευθῶ ἄρχειν τῶν ξύλων;	πορευθῶ ἄρχειν τῶν ξύλων;	והלכתי לנוע על־העצים	πορεύσομαι κινεῖσθαι ἐπὶ τῶν ξύλων;
καὶ εἶπαν τὰ ξύλα τῇ συκῇ	10 καὶ εἶπαν τὰ ξύλα τῇ συκῇ	ויאמרו העצים לתאנה	10 καὶ εἶπον τὰ ξύλα τῇ συκῇ
Δεῦρο βασίλευσον ἐφ᾽ ἡμῶν	Δεῦρο βασίλευσον ἐφ᾽ ἡμῶν	לכי־את מלכי עלינו	Δεῦρο βασίλευσον ἐφ᾽ ἡμῶν
καὶ εἶπεν αὐτοῖς ἡ συκῆ	11 καὶ εἶπεν αὐτοῖς ἡ συκῆ	ויאמר להם התאנה	11 καὶ εἶπεν αὐτοῖς ἡ συκῆ
Ἀφεῖσα τὴν γλυκύτητά μου	Ἀφεῖσα τὴν γλυκύτητά μου	החדלתי את־מתקי	Μὴ ἀπολείψασα ἐγὼ τὴν γλυκύτητά μου
καὶ τὸ γέννημά μου	καὶ τὸ γένημά μου	ואת־תנובתי	καὶ τὰ γενήματά μου
τὸ ἀγαθὸν	τὸ ἀγαθὸν	הטובה	τὰ ἀγαθὰ
πορευθῶ τοῦ ἄρχειν τῶν ξύλων;	πορευθῶ ἄρχειν τῶν ξύλων;	והלכתי לנוע על־העצים	πορεύσομαι κινεῖσθαι ἐπὶ τῶν ξύλων;
	12 καὶ εἶπαν τὰ ξύλα τῇ ἀμπέλῳ	ויאמרו העצים לגפן	12 καὶ εἶπαν τὰ ξύλα πρὸς τὴν ἄμπελον
	Δεῦρο βασίλευσον ἐφ᾽ ἡμῶν	לכי־את מלוכי עלינו	Δεῦρο βασίλευσον ἐφ᾽ ἡμῶν
	13 καὶ εἶπεν αὐτοῖς ἡ ἄμπελος	ותאמר להם הגפן	13 καὶ εἶπεν αὐτοῖς ἡ ἄμπελος
	Ἀφεῖσα τὸν οἶνόν μου,	את־תירושי החדלתי	Μὴ ἀπολείψασα τὸν οἶνόν μου,
	τὴν εὐφροσύνην τὴν παρὰ τοῦ θεοῦ τῶν ἀνθρώπων,	המשמח אלהים ואנשים	τὸν εὐφραίνοντα θεὸν καὶ ἀνθρώπους,
	πορευθῶ ἄρχειν ξύλων;	והלכתי לנוע על־העצים	πορεύσομαι κινεῖσθαι ἐπὶ τῶν ξύλων;

Aesop	LXXA	MT	LXXB
καὶ εἶπαν τὰ ξύλα πρὸς τὴν ῥάμνον	14 καὶ εἶπαν τὰ ξύλα πρὸς τὴν ῥάμνον	וַיֹּאמְרוּ כָל־הָעֵצִים אֶל־הָאָטָד	14 καὶ εἶπαν πάντα τὰ ξύλα τῇ ῥάμνῳ
Δεῦρο, βασίλευσον ἐφ᾽ ἡμῶν	Δεῦρο σὺ βασίλευσον ἐφ᾽ ἡμῶν	אַתָּה מְלָךְ־עָלֵינוּ לֵךְ	Δεῦρο σὺ βασίλευσον ἐφ᾽ ἡμῶν
καὶ εἶπεν ῥάμνον πρὸς τὰ ξύλα	15 καὶ εἶπεν αὐτοῖς ἡ ῥάμνος πρὸς τὰ ξύλα	וַיֹּאמֶר הָאָטָד אֶל־הָעֵצִים	15 καὶ εἶπεν ἡ ῥάμνος πρὸς τὰ ξύλα
Εἰ ἐν ἀληθείᾳ ὑμεῖς χρίετέ με εἰς βασιλέα ἐφ᾽ ἡμῶν, δεῦτε ὑπόστητε ἐν τῇ σκέπῃ μου· καὶ εἰ μή, ἐξέλθοι πῦρ ἐκ τῆς ῥάμνου καὶ καταφάγοι τὰς κέδρους τοῦ Λιβάνου.	Εἰ ἐν ἀληθείᾳ ὑμεῖς χρίετέ με εἰς βασιλέα ἐφ᾽ ἡμῶν, δεῦτε πεποίθατε ἐν τῇ σκέπῃ μου· καὶ εἰ μή, ἐξέλθοι πῦρ ἐκ τῆς ῥάμνου καὶ καταφάγοι τὰς κέδρους τοῦ Λιβάνου.	אִם בֶּאֱמֶת אַתֶּם מֹשְׁחִים אֹתִי לְמֶלֶךְ עֲלֵיכֶם בֹּאוּ חֲסוּ בְצִלִּי וְאִם־אַיִן תֵּצֵא אֵשׁ מִן־הָאָטָד וְתֹאכַל אֶת־אַרְזֵי הַלְּבָנוֹן	Εἰ ἐν ἀληθείᾳ χρίετέ με ὑμεῖς τοῦ βασιλεύειν ἐφ᾽ ὑμᾶς, δεῦτε ὑπόστητε ἐν τῇ σκιᾷ μου· καὶ εἰ μή, ἐξέλθῃ πῦρ ἀπ᾽ ἐμοῦ καὶ καταφάγῃ τὰς κέδρους τοῦ Λιβάνου.

Figure 4. *Jotham's Fable according to MT, LXXA, LXXB and Aesop*

when Aesop offers no parallel, whereas in v. 9 LXXA stayed close to Aesop and MT.[152]

Aesop is more economical, with olive and fig tree but without the vine. This is consistent with the literary genre of such a compendium, used for pedagogical and rhetorical exercises. The beginning and the moral of the story were adaptable to fit the discourse or the composition it was included into.[153] The Bible uses the fable to illustrate the Abimelech narrative; it does not fear repetition, on the contrary, the introduction of the wine delays the punch line and builds up narrative tension.

152. Strangely, LXX B has this dogmatic correction in v. 9 (oil with which humans glorify god) but not in v. 13, possibly because the complicated Hebrew formula of v. 9 allowed more interpretative freedom that the straightforward one in v. 13.

153. See Chambry, *Fables,* 35; A. Theon, *Progymnasmata* (trans. M. Patillon and G. Bolognesi; Budé; Paris: Belles Lettres, 1997), 4.34, describes the different use of fables in schools. In English: J.R. Butts, *The Progymnasmata of Theon: A New Translation and Commentary* (Claremont: Microfilm edition, 1986).

Origin and Date of the Fable

The Greek context. Aesop is not the inventor of the fable genre. The oldest preserved Greek fable goes back to Hesiod, two centuries before Aesop.[154] In the seventh century BCE, Archilochus adopted the process and it led to the emergence of gnomic poetry, condensing observations and wise sayngs into maxims, precepts and enigmas.[155] Fables were collected from different sources and by the time the book of Judges was translated in Alexandria (second century BCE),[156] several Greek collections of fables attributed to Aesop were already available. Jotham's fable found then its way from the Greek text of Judges into the Aesopic corpus.

However, the fable of the Trees and the Olive is only attested in one manuscript, Vaticanus 777 from the 14th century CE, one of the oldest manuscripts of Aesop's fables but also the one containing the largest number of fables. Either the editors of all manuscripts except this one knew the fable from the Bible and did not deem it necessary or theoogically acceptable to include this in a profane collection, or the Jotham fable was added at a much later period into the Greek tradition. Since the 'Trees and the Olive' is found neither in the Syriac nor in the Arabic collection of fables,[157] both inspired by the Greek Aesopic corpus, one may favour the later date, although the evidence is far from binding.

In either case, the evidence speaks in favour of the precedence of Jotham's fable, coined specifically for the purpose of illustrating Judg. 9, then translated into Greek by the LXX and finally integrated into Vaticanus 777 which clearly seeks to be exhaustive and includes fables from different sources.

The Assyrian context. The details of the life of Aesop are disputed,[158] but he was popular in Athens at the time of Aristophanes (c. 400 BCE). A

---

154. 'The Nightingale and the Hawk', Hesiod, *Works and Days* (LCL; Cambridge, MA: Harvard University Press, 1959), l, pp. 200-210.

155. Chambry, *Fables,* 23.

156. M. Harl, G. Dorival and O. Munnich, *La bible grecque des Septante: du judaïsme hellénistique au christianisme ancien* (Initiations au christianisme ancien; Paris: Cerf / CNRS, 1988), pp. 96-98.

157. Sœur Bruno Lefevre, *Une version syriaque des fables d'Esope* (Paris: Firmin-Didot, 1941); Luqman, *Fables de Lokman* (trans. A. Charbonneau; Paris: Imprimerie royale, 1846).

158. Herodotus is the oldest testimony on Aesop (Herodotus, *History*, 2.134). Accordng to Chambry, *Fables,* 16-17: 'there was in Greece in the sixth century BCE an

legend developed round Aesop; the second part of this legend is a transposition of the story of Ahiqar in a Greek context.[159]

Ahiqar contains a short story depicting another bramble in Col VII.7:

]סנ[י]א שד[ר] לרמנ[א] לם

סניא לרמנא מה טב שג[י]א] כבי]ך נ[ג]ע [ש]ב[יך

> The bramble sent a message to the pomegranate as follows:
> 'Dear Pomegranate, what good are all [your] thorns
> [to him who tou]ches your [fru]it?'[160]

]בך וענ]ה [רמנ]א [ו]אמר לסניא

אנת כל]ך] כבן עם זי [נ]גע בך

> The [pome]granate replied to the bramble:
> '[you are nothing but thorns to him who [tou]ches you!'[161]

Before their insertion into the Assyrian story of Ahiqar, a collection of Aramaic proverbs was assembled and fixed between 750 and 650 BCE.[162] A Mesopotamian origin for the *Streitfabel* is accepted[163] based on a Babylonian parallel, 'The Tamarisk and the Date', going back to the Old Babylonian period and Sumerian tradition.[164] The type of dispute between

Aesop who gained popularity by composing or reciting fables; he may have been the slave of Iadmon the Samian together with the famous Rhodopis; he died a violent death in Delphes and the Delphians paid his blood price to Iadmon's grand-son.'

159. Sennacherib becomes Lyceros, Ahiqar Aesop and the nephew Nerdan is Emos.

160. I. Kottsieper, 'Die alttestamentliche Weisheit im Licht aramäischer Weisheits-traditionen', in B. Janowski (ed.), *Weisheit ausserhalb der kanonischen Weisheits-schriften* (VWGT, 10; Gütersloh: Gütersloher Verlagshaus, 1996), pp. 128-62 (10.17): 'Wer (dich) [be]rührt, [ver]fängt sich ja [in dir!]'

161. J.M. Lindenberger, *The Aramaic Proverbs of Ahiqar* (Baltimore: John Hopkins, 1983), p. 167.

162. Date based on the dialectical type of Aramaic which predates the emergence of Imperial Aramaic: Lindenberger, *Proverbs,* 21, 290; I. Kottsieper, *Die Sprache der Ahiqarsprüche* (BZAW, 194; Berlin: W. de Gruyter, 1990), p. 180. W. Burkert, *The Orientalizing Revolution* (Cambridge, MA: Harvard University Press, 1992), p. 121 notes that 'Babrius, who set down the fables of Aesop in verse, states expressly at the beginning of his second book that this type of myth is an invention of the Syrians from the time of Ninos (Nineveh) and Belos; Aesop was the first to relate them to the sons of the Hellenes': Babrius 2.2-3 in *Babrius and Phaedrus* (trans. B.E. Parry; LCL, Cambridge MA: Heinemann, 1965), p. 139.

163. Kottsieper, 'Alttestamentliche Weisheit', p. 147; Lindenberger, *Proverbs,* p. 167.

164. W.G. Lambert, *Babylonian Wisdom Literature* (Oxford: Oxford University Press, 1960), p. 151: three Middle Assyrian examples: pp. 153-64 and 'The Fable of

a thorny bush and trees is a venerable Mesopotamian tradition that found its way, among other Syrian fables and proverbs, into the story of Ahiqar and later into the 'Life of Aesop'.[165]

If the BS was composed in Bethel around 720 BCE,[166] its creators could have simply used a fable circulating in a Syrian collection since 750 BCE. Admittedly, this collection, as we know it from the Elephantine library (the only extant manuscript of the Aramaic Ahiqar)[167] does not contain anything similar to Jotham's fable, but it is far from complete,[168] and such an antimonarchical fable could have easily been deleted from an official royal collection. However, it is perilous to argue out of silence, therefore it is possible to claim only that Judg. 9 did not have to wait for Aesop's fable in order to include 'The Trees and the Olive' in the Abimelech story. That this fable was copied into Aesop's collection from Judg. 9 is more likely than the other way round since Bethel was then under the direct influence of Syro-Mesopotamian culture. The influence of Greece was then still negligable.

Jotham's fable could have been received from an independent model[169] transmitted by a Syrian collection and integrated into Judg. 9 around 720 BCE when the BS was composed. The tale of 'The Tamarisk and the Date' and Aesop's 'Trees and the Olive' are strong evidence against the scholars who doubt that Jotham's fable could have formed an independent unit before its integration into Judg. 9.[170] However, the lack of Aramaisms in

the Willow', pp. 164-67; 'Nisaba [Cereal godess] and wheat', pp. 168-75.

165. Chambry, *Fables*, 29.

166. Knauf, 'Does DH exists?', p. 396.

167. Lindenberger, *Proverbs,* p. 11.

168. Up to half of the proverbs may have been lost: see Lindenberger, *Proverbs,* p. 13.

169. M. Adinolfi, 'Originalità dell apologo di Jotham', *RB* 7 (1959), pp. 322-42 (342); F. Crüsemann, *Der Widerstand gegen das Königtum: Die antiköniglichen Texte des Alten Testaments und der Kampf um den frühen israelitischen Staat* (WMANT, 49; Neukirchen-Vluyn, Neukirchener-Verlag, 1978), p. 19; L. Desnoyers, *Histoire du peuple hébreu des juges à la captivité 1* (Paris: A. Picard, 1922), p. 173; V. Fritz, 'Abimelech und Sichem in Jdc ix', *VT* 32 (1982), pp. 129-44 (132); E.H. Maly, 'The Jotham Fable—Antimonarchical?', *CBQ* 22 (1960), pp. 299-305 (300-304); Richter, *TU*, pp. 308-310; E. Zenger, 'Ein Beispiel exegetischer Methoden aus dem Alten Testament', in J. Schreiner (ed.), *Einführung in die Methoden der biblischen Exegese* (Würzburg: Echter Verlag, 1971), pp. 97-148 (113).

170. R. Bartelmus, 'Die sogenannte Jothamfabel: eine politisch-religiöse Parabeldichtung', *TZ* 2 (1985), pp. 97-120 (108-110): The argument is based mainly on the fact that the etymological figure הלוך הלכו at the onset of the fable cannot indicate the

the 'Trees and the Olive' militates against the straightforward integration of a Syrian fable. It is therefore more likely that the 'Trees and the Olive' was coined by the creators of the BS, imitating the Mesopotamian *Streitfabel*.

Whether v. 15 was part of the fable or was added to smoothen the transition with the narrative in the following verse is difficult to decide.[171] Nothing prevented fable editors and users to adapt and modify not only the beginning and the morale of the fable but also elements in the body of the fable (here adding or removing an actor like the vine) to make it fit their purpose.

The question of the aim of the fable also loses most of its sharpness[172] because each proverb and fable is necessarily general enough to allow its use in vastly differing contexts. However, a few remarks can be made regarding kingship. By using נוע 'to sway over' when the trees decline the throne (vv. 9, 11, 13) instead of מלך 'to be king' (v. 8) Jotham's fable is more critical than Aesop's which uses ἄρχειν 'to lead' to describe the role of the king.[173] On the other hand, the cedar, the most obvious king of the forest, appears only at the end of the fable, in the role of potential victim, like the other trees. This suggests that it is not kingship as such that is considered dangerous, but the usurpation of the throne.[174] Trees, just as loyal (אמת 9, 15.16.19) subjects of a king, are called to produce goods for the general welfare rather than wriggle over the others. Jotham addresses the fable to the men of Shechem (v. 7) whom he blames for having made Abimelech king over the Lords of Shechem on the pretence that he is their brother (v. 18). It is therefore clear that the fable is used in Judg. 9 to reject the crowning of a Shechemite king, not to illustrate a theoretical treatise on the nature of kingship.

Read against the backdrop of the final integration of the kingdom of Israel into the Assyrian Empire and the replacement of the last king of

---

absolute beginning of a story. This infinitive at the beginning of the fable is rather strange, yet it corresponds to ποτὲ 'one day' (indefinite) at the beginning of some Aesop fables. It reveals an absolute start for a fable which is necessarily devoid of context.

171. See H.L. Liss, 'Die Fabel des Yotam in Ri 9, 8-15: Versuch einer strukturellen Deutung', *BN* 89 (1997), pp. 12-21 (13-16).

172. J. Ebach and U. Rütersworden, 'Pointen in der Jothamfabel, *BN* 31 (1986), pp. 11-18; Maly, 'Jotham'.

173. Liss, 'Fabel', p. 18.

174. Maly, 'Jotham', p. 304.

Samaria by a Assyrian governor around 720 BCE, Jotham is not preaching
the return to a pre-monarchic tribal amphictyony, nor the setting up of a
new Israelite king, but the straightforward acceptance of the legitimate
king. More indications on the identity of such a king are found in the
narrative.

Judges 9.16-57: The Rule of Abimelech

If the origin of the fable is bound to remain uncertain, it is quite sure than
the creators of the Abimelech story knew it from the start because most
elements of the fable are used in the narrative: the tree metaphor and the
fire (v. 15) are applied literally to the inhabitants of the Tower of Shechem
(vv. 48-49) and Tebez (v. 52).[175] The 'shade' of the bramble (v. 14) becomes sarcasm in Zebul's mouth who rails Gaal: 'you see the shadow of
the mountain as if they were men' (v. 36). The vine (vv. 12-13) is found
again in v. 27 and the offer of the rule to Gideon (8.22) anticipates the
tree's quest for a king.

The bulk of the Abimelech narrative seems uniform, apart for the last
mentions of Jerubbaal and his 70 sons (minus one!) in vv. 16-19, 24, 57
which are part of the insertion of Jerubbaal in the story of Gideon and
Abimelech to soil Gideon's reputation (see higher). The secondary aspect
of this insertion is confirmed once again by the fact that when v. 17 recalls
the deliverance accomplished by his father, he does not use the usual BS
√ישע 'to save' but √צלה 'to give shade, to protect', thus degrading once
more the saviour Gideon.

Rather than going through the rest of the Abimelech narrative passage
by passage, it will be read against the background of Assyrian politics.

Judges 9 in Assyrian Context

Abimelech's story depicts a complex political reality, a historical context
that would be surprising at the onset of Israelite state formation, but which
is surprisingly congruent with the situation after 720 BCE: Zebul, Abimelech's officer, represents in Shechem an absentee king, as Abimelech
himself seems to reside in Arumah (v. 41). The temples of Baal-berith and
El-berith (vv. 4, 46) point also to the Assyrian domination as the term
Berith is not attested in Palestine before the Assyrian conquests.[176] Berith

---

175. Tree-bearing toponyms are found in vv. 6 and 37.

176. The sole pre-Assyrian attestation would be Judg. 9: E. Kutsch, 'Berit', in E. Jenni
and C. Westermann (eds.), *THAT* 1 (Munich: Chr. Kaiser Verlag, 1971), pp. 256-26
(256).

is the Assyrian technical term for the vassalage treaty imposed on the tributaries. Baal-berith may be nothing else than the image of Yhwh, the god of Israel, guardian of the vassalage treaty that bound the kings of Israel since Jehu,[177] as it is increasingly recognized that Assyrians did not impose their religious beliefs upon their subjects.[178] In fact, how constraining would be an oath sworn by the name of gods other than one's own?

An image of Yhwh, in his role of Baal-berith, was certainly used during a yearly festival similar to the *Akitu* in Samaria. Due to the rapid expansion of the Empire from the ninth century BCE, the Assyrians decentralized this New Year festival, well known in its Babylonian form,[179] and

177. Suggested orally by E.A. Knauf. The title 'Baal' (Hebrew of Akkadian Bêl) rather than a Deuteronomistic note (against Becker, *Richterzeit*, 189) would not have any negative connotation before Josiah's time when Baal became the epithet for every god apart from Yhwh. Moreover it would conform to Assyrian procedures that Yhwh, the local god of Samaria, would be granting his blessing to the king: in Harran it was Sîn, in Kizili and Kurba'il it was Ada who did so: B. Pongratz-Leisten, 'The Interplay of Military Strategy and Cultic Practice in Assyrian Politics', in S. Parpola and R.M. Whiting (eds.), *Assyria 1995* (Helsinki: The Neo-Assyrian Text Corpus Project, 1995), pp. 241-52 (246). The Assyrian did not impose their gods on their new subjects. On the contrary, they used the gods of their new subjects to impose their rule (see the argumentation of Sennacherib's *Rab-shakeh* under the walls of Jerusalem in 701 BCE: 'Is it without Yhwh that I have come up against this place to destroy it?' (1 Kgs 18.25) see Cogan, *Imperialism,* 111). In 720 BCE, Sargon got hold of the gods of Samaria (Becking, *Fall of Samaria*, 29-32, Sargon Nimrud Prism 4.32-33; and Cogan, *Imperialism*, pp. 116-17). The plural cannot be used to prove 'polytheism', as Yhwh probably had a consort: a divine couple is no polytheism. Sargon's mention of the gods of Samaria shows that he attributed too much value to these gods to simply share out the precious metal plating of their images among his soldiers (for this practice see Cogan, *Imperialism*, p. 24). The image of Yhwh and his consort were kept, ready to be brought back once peace and order were established after the campaign and to assume their role again, in the frame of Imperial structures (see Cogan, *Imperialism*, pp. 35-37 for the preregrinations of the divine images of the Arab Ḥazā'il which were confiscated after each defeat and returned afterwards several times over). Assyrian imperialism did not contradict the respect of the principle of divine territoriality. 2 Kgs 17 is based on the same principle: the gods of the populations exiled in Samaria are unable to protect the area against the wrath of Yhwh, the local god of Samaria. The new inhabitants have to be instructed how to serve Yhwh.

178. S. Dalley, 'Yabâ, Atalyâ and the Foreign Policy of Late Assyrian Kings', *SAAB* 12/2 (1998), pp. 82-98 (97-98).

179. But also performed elsewhere: J.A. Black, 'New year ceremonies in Ancient Babylon: "Taking Bel by the Hand" and a Cultic Picnic', *Religion* 11 (1981), pp. 39-59 (40).

performed it in peripheral provincial capitals in order to protect the borders of the realm from external aggressions. Because of the ever increasing distances, the presence of the king was not necessary; he could be represented by a particular kind of coat made for the occasion (*kusuppu*). An *Akitu* temple was built outside the city to house the divine image during its annual sortie into the wilderness to defeat the forces of chaos. In Babylon, this cosmic fight was celebrated by the recitation of *Enuma Elish*. The king or his representative was blessed by the god during his triumphal return to his temple in the city. The king held the hand of the divine image, his chariot drawn by captives.[180] The Assyrians thus reversed the Babylonian logic. Rather than having the images of the peripheral cities go to Babylon and receive the blessing of Marduk during his triumphal return from the *Bit-akiti*, the king went to the periphery in order to receive the blessing of the local gods. In both cases, the festival was closely linked to kingship. In Babylon, at a particular day of the festival,[181] the king was stripped off his regalia and had to swear that he had not done any harm to the city, to the temple and to local privileges. The king was slapped in the face and it was a good omen for the coming year if tears appeared in the eyes of the humiliated king. The ritual emphasized the delicate relation between god and king. A bad omen would announce that the king was in danger and the ritual warned against the dangers that kingship represented for the god and the people.[182]

It would therefore not be surprising to find allusions to the *Akitu* festival in a text dealing with kingship.[183] This could be the case in Judg. 9.27 where a LXX variant reading attests the presence of a hiphil conjugation instead of MT's qal: instead of ויבאו בית אלהיהם 'they went into the house of their god', LXXBC read καὶ εἰσήνεγκαν 'They introduced [something] in the house of their god'. Although the meaning of the variant cannot be established any more due to the loss of the object that was introduced in the temple, it is a possible reference to the *Akitu* temple

180. Pongratz-Leisten, 'Interplay', pp. 247-52.

181. At Babylon, around spring equinox. Some cities may have celebrated a spring and an autumn Akitu: Black, 'Ceremonies', p. 40.

182. Black, 'Ceremonies', pp. 54-56.

183. F. Smyth-Florentin, 'La Bible, mythe fondateur', in M. Detienne (ed.), *Tracés de fondation* (Bibliothèque de l'école des hautes études, 43; Louvain/Paris: Peeters, 1990), pp. 59-66. Page 65 finds other allusions to the new year festival in the Bible: crossings of the Reed Sea and of the Jordan, David's dance in front of the arch and parts of Pss. 77; 114; 144.

at Shechem: v. 27 is set outside, in the fields during a festival celebrating the grape harvest. The *Bit-akiti* was usually built outside the city[184] and a great picnic was organized during the divinity's stay in the *Bit-akiti*.[185] In the hypothesis of such a setting, the revolt of Gaal (vv. 26-41) is fomented during the festival that renewed the blessing of Yhwh over the king. This revolt was meant to overthrow Abimelech who himself had received silver from the Baal-berith temple (v. 4) to revolt against the Shechem senate. At the end, Abimelech kills the Shechemites, razes the city and sows it with salt[186] (v. 45), burns the inhabitants of Migdal-Shechem inside the El-berith temple (v. 49) before dying from a stone thrown by a woman (vv. 53-54).

The whole narrative expresses a deep sense of justice. Those who embezzled money from the Baal-berith temple to break the berith died in the Baal-berith temple. Gaal and his followers who revolted during the festival were either killed or chased out of the city. Abimelech razed the city of Shechem that supported him and a single stone killed him who had killed the senate upon one stone in order to rule alone.[187] All the rebels have been punished, 'god made their wickedness fall back upon their heads and upon them came the curse of Jotham' (Judg. 9.57). The god of Judg. 9 is never called Yhwh (vv. 7, 56), possibly to mark Yhwh's disapproval of Abimelech and Gaal's bloody political feuds.

Shechem 720 BCE

Judges 9 is set in and around Shechem, an important city of the Middle and Late Bronze Age, the base of king Lab'ayu.[188] The city survived in the Iron I and kept its royal status under Jeroboam I (1 Kgs 12.25), before being eclipsed by Samaria as from the reign of Omri (1 Kgs 16.24). Logically, Judg. 9 has always been read in the context of the early Israelite monarchy, before Omri transferred the capital to Samaria. However, in spite of the great deal of topographic information provided by Judg. 9 on Shechem and its immediate surroundings, scholars have not been able to

---

184. Altough it was sometimes part of a large temple complex: J.N. Postgate, 'The Bit Akiti in Nabu Temples', *Sumer* 30 (1974), pp. 51-74 (62).

185. Black, 'Ceremonies'.

186. F.C. Fensham, 'Salt as Curse in the Old Testament and in the Ancient Near East', *BA* 25 (1962), pp. 48-50.

187. J.G. Janzen, 'A Certain Woman in the Rhetoric of Judges 9', *JSOT* 38 (1987), pp. 33-37.

188. Moran, *Amarna*, EA 244.246.249.253-54.280.

match it with the archaeological data of Iron I Shechem.[189] They are not even able to indicate at which gate Gaal and Zebul stood when they saw Abimelech's men running down the mountains (Judg. 9.35-37). This failure indicates either that Judg. 9 is not based on first hand information or that the Iron I setting is wrong.

It is in fact possible to read Judg. 9 against a later historical background, as Shechem continued as administrative centre even after Samaria had become the capital.[190] Stratum VII was destroyed by the Assyrians around 722 BCE and has been well preserved due to this violent end.[191] This is a layer of rich houses, but the tell was not fortified any more, its fortifications having fallen into disuse for a century. In 720 BCE, Shechem had the same aspect than it has in Judg. 9.45: it is razed. In that context, the writers of Judg. 9 knew that Shechem had gates like every other fortified city, but they did not dig through strata VII and VIII (then I and II!) to check out their exact location in stratum IX (ninth century BCE which restored Bronze Age fortifications).[192] It was enough for them to tell a story that explained the present state of the famous city of Shechem, that had once been the seat of the kings of Israel. Shechem was only 10 km from Samaria where resided the Assyrian governor of the province of Samerina.[193] Migdal, Millo, Oak of the Pillar, Centre of the Earth and Diviner's Oak (vv. 6, 37, 46) are therefore devoid of any precise location, only the larger landmarks are identifiable: Thebez (Ṭūbāṣ), Mount Zalmon (*Jebel Salman*), Arumah (*Khirbet el-'Urmeh*). The names of the actors are stereotypes for all the Abimelechs who claim the rule because they are daddy's sons, and for all their challengers who always happen to be close to the throne. Gaal the 'detestable' son of Ebed 'minister' of the previous king dreams to take the place of his father's boss. Zebul 'honoured' is the

189. E.F. Campbell, 'Judges 9 and Biblical Archeology', in C.L. Meyers and M. O'Connor (eds.), *The Word of the Lord Shall Go Forth* (Winona Lake: Eisenbrauns, 1983), pp. 263-71 provides a good overview.

190. Collecting wine (Samaria Ostrakon 44: Lemaire, *Inscriptions hébraïques*, 35) and grain ('granery', in area V: I. Magen, 'Shechem', *NEAEHL*, 4.1347.

191. Magen, 'Shechem', 4.1348.

192. Magen, 'Shechem', 4.1349.

193. Samaria fell to the Assyrians in 720 BCE and was immediately enlarged: Nimrud Prism 4.37-41: 'I repopulated Samerina more than before. People from countries, conquered by my hands, I brought in it. My commissioner, I appointed as governor over them. I counted them as Assyrians': Becking, *Fall of Samaria,* 29; See S. Dalley, 'Chariotry and Cavalry of Tiglath-Pileser III and Sargon II', *Iraq* 47 (1985), pp. 33-41 (36).

only actor who represents the narrator's point of view. He is Abimelech's
פָּקִיד 'officer' (Judg. 9.28) and governor of the town שַׂר הָעִיר (Judg. 9.30),
two realities in Samaria around 720 BCE.[194] Zebul is the sole faithful actor
of the narrative, the only one who does not betray or kill, but also the only
one who has some very ironic words (vv. 36, 38) against Gaal.

Judges 9 is condemning Abimelech's coup as much as Gaal's revolt,
kingship and rebellion are both blamed. There is therefore no objection to
include Judg. 9 in the BS of 720 BCE if one admits that the BS is not
preaching armed resistance to the Assyrians, but peaceful submission to
their rule. Any revolt *à la* Gaal, or any attempt to restore kingship *à la*
Abimelech will end up in the razing of Samaria and the other towns that
were spared when Shechem was destroyed. Judges 9 makes more sense in
the post-royal period, than in the pre-royal one, if such a period ever
existed. Indeed, the fate of Shechem around 722 BCE is a clear warning in
720 BCE for all who would be tempted to follow Hoshea's rebellion which
brought the end of Israelite monarchy (2 Kgs 17.1-6). Shechem then
recovered in the Hellenistic period, a fact that invalidates attempts to read
Judg. 9 in that period.[195]

Shechem and the Israelite Monarchy

As Shechem was a royal Israelite city until Omri, the story of Abimelek
allows sharp criticism of Israel's monarchy without criticising Samaria
and its Assyrian governor. In fact, Judg. 9 can be read as a negative
summary of the achievements of Israelite kings, a compilation of the worst
'hits' of the books of Kings:

> 1 Kgs 16.11-12: slaughter of the house of Baasha by Zimri. 1 Kgs 16.17-18:
> Omri besieges Tirzah. Once the city is taken, Zimri enters the citadel
> (//Judg. 9.50) and sets it on fire (see Judg. 9.49). 2 Kgs 10.1-7: slaughter of
> Ahab's 70 sons (// Judg. 9.5) by Jehu. 2 Kgs 11.1-16: Athaliah slaughters
> the royal family, but Joash is hidden away (//Judg. 9.5), Athaliah is then
> slain. Joash is killed at Beth-Millo (2 Kgs 12.21//Judg. 9.6). King Amaziah

---

194. Two bullae formed with the same seal (unknown origin!) attest the title שַׂר הָעִיר:
N. Avigad, 'The Governor of the City Bulla', in H. Geva (ed.), *Ancient Jerusalem
Revealed* (Jerusalem: Israel Exploration Society, 1994), pp. 138-40; G. Barkay, 'A
Second "Governor of the City" Bulla', in H. Geva (ed.), *Ancient Jerusalem Revealed*
(Jerusalem: Israel Exploration Society, 1994), pp. 141-46. The authors agree on a
seventh century BCE date.

195. Against T. Veijola, *Das Königtum in der Beurteilung der deuteronomistischen
Historiographie: Eine redaktionsgeschichtliche Untersuchung* (AASF, 198; Helsinki:
Suomalainen Tiedeakatemia, 1977), pp. 103-104.

of Judah is killed by his servants in Lachish (2 Kgs 14.19). Shallum kills
Zechariah before being struck by Menahem (2 Kgs 15.10-14). Pekah kills
Pekahiah in the citadel of the king's house (2 Kgs 15.25). At last, Hoshea
kills Pekah (2 Kgs 15.30-33) to become Israel's last king.

The story of Abimelech condenses two centuries of Israelite rule. In 720
BCE, it is the whole of the monarchy which is considered, not just Jehu's
reign,[196] Judg. 9 turns the page of the Israelite monarchy with no regret,
depicting it as a long cycle of usurpation and assassinations. Judges 9
seems to bear the signature of the Bethel writors because of a few details
referring explicitly to the book of Hosea and to the Jacob cycle, two
Bethel compositions.[197]

Judges 9 as the Conclusion of the Book of Saviours
Whatever its date and its origin, Jotham's fable matches the ideological
leanings of the rest of Judg. 9. It proclaims without batting an eyelid that
oil and wine delight gods and humans alike, a view which is hard to
reconcile with the bitter critique of other gods in the schema and the oracle
of the anonymous prophet (Judg. 2.11-19; 6.7-10). No prophet pronounces
any fiery condemnation of foreign gods in Judg. 9.[198] On the contrary,
Yhwh is designated by his title Baal-berith, thus underlining his role in the
Assyrian treaty. The story of Abimelech is comfortable with the dominant
culture, to the point that it may be borrowing an Assyrian or Syrian
proverb to illustrate its condemnation of the Israelite monarchy.

The fable may then constitute a tribute to Assyrian rule in Samaria. The
governor and his board of censors could only be flattered to hear a
favourite story used to denigrate Israel's petty kings, comparing them to
scraggy thorn bushes whose only achievement was to set ablaze the whole
country: the king is dead, long live the Emperor![199]

196. Against Richter, *TU,* p. 340 and Bartelmus, 'Jothamfabel', p. 119.
197. Knauf, 'Does DH exist?', and Bartelmus, 'Jothamfabel', pp. 119-20. Hamor
(Judg. 9.29) refers to Gen. 34; the ambush of Judg. 9.25 points to Hos. 6.9 and Hos 8.4,
14 have striking parallels with Judg. 9 ('They made kings but not through me' and 'I
will send a fire upon his cities and devour his strongholds').
198. Against Maly, 'Jotham', p. 299 who claims that 'The story can be seen as a
type of the prophetic condemnation of later individual kings'.
199. The modern distinction between king and Emperor was not made by the
Assyrians: R. Lamprichs, *Die Westexpansion des neuassyrischen Reiches: eine Strukturanalyse* (AOAT, 239; Kevelaer/Neukirchen-Vluyn: Butzon & Bercker/Neukirchener,
1995). The Assyrians used the title *šar kiššati* = 'king of the totality' to express their
imperial pretentions: P. Garelli, 'L'Etat et la légitimité royale sous l'Empire assyrien',

A book of Saviours telling the stories of Ehud, Barak and Gideon and finishing on the condemnation of local kings cannot be a call to arms to overthrow the Assyrians. It is an official treatise (who else, apart from official court circles, could produce and transmit literature in seventh century BCE Israel?) in favour of a peaceful integration in the Empire. The defeat of 722-720 BCE is interpreted as the consequence of Yhwh's wrath. The culprits are now punished (king Hoshea and his advisors), peace is restored as after all past aggressions by foreign powers (Moabites, Canaanites or Midianites). These setbacks were only temporary, and Yhwh has again sent a saviour to deliver Israel, not to re-establish a king. The saviour has been raised by Yhwh to restore peace and order and to open a new period of calm by removing the tumour that plagued Israel for the last two centuries, its kings. The tales of the saviours make it clear that Israel needs no king and no army. Yhwh himself saves his people with a handful of men, even a woman, equipped with the most unpromising weapons. The war is now finished; Samaria is restored, embellished, its countryside thriving due to direct access to global market. This prosperity is a clear sign of renewed divine favour and a token of the legitimacy of the Assyrian rule.[200] Yhwh has already sent his latest saviour, Sargon is his name.

This may sound an incredible statement in light of the Deuteronomistic vehement rejection of Assyrian rule. Yet, it conforms to 2 Kgs 13.5 which claims that Yhwh gave a saviour to Israel who removed Israel from the hand of Aram. This saviour was Adad-Nirari III, the first Assyrian ruler to reach the Lebanon in 803 BCE. He relieved Israel of Aram's pressure and virtually saved Israel from total conquest by Damascus.[201] The Persians will simply follow suit by convincing the Judaeans that Cyrus was Yhwh's messiah (Isa. 45.1). Unlike States, Empires cannot rely simply on the

in M.G. Larsen (ed.), *Power and Propaganda* (Mesopotamia, 7; Copenhagen: Akademisk Forlag, 1979), pp. 319-28 (320). However, Judg. 9 seems to play on the difference between *šar* and *melech* : God waits for the first mention of *šar* in v. 22 וישר אבימלך על־ישראל in order to send an evil spirit between Abimelech and the men of Shechem (v. 23), a lese-majesty crime against the Assyrians. Before v. 22, Judg. 9 uses משל 'to rule' (v. 2) and מלך 'to make king' (v. 6, 16, 18).

200. The Assyrians presented themselves as deliverers and restorers of divine order: J. Reade, 'Ideology and Propaganda in Assyrian Art', in M.G. Larsen (ed.), *Power and Propaganda* (Mesopotamia, 7; Copenhagen: Akademisk Forlag, 1979), pp. 329-44 and Garelli, 'L'Etat', p. 321.

201. B. Mazar, 'The Aramean Empire and its Relations with Israel', *BA* 35 (1962), pp. 98-120 (115).

power of their armies, the sheer size of their territories requires consent of the ruled populations, active collaboration gained through propaganda.

The Limits of the Book of Saviours

In accordance with Richter, there is no reason to include material beyond ch. 9 into the BS.[202] Noth believed that Jephthah belonged both to the list of saviours and to the list of judges.[203] However, the Jephthah narrative presents none of the characteristics of a saviour narrative: the beginning of the frame is imitated (Judg. 10.6-10) but Israel's cries are rejected by Yhwh (vv. 11-14), there is no mention of Jephthah saving Israel and the narrative ends on ritual cries instead of the assertion of peace (Judg. 11.40). Moreover, the list of foreign gods in Judg. 10.6 ends with the gods of the Ammonites and those of the Philistines, thus introducing both the stories of Jephthah (against the Ammonites) and of Samson (against the Philistines). This introduction is clearly stitching up Judg. 10–16 at the end of the BS (ch. 9) and of the first judges (Judg. 10.1-5). The study of these chapters will point out what differentiates these narratives from the BS.

As for the beginning of the BS, the schema (Judg. 2.11-19) and the following verses that clearly presuppose it (Judg. 2.20–3.6) are secondary. The story of Othniel (Judg. 3.7-11) is theologically close to the saviour narratives, but is set in a different geographical frame. It therefore belongs to an edition of the BS in Jerusalem which will be studied alongside Judg. 1 in Chapter 2.

Israel in the Book of Saviours

A recurrent difficulty is encountered pertaining to the identity of Israel's collectivity in the BS: the different Israelite groups that appear in the stories, are they original or not? The overall logic of the BS lies obviously in the deliverance of Israel through the daring coup of an individual or a very small group. Ehud has an Israelite perspective as he sounds the *shofar* for help in the Mountain of Ephraim (Judg. 3.27); a most general term repeated in the same verse as the 'sons of Israel' come down 'from the mountain'. Only the Moabites casualties are numbered: 10,000 (Judg. 3.29). Ehud is Benjaminite, but this serves more as a pun (his right hand was handicapped v. 15) than to indicate tribal pride and it is a essential

202. Richter, *Bearbeitungen*.
203. Noth, *ÜS*, pp. 47-50.

element of the plot, as he uses his left hand to draw the hidden sword (v. 21). But with Barak the image is getting blurred as he has a group of 10,000 men from Zebulun and Naphtali behind him (Judg. 4.6, 10, 14) and the victory is gained through a military encounter, however unbalanced the numbers: 900 chariots (vv. 3, 7, 13) and המונו 'his crowd' (v. 7) or עם 'militia' (v. 13). Barak originates from Naphtali, which explains why Naphtali is called out, but the presence of Zebulun is unaccounted for, except for the place of honour it holds in the song of Deborah. The Gideon story is even more complicated, a predictable situation since it is the story that received the most additions. Judges 6.33-35, a passage considered original to the BS according to the criteria applied here, presents Abiezer following Gideon (v. 34), v. 35 adds Manasseh, Asher, Zebulun and Naphtali. In Judg. 7.22–8.3, a secondary passage of the BS, Naphtali, Asher and Manasseh pursue Midian towards the Jordan; Zebulun is now left out. The rest of the passage is concerned with the belated mobilization of Ephraim who appears for the first time (as a group, not as a mountain: see Judg. 3.27). Ephraim is furious to have been called out after the others, although he is the one who caught the Midianite princes. Interestingly, this motive is picked up again in Judg. 12.1-6, the same reproach is made against Jephthah, but this time the argument is settled with the slaughter of 42,000 Ephraimites. This heavy emphasis on Ephraim's late calling is the only element that stands out in this confusing situation. This secondary element indicates at least that the absence of Ephraim was a characteristic of the BS and that it was later considered anomalous. Manasseh, the northern part of Samerina is involved in the Gideon story (Judg. 6.35 and 7.23) in a fight at the northeastern limit of its traditional territory, somewhere near Beth-shean. Asher (Judg. 6.35 and 7.23) is likely to be secondary or at least its location is not well established.[204] Naphtali (Judg. 4.6, 10; 6.35; 7.23) and Zebulun (Judg. 4.6, 10; 6.35), the most cited groups are also the most distant, they both originate from Northern Galilee, outside Samaria's jurisdiction.

The point is clearer if we consider not simply the origin of the belligerents but also the actual theatre of fighting: the valleys of the Jordan (Jericho) and of Jezreel (Taanach and Wadi Harod). The only battle fought on Samarian territory is set in Jericho (annexed by Josiah some 80 years later), at one of the most distant towns from the capital. The clashes in Judg. 4 and 7 are set in the territory of the province of Magiddu; they do not concern the Samarian governor.

---

204. See the discussion of its place in the Song of Deborah.

If all these Israelite 'tribes' are mentioned in the BS, the text depicts Israelite victories in peripheral locations. This is congruent with Judg. 9 which denounces Abimelech's revolt right in Israel's heartland.

An Assyrian Book of Saviours

The whole extent of Richter's *Retterbuch* has been recovered using simpler criteria (Richter's war of Yhwh was abandoned), but the results are quite similar and easier to visualize as the text is not atomised and distributed among three or four successive editions. The additions are easily singled out since they form coherent passages. Alongside Beyerlin, the whole composition can be read as a pre-Deuteronomistic, that is a pre-Josianic work.

Three saviour narratives are presented with repetitive frames. *Ehud* is the first and the shortest of the stories. *Barak* is longer, even if the song of Deborah is not included. It is not certain that Judg. 5 was part of the original BS, but it is clear that Judg. 4 knows the song of Deborah and uses it. It is therfore easier to consider it as an integral part of the BS from the beginning. The integration of the song within the BS is the easiest way to explain its transmission after 720 BCE. *Gideon* received extensive additions that more than doubled the length of the original saviour narrative. The collection is concluded by the story of an anti-saviour summarizing the whole of Israelite monarchy in a most critical fashion. Jotham's fable illustrates *Abimelech*, in a similar fashion that the song of Deborah does for *Barak*.

Historically, Knauf's date around 720 BCE is confirmed by the Moabites in ch. 3, the Midianites of chs. 6–7 and the destruction of Shechem. This date and the historical context it implies shed a fascinating light over the BS and provide a well-defined milieu of production. Most surprising and unexpected is the similarity of the BS with official Assyrian propaganda and the role it was meant to play in Israel after 720 BCE.

A post-Assyrian edition is going to take the BS to task, rejecting its conception of an automatic and unconditional salvation. However, before these passages are examined, Othniel, the saviour who came from the South has to be read.

Chapter 2

KING MANASSEH EDITS THE BOOK OF SAVIOURS IN JERUSALEM:
JUDGES 1 AND 3

The aim of this chapter is to clarify the circumstances that led the book of Saviours from Bethel to Jerusalem.

Judges 3.7-11: Othniel, a Saviour from the South

The story of Othniel, placed at the beginning of the book of Saviours, picks up every trait of the saviour narratives (see Figure 1). In fact, it is nothing else than the sum of all the elements of the frame put together in front of the collection. The story itself barely exists: Othniel went to war against Cushan-rishathaim (Judg. 3.10). The Othniel passage has therefore been described as a *Beispielstück*, a kind of prelude heralding the main themes of the composition.[1]

A few secondary elements have been introduced, like the qualification of evil as serving the Baals and Yhwh's wrath which comes from the schema (Judg. 2.13-14//3.7-8). Othniel is also presented as judge (v. 10). Apart from these slight additions, Othniel is a saviour who saved Israel (v. 9).

However scanty its narrative, Judg. 3.7-11 offers crucial information on the first editorial stage of the BS. The story is as extravagant as it is short: its only specifics are that the hero comes from an obscure Calebite clan and that he vanquished an enemy dubbed with the most grandiloquent name of Double-Evil Kushite King of Aram of the Two Rivers. This bombastic title reflects a definite historical reality, which is now going to be presented.

Cushan-rishathaim and the Yamani Affair

Double-Evil Kushite is a nickname for a king of Kush, the traditional

---

1. Richter, *Bearbeitungen,* pp. 90-91.

Biblical designation of Ethiopia or Nubia, the southernmost extremity of any known territory in the Ancient Orient. This civilization reached its apex at the end of the eighth century BCE when it dominated Egypt with the 25th dynasty (715-663 BCE). Double-Evil, the dual form of רשע 'nasty, culprit',[2] indicates the feelings of the text towards this Kushite, but does not help to identify him, as obviously no 25th dynasty pharaoh ever held such title. But the Kushites became important actors on the Palestinian political scene when they appeared as challengers of the Assyrians in the area. The two Empires first met in Philistia during the rule of Sargon II (722-705 BCE). Sargon had just completed the integration of Aram and Israel; Assyria was tightening its control over Judah and the Philistine kingdoms. At that time, the Kushites, who struggled to dominate the Nile delta, were faced with a delicate diplomatic incident: King Yamani of Ashdod (721-713 BCE) had rebelled against his Assyrian overlord and fled to Egypt. The Kushites decided to extradite the rebel and turned him over to Assyrian border guards.[3] To thank them for this show of goodwill, Sargon recognized Shabako (715-700 BCE) as the legitimate ruler of Egypt against Neko I, who was then murdered. The Assyrians thus sided with the most promising party and so hoped to strengthen Kushite rule over northern Egypt in order to gain a meaningful partner. But, in spite of Assyrian indirect support, the Kushites did not manage to establish their rule over the delta. Worse, viceroy Tirhakah[4] put an end to the *entente cordiale* in 701 BCE by attacking Sennacherib in Elteqeh.[5] Further Egyptian involvement in Southern Palestine between 690 and 680 BCE led Esarhaddon to invade Egypt. The Kushites were chased from Memphis in 671 BCE and Egypt was reorganized from Sais, the centre of anti-Kushite resistance. The 26th dynasty was then established (663-525 BCE) and Psametek I (663-609 BCE) managed to unify Egypt and push the Kushites south of Elephantine (656 BCE). Kush then declined steadily never to threaten Egypt again.[6]

2.   B. Oded, 'Cushan-Rishathaim (Judges 3.8-11): an Implicit Polemic', in M.V. Fox, V.A. Hurowitz and A. Hurvitz (eds.), *Texts, Temples and Traditions* (Winona Lake: Eisenbrauns, 1996), pp. 89*-94*.

3.   See Isa. 20 for a vivid description of the scene. L. Török, *The Kingdom of Kush* (HdO, 1.31; Leiden: E.J. Brill, 1997), p. 167.

4.   Who became king in 681 BCE: K.A. Kitchen, 'Egypt, the Levant and Assyria in 701', in M. Görg (ed.), *Fontes atque pontes* (AAT, 5; Wiesbaden: Otto Harrassowitz, 1983), pp. 243-53 (251).

5.   Isa. 37.9 and Kitchen, 'Egypt, the Levant', pp. 243-53.

6.   D.B. Redford, 'Kush', *ABD* 4, pp. 109-111 (110).

This historical background provides information on the Kushites, but not on Aram of the Two Rivers over which Cushan-rishathaim is supposed to rule. These are recognized as an allusion to Syria and Mesopotamia, but no Kushite ever ruled over Palestine, let alone Mesopotamia. Cushan-rishathaim king of Aram of the two rivers is therefore a code uniting Kushite and Mesopotamian powers into one fictitious figure. The most likely period designated by such a union is the period of the *entente cordiale* between the extradition of Yamani in 712 BCE and the aggression of Tirhakah in 701 BCE. There was then no single ruler dominating over both Mesopotamia and Kush, but these years are the only ones in the whole history of the Orient when from Babylon to Napata (the Kushite capital) two powers seemed to rule the world of one accord. To Palestinian eyes, the beginning of the reign of Neko II (c. 609–594), before his defeat by the Babylonians (605 BCE) could have also appeared as a Egypto-Assyrian coalition, but no one ignored the fact that Neko intervened in a very troubled Mesopotamian context. Neko's involvement clearly demonstrated Assyria's loss of control over Mesopotamia. In Neko's days, the presence of several antagonistic powers was all too clear and therefore unlikely to create the illusion that a single Empire ruled from Mesopotamia to Kush.

However, between 712 and 701 BCE, the illusion of one united power would have been convincing. All the more convincing if one sat in Jerusalem (a mere 50 km from Ashdod), at the front seat to follow the developments of the Yamani affair, how the rebel escaped and the news of his return and delivery to the Assyrian police. Each ruler of Philistia, Judah and Transjordan pondered very seriously over the meaning and the consequences of such a new diplomatic situation that seriously curtailed their options. Egypt, a traditional refuge for Palestinians (from Jacob to Jeroboam and Jesus), was not to be relied upon any more; Yamani had proven, albeit against his will, that a kind of super-power united Kush and Mesopotamia, from the source of the Nile to the mouth of the Tigris.

However extraordinary this super-power may seem to modern eyes, it left some traces in Biblical literature as Isa. 19.24 suggests:

> That day, Israel, making the third with Egypt and Assyria, will be blessed in the centre of the world. Yhwh Sabaoth will give his blessing in the words: 'blessed be my people Egypt, Assyria my creation and Israel my heritage'.[7]

---

7. See P. Machinist, 'Assyria and its Image in the First Isaiah', *JAOS* 103 (1983), pp. 719-37; Dalley, 'Yabâ, Atalyâ', p. 87.

From 740 to 701 BCE, Assyro-Judaean relations were extremely good,
the Assyrians played their usual role of defenders of the weak and
restorers of order when Ahaz asked Tiglath-pileser III to save (יש׳!) him
from Israel and Aram (2 Kgs 16.7). Ahaz is presented as servant and even
son of the Assyrian king (2 Kgs 16.7), quite an appropriate title if Yabâ
and Atalyâ, the two queens found in Nimrud, were Judaean princesses
married by Tiglath-pileser and Sargon respectively.[8] Ahaz and Isaiah are
simply witnessing the new Assyrian policy that came into effect at the
middle of the eighth century BCE. Assyria started to seek compliance of
vassals through rewards and not simply by terror as previously.[9]

Hezekiah versus Sennacherib

The bombastic title of Cushan King of Aram of the Two Rivers is therefore coherent with Palestinian political reality at the end of the eighth century. The only disturbing detail in Judg. 3 is the epithet *rishathaim* 'double
evil' that does not match the good relations between Assyria and Judah.
But the situation changed radically when Hezekiah (716–687 BCE) joined
the rebellion that broke out at the death of Sargon in 705 BCE. That Judah
joined this rebellion when it had staunchly remained loyal for the previous
half-century requires an explanation found simply in the circumstances of
Sargon's death. Sargon died in battle (705 BCE) in far away Cilicia, his
body was not recovered and was therefore deprived of a funeral. This was
a catastrophe which proved that the gods (among them Yhwh) had with-
drawn their support from the Assyrian king and absolved the vassal kings,
even the most loyal ones, from their oaths of loyalty.[10] Almost overnight,
Sargon became, in the eyes of the Assyrian vassals, the embodiment of
evil, he could therefore have been labelled 'rishataim' in Jerusalem as
soon as 705 BCE.

Once he had managed to secure the throne, Sennacherib conducted his
third campaign against the rebels of the West in 701 BCE. Luli of Sidon
escaped to his Cyprian colony; Sennacherib replaced him with Ittobaal II
and received the tribute of Sidon, Arwad, Gubla, Ashdod, Ammon, Moab

---

8.   Dalley, 'Yabâ, Atalyâ'.
9.   G.B. Lanfranchi, 'Consensus to Empire: Some Aspects of Sargon II's Foreign
Policy', in H. Waetzoldt and H. Hauptmann (eds.), *Assyrien im Wandel der Zeiten:
XXXIXe RAI* (HSAO, 6; Heidelberg: Heidelberger Orientverlag, 1997), pp. 81-87.
10.   Isa. 14.18-19: 'All the kings of the nations lie honourably, each in his tomb.
But you, you have been repelled from your grave like loathsome dung, buried under
the slaughtered, under those cut down by the sword'; Dalley, 'Yabâ, Atalyâ', p. 90.

and Edom. He then proceeded south to mop up the last pockets of resistance. The king of Ashkelon was deported and replaced. A Kushite army met Sennacherib near Eltekeh and the conflict ended up in a 20 year stalemate. Jerusalem was blockaded until Hezekiah agreed to pay a heavy tribute and to liberate Padi, the king of Ekron who had been jailed in Jerusalem during the uprising. Padi was reinstated. Gaza probably remained a Egyptian outpost while the Assyrians had to re-establish Ashdod as a vassal kingdom (they had turned it into a province in 711 BCE).[11] The Judaean Shephelah was destroyed, its land handed over to Gaza, Ashdod and Ekron.[12] In all, 200,000 people were deported from Palestine, leaving large expanses of the countryside empty.[13]

Hezekiah was the first Judaean king to rebel against Assyria, and his 'victory' gave rise to differing interpretations. 2 Kings 18.14-16 records the paying of a tribute similar in size to the one mentioned by Sennacherib.[14] Isaiah 36–38 offer a more elaborate version laying the foundations of the invincibility of Zion:[15] Yhwh sends a messenger who strikes

11. For a new understanding of this campaign see E.A. Knauf, 'Who Destroyed Beersheba II?', in U. Hübner (ed.), *FS Manfred Weippert* (OBO, 186; Fribourg/ Göttingen: Universitätsverlag/Vandenhoeck & Ruprecht, 2002), pp. 181-95.

12. 2 Kings 18 and D.D. Luckenbill, *The Annals of Sennacherib* (Chicago: University of Chicago Press, 1924), pp. 29-31: 'The officials, nobles and peoples of Ekron, who had thrown Padî, their king, bound by oath and curse to Assyria, into fetters of iron and had given him over to Hezekiah the Jew, he kept him in confinement like an enemy...'

13. The Annals mention 200,150 persons (Luckenbill, *Sennacherib,* 33), a number often considered totally unrealistic: A. Ungnad, 'Die Zahl der von Sanherib deportierten Judäer', *ZAW* 59 (1941), pp. 199-202. However, A.R. Millard, 'Large Numbers in the Assyrian Royal Inscriptions', in M. Cogan and I. Eph'al (eds.), *Ah Assyria...* (SH, 33; Jerusalem: Magnes Press, 1991), pp. 213-22, compares it with similar campaigns and reckons that it must be fairly close to reality. 200,000 are too many if they concern only the inhabitants of the Shephelah, but placed at the end of the account of the third campaign, it can be the sum of all the deportees for that campaign against Syria-Palestine. It is then realistic.

14. 300 talents of silver and 30 talents of gold (2 Kgs 18.14), 800 talents of silver and 30 talents of gold (Luckenbill, *Sennacherib,* 33).

15. There is no need here to enter the debate over the date of 2 Kgs 18 and Isa. 36–38. See Ch. Hardmeier, *Prophetie im Streit vor dem Untergang Judas: Erzählkommunikative Studien zur Entstehungssituation der Jesaja- und Jeremiaerzählungen in II Reg 18–20 und Jer 37–40* (BZAW, 187; Berlin: W. de Gruyter, 1990); U. Becker, *Jesaja, von der Botschaft zum Buch* (FRLANT, 178; Göttingen: Vandenhoeck und Ruprecht, 1997), pp. 220-22.

185,000 Assyrian soldiers in one night (compare with Sennacherib's 200,150 deportees!), Sennacherib then returns home to be murdered by his son (Isa. 19.35-37). Considered from this vantage point, Hezekiah could be considered as the victor of the twice-wicked king of Aram and Mesopotamia. However, can Othniel be simply equated with Hezekiah?

Othniel the Calebite

The trouble with identifying Othniel with Hezekiah, the 'victor' of Sennacherib in 701 BCE, is that Othniel is of Calebite or Kenazite descent (Judg. 1.13//3.9) which makes it impossible to consider him simply as Judaean.[16] The books of Kings have Hezekiah and all his predecessors descending from David through Maacah the daughter of Absalom.[17] As Absalom is crowned in Hebron, the first capital of David, he seems to be a pure Judaean, unlike Othniel who is son of Kenaz, a brother of Caleb. Considering that the Calebites appear as the most resilient opponents of David's hegemony over Southern Judah,[18] it is very unlikely that Othniel is to be understood as a Judaean, a descendant of David like Hezekiah.

If Othniel cannot be Hezekiah, the saviour of Judg. 3.7-11 could have been anonymous as the name Othniel appears to have been inserted after v. 9a: it is introduced by the particle את and vv. 9-10 make sense without the naming of the saviour:

ויקם יהוה מושיע לבני ישראל ויושיעם
את עתניאל בן־קנז אחי כלב הקטן ממנו:
ותהי עליו רוח־יהוה [וישפט את־ישראל] ויצא למלחמה
ויתן יהוה בידו

It is therefore possible that Judg. 3.7-11 introduced the book of Saviours naming neither saviour nor enemy nor the eight years of oppression. This

16. Against Becker, *Richterzeit*, p. 104.

17. 1 Kgs 15.10, thus bypassing the 'Jebusite' Solomon and the pathetic Rehoboam. 2 Chronicles 11.19 resolves this difficulty by marrying Maacah to Rehoboam: Z. Ben-Barak, 'The Queen Consort and the Struggle for Succession to the Throne', in J.-M. Durand (ed.), *La femme dans le Proche-Orient Ancien* (Paris: Recherche sur les civilisations, 1987), p. 34; T. Ishida, *The Royal Dynasties in Ancient Israel* (BZAW, 142; Berlin: W. de Gruyter, 1977), pp. 158-59.

18. 1 Samuel 25 witnesses the bitter fight between David and the Calebites for the control of the Negeb. David has the support of the Judaeans, the Jerahmelites and the Kenites (1 Sam. 27.10), but the Calebites remained enemies as they did not receive 'presents' in 1 Sam. 30.27-31. However, they were a powerful tribe 1 Sam. 30.14 and later Judaean traditions had to negotiate with the Calebites and finally 'gave' Hebron to Caleb (Josh. 14.6-15; 15.13-16; 20.11-12).

passage without names would then belong to the original BS. However, it is also conceivable that the whole of Judg. 3.7-11 was created later, telling from the start the story of Othniel. The strange construction introduced with אֵת in v. 9b would then be a literary device to put the emphasis on Othniel. It seems impossible to decide between the two options. However, Othniel and Cushan-rishathaim are now present and this fact has to be accounted for.

A solution is found in the other text that mentions Othniel (Judg. 1), where Judah is not presented as a monolithic whole but as a society torn by the conflicting interests of two well-defined groups.

Judges 1

Contents of Judges 1

I Conquests in Judah (vv. 1-21)
   1-3 Preparing the conquest: Judah and Simeon
   4-7 Against Adoni-bezek: Judah
   8-9 Against Jerusalem and Judaean country: Bene-Judah
   10-15 Against Hebron and Debir: Judah, Caleb, Othniel
   16 Against Negeb of Arad: Kenites, Bene-Judah, Amalek
   17 Against Hormah:[19] Judah and Simeon
   18 Against Gaza, Ashkelon and Ekron: Judah
   19-21 The Mountain only, not Jerusalem

II Conquest of Bethel (vv. 22-26): Beth-Joseph

III Progressive conquest in Israel (vv. 27-36)
   27-28 Manasseh did not take Beth-shean, Taanach, Dor, Ibleam, Megiddo
   29 Ephraim did not take Gezer
   30 Zebulun did not take Kitron, Nahalol
   31-32 Asher did not take Acco, Sidon, Ahlab, Achzib, Helbah, Aphik, Rehob
   33 Naphtali did not take Beth-shemesh, Beth-anath
   34 Amorites pressed Dan who did not take anything
   35-36 Amorite territory

Each of the three sections is dealing with a well-defined geographical zone: Judah, Bethel, Israel. Southern leanings are clearly at work throughout the chapter as the conquest of Judah is successful, while the Israelite one starts with the description of the conquest of Bethel but then lists the cities that were not taken. In spite of this apparent thematic unity, Judg. 1 is composed of disparate material. However, before entering a detailed

---

19. Possible location at Khirbet Mshash: Knauf, 'Low Chronology', n. 31.

analysis, the result of the work of a few scholars on Judg. 1 should be presented.

History of Research on Judges 1

Research on Judg. 1 is a free-for-all situation where the most blatant shortcomings of modern exegesis are held as common sense. Judges 1 is dubbed 'late', due to its position in front of the book and its similarities with the conquest theme in Joshua, while admitting that this late chapter holds some very 'old' traditions. Albrecht Alt held that the incomplete or gradual conquest depicted in Judg. 1.27-36 is closer to historical truth than the ideological presentation of the total and once-for-all invasion of Canaan described in the book of Joshua. Judges 1 would then serve as transition to smooth out the difficulties caused by the juxtaposition of these two irreconcilable conceptions of Israel's settling in Canaan.

However, once the text is studied in detail, the consensus disintegrates in front of the complexity of Judg. 1, one is forced to admit that if Judg. 1 was meant as a transition between Joshua and Judges, the whole endeavour failed.[20] A few pages have to be committed to presenting the latest attempts to explain Judg. 1.

Rofé and the Ephraimite Historiography. In 1991, Rofé tried to refute the Deuteronomistic Historiography hypothesis, noting that Noth affirmed the unity of DH, without ever demonstrating it.[21] He followed Charles Burney[22] who identified a first form of the book of Judges extending from Josh. 24 to 1 Sam. 12. From this 'proto-Judges', Rofé removed chapters 17–21 where neither saviour nor judge appear, plus the introductions of the book in chs. 1 and 2. The Othniel passage (Judg. 3.7-11) is also removed, as a LXX plus in Josh. 24.33 introduces the story of Ehud directly at the end of the book of Joshua.[23] This LXX plus shows that a form of

20. Lindars, *Judges 1–5*, p. 92.

21. A. Rofé, 'Ephraimite versus Deuteronomistic History', in D. Garrone and F. Israel (eds.), *Storia e tradizioni di Israele: Scritti in onore di J. Alberto Soggin* (Brescia: Paideia, 1991), pp. 221-35.

22. C.F. Burney, *The Book of Judges* (London: Rivingtons, 1918).

23. A. Rofé, 'The End of the Book of Joshua According to the Septuagint', *Shnaton* 2 (1977), pp. 217-27, see H.N. Rösel, 'Die Überleitungen vom Josua zum Richterbuch', *VT* 30 (1980), pp. 342-50, also A. Moenikes, *Die grundsätzliche Ablehnung des Königstums in der hebräischen Bibel* (BBB, 99; Weinheim: Belz Athenäum, 1995).

Judges starting with the story of Ehud existed at one point omitting Judg. 1.1–3.11. This LXX plus is usually considered as a summary, therefore secondary rather than original, however, A. Graeme Auld, a specialist of the Greek text, suggests that the argument can be reversed.[24]

According to Rofé, Josh. 24, Judg. 3–16 and 1 Sam. 1–12 constituted an Ephraimite Historiography (Ephr.) telling the stories of northern tribes, Manasseh, Ephraim, Benjamin, Gad, Dan (Samson is kept in Ephr.) and Naphtali, among which Ephraim holds a dominant position, indicating a date before 722 BCE. Joshua and Samuel who frame Ephr. are Ephraimites just as Deborah is.

Rofé compares Ephr. with Deuteronomistic theologies to establish its main themes. Ephr. ignores the centralization of the cult,[25] situated by the first Deuteronomists under Solomon (Deut. 12.10; 1 Kgs 5.18) or during the conquest by later Deuteronomists (Deut. 11.31–12.7, in Shiloh waiting for the building of the Jerusalem temple). Ephr. mentions no less than seven sanctuaries (Shechem, Ophrah, Mizpah of Gilead, Shiloh, Mizpah of Benjamin, Ramah and Gilgal). Although Rofé finds only nine critical verses against kingship, he does not hesitate to characterize Ephr. as fundamentally antimonarchical.[26] Regarding war, Ephr. is quietist,[27] it is Yhwh himself who fights while Israel stands by (Josh. 24, Gideon and Samuel at Mizpah).[28] Ephr. shares with DH the exclusive adoration for Yhwh and the condemnation of idolatry.[29]

Rofé is therefore close to Richter in his attempt to define an Israelite collection and closer to Knauf with a date around 720 BCE (see Chapter 1). However, he tries to overthrow the yoke of the Nothian DH by creating another historiography, dated more than a century earlier than Noth's.[30] This is a methodical flaw.

24. A.G. Auld, 'What Makes Judges Deuteronomistic?', in *idem* (ed.), *Joshua Retold* (Edinburgh: T. & T. Clark, 1998), pp. 120-26 (125).

25. A. Rofé, 'The Strata of the Law about the Centralisation of Worship and the History of the Deuteronomic Mouvement', in *Congress Volume, Uppsala 1971* (VTSup, 22; Leiden: E.J. Brill, 1972), pp. 221-26.

26. Rofé, 'Ephraimite History', p. 228.

27. Rofé, 'Ephraimite History', p. 229.

28. 1 Sam. 7.7-14; Rofé, 'Ephraimite History', p. 230.

29. Critique of Jeroboam's golden calves (1 Kgs 12), ark without cherubim (Deut. 10.1-5), aniconic cult (Deut. 4.9-31; 2 Kgs 17.16): Rofé, 'Ephraimite History', p. 234.

30. Rofé, 'Ephraimite History', p. 234.

Rösel turns Rofé's argument upside down. Hartmut Rösel rejects Rofé's thesis and considers that Josh. 24 and Judg. 1–2.5 are the original transition between Joshua and Judges. Joshua 23 and Judg. 2.6-10 organize a later transition because the note on Joshua's death in Judg. 2.6-9 clearly depends on Josh. 24.28-33.[31] This last remark is acceptable, however, Rösel is left with the intricate problem of Josh. 23 being secondary to Josh. 24. The historiographic model prevents him to be satisfied with Judg. 2.6-9 as the transition between the books of Joshua and Judges and leads him to postulate such a transitional function for both Josh. 23 and 24 which they probably never had.

Blum uses Judges to explain Joshua. Recently Erhard Blum has proposed an impressive compositional model combining the first chapters of Judges with Joshua and with the composition of the Pentateuch. Blum observes that the concept of the conquest found in Josh. 23 differs as much from the one in Josh. 1–12 as from the one in Judg. 1 and that these three passages have to be attributed to different stages. Judges 1 is also very different from Judg. 2.1-5 so that Judg. 2.1-5 cannot be the conclusion of ch. 1. Joshua 24 corresponds to none of the previous passages and has to be considered separately. Joshua 21–Judges 3 is therefore the result of an editorial process in seven stages.

1.   DtrG, main DH layer: total conquest (Josh. 1-12; 13.1a*, 7ss*) and allotment of the land (Josh. 21.43-45). Judg. 2.8-10* performs the transition between this first form of Joshua and the first form of Judges.

2.   DtrG2, DH supplements: unconquered periphery around the Israelite cradle (Josh. 13.1b-6; 23; Judg. 2.20-21, 23; 3.1a*, 3). This minimalist conception of the conquest serves to counter the ideal image at the end of the exilic period,[32] the remaining Canaanites on the margins of Israel do not constitute Israel's guilt, nor Yhwh's punishment, but a threat.

3.   Mal'ak-Yhwh addition (Judg. 2.1-5): an allusion to Josh. 9, but not the conclusion of Judg. 1. The difference between centre and periphery is cancelled, the Canaanites are everywhere. This conception is post-exilic, post-Deuteronomistic:[33] it presupposes the pre-Priestly edition of the

---

31. Rösel, 'Überleitung', pp. 342-50.

32. E. Blum, 'Der kompositionelle Knoten am Übergang von Josua zu Richter: Ein Entflechtungsvorschlag', in M. Vervenne and J. Lust (eds.), *Deuteronomy and Deuteronomic Literature* (BETL, 133; Leuven: Peeters, 1997), pp. 181-212 (189).

33. Blum, 'Knoten', p. 192.

Torah (KD)[34] and reflects the 'second conquest'.[35]

4.   Hexateuch complements (Josh. 24): the book of the Law of God. The Samaritans are called to adopt the Torah as their constitution.[36] The aim is to serve Yhwh, not to conquer other people. Joshua 24 concludes the Hexateuch by establishing links with the stories of Jacob and Joseph in order to transform Moses' Torah into God's (vv. 26-32). Joshua 24 marks the end of the Hexateuch and separates Joshua from Judges.[37]

5.   Unconquered centre (Judg. 1): parallels are made with Judg. 17–21 to turn Judges (now rejected from the Hexateuch) into an independent unit.[38] Blum admits that it is difficult to know exactly how Judg. 1 considers the survival of the Canaanite cities, but notes that this surprising feature is not necessarily to be understood as a reproach, but rather as an acknowledgement of failure.[39]

6.   Divine pedagogy (Judg. 2.17, 22; 3.4): *Fürsorge* theodicy[40] to explain that the conquest has been delayed due to the small numbers of the Jewish population of Persian *Yehud.*

7.   Priestly additions (Josh. 14.1; 17.4; 19.51; 21.1; 24.33): the priest Eleazar is raised to the same rank as Joshua.

Blum manages the remarkable feat of synthesizing the work of Smend, Lohfink, Anbar, Van Seters, Rösel, Rofé, Auld, Becker and his own studies of the Pentateuch[41] but opens no new vista as he remains sticks to the traditional Nothian frame. This *Entflechtungsvorschlag* adds another loop to the Gordian knot that entangles Joshua, Judges, the Pentateuch and the Former Prophets. He studies Judges in the light of Joshua and cannot imagine the existence of parts of Judg. 1–3 independent from Joshua and DH. His study is therefore much more convincing on Joshua than it is on Judges.

Lindars and the failed harmonization. Barnabas Lindars applies to Joshua and Judges the literary device of *catch-lines* first presented by Menahem

34.   Blum, 'Knoten', p. 193.
35.   Blum, 'Knoten', p. 189.
36.   Blum, 'Knoten', p. 198.
37.   Blum, 'Knoten', p. 205.
38.   Blum, 'Knoten', p. 207.
39.   Blum, 'Knoten', p. 207.
40.   Blum, 'Knoten', p. 210.
41.   E. Blum, *Die Komposition der Vätergeschichte* (WMANT, 57; Neukirchen-Vluyn: Neukirchener, 1984).

Haran between Chronicles and Ezra.[42] Judges 2.7, 10 would be the first introduction to Judges and Josh. 24.31 a *catch-line* indicating the end of Joshua and the beginning of the next book. This shrewd solution, a reversal of Rösel's theory,[43] implies that Judges started at Judg. 2.7 when Joshua ended at Josh. 24.31, a most unlikely situation as Josh. 24 is generally considered as a very late chapter.[44] Moreover, the results are not convincing as Lindars himself admits: Judg. 2.6, 8-9 are rather inadequate to harmonize Joshua and Judges after the addition of Judg. 1.1–2.5 and 2.20–3.6.[45] Does the fault lie with the redactors of the text or with its modern explanatory systems?

Back to Noth with Becker. Becker attributes Josh. 21.43-45; 24.31 and Judg. 2.8-23 to DtrH, the author of the Deuteronomistic Historiography, still not divided into separate books. DtrN inserted Josh. 22.1-6; Josh. 23 and the negative passages of Judg. 1.21, 27-31; 2.1-5, 6-7 which sever Judg. 2.8 from Josh. 24.31. A post-Deuteronomistic editor (R[P]) added Josh. 22.7-34; 24.1-30, 32-33; Judg. 1.1-18, 22-26.

Becker's proposal is attractive as it conveniently escapes the confusion affecting the field by simply returning to Noth's intuitions. However, Becker has not produced confirming evidence of his master's intuitions. In fact, despite the abundance of propositions, they all follow the Nothian model that forces them to understand Joshua and Judges as part of a continuous historiography before becoming separate books. All hypotheses seek the transition before the books were ever separated, which is a rather odd way to proceed. Transitions become necessary only when independant and self-sufficient units are juxtaposed.

Times are changing and the aforementioned study by K. Schmid is now offering a later date for the composition of the Former Prophets. This new theory will be presented in Chapter 7, but let it be said here already that Schmid claims that the book of Judges is a late-comer in the chronography of the Former Prophets. *Judges* existed first as an independant work before it was inserted between *Joshua* and *1 Samuel* to represent a particular period of Israel's past. Joshua 24 was drafted as a last conclusion to the book of Joshua, but not as a transition between Joshua and Judges.[46]

---

42. M. Haran, 'Book Size and the Device of Catchline', *JJS* 36 (1985), pp. 1-11.
43. Rösel, 'Überleitungen', pp. 342-50.
44. Becker, *Richterzeit*, p. 69.
45. Lindars, *Judges 1–5*, p. 92.
46. Schmid, *Erzväter*, p. 220.

Consequently, Judg. 1 is freed from the burden of harmonizing the content of Judges with that of Joshua.

However, Joshua and Judges are now following each other and it is obvious that some verses in Judges do perform a transition with the book of Joshua. These verses are quite simply those that mention Joshua in the book of Judges, namely Judg. 1.1; 2.6-10, 20–3.6. Moreover, two glosses in Judg. 1.19-21, 35-36 harmonize the most blatant contradictions between Joshua and Judges.

Those explicit mentions of Joshua in Judges are framing two textual blocks (Judg. 1.2–2.5 and 2.11-19, the schema already encountered in Chapter 1) which present many parallels with the book of Joshua[47] but follow their own logic. In fact, these two blocks organize an internal disputation within Judges and do not directly address issues contained in the book of Joshua. Therefore, instead of comparing Joshua and Judges, the enquiry must first focus on the tensions within Judg. 1–3. Once the transitional material with Joshua is removed (see Chapter 7), the remaining verses can be dealt with. Judges 1.4-34 are analysed in the remaining part of the present chapter, except for the central part (vv. 22-26, the conquest of Bethel) which is kept for Chapter 6 for reasons that will be exposed there and then. Judges 2 will be considered in Chapter 3.

However, before entering the literary arena, the historical situation prevailing in Judah after Hezekiah's rebellion (705 BCE) has to be presented in the hope of gaining some external guidelines.

Jerusalem 701-640 BCE, the Reign of Manasseh

A co-regency. The end of Sennacherib's blockade of Jerusalem became the basis of the myth of the invincibility of Zion, but it also provoked, directly or indirectly, a change of majority at the court of Hezekiah. The report of these events in 2 Kgs 18–19 is followed immediately by the narration of a sickness that threatened Hezekiah's life. The king was finally cured when Isaiah applied a cake of figs on the royal boil and Hezekiah gained a 15 years' lease of life (2 Kgs 20.6-7). The figs represent the healing power of his submission to Assyria, and the 15 years are those of his semi-retirement from the rule after 701 BCE.[48] Although 2 Kgs 20 gives the

---

47. Becker, *Richterzeit*, p. 23.

48. S.W. Bulbach, 'Judah in the reign of Manasseh as Evidenced in Texts during the Neo-Assyrian Period and in the Archeology of the Iron Age' (PhD dissertation; University of New York, Ann Arbor, MI: University Microfilms, 1981), p. 128.

impression that Hezekiah ruled until his death in 687 BCE, the chronology of Manasseh's reign shows that he started to rule well before his father's death, shortly after 701.[49] Manasseh was then only 12 years old (2 Kgs 21.1) and may only have held the title *BN HMLK* 'son of the king'.[50] A co-regency was set up and if Hezekiah remained king, the effective power was in the hands of an Assyrian-friendly group of advisers.[51] In the meantime, Hezekiah remained nominal ruler, a face-saving move to avoid pushing the rebellious party into near-by Kushite arms.[52] In fact, the Assyrian kept local dynasties on their throne as long as possible, especially in sensitive border-areas like Palestine where they preferred to maintain small buffer states rather than setting up provinces under direct administration.[53]

The golden age of the kingdom of Judah. The long reign of Manasseh was also a time of rapid economical change. In fact, it coincided with the reigns of the greatest Sargonid kings (Sennacherib, Esarhaddon and Assurbanipal) and the apex of the Assyrian Empire, characterized by internal stability (apart from Babylon) and prosperity that permitted the successful integration of the last valuable part of the Orient: Egypt. Contrary to what is sometimes claimed, Manasseh did not rebel,[54] this presumed rebellion is based on Manasseh's alleged exile (!) to Babylon (!) and his subsequent repentance in 2 Chron. 33.10-13. This story is clearly meant to explain how such an impious king as Manasseh could achieve so much: the next verse describes the expansion of Jerusalem and the enlargement of the walls (2 Chron. 33.14). According to the Chronicler's historiographical

49. Bulbach, 'Judah', p. 120 and E.R. Thiele, *The Mysterious Numbers of the Hebrew Kings* (Grand Rapids, Eerdman, 1965), pp. 128-39.

50. According to a seal of unknown origin: למנשה בן המלך. Title also attributed to King Jotham, in addition to על הבית (2 Kgs 15.5): N. Avigad, 'A Seal of Manasseh, Son of the King', *IEJ* 13 (1963), pp. 133-36, and M. Görg, 'Zum Titel BN HMLK', *BN* 29 (1985), pp. 7-11.

51. Some members of Hezekiah's family were deported as Sennacherib claims that Hezekiah sent to Nineveh 'his daughters, his harem, his male and female musicians...' (Luckenbill, *Sennacherib*, p. 34).

52. Bulbach, 'Judah', pp. 119-28.

53. E. Ben Zvi, 'Prelude to a Reconstruction of the Historical Manassic Judah', *BN* 81 (1996), pp. 31-44 (33); and B. Otzen, 'Israel under the Assyrians', in M.G. Larsen (ed.), *Power and Propaganda* (Mesopotamia, 7; Copenhagen: Akademisk Forlag, 1979), pp. 251-62 (256).

54. A.T. Olmstead, *History of Assyria* (Chicago: University of Chicago Press, 1923), p. 380.

conception, only good kings can be successful.[55] However, there is no indication of trouble in Judah during Manasseh's reign, neither in connection with Shamash-shum-ukin's revolt in Babylon (652-648 BCE), nor in 644 BCE during the rebellion of Acco and Ushu.[56] The Assyrian Annals record simply that the 22 kings of the West sent building materials to Nineveh;[57] the hooks and fetters of bronze mentioned in 2 Chron. 33.11 served to fasten the beams and the stones for the new palace rather than to bind Manasseh.

The transport of these materials indicates the development of long-distance trade and the booming economy from which the small kingdom of Judah got its share. Like the rest of the Empire, Judah experienced a vast urbanization programme and the population of Jerusalem exploded,[58] due to the arrival of refugees, not from Israel but from the Judaean countryside.[59] For the first time in its history, Jerusalem became the real capital of Judah, Hebron being relegated to a secondary role. International trade and subsequent prosperity, combined with political and cultural domination of Assyria, encouraged a spurt of literary production across the Empire. Old cultures felt threatened by this border-erasing Empire, but at the same time, they benefited from favourable financial conditions that allowed them to protect their traditions by putting them in writing.[60] The Phoenician Chronicles and the book of the Chronicles of the Kings of Israel and Judah quoted by 1 and 2 Kings appeared;[61] the Assyrian Annals became models that still inspired Manetho three centuries later in Egypt.[62]

55. Ahlström, *History,* p. 737.

56. D.D. Luckenbill, *Ancient Records of Assyria and Babylonia* (Chicago: University of Chicago Press, 1926), p. 2 §830.

57. R. Borger, *Die Inschriften Asahaddons* (AfO Beihefte, 9; Graz: Selbstverlage des Herausgebers, 1956), p. 60: 2 §698.

58. From 6 to 25% of the total population of the kingdom: Finkelstein, 'Manasseh', p. 177; M. Broshi, 'The Expansion of Jerusalem in the Reigns of Hezekiah and Manasseh', *IEJ* 24 (1974), pp. 21-26.

59. Ben Zvi, 'Prelude', pp. 31-44.

60. Knauf, *Umwelt*, p. 234.

61. Kitchen, 'Egypt, the Levant', p. 252: Tirhakah is called king in 2 Kgs 19.9 but only received the crown 10 years after the events (690 BCE) whilst 2 Kgs 19.37 knows of Sennacherib's murder which only happens in 681 BCE. 2 Kings 19 and the previous chapters are therefore likely to have been written in 680 BCE at the earliest.

62. D.B. Redford, *Egypt, Canaan and Israel in Ancient Times* (Princeton: Princeton University Press, 1992), p. 332.

The roots of nationalism. The rebellion of 705-701 BCE was quenched, but its actors instigators remained in the country: Manasseh is accused *inter alia* to have shed much innocent blood in Jerusalem (2 Kgs 21.16; 24.4). The books of Kings are dominated by Deuteronomistic ideology, an ideology bent on turning Manasseh into the worst villain of all the Judaean kings.

Manasseh was caught between two opposite forces. On the level of foreign affairs, his survival was tied to strict respect of the stipulations of the *berith*. Compliance of the ruling elite was secured by direct benefit from the prosperity that resulted from political stability and the absence of military interventions. Tax pressure (tribute) stimulated production and an Empire-wide market absorbed the surplus. But in Judah, the stability was understood as treason by the traditional country elite which was losing power to the *nouveaux riches* of the capital, in a process similar to the one found a century earlier in Israel. The prosperity generated by this stability aggravated the resentment of the countryside as the Assyrians gained the active participation of the new ruling elite by allowing it a bigger share of the profit than the one received by the other segments of society.[63] The 'people of the land' had probably supported Hezekiah's revolt in 705 BCE and continued to exalt his courage and his piety against Manasseh and 'those fellows in Jerusalem' who were selling out the country to foreigners. The voice of the reactionary groups is still audible in the Biblical text accusing Manasseh of having shed much blood in Jerusalem, to the point of filling the city from one end to the other (2 Kgs 21.16)! Behind the hyperbole, the reality of the repression of the internal enemy is obvious. The price of peace with the Assyrians was the ruthless suppression of the anti-Assyrian opposition, the viciousness of the fight being proportional to the magnitude and the speed of the changes that transformed Judaean society. Baruch Halpern does not hesitate to describe this period as a

63. In fact, Assyrian Imperialism, like most imperialisms, was based on varying degrees of harmony and disharmony of interest between center and periphery. This fostered centripetal cohesion forces: the highest harmony of interest was found between the elite of the capital of the Empire and the elites of the provincial capitals, the highest level of disharmony of interest was between the Imperial capital's periphery of the Empire and all the provincial peripheries. The system holds as long as the level of harmony between the centre and the periphery of the Imperial capital is kept at a higher level than between provincial elites and their own periphery. Therefore, the Empire requires to maintain a high level of *Interessendisharmonie* between the provincial elites and the people they dominate, which is precisely the point under Manasseh: Lamprichs, *Westexpansion*, pp. 33-45 and Abb. 1.

Kulturkampf[64] as the backward and peripheral kingdom of Judah was suddenly sucked into an Empire that had reached its highest development. The survival of nationalistic aspirations during Manasseh's reign is also brought to light by their immediate resurgence under Josiah, as soon as the Empire showed its first signs of weakness. Hezekiah will then be understood as Josiah's forerunner, thus framing the odious Manasseh with the best kings since David in order to underline the evil of the Assyrian period.[65]

In this context, the book of Saviours produced at near-by Bethel, could have aroused the interest of Manasseh's advisers as the BS conveyed a message of appeasement towards the Assyrians. The BS would have been used in Jerusalem with a new introduction to make it pertinent to the Judaean context. Such could be the function of Othniel in the *Beispielstück* and in Judg. 1 as vv. 4-18 seem to oppose two parties in Judah while vv. 27-34 offer a most unusual vision of the settlement of Israel in the land. These two sections of Judg. 1 are now to be examined.

Judges 1.4-18: Judah versus the Sons of Judah

Judges 1.4-7 form a small literary unit telling Judah's victory over the Canaanites and the Perizzites with special emphasis on the defeat of Adoni-bezek in vv. 5-7. The relationship of this Adoni-bezek with Adonizedek (Josh. 10) and Melchizedek (Gen. 14) is unclear, but as all three texts are connected with Jerusalem, it is safe to assume that a mythical ruler of Jerusalem is referred to. Judges 1 seems to purposely misspell his name although the exact meaning of the pun can only be guessed.[66]

Beside twisting his name, Judg. 1 removes Adoni-bezek from Jerusalem by setting Judah's first victory in Bezek (Judg. 1.4) thus making him Lord of an unknown place called Bezek and it is Judah who brings him to Jerusalem (v. 7). In this way, a king Zedek or Bezek did reside in Jerusalem

---

64. B. Halpern, 'Jerusalem and the Lineages in the Seventh Century BCE', in B. Halpern and D.W. Hobson (eds.), *Law and Ideology in Monarchic Israel* (JSOTSup, 124; Sheffield: JSOT Press, 1991), pp. 11-107 (86, 91).

65. L.K. Handy, 'Hezekiah's Unlikely Reform', *ZAW* 100 (1988), pp. 111-15.

66. According to the parallelism ברק/בזק (Ezek. 1.16-17), Adoni-bezek could be understood as a divine epithet 'Lord of the thunderbolt'. But בזק is also attested in a proverb from the Ahiqar collection (n° 107): Lindenberger, *Proverbs*, p. 205, translated 'pebble' on the basis of Syriac *bizqâ'* 'pebble, fragment of broken pottery' or 'Steinchen, Kiesel' (Kottsieper, *Sprache*, p. 192). The title Adoni-bezek, 'Lord of the crumbs' may then be announcing the final destiny of the king who ended up picking crumbs under his own table (Judg. 1.7).

but as prisoner, brought to Jerusalem by Judah, who thus reveals himself as the real master of Jerusalem and as a native of Jerusalem from the very beginning.

However, in v. 8 a new actors intervene, the sons of Judah, who put Jerusalem to fire and sword before turning against the Canaanites in the Mountain, the Negeb and the Shephelah (v. 9). One may consider that the narrative goes back from the action told in the previous verse and that the sons of Judah are only another designation of Judah[67] or that Judg. 1 has been compiled by clumsy scribes who did not understand what they were doing.[68] Before blaming the text, we should try to understand it.

In fact, the sons of Judah reappear in v. 16 alongside the Kenites and a mysterious עַם (people) which could be an improved form of the offensive reading Amalek עֲמָלֵק.[69] As the David cycle locates Amalek in the Negeb with the Judaeans, the Kenites and the Calebites, and as Amalek was later styled as the archetype of Israel's enemy,[70] it is understandable that Amalek was turned into a neutral 'people' as the next door neighbour of the sons of Judah.[71] In spite of this difficult verse, the narrative is coherent. After the celebration of the mythical origin of Judah from Jerusalem and after the transformation of the traditional master of Jerusalem into a resident prisoner, a group of sons of Judah destroys Jerusalem and ends up in the far side of the Negeb, next to the most undesirable Amalekites. A certain amount of military success is granted to the sons of Judah, but the opposition between Judah and the sons of Judah increases. Judah's campaign against Hebron (v. 10), Debir (vv. 11-15), Zephath (v. 17), Gaza, Ashkelon and Ekron (v. 18) shows that the sons of Judah did not conquer any city. Judah's move, on the contrary, is presented as a campaign of liberation limited to defeating tyrants (Adoni-bezek in Jerusalem, Sheshai, Ahiman and Talmai in Hebron) and the taking לָקַד (vv. 13, 18) of Debir and of three Philistine cities. Judah is only reported to shed blood at Zephath (v. 17) which is utterly destroyed חרם, although this is motivated by the etymology of the name of Hormah חָרְמָה. Compared to the sons of Judah who kill and burn in Jerusalem and wage war לְחֹם against the rest of

---

67. Becker, *Richterzeit*, p. 39.

68. Lindars, *Judges 1–5*, p. 6.

69. Against B. Mazar, *Biblical Israel* (Jerusalem: Magnes Press, 1992), p. 71. See S. Mittmann, 'Ri. 1, 16f u.d. Siedlungsgebiet d. Kenitischen Sippe Hobab', *ZDPV* 93 (1977), pp. 213-35.

70. Knauf, 'Amalekiter'.

71. The town of Palms, Tamar, *'Ain el-'Arus*: Mittmann, 'Ri. 1, 16', p. 120.

the Judaean country (vv. 8-9), Judah's role appears as peaceful, all the more so since vv. 14-15 are devoted to the settlement of watering rights. The distinction between Judah and the sons of Judah serves to establish the legitimacy of a ruling group in Jerusalem against another group, a group described as leading violent raids against the capital, a group eventually banished to the Negeb. This polemic around Jerusalem could reflect the tension that afflicted the kingdom of Judah during the reign of Manasseh along the lines presented in the historical reconstruction in the previous paragraph. Admittedly, the evidence is slight, but the three Philistine cities mentioned in v. 18 should allow for a more convincing case.

Gaza, Ashkelon, Ekron and the Date of Judges 1.4-18
The conquest of Gaza, Ashkelon and Ekron is attributed to Judah at the end of the passage (v. 18).[72] This note appears as ludicrously boastful: Judah never was able to effectively control the Philistine cities before the Hasmonaean period. However, these three cities correspond exactly to the ones that came under Hezekiah's influence during the revolt in 705–701 BCE. Hezekiah did not actually conquer them, but he certainly was involved in a campaign of intimidation aimed at coercing his unwilling neighbours into the rebellion.[73] 2 Kings 18.8 affirms that Hezekiah smote the Philistines as far as Gaza, and this claim is indirectly confirmed by Sennacherib when he allocates a share of the Judaean Shephelah to Gaza,[74] thus recognizing that Gaza had not joined the rebellion willingly. Ṣidqa of Ashkelon seems to have joined the rebels of his own accord and was consequently overthrown by his own subjects upon the approach of Sennacherib.[75] Hezekiah's involvement in Ekron is obvious as king Padi of Ekron was locked up in Jerusalem until Sennacherib had him released and reinstalled. As for the two remaining Philistine cities not mentioned in Judg. 1.18, Gath was part of the kingdom of Ashdod at least since 712 BCE.[76] Mitinti of Ashdod had remained loyal because he was the only

72. Verses 19-21 harmonize Judg. 1.4-18 with Josh. 13.3 and will be considered in Chapter 8.
73. N. Na'aman, 'Forced Participation in Alliances in the Course of the Assyrian Campaigns to the West', in M. Cogan and I. Eph'al (eds.), *Ah Assyria...* (SH, 33; Jerusalem: Magnes Press, 1991), pp. 80-98.
74. Luckenbill, *Sennacherib*, pp. 29-31.
75. Kitchen, 'Egypt, the Levant', p. 246.
76. Sargon conquered Gath with Ashdod in 712 BCE: A. Fuchs, *Die Inschriften Sargons II aus Khorsabad* (Göttingen: Cuvillier Verlag, 1994), pp. 132-33, 326.

Philistine ruler to present his submission spontaneously at Ushu before Sennacherib proceeded South to sort out the wheat from the chaff. Judges 1.18 is therefore coherent with the political configuration in Palestine between the death of Sargon and Sennacherib's third campaign: Gaza, Ashkelon and Ekron joined the rebellion with Hezekiah and others, whilst Ashdod managed to remain loyal.[77] Hezekiah did not really conquer Gaza, Ashkelon and Ekron, but he could have claimed to have forced his will on them, to the point of taking into custody the king of Ekron.

We may now attempt to determine the aim of Judg. 1.18. In the context of Judg. 1, the boastful claim to have conquered Gaza, Ashkelon and Ekron underlines the superiority of Judah over the sons of Judah who are just good at raiding the land.

Since Hezekiah lost most of his power after 701 BCE, it is likely that this claim was put forward during the reign of Manasseh. However, this seems rather odd for a king as loyal to his Assyrian overlord as Manasseh to boast about his father's greatest achievement during his revolt against Assyria. This apparent difficulty may be cleared if Judg. 1.18 is considered in the light of the whole of Judg. 1.4-18: Manasseh's propagandists are using Hezekiah's only 'success' to bolster up the legitimacy of his son's rule against a growing opposition which may be tempted to use the events of 705-701 BCE to prove that rebellion pays. By attributing to peaceful Judah the temporary control of Gaza, Ashkelon and Ekron, Manasseh cashes in on his father's prestige in the eyes of his own people who remembered Hezekiah as the conqueror of the Philistines. The aim was to transfer on Manasseh some of this prestige in order to gain support for Manasseh's Assyrian-friendly policies that were bound to be less popular than his father's short lived successes against Philistia.

The analysis of vv. 27-34 will clarify Manasseh's aim.

Judges 1.27-34: Insignificance of the Plains

If a first polemical front opposes Judah to the sons of Judah in vv. 4-18, what about the widely recognized contrast between a victorious Judah and a failing Israel in vv. 27-34? Such an exaltation of Judah would make sense if Judah had territorial claims over Israel, possibly under Josiah or under the Hasmonaeans. On the contrary, during Manasseh's reign, the survival of the kingdom of Judah was only possible in the absence of any such claims. Is Judg. 1.27-34 to be understood as produced by Josiah or by the Hasmonaeans?

---

77. Yamani's lesson was not lost on his successor!

The answer is that Judg. 1.27-34 cannot be attributed to either Josiah or the Hasmonaeans since nothing in this passage stresses the superiority of Judah over against Israel. In fact, it is only Judg. 2.1-5 that throws a negative light on Israel's non-conquest of the cities cited in Judg. 1.27-34 (see Chapter 3). Without Judg. 2.1-5, the progressive conquest of the cities of the plains needs not be understood as a failure on the part of Israel. These verses respond to the requirements of the internal affairs of the kingdom of Judah during Manasseh's reign. It was vital for Manasseh to convince his subjects that collaboration with the Assyrians was better than rebellion. However, the demonstration was arduous, there were undoubtedly countless Judaeans who would have drawn the opposite conclusion: if Judah did not resist, the Assyrians would soon swallow it, as they had done with Israel. To refute this obvious reading of the events between 735 and 720 BCE, it was necessary to go back much earlier, to the mythical times of the origins, when Israel's forefathers lived in the mountains, as the song of Deborah had depicted them so vividly, coming down from the hill country to harry the troops of the cities in the plain.[78] In those days, Israel did not control these cities and it is only later that they came under direct Israelite rule, albeit progressively and temporarily.

Therefore, Manasseh's propagandists draw a list of the main cities of the lowland around the hill country of Ephraim: Beth-shean, Taanach, Yibleam, Megiddo, Kitron and Nahalol[79] in the Jezreel valley; Dor and Gezer in the Sharon and Acco, Ahlab, Achzib, Helbah, Aphik and Rehob on the Phoenician coast. Neither Shechem nor Samaria nor any town of the Israelite cradle is mentioned, the focus is on the plains to underline their secondary aspect and to minimize the gravity of the Assyrian conquest. Granted, the Assyrians had also conquered the Israelite mountain and they had turned Samaria into a provincial capital. But Manasseh's audience was Judaean, not Israelite, and it was the loss of the Shephelah by Judah after 701 BCE that had to be played down. Manasseh boasts about his father's control over three Philistine cities in vv. 4-18, and in vv. 27-34

---

78. The conquest under Joshua is not yet conceptualized and it is probably only under Josiah that the conquest of Benjamin will be justified by connecting it with the coming out of Egypt and the crossing of the Jordan in Josh. 3–10: Th. Römer, 'Le livre de Josué, histoire d'une propagande. Propagande d'une histoire', *FVCb* 37 (1998), pp. 5-20 (12-14). For the reception of the Exodus in Judah see Y. Hoffman, 'A North Israelite Typological Myth and a Judaean Historical Tradition: The Exodus in Hosea and Amos', *VT* 39 (1989), pp. 169-82.

79. Lindars, *Judges 1–5*, p. 64.

he claims that the loss of these territories is no catastrophe. After all, Yhwh was essentially a god of the mountain (1 Kgs 20.23), and it is only under Josiah that official Deuteronomistic doctrine will turn him into a universal god.[80] However, we are well before Josiah's reign. The Assyrian Empire is reaching the apex of its power and Manasseh has to choke internal resistance. Hezekiah's supporters must be banned to the Negeb, literally or not there is no way to tell. Because they only brought destruction to Jerusalem and in the rest of the country (Judg. 1.8-9), they must now let Judah, that is Manasseh and his advisers, run the kingdom without interfering and putting everyone in danger.

This reading of Judg. 1.27-36 in the light of vv. 4-18 may seem extremely hypothetical, given the fact that this list of unconquered cities remains factual, devoid of any parenetic material that would reveal the aim of those who composed it. We are left with the Bible text, but the sermon that was preached from it is lost.

However, history can be called again to the witness box in order to recover part of the lost sermon. This time, it is the information given about the tribe of Asher that will confirm the validity of the interpretation of Judg. 1.27-34 during the reign of Manasseh.

The Date of the Progressive Conquest
Judges 1.31 indicates that 'Asher did not drive out the inhabitants of Acco, or the inhabitants of Sidon, or of Ahlab, or of Achzib, or of Helbah, or of Aphik, or of Rehob'.

Acco and Sidon seem to indicate the length of the Asherite territory, representing its Southern and Northern limits, while Tyre is not mentioned, in spite of its importance. Lindars explained that this silence is due to Tyre's situation between Acco and Sidon and that Tyre is included *de facto*.[81] The problem with this explanation is that the second half of the verse lists five towns, all situated between Acco and Sidon and all of secondary importance compared to Tyre. Ahlab is Ḥirbet el-Maḥalib south of the mouth of the Litani River or Ras el-Abyad 12 km south of Tyre.[82]

---

80. In 1 Kgs 20 an anonymous prophet (// Judg. 6.7-10) encourages Ahab to dare a flat-land battle to prove that Yhwh is also at home in the plain.

81. Lindars, *Judges 1–5*, p. 65.

82. מחלב in Josh 19.29 or Mahalliba (LXXB Λεβ LXXA σχοινίσματος =חלק). N. Na'aman, 'Tiglath-pileser III's Campaigns against Tyre and Israel', *TA* 22 (1995), p. 270 n. 4.

Helbah is a corruption of Ahlab[83] and should be dropped, Achzib is *ez-Zib* 15 km north of Acco. There are several candidates for Rehob in the Phoenician zone: Tell el-Balāṭ 5 Km north of Iqrīt, Tell er Râḥib 5 km east of the same Iqrīt,[84] et-Tell site of Kabri, one of the largest cities of the Bronze Age[85] or Tell Bīr el-Gharbī 9 km south-east of Acco.[86] Aphik is Tell Kurdāneh south of Achzib in the Jezreel plain or Tell Kabrī.[87]

Such a detailed enumeration of towns around Tyre renders the absence of the main city all the more puzzling. Is the author of Judg. 1.31 inferring that Asher actually conquered Tyre? Alternatively, was there any particular reason to omit Tyre while mentioning Sidon? The following is a tentative reconstitution of the political situation in the area covered by Judg. 1.31 in order to determine the most likely period reflected by the particular set of towns and cities enumerated in this verse.

The political situation in the area between Sidon and Acco. Before the Neo-Babylonian period, there are only two time slots when Sidon could have ruled over all the sites mentioned by Judg. 1.31.

Firstly, between Tiglath-pileser I (1114–1076 BCE), the first Assyrian ruler to receive Sidonian tribute, and Ashurnasirpal II (883–859 BCE) who records the first Tyrian tribute,[88] Tyre seems to have been eclipsed by Sidon. While the Late Bronze Age was characterized by continual competition between Tyre and Sidon[89] and although the two rivals seem to have escaped the fate of Ugarit, one can surmise that Sidon took the advantage over Tyre and ruled over the whole of the coastal track. Unfortunately, the lack of sources does not permit the reconstruction of a reliable historical sequence. Moreover, these two centuries are unlikely settings for the composition of Judg. 1, as Israelite or Judaean literary production was quasi non-existent at the time.

From Ashurnasirpal II onwards, Tyre and Sidon are mentioned together

---

83. Lindars, *Judges 1–5*, p. 65.

84. S. Ahituv, *Canaanite Toponyms in Ancient Egyptian Documents* (Jerusalem/Leiden: Magnes Press/E.J. Brill, 1984), pp. 163-64.

85. A. Kempinski, 'Kabri', *NEAEHL*, 3 (Jerusalem: Israel Exploration Society and Carta, 1993), pp. 839-41(839).

86. Lindars, *Judges 1–5*, p. 65.

87. R. Frankel, 'Aphek', *ABD* 1, p. 276.

88. A.K. Grayson, *Assyrian Rulers of the Early First Millenium (1114-859)* (RIMA, 2; Toronto: University of Toronto Press, 1975), 1 §479.

89. *EA* 147.154.

in the tribute lists, except under Tiglath-pileser III (744–727 BCE) who mentions Damascus, Samaria, Tyre and Gubla but not Sidon.[90] Salmanazar V (726–722 BCE) or Sargon II (722–705 BCE)[91] receives the subjection of Sidon, Acco and Ushu (mainland Tyre). Tyre is blockaded for five years[92] around 709–705 BCE.[93] This blockade opens the second period, which could be reflected in Judg. 1.31. At that time indeed, Tyre had lost its continental possessions. Sargon handed to Sidon the Tyrian coast down to Acco. This is why Sennacherib crushed Sidon's rebellion in 701 BCE by storming Sidonian logistic centres down to Acco. In fact, Sennacherib's inscriptions offer a list of Sidonian fortresses covering the same area as Judg. 1.31:[94] Sidon the Great, Little Sidon, Bit-Zitti, Zarephath, Mahalliba, Ushu, Achzib and Acco. Tyre recovered its continental possessions between the Litani and the Carmel following Sidon's destruction by Esarhaddon in 677 BCE.[95] There is no indication that Tyre lost Acco to Sidon in the Babylonian period for, in spite of the restoration of Sidon, Tyre kept the upper hand over Sidon. The king of Tyre, who had been replaced by a Babylonian governor,[96] was re-established by

90. Grayson, *Assyrian Rulers*, 1 §772.

91. J. Elayi, 'Les relations entre les cités phéniciennes et l'Empire assyrien sous le règne de Sennakérib', *Semitica* 35 (1986), pp. 19-26 (21 n. 15).

92. F. Josephus, 'Jewish Antiquities', in P. Maier (ed.), *The New Complete Works of Josephus* (Grand Rapids: Kregel, 1999), pp. 49-661 (9.285) and J. Elayi and A. Cavigneaux, *Sargon II et les Ioniens* (OA, 18; Paris, 1979), p. 67.

93. Elayi, 'Relations', p. 21.

94. 'In my third campaign I went against the Hittite-land (Syria). Lulê (Elulæus), king of Sidon, the terrifying splendour (*lit.,* terrors of the splendours) of my sovereignty overcame him and far off into the midst of the sea he fled. (There) he died. Great Sidon, Little Sidon, Bît-Zitti, Zaribtu, Mahalliba, Ushu, Akzib, Akkû, his strong walled cities, where there were supplies (*lit.,* fodder and drinking-places) for his garrisons, the terrors of the weapons of Ashur, my lord, overpowered them and they bowed in submission at my feet. Tuba' lu (Ethbaal, Ithobalus) I seated on the royal throne over them, and tribute, gift(s) for my majesty, I imposed upon him for all time, without ceasing': Luckenbill, *Sennakerib,* pp. 29-30 or *idem, Ancient Records*, 2 § 239.

95. Luckenbill, *Ancient Records*, 2 § 512, H. Sader, 'Tell Burak: An Unidentified City of Phoenician Sidon', in B. Pongratz-Leisten, H. Kühne and P. Xella (eds.), *Ana šadī Labnāni lū allik* (Kevelaer/Neukirchen-Vluyn: Butzon & Bercker/Neukirchener, 1997), pp. 363-78.

96. H.J. Katzenstein, *The History of Tyre: From the Beginning of the Second Millenium B.C.E. until the Fall of the Neo-Babylonian Empire in 538 B.C.E.* (Jerusalem: Schocken Institute for Jewish Research of the Jewish Theological Seminary of America, 1973), p. 333.

Nabonidus and maintained itself until the Persian era.[97] Sidon took the lead again only under Persian rule, when it became the base of the Achemenid naval forces.[98] The hegemony of Sidon over the other cities of the coast lasted until its destruction by Artaxerxes III around 350 BCE.[99] Despite its decline, Tyre was still active under the Persians and probably managed to keep Acco, for when the Great King decided to reward Sidon, he gave Dor and Jaffo, south of the Carmel, because Tyre ruled as far as Acco and the Persians had no reason to reduce Tyrian territory. Moreover, archaeological sources tend to favour a Tyrian domination for the whole of the Acco plain throughout the Persian era.[100] If Judg. 1.31 was to be dated during the Persian period, the absence de Tyre would be inexplicable, as Tyre controlled the area between the Litani and the Carmel.

Sidon was sacked between 351 and 345 BCE following a revolt caused by the ever-increasing pressure of the Persian campaigns against Egypt. King Tennes of Sidon was executed with the council members and part of the population[101] while other Sidonians were deported to Babylon.[102] A tyranny was established and the city was quickly repaired. An autonomous king soon reappeared (Straton II) and new Sidonian coins were minted.[103] However, Sidon had lost most of its Palestinian territories because at the arrival of Alexander, Sidon only controlled a very limited zone around the city[104] and Tyre was the only city able to resist the Macedonians.[105] After 350 BCE (Tennes' revolt) the mention of Acco and Sidon as one territorial

97. Katzenstein, *History of Tyre,* p. 342.

98. J. Elayi, *Recherches sur les cités phéniciennes à l'époque perse* (Napoli: Istituto Universitario Orientale, 1983), pp. 73-74.

99. J. Elayi, *Sidon, cité autonome de l'Empire perse* (Paris: Idéphane, 1989), p. 123. The Sidonians won the regatta organised for Xerxes I in Abydos: Herodotus, *History* (trans. A.D. Godley, LCL, 120; Cambridge, MA: Harvard University Press, 1981), 9.7.44, 67-68, 96-100, 128. The Sidonian King and the Athenian Conon were in charge of the royal navy at the battle of Cnidos: P. Briant, *Histoire de l'Empire perse* (Paris: Fayard, 1996), pp. 655-64.

100. A. Lemaire, 'Populations et territoires de la Palestine à l'époque perse', *Transeuphratène* 3 (1990), pp. 60-63.

101. Elayi, *Sidon,* pp. 120, 130 n. 96: 600 citizens + 45,000 inhabitants compared to the 23,000 men of the Sidonian contingent (out of which 4000 were mercenaries).

102. A.K. Grayson, *Assyrian and Babylonian Chronicles* (TCS, 5; Locust Valley New York: J.J. Augustin, 1975), n° 9, 114.

103. Briant, *Empire perse,* 734.104-1042.

104. Quintus Curtius Rufus, *Alexander,* 4.1.26.

105. Elayi, *Sidon,* p. 186.

unit by Judg. 1.31 is unlikely as Sidon's power and territory had been sharply reduced.

It is therefore obvious that the reign of Sennacherib is the period that offers the best correlation with Judg. 1. Admittedly, the list of Sidonian fortresses from Sennacherib's annals does not exactly match Judg. 1.31. Yet, both lists consider the whole of the coastal plain between Sidon and Acco as Sidonian, both ignore Tyre as it had lost all its Palestinian possessions following Sargon's land blockade (c. 710 BCE). Before this date, the coastal zone between Sidon and Acco was split along the traditional border of the Litani River: Tyrian territory in the South down to Acco, Sidonian to the North. Apart from Sidon, all the sites of Judg. 1.31 are near Tyre, the silence over Tyre being thus difficult to explain. However, from 710 BCE to its destruction by Esarhaddon (c. 677 BCE), Sidon received all the Tyrian continental territory and ruled the coast from Sidon to Acco. When Sidon rebelled, Sennacherib sacked eight Sidonian fortresses. Four of which are also mentioned in Judg. 1.31 (Sidon, Ahlab, Achzib, and Acco). Sennacherib also mentions Ushu (Palaiotyros) and Zarephath who, like Sidon is north of the Litani. The Israelites probably considered the Litani River as the natural northern border of Galilee, hence they did not mention Zarephath. Ushu was also omitted due to its connections to Tyre. Lastly, Judg. 1.31 mentions Aphik and Rehob but Sennacherib does not. They are difficult to locate, but one thing is sure, they are not situated directly on the coast as the others are. This explains why they did not serve as military stores and for this very reason did not attract Assyrian attention. However, they were well known to Galilaeans for whom they served as intermediaries in their dealings with the main centres on the coast.

The reason why Tyre is omitted from Judg. 1.31 is that at the time of writing, Sidon controlled the entire Galilaean coast, down to Acco and Tyre was completely isolated on its island.

Yet, two objections stemming from understandings of Phoenician history at variance from the one offered here have to be dealt with.

First objection: the existence of a Tyro-Sidonian confederation. Phoenicia is often understood as a unified political entity. In that case, the absence of Tyre in Judg 1.31 would not be surprising, Sidon would be a metonymy for both Tyre and Sidon. According to Kestemont, Southern Phoenicia consisted of a single kingdom whose throne was normally in Tyre excepted from the time of Sennacherib to Esarhaddon when it was in

Sidon.[106] This kingdom was centred round Tyre, but with an autonomous internal kingdom in Gubla, and a second important district in Sidon.[107] Tyre would have been the capital and Sidon the generic of the whole country. Kestemont admits that this supposition goes against the Assyrian sources, which regularly cite either the capital or the country but do not mix the two,[108] but he maintains his confederation controlled by Tyre.[109] Discussing the Limassol inscription which attests to the existence of a vice-Roy in Carthage of Cyprus, he considers that it shows the extent of the confederate State of Southern Phoenicia. Tyre would be the head of this confederation in spite of the fact that the *sâkin* in question is expressly presented as servant of King Hiram of Sidon![110] Concepts of Confederation or Confederate State are likely to be anachronistic, even for Tripolis.[111] The El-Amarna letters show without doubt that Tyre and Sidon, far from being federated, were constantly competing with each other. The Assyrian sources attest to the persistence of this competition into the Iron Age until Sidon was turned into an Assyrian province (677 BCE). Tyre maintained a relative level of autonomy after the replacement of Sidon by Kar-Esarhaddon. Due to the collapse of Assyria, Tyre escaped being turned into a province.[112] Like Josiah of Jerusalem, Tyre used the interim between the fall of Nineveh (612 BCE) and its siege in 585 BCE to recover its continental territory.[113] It seems safer to consider each city of the coast as a separate political entity rather than lumping them together into a federal model and shifting the capital around to fit the sources. Faced with a common enemy, Tyre and Sidon could create a common front, but each jealously kept its prerogatives, ready to abandon its rival at the hands of

---

106. G. Kestemont, 'Tyr et les Assyriens', in E. Gubel, E. Lipinsky and B. Servais-Soyez (eds.), *Redt Tyrus/Sauvons Tyr Histoire phénicienne/Fenicische Geschiedenis* (SP, 1.2; Leuven: Peeters, 1983), pp. 53-78 (57).

107. Kestemont, 'Tyr', p. 58.

108. Kestemont, 'Tyr', p. 58.

109. Kestemont, 'Tyr', pp. 59-61.

110. Kestemont, 'Tyr', p. 66.

111. Kestemont, 'Tyr', p. 59 n. 16. Tripolis was governed by its 3 founding towns (Sidon, Tyr and Arwad). A kind of 'federal council' met regularly: J. Elayi, 'Tripoli (Liban) à l'époque perse', *Transeuphratène* 2 (1990), pp. 59-72.

112. Tyre may have lost its continental possessions after Baal's revolt in 668 BCE: Elayi, 'Cités', pp. 45-46.

113. M. Liverani, 'The Trade Network of Tyre', in M. Cogan and I. Eph'al (eds.), *Ah Assyria...* (SH, 33; Jerusalem: Magnes Press, 1991), pp. 65-79.

the enemy when it decided that submission was in its best interest.[114] Therefore, Tyre and Sidon are not interchangeable names for the coastal stretch between Gubla and Acco. In that case, the mention of Sidon and the absence of Tyre in Judg. 1.31 remains a valid indicator for the dating of Judg. 1.27-34.

Second objection: a united kingdom of Tyre and Sidon? Based on a hypothesis of Katzenstein,[115] Elayi postulates a united kingdom or double kingdom of Sidon and Tyre in the time of Luli and Sennacherib,[116] although Sennacherib never mentions Tyre.[117] In 738 BCE, Tiglath-Pileser III received the tribute of Hiram of Tyre while Sidon is not mentioned. Since, according to this theory, Sidon belonged to Tyre, although the Limassol bowl calls Hiram, king of the Sidonians.[118] Katzenstein dates the merger of Tyre and Sidon under Ethbaal (887–856 BCE), father of Jezebel, called king of the Sidonians in 1 Kgs 16.31 but king of the Tyrians and Sidonians by Josephus.[119] 'Sidonian' would mean dweller of Sidon or of any Phoenician city. This united kingdom would have ended precisely under Eloulaeos, considered by Josephus as king of the Tyrians, based on Menander, who 'wrote the archives of the Tyrians and translated them into Greek'. Josephus claims that 'Selampsas, king of the Assyrians, invaded Phoenicia, dealt with each of the cities and went back home. At the time, Sidon, Arcé, Palae-Tyros, and many others detached themselves from Tyre to give themselves to the king of the Assyrians.'[120] Josephus offers a fine testimony of the confusion prevalent in his time pertaining to the history of Palestine. However, he cannot be used to prove the existence of a united kingdom. He is trying to harmonize the contradictory evidence available. Moreover, in an earlier study, Elayi demonstrates that the Assyrians systematically played on the competition between the two cities.[121] Sennacherib ruined Tyre, who refused Assyrian control of Mediterranean trade,

114. J.T. Strong, 'Tyre's Isolationist Policies in the Early Sixth Century BCE: Evidence from the Prophets', *VT* 47 (1997), pp. 207-219 (215).

115. Katzenstein, *History of Tyre*, pp. 130-34, 224.

116. Elayi, *Sidon*, p. 88.

117. Apart from Tyrian prisoners, Luckenbill, *Ancient Records,* 2 §319.383.

118. E. Honigmann, 'Sidon', *PW* 1972, 2.2.2218.

119. Josephus, *Ant.,* 8.317; 9.138. In 8.324 Ethbaal is only king of the Tyrians. Katzenstein considers it as a contracted form: *History of Tyre*, p. 130.

120. Josephus, *Ant.,* 9.284-286. Josephus may have mixed Salmanazar and Sennacherib: Honigmann, 'Sidon', 2.2.2218.

121. Elayi, 'Relations', pp. 19-26.

by fostering an Assyrian-friendly regime in Sidon.[122] In spite of this, Elayi claims that the list of Luli's fortresses taken by Sennacherib 'clearly shows that Luli was king over both Tyre and Sidon'.[123]

It is much more likely that these towns were taken precisely because they belonged to Sidon at the time. Tyre is not mentioned because it is totally isolated on its island and did not represent any threat.[124] It could not rebel since it had already suffered under Sargon II.[125] Luli had received all the Tyrian continental territory but rebelled with other rulers of Palestine in 705 BCE and became Sennacherib's first target in 701 BCE. He then ran away 'in the midst of the sea',[126] probably to his Cypriot colony. Ethbaal was then seated on Luli's throne. Abdi-Milkuti's revolt led Esarhaddon to destroy Sidon, to transform its continental territory into a province and to return the southern part of the coast to Tyre.[127]

Therefore, Kestemont's and Elayi's hypotheses needlessly complicate the relations between Tyre and Sidon. Although correspondences are approximate, and in spite of a limited amount of sources, the list of Sidonian fortresses taken by Sennacherib reflects the same political situation than the one described by Judg. 1.31. This is all the more likely as this period is the only time when Sidonian rule down to Acco is certain.

Recapitulation

The analysis of the Othniel passage in Judg. 3.7-11 leads to the conclusion that the *Beispielstück* could have been anonymous at first, without either Othniel nor Cushan-rishathaim, and that such an anonymous introduction should then be attributed to the Bethel book of Saviours around 720 BCE.

The addition of Othniel and Cushan-rishathaim appears as a clear reference to the *entente cordiale* between the Kushite and Assyrian Empire at the end of the eighth century BCE. However, this does not provide any satisfactory answer for the identity of Othniel.

A close look at Judg. 1 which mentions the same Othniel, revealed that this baffling chapter clearly reflects the social struggles that tore Judaean

---

122. Elayi, 'Relations', p. 26.

123. Elayi, 'Relations', p. 20. She compares this united kingdom with David's and Solomon's: Elayi, *Recherches*, p. 122 n. 553!

124. Elayi, 'Relations', p. 23 and Katzenstein, *History of Tyre*, pp. 248-49.

125. Elayi, 'Relations', p. 21.

126. Luckenbill, *Ancient Records*, 2 §239.

127. Sader, 'Tell Burak', pp. 368-69, Esarhaddon cites 'Ma'rub(?)... Sariptu' given to Ba'ali of Tyre (Luckenbill, *Ancient Records*, 2 § 512).

society apart in the seventh century BCE, in particular during the long and prosperous reign of Manasseh. The small kingdom of Judah then came under the direct influence of the Empire, experiencing deep and rapid transformations due to political stability and tax pressure. Centralization favoured Jerusalem against the venerable tribal structures of the traditional rural centres, which lost much of their prerogatives. Upheavals of such speed and amplitude could only provoke a violent backlash in the next generation, during the reign of Josiah, which coincides with the disintegration of the Assyrian Empire. This will be the subject of Chapters 3 and 4.

Before considering Josiah's Judah, one last conclusion has to be drawn about Othniel. One of Manasseh's wives, the mother of Amon (a pure Egyptian name),[128] came from Jotbah (today's Ṭaba) some thirty kilometres north of Aqabah in southern Edom.[129] This Edomite princess status as queen mother and her son's Egyptian name indicate the level of internationalism reached by Manasseh's court. This throws an interesting light on the fact that Othniel's name bears an Arabian origin, close to Edomite.[130] Moreover, in the seventh century BCE, the Beer-sheba valley became vital for Judah's economy and was intensively farmed, in order to

128. Manasseh may have so named his heir in memory of the campaign of Esarhaddon against the Kushites and the liberation of Thebes, No' 'Amôn (Nah. 3.8). Manasseh was probably personally involved in this campaign, along the other western vassal kings of Hatti-land. Esarhaddon reports: 'In the course of my march, 22 kings of the seacoast, of the midst of the sea and of the mainland, servants subject to me, brought their rich (heavy) presents before me and kissed my feet. Those kings, together with their forces, on their ships by sea, on the dry land with my armies, I caused to take path and road…' Luckenbill, *Ancient records*, 2 §771, prism A not published anew by A.C. Piepkorn, *Historical Prisms: Inscriptions of Ashurbanipal* (Assyriological Studies, 5/1; Chicago: 1933). See also R.B. and M.P. Coote, *Power, Politics and the Making of the Bible* (Minneapolis: Augsburg Fortress, 1990), p. 58; R. Nelson, 'Realpolitik in Judah (687-609 B.C.E.)', in W.W. Hallo, J.C. Moyer and L.G. Perdue (eds.), *Scripture in Contex. II. More Essays on the Comparative Method* (Winona Lake: Eisenbrauns, 1983), pp. 177-89 (181); D. Rudman, 'Note on the Personal Name Amon', *Biblica* 81 (2000), pp. 403-405.

129. Ahlström, *History of Ancient Palestine*, p. 734. But Dalley, 'Yabâ, Atalyâ', follows M. Cogan and H. Tadmor, *II Kings: A New Translation with Introduction and Commentary* (AB, 11; New York: Doubleday, 1988), p. 275, who thought Jotbah in lower Galilee was preferable to the one in Edom.

130. Etymological ġ and ṭ were preserved: *Ġōṭà-nī-'ēl* 'God helped me': A. Sima, 'Nochmals zur Deutung des hebräischen Namens Otniel', *BN* 106 (2001), pp. 47-51.

compensate for the loss of the Shephelah after 701 BCE.[131] If Othniel does not represent any particular Judaean king, he can be understood as a fitting tribute to Amon's mother Meshullemeth and to the South Negeb populations, an attempt to counter-balance the Judaean pressure-group based in Hebron with even more southern groups. Manasseh's active collaboration with Assyria allowed Judah to benefit from the general economical prosperity while the kingdom kept as much 'autonomy' as was deemed possible by its Assyrian overlords. In this way, Othniel, that is Manasseh's pro-Assyrian policy, halted the progression of the frightful Assyrian machinery, turned it into an ally and literally saved Judah from Cushan-rishathaim.

Before turning to the next editorial stage, a provisional overview of the results reached so far for Judg. 1 can be provided:

vv. 1-3:   Transition with the book of Joshua (see Chapter 7)
vv. 4-18:   Superiority of Judah (reign of Manasseh)
vv. 19-21: Harmonization (see Chapter 7)
vv. 22-26: Conquest of Bethel, Persian period (see Chapter 6)
vv. 27-34: Israel's progressive conquest (reign of Manasseh)
vv. 35-36: Southern Danites (see Chapter 4) and harmonization (see Chapter 7)

---

131. 5000 tons of grain were produced while local consumption only required 5 per cent of this amount: Finkelstein, 'Manasseh', p. 177.

Chapter 3

JOSIAH TURNS MANASSEH'S BOOK OF SAVIOURS INTO A BOOK OF JUDGES: JUDGES 2; 6; 10 AND 12

Political Context from Amon to Josiah

Manasseh died in 642 BCE and his son succeeded him. But Amon was murdered in his second year of reign at the age of 24 and replaced by his son Josiah, then eight years old (2 Kgs 21.19-24). In spite of his short reign, Amon is considered by the Biblical writers as bad as his father (2 Kgs 21.20-22). His son Josiah, on the other hand, is presented as the best king since David.

Josiah is said to have been enthroned by the people of the land (עם הארץ) after the murder of Amon (2 Kgs 21.24). The writers manifestly seek to exonerate the people of the land from any involvement in the murder by attributing it to a conspiracy of Amon's own servants. The people of the land, who got all the benefits from the murder by taking control of the affairs of the kingdom, are said to have executed Amon's murderers. This is the neat official version of a putsch that overthrew the pro-Assyrian elite which had governed the kingdom since 701 BCE.

640 BCE: International Context

Amon's murder takes place ten years before the death of Assurbanipal. It thus seems to happen a decade too early to be set in the context of the first signs of Assyria's decline which did not become apparent before 626 BCE when Nabopolassar established the Neo-Babylonian dynasty. The Assyrians resisted the Babylonian pressure even after the destruction of Niniveh in 612 BCE. The issue of Assyria's lingering Babylonian problem was finally settled by the Medes who decided to place their bet on the Babylonian side.[1] In Palestine, Assyrian control was gradually taken over

---

1. S. Zawazki, *The Fall of Assyria and Median-Babylonian Relations in Light of the Nabopolassar Chronicle* (Poznan: Adam Mickiewicz University Press, 1988).

by the Egyptians of the 26th Saite dynasty, most probably with Assyria's consent.[2] However, this Egyptian interim was not manifest before 609 BCE, three years after the fall of Niniveh, when Neko II executed Josiah in Megiddo, on his way to help the Assyrians against the Babylonians.[3] It is therefore clear that Josiah benefited from a power vacuum that left him free to conduct an independent programme. However, this is not quite the case for the decade of his minority, between Amon's murder and Assurbanipal's death. If Amon's murder cannot simply be explained as a revolt against a failing Empire, then the possibility of internal pressure has to be reckoned with.

The People of the Land
That Amon was murdered after two years of reign and not right at the beginning is significant. The country elite may have expected a change of policy and it is only after two years that it realized that this hope was unfounded. Moreover, the conditions were likely to be more favourable for an uprising in 640 than in 642 BCE. The Scythian raids in the northern parts of the Empire may have triggered the murder, as they would have been interpreted by the Judaean opposition as a first sign of weakness on the part of the Assyrian overlord.[4]

Amon's murderers were certainly supported by a wave of popular restlessness,[5] but whatever the responsibility of Amon's servants, the people of the land managed to take over from Manasseh's advisors[6] and

2. Nelson, '*Realpolitik*', pp. 183-89.

3. It is therefore unlikely that the putsch against Amon was supported by the Egyptians as claimed by T. Ishida, 'The People of the Land', in *idem* (ed.), *History and Historical Writing in Ancient Israel* (SHCANE, 16; Leiden: E.J. Brill, 1999), pp. 81-96. This claim is based on the belief that Egypt rebelled against Assyria as from 656 BCE, before deciding to help the remnants of Assyria against the Medo-Babylonians at Carchemish in 609 BCE! In this case, one would expect Egypt to intervene in Palestine well before 609 BCE (which may not have been possible due to the state of Egyptian internal affairs). On the contrary, the evidence points to a 26th dynasty loyal to its Assyrian overlord until the end, very conscious of the fact that it was the Assyrians who repelled the Kushites and established the dynasty.

4. Redford, *Egypt*, p. 441. However, the Scythians did not penetrate 'usque ad Palaestinam': R.W.O. Helm, *Die Chronik des Hieronymus* (Eusebius Werke, 7/1; Leipzig, 2nd. edn, 1913), p. 96, and N. Na'aman, 'The Kingdom of Judah under Josiah', *TA* 18 (1991), pp. 3-71 (37).

5. Redford, *Egypt*, p. 441.

6. A. Malamat, 'The Historical Background of the Assassination of Amon, King

installed a new majority in Jerusalem. Amon's servants were convenient scapegoats and their execution allowed the people behind Amon's murder to wash their hands and present themselves as restorers of public order.[7] This new majority attests the level of discontent of the rural elite after more than half a century of intense urbanization that favoured the city of Jerusalem against the rest of the kingdom.[8] It was seen in the previous chapter that this discontent was a structural requirement of Imperial dynamics,[9] and it is no wonder that due to the rapid changes, the *Interessendisharmonie* had reached such proportions in Judah that it provoked the overthrow of the pro-Assyrian urban elite. Thanks to the relative unimportance of Judah on the international scene since the integration of Egypt into the Assyrian Empire and thanks to the diplomatic skills of the new leaders in Jerusalem,[10] the change of majority did not provoke any military intervention on the part of Assyria or Egypt. However, the people of the land did not try to revert to the old order, but clearly assumed the new situation by moving into the capital and taking into their own hands the reins of the entire kingdom. Traditionally centred on Hebron,[11] the people of the land turned from now on into an urban elite and gradually took over the Imperial programme to serve its own interest. Jerusalem was to become the centre of the counter-Empire conceptualized in Josh. 3–11 as Josiah's blue print to restore (in fact, to establish) Solomon's Empire. The first steps of this programme were implemented with the conquest of Benjamin.

The people of the land were not the farming populace of the Judaean countryside, but a small segment of the population of the kingdom, a few hundred individuals of the landed aristocracy who had taken over from the previous elite. They prospered to the point that, in 609 BCE, they were the

of Judah', *IEJ* 3 (1953), pp. 26-29 (26) had already challenged the common opinion that follows 2 Kgs 21.24 too closely, claiming that the people of the land avenged Amon and restored the *status quo*.

7.   P. Dutcher-Walls, 'The Social Location of the Deuteronomists: A Sociological Study of Factional Politics in Late Pre-Exilic Judah', *JSOT* 52 (1991), pp. 77-94 (85).

8.   By favouring the city elite, the Assyrians bought the compliance of the ruling group and saved themselves the expenses of running a poor kingdom: Ben Zvi, 'Prelude', p. 33; Assyrian as Mesopotamian politics were always city-centered: Oppenheim, *Mesopotamia*, pp. 118-24.

9.   Lamprichs, *Westexpansion*.

10. 2 Kgs 21.19-24 may be a fine witness of their skill as it is markedly more subtle than the usual brash style of the rest of 1 and 2 Kings.

11. Knauf, *Umwelt*, p. 236.

only Judaeans capable of paying the tribute imposed by Neko.[12] They were no more inclined towards the poor than their predecessors. They were soon criticized by the 'prophets' (Jer. 34.19; Ezek. 22.29) and resisted the land reforms attempted by Zedekiah (Jer. 34) and Gedaliah (Jer. 40.10).

The people of the land thus represented much more than a popular uprising, and if it is anachronistic to see it as one of the chambers of the bicameral parliamentary regime imagined by Sulzberger,[13] they were nevertheless a well organized pressure-group with a long tradition of forceful interventions in state affairs at the highest level. The people of the land regularly show up in the books of Kings, embroiled in ruthless coups when their interests are jeopardised.[14] After the murder of Athaliah, the people of the land acclaimed the young Jehoash (seven years old).[15] After the murder of Amaziah the people of the land crowned his son Azariah (sixteen years old).[16] The people of the land confined the same Azariah after a strange bout of leprosy and replaced him with Jotham, who was previously ruling over the people of the land עם הארץ שפט את.[17] As vassals of the northern kingdom of Israel (Athaliah and Amaziah) or simply as members of the Jerusalem aristocracy (Amaziah and Azariah), these unfortunate rulers soon found themselves defending interests that set them in direct confrontation with the landed aristocracy of the Judaean countryside. Athaliah, Amaziah and Azariah had to bear the full consequences of such an uneasy position.

12. 2 Kgs 23.35. S. Talmon, 'The Judean 'am ha'ares in Historical Perspective', in *4th World Congress of Jewish Studies 1* (Jerusalem: Magnes Press, 1967), pp. 71-76. Against T.N.D. Mettinger, *King and Messiah* (ConBOT, 8; Lund: C.W.K. Gleerup, 1976), p. 126, who thinks that the large sum involved could only have been paid by the majority of the population. The argument is void since before the generalization of coinage, only the top tier of any given society owned a significant amount of precious metal.

13. M. Sulzberger, *The AM HA-ARETZ: The Ancient Hebrew Parliament* (Philadelphia: 1909).

14. See Ishida, 'People of the Land', pp. 82-95.

15. 2 Kgs 11.17-20: three mentions of the עם הארץ and two of the עם in order to produce the impression of popular unanimity. But v. 20 indicates the presence of two factions: the people of the land rejoiced while the town was quiet. Jerusalem was regularly opposed to the people of the land and therefore had no reason to rejoice.

16. 2 Kgs 14.19-21. Amaziah's mother is from Jerusalem (2 Kgs 14.2) which explains the opposition of the עם יהודה probably a variant for עם הארץ.

17. 2 Kgs 15.5. The leper king is kept in a separate house. √חפש can also be translated 'to be freed, liberated, discharged' and could indicate something other than sanitary quarantine as Azariah suffered also from the opposition of the people of the land.

The involvement of the people of the land in the murder of Amon is therefore just one episode in a long chain of involvement of the people of the land in the kingdom's affairs. Logically, in the seventh century BCE, the people of the land were the backbone of anti-Assyrianism as previously it had resisted the Jerusalem aristocracy.[18] Under Josiah, it went a step forward, it moved into Jerusalem and developed its organization in order to face the new reality.

Josiah's Coronation and the Book of Saviours
Isaiah 9.1-6 could be part of a hymn composed for Josiah's coronation ceremony in 640 BCE.[19] The day of Midian mentioned in Isa. 9.4 is likely be quoting Judg. 6–9, and if this is the case, Isa. 9 could be taken as indicating that the book of Saviours was known in Jerusalem at the beginning of Josiah's reign. This is an argument in favour of Manasseh's introduction and enlargment of the BS, postulated in Chapter 2.

The Death of Josiah
After a 30-year rule (640-609 BCE), Josiah, the strong man of the people of the land, had to face his judge. Josiah did not die on the battle field as 2 Chron. 3.20-23 would have us think, but even less gloriously when Neko sent for him during his stay in the Assyrian provincial capital of Megiddo to arbitrate the affairs of the Assyrian vassals of the area. The Samaria authorities may have filed a complaint against Josiah about his annexation of Benjamin and this was deemed sufficiently grave for Neko to slay Josiah as soon as he saw him (2 Kgs 23.29).[20]

The fact that, at one point in the seventh century BCE, the whole of Benjamin was integrated into Judah can be considered as established because it is in Benjaminite Mizpah that the Babylonians set up Judah's new capital after the destruction of Jerusalem. Southern Benjamin was probably part of the kingdom of Judah since the independent Benjaminite kingdom was integrated into Judah by Pharao Shishak.[21] According to 1 Kgs 15.17, 22, the war between Asa and Ba'asha king of Israel (c. 900–

---

18. R. Gordis, 'Sectional Rivalry in the Kingdom of Judah', *JQR* 25 (1934), pp. 237-59.

19. E.A. Knauf, 'Vom Prophetinnenwort zum Propheten Buch: Jesaja 8, 3f im Kontext vom Jes 6, 1–8, 16: lectio difficilior', *European Electronic Journal for Feminist Exegesis* 2/2000 (www.lectio.unibe. ch).

20. For a slightly different scenario see Nelson, '*Realpolitik*'.

21. Na'aman, 'Israel, Edom', p. 81; Knauf, 'Low Chronology', p. 62 n. 30.

890 BCE) ended with Israel's conquest of the northern part of Benjamin as far as Ramah and Bethel. The new border was established between Bethel and Mizpah because, in spite of the triumphalistic tone of the text, Asa of Judah has to fortify Mizpah (1 Kgs 15.22), a fact that indicates that Mizpah then became a border post, which it had not been previously. Slight variations of the border between Israel and Judah during the ninth and eighth centuries BCE may have taken place, but the amplitude of those changes was small, they were restricted to the southern part of Benjamin.[22] However, it is almost certain that Gibeon and Mizpah were Judaean during Hezekiah's reign because over 80 LMLK impressions were discovered in both places. These royal stamps are interpreted as provisions stored by Hezekiah to face Sennacherib's attack in 701 BCE.[23] Judah probably did not recover Northern Benjamin before the second part of Josiah's reign.[24] At the same time, Judah probably took back the Shephelah because Lakish was once again part of the kingdom of Judah when the Babylonians attacked it.

In spite of Josiah's execution, Judah managed to hold on to Benjamin. Obviously, his defeat at Carchemish and his hasty retreat to Egypt gave Neko no time to erase Josiah's achievements. The northern extension of the kingdom of Judah was endorsed by the Babylonians who eventually replaced Jerusalem by Mizpah (see Chapter 6), and later by the Persians as Benjamin remained in the province of *Yehud*.

Josiah was thus more successful than Hezekiah was, even if his territorial gains eventually cost him his life. Those gains obviously left their mark on contemporary literary production: Benjamin's annexation is the backdrop of Josh. 3–9.[25] Manasseh's book of Saviours had also to be dealt with as its message was not conducive to military adventures. The BS was thus subjected to a new thrust of literary activity in order to fit the new borders of the kingdom. Until then, Manasseh had only added a modest introduction (Judg. 1.4-18, 27-34 and possibly 3.7-11; see Chapter 2) to Bethel's BS. Josiah's scribes did now venture to corset the BS in order to

---

22. See K.-D. Schunck, *Benjamin* (BZAW, 86; Berlin: Töpelmann, 1963), map p. 170.

23. E.A. Knauf, 'Who Destroyed Beersheba II?', in Hüber and Knauf (eds.), *Kein Land für sich allein. Studien zum Kulturkontakt in Kanaan, Israel/Palastina und Ebirnari für Manfred Weippert zum 65. Geburtstag. FS Weippert, Manfred* (OBO, 186; Freiberg, Schweiz: Universitätsverlag, 2002), pp. 181-95.

24. Na'aman, 'Kingdom of Judah', p. 41.

25. Römer, 'Livre de Josué'.

put it in line with Josiah's aggressive policies and Deuteronomistic
theology. Instead of simply adding a second introduction, the Josianic
edition seem much more intrusive. Under their hands, the composition
eventually doubled its size. It is time to turn to the text.

Judges 2.1-5: Indictment of Judges 1

An envoy of Yhwh[26] goes from Gilgal to Bochim[27] to deliver a devastating
message. Yhwh declares that his oath to provide a land for his people is
now null and void because, in spite of Yhwh's promise never to violate his
berith,[28] 'you' have not obeyed orders to destroy the altars of the inhabitants of the land. Therefore, Yhwh announces that he will not chase the
enemies in front of 'them' and that the enemies will become snares. The
addressees of the message are only specified in v. 4: the sons of Israel and
the people who duly burst into tears (√בכה), thus providing an etymology
for Bochim.

This extremely concise passage raises a few problems. First, no berith
has so far been mentioned in the narrative of Judges. The allusion must
refer therefore to a passage outside the book of Judges. In the context of
the Nothian Deuteronomistic Historiography, the answer is obviously
found in Joshua.[29] However, in the hypothesis of the BS, this berith refers
to any one of the many vassal treaty established between the Israelite and
Assyrian kings, in particular the one mentioned in Judg. 9.4 (see Chapter

26. On this messenger see M. Weinfeld, 'The Period of the Conquest and of the
Judges as Seen by the Earliest and the Later Sources', *VT* 17 (1967), pp. 93-113 (95)
and Exod. 23.20-23; 32.34; 33.2; Num. 20.16. For the links between Exod. 32.34; 33.2
and Judg. 2.1-5 see A. Marx, 'Forme et fonction de Juges 2, 1-5', *RHPR* 59 (1979), pp.
341-50 (346).

27. Marx, 'Forme', p. 348, understands Bochim as *athbash* for Shiloh. *BHK* signals
a LXX plus after Bochim καὶ ἐπὶ Βαιθηλ καὶ ἐπὶ τὸν οἶκον Ἰσραηλ, probably a gloss
to site Bochim in the light of Deborah's oak in Gen. 35.8: Lindars, *Judges 1-5*, p. 76;
Marx, 'Forme', pp. 341-42. Οἶκον Ἰσραηλ compensates MT's ambiguity and aggra-
vates Israel's guilt: 'Ces tentatives d'explicitations témoignent de la perplexité des
anciens traducteurs, gênés eux aussi par le fait qu'un lieu si important soit à ce point
inconnu' Marx, 'Forme', p. 342.

28. See W. Thiel, 'HEFER BERIT: Zum Bundbrechen im Alten Testament' *VT* 20
(1970), pp. 214-29. *Berith* is a clear Assyrian concept taken over by Ezek. 17.15-19,
the treaty between the kings of Babylon and Jerusalem is called 'my berith' in v. 19.

29. According to Marx, 'Forme', p. 347, Judg. 2.1-5 presupposes the Gibeonite
episode in Josh. 9.

1). Secondly, the whole passage is often considered as refering to some ancient founding legend of a cult performed in Bochim, wherever this place may be. Ritual wailing was certainly part of some liturgies,[30] but if such a ceremony is alluded to here, one has to admit that it is in a most derogatory manner, as Judg. 2.1-5 is hardly appropriate as a founding legend for any cult worth taking about. In fact, this miserable passage is more likely to allude directly to another type of weeping, namely the cries of the book of Saviours. The cries (√זעק) of Israel towards Yhwh were the backbone of the theology of the BS as they were systematically heard favourably by Yhwh (see Chapter 1). On the contrary, the Bochim tears establish the hopelessness of all cries, as Yhwh now declares that he will not be intervening to save Israel from its enemies but that the enemies and their gods will now remain dangerously present.

There is therefore no need to consider Judg. 2.1-5 as part of the transition between Joshua and Judges.[31] This passage bears all the theological marks of Josianic theology, it was probably composed by the same school than the oldest part of the books of Joshua and Kings, but this does not imply that these works were part of a 'historiography'. The only element within Judg. 2.1-5 that could well be part of a secondary harmonizing process establishing links between Joshua and Judges is Gilgal, which is not attested by the Old Latin versions[32] Since the 'Old Latin in Judges is often the surest guide to the earlier form of the Old Greek',[33] Gilgal could have been added after the first Greek translations of Judges, in order to connect Judg. 2.1 to Josh. 4.19.

The Bochim episode comes just after the list of unconquered cities (Judg. 1.27-34) and throws a negative light on the list, which can now be properly termed 'negative conquest'. Instead of playing down the loss of the Shephelah in 701 BCE (see Chapter 2), the fact that Israel did not immediately conquer those cities becomes Israel's original sin that leads Yhwh to abandon his people.

Josiah has regained the territories lost in 701 BCE and is about to conquer Benjamin. This triumphant Judah is comparing its glorious

---

30. F.F. Hvidberg, *Weeping and Laughter* (Leiden: E.J. Brill, 1962), pp. 98-137.

31. E. Blum, *Studien zur Komposition des Pentateuch* (BZAW, 189; Berlin: W. de Gruyter, 1990), p. 366.

32. Vetus Latina: 'et ascendit angelus Domini super Clauthmona montem' does not mention Gilgal.

33. W.R. Bodine, *The Greek Text of Judges: Recensional Developments* (Chico, CA: Scholars Press, 1980), p. 32.

situation with what has been the fate of the Israelite provinces under the thumb of the governors of Samaria, Dor and Megiddo since a century. The sons of Israel have every reason to shed tears at Bochim!

Theologically, a long way has been trodden. Divine wrath, which was used to justify Assyrian exactions,[34] is now used to justify Judah's own territorial claims. Yhwh has clearly abandoned Israel while Judah still benefits from his divine favour. Post-Assyrian theology is emerging, Judah turns Assyrian expansionism against Assyrian provinces. As Israel has lost Yhwh's favour by not conquering the cities of the plains, Judah must retain Yhwh's favour by accomplishing this conquest. The message of the book of Saviours is interpreted to justify Josiah's conquests. The Josianic Deuteronomists present themselves as the legitimate heirs of Yhwh's Israel by claiming for themselves the sacred mission of expelling the enemies which Israel has obviously been unable to vanquish, thus proving the BS wrong.

Judges 2.11-19: The Schema

This passage has already been considered in Chapter 1 in relation to the frame of the BS. It can now be viewed in the context of Josiah's edition of the BS. Before the insertion of the notice concerning Joshua's death (Judg. 2.6-10//Josh. 24.28-31), the schema followed immediately upon Judg. 2.1-5. The schema carries on the same purpose of 'deuteronomization' than the Bochim episode. Compared to the frame of the BS, the schema of Judg. 2.11-19 develops four major differences.

Evil Qualified as Apostasy

Like the frames of the saviour narratives, the schema starts with the evil that was committed by Israel. However, the evil that the frames mentioned merely to explain why Yhwh abandoned Israel into the hands of an enemy is now specified by the schema as refering to the service of the Baals ויעבדו את־הבעלים (Judg. 2.11, 13). To serve Baal had no negative connotation for a seventh century BCE Israelite, as Baal was one recognized title for Yhwh.[35] The title is therefore used in the plural to convey a

---

34. Or simply to explain a difficult situation as Mesha does. The evolution of the concept can be plotted: Statehood explains unfavourable situations by divine wrath. The Empire uses divine wrath to justify Assyrian intervention. Deuteronomism justifies the creation of Josiah's counter-Empire with Yhwh's wrath against Israel.

35. See E.A. Knauf, 'Dushara and Shai' al-Qaum: Yhwh und Baal. Dieu', in

polytheistic note to Israelite cult. Lindars suggested that this plural refer-red to the various local manifestations of Yhwh rather than to a plurality of gods[36] but this may be too learned a solution for a simple polemical note. The text ridicules its opponents by misspelling and misusing divine names, with no concern for historical reality. However overrated, the idea of a large pantheon in Israel has too often been taken at face value.

If the Baalim do not refer to a multiplicity of gods adored by the Israelites, they nonetheless address the divine witnesses enumerated in the vassalage treaties imposed by the Assyrians. The berith evoked the gods of both sides, and there is no reason why, in Israel as much as in Judah, Yhwh would not have been called upon, alongside a large range of more or less Assyrian gods, to give his divine guarantee to the treaty.[37] Serving the Baals did not originally mean to abandon Yhwh and worship foreign gods, but to accomplish all the requirements of the berith. To revolt against the Assyrian overlord was to become unfaithful to one's own god who was evoked by the berith.[38]

It therefore required a theological *tour de force* for Josiah's advisors to free themselves from this most comprehensive and binding conception, to turn it upside down and justify rebellion as faithfulness to Yhwh.

No Cries

As it is the case in the frames, Israel is abandoned into the hands of enemies (Judg. 2.14) generally presented here as raiders and round about enemies. Israel is greatly distressed as Yhwh's hand is now acting against his people (v. 15), but in spite of this extremely difficult situation, Israel does not cry to Yhwh as it always did in the BS.[39] Suffering provokes groans נאקתם instead of cries (v. 18). Eventually, Yhwh does intervene in spite of Israel's silence, but motivated solely by pity כי־ינחם יהוה for the sufferings endured by his people (v. 18). Such unsolicited relief is so unexpected compared to the saviour's narratives that the *BHS* editor

Th. Römer (ed.), *Lectio difficilior probabilior* (BDBAT, 12; Heidelberg: Esprint, 1991), pp. 19-29, Knauf, *Midian*, pp. 43-48.

36. Lindars, *Judges 1–5*, p. 102.

37. See S. Parpola and K. Watanabe, *Neo-Assyrian Treaties and Loyalty Oaths* (SAA, 2; Helsinki: Helsinki University Press, 1988); G.B. Lanfranchi, 'Esarhaddon, Assyria and Media', *SAAB* 12/2 (1998), pp. 99-110 (101-102).

38. Dalley, 'Yabâ, Atalyâ', p. 98 and Ezek. 17.

39. See Judg. 3.9 (Othniel); 3.15 (Ehud); (6.6, 7) Gideon. In Judg. 10.10 (Jephthah), Israel cries again but Yhwh refuses to listen (Judg. 10.11-14).

suggests to insert ויזעקו אל־יהוה 'They cried to Yhwh' between vv. 16 and 17. The temptation to harmonize the schema with the frames should be resisted. The lack of cries in the schema is consistent with the deconstruction of the theology of the BS operated here and in v. 4, where the cries of the BS are scoffed at by being called Bochim. In the schema, the cries are carefully omitted. This loud silence expresses Josiah's rejection of the BS 'crying theology' due to the unconditional nature of the salvation that it offers (the same critique will be found later in Judg. 6.7-10; 10.10-16).

Judges Instead of Saviours
Salvation is now brought through the agency of judges (vv. 16, 18), the first mention of the figures that will give their name to the book. The title 'judge' will be discussed later in this chapter with the list of Judges, but it should be noted that it only appears here and, for Yhwh, in Judg. 10.27. Elsewhere it is the verb that is used: both in Judg. 10 and 12 and in the additions to the saviour narratives of Othniel and Barak (Judg. 3.10; 4.4). The function of the judges will come to light with the analysis of Judges 13 (see Chapter 6), while the bucolic depiction of Deborah judging under her tree (Judg. 4.5) will be considered in Chapter 7 with the transition between Judges and 1 Samuel.

From a Cycle of Salvation to an Infernal Spiral of Corruption
Instead of crying to Yhwh for salvation, Israel sinks into apostasy without ever turning back to a god that nevertheless sends judges to save him. Where the BS is built on the alternation of abandon and deliverance, the schema underlines Israel's stubbornness and lack of gratitude. On top of not crying for help, Israel does not even listen to the judges (v. 17); in spite of the fact that Yhwh was with the judge all the days of his life (v. 18), Israel did not stop going a whoring after other gods (v. 17). There never was any repentance, and the verb שוב√ 'to return' in v. 19 is not used as it often is to denote repentance, but stands for returning to corruption. The implied conclusion is that apostasy did not aggravate during the life of the judge, but just went on worse than ever after his death.[40] The BS is herewith stripped of any pedagogical value, as the successive trials that it presents never produce any return to Yhwh. On the contrary, by

---

40. וישתחוו להם (Judg. 2.17) last verb in narrative mode. The following is grammatically a non narrative, a maddening repetition.

refusing to listen to the judges who saved them, the Israelites' guilt grows after each episode presented by the BS.

The deconstruction of the BS could hardly have been more thorough: its downplay of the effects of the integration of Israel within the Empire is turned upside down to demonstrate that Israel's integration proves Israel's essential unfaithfulness to Yhwh. The schema thus reveals the emergence of a post-Assyrian theology that takes roots in Josiah's rejection of the Assyrian Empire. Samaria's takeover in 720 BCE is now understood as Israel's 'downfall', the direct consequence of Israel's forsaking of Yhwh and following other gods.

Judges 6.7-10: Echoing Judges 2, an Anonymous Prophet

The schema's accusations are relayed by the sermon preached by the anonymous prophet inserted halfway through the book of Saviours, precisely when the Israelites are crying to Yhwh at the beginning of the Gideon narrative. The cries of the BS (ויזעקו בני־ישראל אל־יהוה 'The sons of Israel cried towards Yhwh' v. 6) are repeated in front of v. 7: ויהי כי־זעקו בני־ישראל אל־יהוה 'It happened, when the sons of Israel cried towards Yhwh' to indicate clearly the target of the critique. For this reason, the suggestion of *BHS* (note 7a-a) should be rejected.

After the obliteration of those cries in the schema, the last mention of the cries within the BS now comes directly under the fire of a certain prophet איש נביא. The sons of Israel are accused of having feared the gods of the Amorites in spite of Yhwh's explicit order not to do so (v. 9) and in spite of the fact that Yhwh had brought them out of the Egyptian servitude (v. 8) and had given them the land of their oppressors (לחציכם v. 9). The identity of the oppressors is not clear: they can't be Egyptians as Israel did not take over Egypt. So they should refer to the enemies described by the BS (Moabites, Canaanites and Midianites), although it seems far-fetched to assume that Israel should have conquered Midianite territory.[41] The last verse of the sermon takes over the devastating conclusion of the Bochim messenger: 'but you did not listen to my voice!' (Judg. 2.2//6.10). The cycle of deliverance of the BS is turned into a chain of proofs that Israel never repented and sank deeper and deeper into apostasy. In such circumstances, it is now pointless to carry on crying to Yhwh.

---

41. This uncertainty may indicate that the Joshuan conquest is not yet fully conceptualized.

Judges 10.1-5 and 12.8-15: The Judges

We now go beyond the BS and reach material added after the Abimelech narrative: a list of five judges cut in half by the Jephthah story (Judg. 10.6–12.7).

'Minor' Judges?

The saviour narratives are structured around the verbs זעק√ 'to cry out' and ישׁע 'to save' (see Chapter 1). Two of them also mention שׁפט√ 'to rule, to judge' (Judg. 3.10; 4.4), but these mentions can be considered as secondary as they are limited to a few words out of context, intruding into the flow of narratives that have no connection with governing or legal activities whatsoever.[42] On the contrary, the title 'judge' attributed to Yhwh by Jephthah (Judg. 11.27 ישׁפט יהוה השׁפט) lies within a legal argument and is perfectly in place there, just as it is in the small notices devoted to those traditionally called 'minor' judges.[43] In fact, the act of judging, whatever the meaning of such an activity,[44] is the only activity recorded by the text for these five characters, apart from making children and marrying them.[45] The judging activity is therefore essential to their short narratives, even though there is no indication of what judging entails.

Two categories of figures are therefore well defined. On one hand, the saviours are saving, while on the other, the judges judge; the distinction between judges and 'minor' judges is confusing[46] as, strictly speaking, there are no 'major' judges.[47] Othniel, Barak, Ehud and Gideon are noth-

---

42. T. Ishida, 'SOFET: The Leaders of the Tribal League "Israel" in the Pre-Monarchical Period', in T. Ishida (ed.), *History and Historical Writing in Ancient Israel* (Leiden: E.J. Brill, 1999), pp. 36-56 (46), wonders why Ehud, Shamgar, Gideon and Abimelech have no judging formula. The Josianic Deuteronomists selected only the 'clean' candidates.

43. Noth, 'Amt', pp. 389-412

44. See W. Richter, 'Zu den "Richtern Israels"', *ZAW* 77 (1965), pp. 40-72 (58-70) and Ishida, 'SOPET', pp. 41-44; E. Easterlly, 'A Case of Mistaken Identity: The Judges in Judges Don't Judge', *BR* 13 (1997), pp. 40-43; H. Niehr, *Herrschen und Richten: die Wurzel špt im Alten Orient und im Alten Testament* (FzB, 54; Würzburg: Echter Verlag, 1986), pp. 84-88.

45. O. Eissfeldt, *The Old Testament: An Introduction* (Oxford: Basil Blackwell, 1965), pp. 258-60.

46. T. Nöldeke, *Untersuchungen zur Kritik des AT* (Hildesheim: 1869), pp. 181-84, Noth, 'Amt'.

47. Ishida, 'Leaders', pp. 514-30; K.-D. Schunck, 'Falsche Richter im Richter-

ing else than saviours in spite of the fact that judging activities are attributed to Othniel and to Deborah. Tola, Jair, Ibzan, Elon and Abdon judge and do little else. Of Tola, it is true, it is said also that he 'arose to save Israel' (Judg. 10.1) but no saving act is recorded for Tola. This note about Tola looks rather like a literary device to hook the list of judges at the end of the BS, but it does not turn Tola into a 'minor' saviour. Three figures do not fit the saviour/judge distinction: Shamgar is a saviour with a story as short as the shortest judge stories, Jephthah and Samson are figures closer to the anti-saviour type of Abimelech than to either the judges or the saviours (see Chapter 6). For clarity's sake, the title 'judge' will be reserved to the five figures found on each side of Jephthah's story as they form a uniform group. The expression 'minor' judge is abandoned.

The Five Judges

The judges cover a mere 14 verses, providing very sketchy information. Indications about the length of 'office' and the burial place form the main information provided by these notices (see Figure 5).

	Tola	Jair	Ibzan	Elon	Abdon
Judges	10.1-2	10.3-5	12.8-10	12.11-12	12.13-15
Father	Puah				Hillel
	Dodo				
Home	Shamir,		Bethlehem		Pirathon
	Ephraim				
Tribe	Issachar	Gilead		Zebulun	
Year	23	22	7	10	8
Children		30 sons	30 sons		40 sons
			30 daughters		
			30 daughters-in-law		30 grandsons
Donkeys		30			70
Burial	Shamir	Kamon	Bethlehem	Ayyalon	Pirathon
					Ephraim

Figure 5. *The Judges*

Tola is the only judge whose grandfather is mentioned. His term is the longest (23 years). LXX reads Σαμαρεία instead of שמיר for his residence,

buch', in R. Liwak (ed.), *Prophetie und geschichtliche Wirklichkeit im alten Israel* (Stuttgart: Kohlhammer, 1991), pp. 364-70 suggests a distinction between 'true' and 'false, fictitious, anhistorical' judges.

which corresponds probably to the replacement of an obscure place by a very well known one: all the other judges come from peripheral places. The saving formula ויקם להושיע 'he arose to save' links the judges to Judg. 9: Tola and his colleges open a new era of salvation after Abimelech's disastrous times.

Jair, with his 30 sons, 30 donkeys and 30 towns, transfers the focus from the past to the future.[48] Like Tola and unlike the other judges, his notice starts with ויקם (qal) 'he arose', indicating that Tola and Jair were self-appointed and independent from any central government. The location of Jair's residence is not indicated, as the focus is entirely on Jair's possessions. The sons add up to the word-play between the 'donkeys' and the 'villages' (עירים same word pronounced *'ayarim*), two unusual forms for either donkeys or village, to explain the origin of the name Havvoth-jair 'Jair's camps' as Jair יאיר is a kind of aliteration of עירים.[49] The rare word עירים is based on a Gileadite or an Israelite form,[50] intended to give a northern shade to the stories of the judges. The word play should alert the modern reader not to attribute any historical value to the information conveyed by the list.[51]

Ibzan is the first judge of the second part of the list, placed after the Jephthah narrative (see Chapter 6), which itself also ends on a judge notice (Judg. 12.7). Jephthah the Gileadite is thus placed after Jair the Gileadite. Each of the last three judge notices starts with the words וישפט אחריו את-ישראל 'he judged Israel after him' to produce a picture of continuity with a smooth transition between each figure that judged Israel. Ibzan comes from a Bethlehem, which is more likely to be in Israel, possibly in Zebulun (see Josh. 19.15), than in Judah due to the overall Israelite context of the list. Ibzan is even more prolific than Jair as, in addition to his 30 sons he also has 30 daughters and 30 daughters-in-law. Here the focus is on the outside, to where the daughters were sent and from where the daughters-in-law came.

Elon the Zebulunite is buried in Aijalon, a town of approximately the

48. B. Beem, 'The Minor Judges: A Literary Reading of Some Very Short Stories', in K.L. Younger (ed.), *The Biblical Canon in Comparative Perspective* (ANETS, 11; Lewiston: Edwin Mellen, 1991), pp. 147-72 (151).

49. Villages that kept the name of the temporary harvesting camps upon which they were built: E.A. Knauf, 'Jair', *NBL*, 2.7.271-272; 1 Kgs 4.13; 1 Chron. 2.21-23.

50. G.A. Rendsburg, 'Notes on Israelian Hebrew 2', *JNSL* 26 (2000), pp. 33-45.

51. The fictitious character of the list has been stressed by M. Görg, *Richter* (NEB, 31; Würzburg: Echter Verlag, 1993), pp. 6, 59 and 70-71.

same name. He belongs so much to his native heath that the onomastic hardly distinguish between the place and the man. Elon is a worthy member of the country elite, established on the land since immemorial times.

Abdon is the last but certainly not the least of the five judges as the text indicates not only his father but also his grandsons. Thus, Abdon's father at the end of the list corresponds to Tola's father at the beginning, while Tola's grandfather corresponds to Abdon's grandchildren, four generations to underline continuity. Coming from Pirathon,[52] Abdon is buried in the land of Ephraim. The mention of Amalek at the end of v. 15 is best understood as a secondary and hostile note aimed at the Samaritans, as was already the case in Judg. 5.14.[53]

The list ends where it started, in Ephraim, the traditional Israelite heartland, after Southern Galilee (Issachar, Zebulun) and Gilead. The men who judged Israel (they are never called judges here) produced a large descent that they equipped with donkeys and wives. They depict an era of stability, with neither war nor orphans. Their greatest achievement as leaders is to be buried in their place of origin.[54] They are not saviours since there is no aggression, they describe what the BS only mentions at the end of the deliverance accounts, the period of peace and tranquillity. Linking each judge to the preceding one with אחריו 'after him' (10.1, 3; 12.8, 11, 13), the list creates a 70 years long era of peace broken only once by the Jephthah narrative.[55] This literary device led Noth to consider the judges as magistrates of a premonarchical amphyctiony[56] because one gets the impression that the judges succeeded each other to assume a charge than was not yet linked to a well defined centre. The apparent precentralization lent some likelihood to Noth's hypothesis. However, both the Israelite amphyctiony and the premonarchical judge office are now out of favour.[57]

---

52. *Far'ata*, south of Nablus. See E.A. Knauf, 'Pireathon—Fer'ata', *BN* 51 (1990), pp. 19-24.

53. R.J. Tournay, 'Polémique antisamaritaine et le feu du *Tofet*', *RB* 104 (1997), pp. 354-67.

54. Although the location of Kamon, Jair's burial place is unknown, but there are several candidates in his native Gilead: H.O. Thompson, 'Kamon', *ABD* 4, p. 5.

55. The round number of 70 years indicates that Jephthah was not considered as a judge (see discussion of the chronology in Chapter 5).

56. M. Noth, *Das System der zwölf Stämme Israels* (BWANT, 4/1; Stuttgart: Kohlhammer, 1930).

57. A.J. Hauser, 'The "Minor Judges"—a Re-Evaluation', *JBL* 94 (1975), pp. 190-200; T. Mullen, 'The "Minor Judges": Some Literary and Historical Considerations',

Contrarily to the saviours who come unexpectedly and disappear as soon as they finished their mission, the list of judges insists on generation continuity as for each one, at least two generations are presented.[58] 'Tola built for one generation; Jair for two, Ibzan for two, but with sixty arranged marriages there is certainly the expectation of more; and now, with Abdon, the grandchildren have arrived, and he clearly builds for three generations'.[59]

Israelite Judges from Josiah's Vantage Point
The overall picture of stability unfolded by the list of Israelite judges, in particular their burial in their home town, can be understood as a nostalgic note in a seventh century BCE society that is barely recovering from the uprooting effects of deportations and immigrations.[60] Salmanazar had exiled some Israelites in 722 BCE and Sargon replaced them by Arabs around 715 BCE. Sennacherib had removed 200, 000 people from Palestine in 701 BCE and 46 towns and villages of the Judaean Shephelah were razed. To offset the loss of the Shephelah, Manasseh farmed the Beer-sheva area intensively[61] and this must have led to the transfer of large numbers of Judaeans to new settlements in the South. To be buried in the family vault after the Assyrian upheavals must have become a rare privilege and was thus insisted upon in the list of judges. Moreover, the burial notice qualifies the judges as 'real' Israelites, native sons of natives (Tola), in opposition to the foreigners, Assyrians and Arabs who were now mingling with the Israelite population.

Could the list of judges be an answer to the BS? The lives of the men who judged Israel, peaceful and prosperous as they are, create a sharp contrast with the saviours, for whom family matters are simply ignored, and with Abimelech, Jephthah or Samson for whom family matters end up in disaster.

The judges do not come from Judah, nor from Benjamin for that matter, and this could be a first clue that Benjamin is part of Judah when the list of judges is drawn. With the judges' list, the rest of Israel is invited to join Josiah's cause, soon after the annexation of Benjamin. Josiah's daring

CBQ 44 (1982), pp. 185-201.
    58. Beem, 'Minor Judges', p. 151.
    59. Beem, 'Minor Judges', p. 157.
    60. Vividly described by Halpern, 'Lineages'.
    61. Finkelstein, 'Manasseh', p. 177.

move did not provoke any immediate Assyrian response,[62] and if it is impossible to know exactly how much time elapsed before Neko's retaliation in 609 BCE at Megiddo, it can safely be affirmed that it was a matter of several years. The campaign in Benjamin may have served Josiah as a test of Assyrian resistance before launching a larger move against the rest of the Assyrian Israelite provinces. The lack of Assyrian response did not mean victory, for local Israelite sensibilities had to be coaxed in order to win the support of the populations or at least of their elite. Wholehearted Israelite support would have allowed Josiah to present himself as a loyal Assyrian vassal, as a helper merely taking over the administration of the Israelite provinces and thus relieving the imperial administration, overburdened as it was with problems in the northern and eastern parts of the Empire. A parallel move by the Egyptians would best explain Neko's support of Assyria at Carchemish and his liquidation of Josiah as a rival heir for the Assyrian realm in Palestine.

However, the Israelites may have proved more difficult to convince than the Assyrians. In fact, Josiah would have had very few arguments at his disposal to justify a new Israel governed from Jerusalem. Memory and traditions pointed rather to the opposite direction, towards a Judaean petty kingdom under strong Israelite control. Moreover, after a century of Assyrian rule, Israelites became acquainted with the benefits of world economy, new opportunities abroad, large investments at home and the overall advantages of serving an Empire rather than a small kingdom.[63] To force Israel to accept Judaean hegemony over Israel would have been as difficult then than it is now for today's Israeli leaders to impose their rule on the Palestinians. To make things worse, the BS had preached an Israel without king as its religious ideal! The BS had therefore to be tackled head on; and this apparently was the role thought out for the men who judged Israel. The sheer ambiguity of their function could reflect a reinterpretation of the situation of Israel after 720 BCE, once the Israelite monarchy had been replaced by direct Assyrian rule. Rather than continuing to exalt saviours to obtain acceptance of the post-royal situation, Josiah's ideologues introduced within the ranks of the saviours a new kind of hero, embodying a totally different set of values. No daring warriors, the men who judged

62. The peaceful covenant with the Gibeonites suggests that Benjamin was annexed without fighting.

63. Examples of wholehearted support of the Empire by vassals in Lanfranchi, 'Esarhaddon', pp. 109-110, also Habakkuk's despair when the Chaldeans destroyed the Assyrian Empire and the stability it had provided.

Israel reflect the best of traditional rural elite, wise and cautious village leaders from backdoor Israelite places, far away from the compromises of the capital. This is the real Israel, the only one worth talking about, the pure Israel where sound tribal values are preserved and practised: careful land husbandry, wise intermarrying with good families, preserving the ancestral estate and dying in one's own bed, to be buried in the family vault. Quite the opposite of the reality experienced by the majority of Israelites, but a most convenient manner to avoid mentioning the Assyrian reality. One way to cancel an unacceptable reality is not to talk about it. The Assyrian rule was not mentioned, but neither was the Judaean rule that Josiah intended to impose on Israel. It was wiser to present the Judaean takeover of Israel as the restoration of ancient tribal structures. Leaders chosen within village aristocracies would be the backbone of a most decentralized structure, a local administration in the hands of locals, which would rule the land with no visible links with Jerusalem or Assyria. Certainly a most unrealistic system, but it was meant as propaganda rather than as a blueprint to be put in effect. The men who judged Israel are men of straw in the hands of a king who prefers to remain in the dark not to frighten his would be subjects, the velvet glove of local autonomy to hide the iron grasp of Jerusalem over Israel.

Israel escaped Judaean rule since Neko was called to the rescue. Josiah was executed before he could proceed any further than Benjamin. The plan, however, would not be forgotten: the Hasmonaeans did indeed accomplish it.

The men who judged Israel can also be considered as the extension to Israel of Josiah's famous administrative centralization in Judah. Arguing from Deut. 14–17, Niehr has shown that Josiah centralized justice and cult in Jerusalem[64] in order to gain full control over the kingdom's affairs. Sacrifices would be reserved for the Jerusalem temple, and a high court of justice was established in Jerusalem to which local judges (Deut. 16.18-20) had to refer important cases (Deut. 17.8-12). Local justice was therefore put under the control of the capital[65] and the men 'who judged Israel'

---

64. H. Niehr, *Rechtsprechung in Israel: Untersuchung zur Geschichte des Gerichtsorganisation im Alten Testament* (SBS, 130; Stuttgart: Verlag Katholisches Bibelwerk, 1987).

65. E. Junge, *Der Wiederaufbau des Heerwesens der Reiches Juda unter Josia* (BWANT, 75; Stuttgart: Kohlhammer, 1937), pp. 81-93; Niehr, *Herrschen; idem, Rechtsprechung.* Josianic centralization could have been justified in 2 Chron. 19 by attributing it first to King Jehoshaphat 'Yhwh judges': J.A. Dearman, *Property Rights*

in Judg. 10 and 12 could refer to the local level of that institution of centralized justice. Josiah insists on the local level in order to underline the
restoration of local authorities after the removal of the Assyrian administration. Of course, he leaves the delicate matter of the central government
in the dark rather than admitting that his aim is to transfer the centre from
Niniveh and Samaria to Jerusalem.

Josiah's advisors thus pursue their editing of the book of Saviours by
integrating a list of judges into it. After presenting Israelite 'history' as a
sequence of systematic unfaithfulness in the schema, after rejecting the
validity of cries through the anonymous prophet, after turning Gideon into
a coward by means of all the procrastinating material in Judg. 6–8,
Josiah's men turn the saviours into judges by adding two notices in Judg.
3.10; 4.4 that interpret the saviour's mission as 'judging' and by append-
ing the five judges at the end of the BS. These 'later' rather than 'minor'
judges are the real heroes of the Josianic edition of the BS, that is of the
first book that can be legitimately called the 'book of judges'. They are the
ideal civil servants of the Josianic Greater Israel. Their rule would mark
the end of violence, a time of prosperity without cities, corvée-work,
deportations, each one living under his own tree, feeding on the fat of his
tribal land, begetting and marrying hosts of children, gambolling on proud
donkeys before being laid to rest alongside one's own ancestors.

Judging or Ruling?
This bucolic presentation was likely to get some audience in Israel as it
must have been somehow in line with the longings of the Israelite 'people
of the land', the tribal elite that suffered most from Statehood and Empire.
In this context, the question of the exact meaning of √שׁפט 'to judge' loses
most of its relevance: the aim was not to describe a realistic mode of
government but to blur Josiah's real intentions behind a vague demagogic
programme that drew its inspiration from timeless cravings for peace and
prosperity.

However non-specific, the description of the judges in Judg. 10 and 12
draws on well known realities that have been studied in detail to understand the Biblical judges. The Edict of king Haremhab is an Egyptian text,
dated a few years after the Amarna period (end of the fourteenth century

in the Eighth-Century Prophets (SBLDS, 106; Atlanta: Scholars Press, 1988), p. 86.
Exod. 18.13-27 would have the same function going back to Moses: R. Knierim,
'Exodus 18 und die Neuordnung der mosaischen Gerichtsbarkeit', *ZAW* 73 (1961), pp.
146-71.

BCE), requiring the nomination of well-bred and respected priests as judges to reduce corruption.[66] The Amenemope Instruction (eleventh century BCE) similarly discusses the problem of the venality of judges[67] and offers some interesting parallels with Biblical proverbs.[68] The Installation of the vizier also contains recommendations by Thoutmoses III to ensure equity.[69] These texts show that the exercise of justice was a recurrent problem. However, they do not bring any light on Judg. 10 and 12 since our list of judges offers no consideration on the exercise of justice.

The Tale of the Queen of Kaniš found in old Hittite archives in Bogazköy (1900–1700 BCE)[70] has been mentioned in connection with the Biblical judges as it holds all the details found in Judg. 10 and 12 (donkeys, sons and daughters). Tsevat affirms that this tale is the source of the Biblical judges or that both texts are based on the same source.[71] The aim

---

66. K. Pfluger, 'The Edict of king Haremhab', *JNES* 5 (1946), pp. 260-66; W.H. Helck, 'Das Dekret des Königs Haremheb', *ZÄSA* 80 (1955), pp. 109-136.

67. H. Brunner, 'Die religiöse Antwort auf die Korruption in Ägypten', in W. Röllig (eds.), *Das Hörende Herz* (OBO, 80; Freiburg/Göttingen: Universitäts-verlag/ Vandenhoeck & Ruprecht, 1988), pp. 103-109.

68. Weinfeld, *Deuteronomy*, pp. 265-72.

69. R.O. Faulkner, 'The Installation of the Vizier', *JEA* 41 (1955), pp. 18-29.

70. H. Otten and C. Rüster, *Keilschrifttexte aus Bogasköy H. 22 aus dem Bezirk des grossen Tempels* (WVDOG, 90; Berlin: Mann Verl., 1974); idem, *Eine althe-thitische Erzählung um die Stadt Zalpa* (SBT, 17; Wiesbaden: Otto Harrassowitz, 1973), pp. 6-9, 14-36.

71. M. Tsevat, 'Two Old Testament Stories and their Hittite Analogues', *JAOS* 103 (1983), pp. 35-42:

> 'The queen of Kaniš gave birth to 30 sons in a single year. She said: 'What is this? I have born a gang'. She filled containers with excrements, put her sons in them and turned them over to the river. The river carried them to the sea to the land of Zalpuwa. The [Gods], however, took the sons out of the sea and reared them. In the meantime, as the years went by, the q[ueen] gave birth again, to thirty daughters. Those she reared herself. The sons went back to Neša. They drove an ass/asses, and when they arrived at Tamar[mara], they said, 'here you have heated the room, and an ass/asses mates'. This is what the men of the city said, 'wherever we have come, an ass-asses mates [...]' This is what the sons said: 'wherever we have come, a woman [bea]rs a child [only once a year], as however she bore at once one time'. This is what the men of the city said: 'once o[ur quee]n of Kaniš bore 30 daughters at one time, but the sons have disappeared'. Thereupon the sons said before their ears: 'whom are we seeking? We have found our mother. Come, let us go to Neša'. As they were travelling to Neša the God made them an other heart; their mother [...] did not recognise them, and she gave the daughters to her sons. [The fi]rst ones did not recognise their sisters, the last one, however [said], 'let us [not] take our sisters. Do not commit an abomination!' [...] right. And s[lept] w[ith t]hem. [Large lacuna].'

of the Hittite tale is obviously to warn against unintentional incest, which is not the case in the Bible, except with Ibzan who takes the trouble to send his 30 daughters outside and to bring in from outside 30 wives for his sons (Judg. 12.9).[72] This fascinating parallel confirms the antiquarian character of the list of judges which consciously draws on ancient material to evoke a kind of golden age rather than offering a realistic programme. It does not provide information on the function of Israelite judges in the premonarchical period.

If Bronze Age parallels are unable to provide guidance on the Biblical judges, the analogy with Iron II Phoenician *suffets* is more promising. The oldest attestation of their existence comes from Josephus who claims to cite the records of the Phoenicians and reports that the διδάσκοι governed Tyre during Nebuchadnezzar's blockade:

'Nebuchadnezzar besieged Tyre for thirteen years in the days of Ithobal, their king; after him reigned Baal ten years; after him were judges appointed, who judged the people: Ecnibalus, the son of Balascus, two months; Chelbes, the son of Abdeus, ten months; Abbar the high priest, three months; Mitgonus and Gerastratus, the sons of Abdelemus, were judges six years; after whom Balatorus reigned one year; after his death they sent and fetched Merbalus from Babylon, who reigned four years; after his death they sent for his brother Hiram, who reigned twenty years. Under his reign, Cyrus became king of Persia.'[73]

The reliability of this information is difficult to evaluate. The claim has to be taken with great caution as Josephus is comparing Chaldean and Tyrian records to show that they agree with Biblical writings on the Jerusalem temple, his aim being to prove the antiquity of the Jewish nation.[74] Although the details of Tyrians chronology offered here are not necessarily trustworthy, it is significant that the rule of Tyre is conveyed by 'judges' in a crisis situation around 600 BCE. This fact, reliable enough, provides a most interesting parallel with Judg. 10 and 12. The Tyrian judges served as an interim government while the king was missing. In normal times, they seem to have represented a kind of municipal authority

See H.A. Hoffner, 'The Queen of Kanesh and the Tale of Zalpa', *CoS* 1, pp. 181-82.

72. Tsevat, 'Stories', p. 235.

73. F. Josephus, 'Against Apion', in P. Maier (ed.), *The New Complete Works of Josephus* (Grand Rapids: Kregel, 1999), pp. 937-81: 1, pp. 156-58.

74. Josephus, *Apion* 1.160.

beside the royal power, limited to the local administration and justice.[75] It is not far-fetched to postulate that the Tyrian *suffets* were known in Jerusalem, less than 200 km to the South and only a few decades earlier, during Josiah's reign. In the light of the *suffets*, the Biblical judges could be interpreted as a temporary authority, covering, from Jerusalem's vantage point, the whole of the Assyrian period. Instead of naming the Empire (why name a waning power when one is about to take its place?), the period of the judges is a euphemism referring to a time in Israel when there was no more king, until Josiah would restore order and offer himself as king to Israel.

Conclusion

To attribute the list of judges to Josiah's court leads to an understanding of the judges not as the description of a premonarchical political system rooted in Iron I Israel, but as a code-word for the Assyrian period. This is a rather novel conclusion, but the Tyrian judges system give it a certain credibility, in spite of the fact that the list bears no Deuteronomistic traits.[76] Moreover, this understanding is in line with the schema, which also mentions judges in front of the book of Saviours in order to streamline the saviours with a layer of judges. This process is clearly opposed to the theology of the BS, in particular to the unconditional saving effect of its cries, as these are rejected by the anonymous prophet. The typically Deuteronomistic nature of the Bochim episode, the schema and of the passage of the anonymous prophet gives weight to a Josianic date for this vast editing process. Manasseh's book of Saviours had become Josiah's book of Judges.

However, this is not the end of this Josianic edition. Judges 17–18, which are considered by most interpreters as an appendix to the book of Judges are likely to conclude the Josianic edition of the book of Judges. Chapter 4 is therefore devoted to the presentation of this hypothesis.

---

75. E. Lipinski, 'Suffètes', *DCPP*, p. 429.

76. For this reason Görg, *Richter,* pp. 6, 59 and 70-71 attributes the list to a post-Deuteronomistic edition.

Chapter 4

JOSIAH'S GREAT ISRAEL, THE DANITES: JUDGES 17–18

After the saviours of Judg. 3–8, the judges of the schema (Judg. 2.11-19) and the judges of Judg. 10–12, the book of Judges seems bent on introducing a gallery of non-heroic figures.

Jephthah and Samson (Judg. 10–16) do share some characteristics of the saviours and of the judges, yet their narratives end tragically. Jephthah kills his own daughter (Judg. 11.3) and Samson commits suicide (Judg. 16.30).

In Judg. 17, Micah's mother is the victim of a theft committed by Micah himself, who then becomes afraid of his mother's curse and returns the stolen silver. The mother hands over part of the silver to a silversmith to plate an idol with it.

Judges 18 tells how Micah is robbed of the idol (and of the Levite he had hired to serve it) by the Danites who were migrating from Samson's land to the city of Dan at the sources of the Jordan.

In Judg. 19–21, another Levite, just as anonymous as the first one, falls victim to Benjaminite xenophobia in an ugly episode which costs the life of his concubine. Apart from the presence of those Levites and a pro-monarchical refrain (Judg. 17.6; 18.1; 19.1; 21.25), Judg. 17–18 and Judg. 19–21 have nothing in common.[1] For this reason, the Benjaminite problem will be considered separately (Chapter 6), while the present chapter is devoted to the Danites in Judg. 17–18 (for the Jephthah and Samson narratives see Chapter 5).

In Judg. 17–18, Becker found an exilic or early postexilic narrative criticizing the cult in Dan;[2] just as 1 Kgs 12 criticized Jeroboam setting up one of his golden 'calves' in Dan. Here, the critique is harsher as it traces the illegitimacy of the Danite cult to a time way before Jeroboam: the

---

1. See A.D.H. Mayes, 'Deuteronomistic Royal Ideology in Judges 17–21', *BibInt* 9 (2001), pp. 243-58 (254).

2. Becker, *Richterzeit*, p. 253.

illegitimacy is there, from the origin, as soon as the Danites have taken hold of the city of Dan.

Becker's exilic-to-early-postexilic date is based mainly on the word צוֹרֵף 'silversmith' (Judg. 17.4) which is not found in texts considered older.[3] This argument is obviously most convenient if one wishes to push Judg. 17–18 beyond the fateful year 586 BCE. Becker claims that the prohibition of images was not formulated in such a stringent way before the exile.[4] However, even if צוֹרֵף was only attested in Neh. 3.8, 32 and Prov. 25.4, the association of the verb צרף with the polemic against idols in Isa. 40.19; 41.7; 46.6; Jer. 10.9, 14; 51.17 opens the possibility to earlier dates. One may wonder how valid can a criterion be when it is based on one word only. It is necessary to combine literary analysis with information drawn from the political context of the area described by the text.

The Danites, a Geographical Problem

The story of the Danite migration seems to seek to conciliate contradictory statements of biblical texts about the location of the tribe of Dan. According to Josh. 15–19 and to Judg. 1.27-34, which present Dan last, as the northernmost Israelite group, the Danites seem to be the inhabitants of the city of Dan.[5] Another group of texts (Josh. 19.41-46; Judg. 13–16) locates the Danites in the Soreq valley, west of Jerusalem. Lastly, Josh. 19.47// Judg. 1.35 and Judg. 17–18 explain this contradiction by reporting a migration that led the Danites to move from the Soreq to Dan.

Judges 1.34-35: Danites from North to South

One can see at first glance that Judg. 1 occupies a particular position among the texts concerned with Dan. This text belongs to the first group in so far as it mentions Dan after all the other tribes (v. 34 Dan, after Asher and Naphtali), while its last verses (vv. 35-36) presuppose Dan back in the Soreq region, thus anticipating the cycle of the Danite Samson (Judg. 13–16) and the migration from the Soreq to Dan in Judg. 17–18. The presence of a caesura is likely between Judg. 1.34 and 35-36. Verse 34 belongs to King Manasseh's presentation of Israel's progressive domination over the lowland cities (see Chapter 2). But vv. 35-36 must be later, belonging, at

---

3.   Becker, *Richterzeit*, p. 231. Bauer, *Warum nur übertretet*, p. 444.
4.   Becker, *Richterzeit*, p. 231.
5.   Genesis 30; 49; and Deut. 33 follow a genealogical rather than a geographical logic and are therefore not pertinent to the present dicussion.

the earliest, to the same editorial stage that produced *Samson* and the migration narrative (Judg. 13–18).

In Manasseh's version of Judg. 1, the Danites offer the most vivid illustration of his political understanding of Israel's origins. As the nor-thernmost Israelite group, the Danites had even less success against the cities in the plain than Asher and Naphtali who had settled among the Canaanites (Judg. 1.31-33): 'The Amorites pressed the Danites back to the mountains and did not let them go down to the plain' (Judg. 1.34). On the basis of the northward progression followed by Judg. 1.27-34, the plain in which the Danites could not settle must be the area around the city of Dan, in the upper Jordan valley (Judg. 18.7, 14, 27, 29).[6] The Danites were thus unable to take control of Dan, the city around which they lived. Calling the Danite's enemies Amorites instead of Canaanites (as they are called in Judg. 1.27-33), Judg. 1.34 clearly distinguishes the upper valley of the Jordan from the Jezreel and Sharon plains. It thus coheres with a long forgotten truth that archaeology is slowly rediscovering, namely that the Syrian cultural sphere spread southward down to Hazor[7] even as far as pseudo-Beth-Saida.[8] For this very reason, Judg. 1 does not call the masters of the city of Dan 'Canaanites': Dan is set in a geographical and cultural zone distinct from Israel. From every point of view, Dan is closer to Damascus than to Samaria. The mention of the 'Amorites' therefore indicates clearly that the sons of Dan in v. 34 lived in the hills of Upper Galilee and on the slopes of Mount Hermon.

---

6. Was Dan called Laish before its conquest by the Danites as Judg. 18.29 claims? A Laish is attested next to a Hazor and a Beth-Shemesh in Egyptian execration texts: G. Posener, *Princes et pays d'Asie et de Nubie* (Bruxelles: 1940), p. 92 (E 59). A Laish is also attested in a tin delivery at Mari: A. Malamat, 'Syro-Palestinian Destination in a Mari Tin Inventory', *IEJ* 21 (1971), pp. 31-38 and in a list from Thoutmoses III: *ANET*, p. 242. But J.M. Sasson, 'Yarim-Lim Takes the Grand Tour', *BA* 47 (1986), pp. 246-51, has identified this Laish in the Aleppo area and has therefore no connection whatsoever with Dan. ליש is recalled in Judg. 18 as an Aramaic pun based on ליה 'Does not exist' contraction of לא איתי = Heb. אין: see Barrakkab stele 1 in Zenjirli l. 16: ליתה: Gibson, *Textbook,* 90-91. Josh. 19.47 translated the pun, replacing Laish by Leshem, לשם contraction of לא שם 'no name', cf. Arabic *laïsa* 'there is not'.

7. A. Ben Tor, director of the Hazor excavations, oral presentation Freiburg, Switzerland (November 1999).

8. S. Schorch, 'Der Name des Gottes von et-Tell/Bethsaida', *BN* 103 (2000), pp. 36-38 (36); R. Arav, 'Bethsaida Preliminary Report' in R. Arav and R.A. Freund (eds.), *Bethsaida: A City by the North Shore of the Sea of Galilee* (Kirksville, MI: Truman State University Press, 1999), pp. 3-114.

Judges 1.35-36 introduces a completely different perspective. As v. 34 did not expressly name the city coveted by the Danites, the Amorites are said to be living in Har-heres, Aijalon and Shaalbim (Judg. 1.35a) inferring that the Danites lived in the hills overlooking the Shephelah. Beth-Shemesh is called Har-Heres 'scabby mound'[9] to avoid confusion with another Beth-Shemesh in Naphtali. However, Har-heres is also a fitting seventh century BCE description of the aspect of Tell er-Rumēle (the name of the tell traditionally considered as the location of Beth-She-mesh[10]) because after its destruction in 701 BCE, the tell was only partially reoccupied, to be deserted for good around 670 BCE.[11] Transferring the Amorites, and along with them the Danites, from Dan to the west of Jerusalem allows Judg. 17–18 to explain how the Danites ended up conquering Dan while they had previously been prevented from doing so by the Amorites.

Unexpectedly, the tale of the Danite migration reveals that the end of Judg. 1 has been produced in several stages. In addition to the geographical transfer, v. 35b presents the 'house of Joseph' as the group that finally subdued the Amorites. As this house of Joseph first appears in the

9.   H.M. Niemann, 'Zorah, Eshtaol, Beth-Shemesh and Dan's Migration to the South: A Region and its Traditions in the Late Bronze and Iron Ages', *JSOT* 86 (1999), pp. 25-48 (39); K.-D. Schunck, 'Wo lag Har Heres?', in *idem* (ed.), *Altes Testament und Heiliges Land,* 1 (BEAT, 17; Frankfurt am Main: Lang, 1989), pp. 177-81; S. Bunimovitz and Z. Lederman, 'Beth-Shemesh: Culture Conflict on Judah's Frontier', *BARev* 23 (1997), pp. 42-49 (42-43).

10.   That Tell er-Rumēle is Beth-shemesh is not sure. E. Robinson (1841) based this identification on the name of the nearby village of 'Ain Shems: Bunimovitz & Lederman, 'Beth-Shemesh', p. 43. Strangely, the Samson cycle never mentions Beth-shemesh, in spite of the fact that Tell er-Rumele is very close to Zorah and Eshtaol and would have made a perfect onomastic link with Samson's name. Excavations at Tell er-Rumēle have so far failed to establish its ancient name. EA 273.21 mentions Ṣarḫa as a strategic site near Aijalon and Niemann, 'Zorah', pp. 40-45 suggests that Khirbet er-Rumēle was called Ṣarḫa in the Bronze Age and in the Iron I. Zorah (Tell Ṣar'a) would then be a dependency of Ṣarḫa that developped after the destruction of Ṣarḫa/Beth-shemesh. The ark narrative (1 Sam. 6), that of the conquest of Beth-shemesh by the Philistines (2 Chron. 28.18) and the levitical city of Josh. 21.16 can all be secondary to Judg. 13–18. The story of Amaziah's capture at Beth-shemesh (2 Kgs 14.11-13) and Solomon's first prefect over Makaz, Shaalbim, Beth-shemesh and Elon-beth-hanan (1 Kgs 4.9) provide no extra information for the localization of Beth-shemesh. Josh. 15.10 is slightly more precise, locating Judah's northern border in Beth-shemesh near Timnah.

11.   Niemann, 'Zorah', p. 45.

account of the conquest of Bethel (Judg. 1.22-26) we may presume that Judg. 1.22-26 and 35b all belong to the same editorial stage. The story of the conquest of Bethel will be considered in Chapter 6 and dated to the Persian period. It will be necessary to inquire whether Judg. 17–18 should also be attributed to the Persian period or if there are clues favouring an earlier date.

Niemann's Migration in Reverse
Michael Niemann has recently put forward a new hypothesis which, compared with his thesis published in 1985, lowers the date of the Danite migration from 1200–1160 BCE[12] to 735 BCE. According to this new hypothesis, the Danites would have moved from the city of Dan towards a refugee camp called Mahaneh-dan (Judg. 18.12) near Kiriath-jearim to escape from Tiglath-pileser's attack on Northern Israel in 733 BCE.[13] Hezekiah would have then settled these Danite refugees in Zorah and Eshtaol. They would have integrated the local Samson folklore into their own traditions and produced an Exodus narrative towards Dan in order to reinterpret and justify their recent arrival in the Soreq valley as a 'return' to their original territory. They would placate the criticisms of their new neighbours by claiming that they were entitled to live in and around Zorah and Eshtaol since their ancestors had been natives of the area. Finally, the Assyrians would have caught up with them and Sennacherib would have deported them in 701 BCE.

This new hypothesis is very innovative, it squarely turns it back to the famous pre-monarchical 'period of the judges' to seek a background for the migration towards the end of the royal period.

However, the concept of refugees fleeing from advancing armies is problematic. Although it is a well known phenomenon in the modern world, it is not sure that populations in Antiquity were inclined to leave their homes, even at the approach of foreign armies. Before the creation of specialized humanitarian agencies, no one would provide for people who had left their land, usually their only means of subsistence. The only indisputable massive population transfers were deportations, which uprooted people by force. Populations survived war by hiding crops, animals, valuables and themselves in caves, underground silos or fortresses (Judg.

---

12. H.M. Niemann, *Die Daniten: Studien zur Geschichte e. altisraelitischen Stämmes* (FRLANT, 135; Göttingen: Vandenhoeck & Ruprecht, 1985), p. 143.

13. Niemann, 'Zorah', p. 35.

6.2).[14] Large-scale migrations in the ancient Orient are not attested although the concept is still extremely popular in Biblical studies. The famous migration of the Sea People is disputed[15] and it may finally turn up to be understood as a literary construct like its Biblical counterpart, the mass Exodus out of Egypt. The alleged evidence concerning large population movements at the end of the Hittite Empire is also far from convincing. Raids by confederated gangs equipped with new weapons would have provoked the flight of whole populations like in Ugarit.[16] But excavations at Ugarit have revealed that some inhabitants had hidden their valuables underground, thus showing that if they fled, they intended to come back as soon as possible. Sixty arrowheads indicate that the city was not deserted: fighting did take place. The small number of skeletons found shows that the number of casualties was kept minimal, for prisoners were a valuable part of the booty.[17] To come back to the Iron Age, the sheer number of deportees moved by the Assyrians shows that populations did not escape but simply stayed put and waited to see what would happen.

If Niemann's date for the Danite move is attractive, the flight of the inhabitants of the city of Dan before the arrival of Assyria troops is unconvincing. It is therefore necessary to improve Niemann's scenario.

The Migration in Reverse Put Straight

Seeking an historical background for Judg. 17–18 around the Assyrian conquest of Dan in 733 BCE has the unfortunate consequence of reversing the direction of the population transfer. To overcome this difficulty, one could connect the migration of the Danites with a large demographic movement in the opposite direction, from Zorah and Eshtaol towards the North, as indicated by the text. Sennacherib's destruction and deportation

14. A survival technique that has provided great archaeological finds: among others Nahal Hever, Wadi ed-Daliyeh, 'Arâq en-Na'sâneh, Wadi Murabbaat and of course Qumrân.

15. R. Drews, 'Medinet Habu: Oxcarts, Ships and Migration Theories', *JNES* 59 (2000), pp. 161-90: in spite of the reliefs from Medinet Habu, Ramses III may have intercepted a local Shasou group rather than a migrating people.

16. J. Freu, 'La fin d'Ugarit et de l'Empire hittite', *Semitica* 47 (1997), pp. 17-37 (35) citing J. and E. Lagarce, *The Intrusion of the Sea People and their Acculturation: A Parallel between Palestinian and Ras Ibn Hani Data* (SHAP, 3; Aleppo: Aleppo University Press, 1988), pp. 137-69, 308-333.

17. M. Yon, 'The End of the Kingdom of Ugarit', in M.S. Joukowsky (ed.), *The Crisis Years: The 12th Century B.C.* (Dubuque, Io: Kendall/Hunt, 1992), pp. 111-22 (117).

of the inhabitants of the Shephelah in 701 BCE comes naturally to mind.

Instead of taking Judg. 17–18 from a Danite point of view, a Judaean or Philistine[18] vantage point may be more appropriate. The story is indeed told by an outsider: glorification of the 'heroes' is missing so badly that Judg. 18 has been read as an anti-conquest narrative.[19] Throughout the story, the Danites take no risks, in Micah's house or at Dan they fall on easy preys, the absence of heroic deeds is conspicuous. The name Micah itself, in spite of its frequency,[20] could, in the context of Judg. 17–18 bear ironic traits: the Israelites in general are rather unsure about the identity of their god, they are still asking themselves the question: מיכיהו or מי כה יהוה 'Who is like Yhwh?'

What would the Danites departure from Zorah and Eshtaol mean from a Judaean point of view? It is likely to be related to the Assyrian reorga-

18. S. Ackerman, 'What If Judges Had Been Written by a Philistine?', in J.C. Exum (ed.), *Virtual History and the Bible* (Leiden: E.J. Brill, 2000), pp. 33-41.

19. U.F.W. Bauer, 'Judges 18 as an Anti-Spy Story in the Context of an Anti-Conquest Story', *JSOT* 88 (2000), pp. 37-47.

20. The name Micah is widespread. *Mykyhw* is attested more than 10 times on seals and impressions, F. Vattioni, 'I sigilli ebraici', *Biblica* 50 (1969), pp. 357-88, n° 30; P. Bordreuil and A. Lemaire, 'Nouveaux sceaux hébreux, araméens and ammonites', *Semitica* 26 (1976), pp. 45-63 n° 10; למכיהו בן שלם: N. Avigad, *Hebrew Bullae from the Time of Jeremiah* (Jerusalem: Israel Exploration Society, 1986), pp. 70-73 n° 90-92.94-97), on inscriptions (Jerusalem, seventh century BCE): N. Avigad, 'Chronique archéologique', *RB* 80 (1973), pp. 576-79 (מכיהו 579); Lakish: Lemaire, *Inscriptions hébraïques* I, pp. 128-29 n° 11 l. 3; Wadi ed-Daliyeh (fourth century BCE Samaria): J. Zsengellér, 'Personal Names in the Wadi ed-Daliyeh Papyri', *ZAH* 9 (1996), pp. 182-89 (183).

Mykyh in Jerusalem: Avigad, *Hebrew Bullae*, 41 n° 27.

Mykh around Jerusalem: N. Avigad, *Bullae and Seals from a Post-Exilic Judean Archive* (Qedem, 4; Jerusalem: Institute of Archeology, 1976), p. 10 n° 12; in Elephantine: B. Porten and A. Yardeni, 'Three Unpublished Aramaic Ostraka', *Maarav* 7 (1991), pp. 207-227 (211 BM 45035).

mì-ka-ya-a: M.D. Coogan, *West Semitic Personnal Names in the Murashu Documents* (Missoula, MT: Scholars Press, 1976), p. 28.

מיכיה: Jer. 26.18; 2 Kgs 22.12//2 Chron. 34.20.

מיכה: Neh. 11.17.

לחדק בן מכא and reverse כהן דאר [מ]כהיו, : N. Avigad, 'The Priest of Dor', *IEJ* 25 (1975), pp. 101-105 (102).

m]ika'il: K.P. Jackson, 'Ammonite Personal Names in the Context of the West Semitic Onomasticon' in C.L. Meyers and M. O'Connor (eds.), *The Word of the Lord Shall Go Forth* (Winona Lake: Eisenbrauns, 1983), pp. 507-521 (509 Nimrud Ostrakon n° 12).

מכי Arav, 'Bethsaida Preliminary Report', p.47.

nization of the area after 701 BCE. The area had been handed over to the Philistines until it came again under Judaean rule, either during the reign of Manasseh or under Josiah.[21] Timnah, mentioned in Sennacherib's annals, was rebuilt immediately according to a very elaborate plan[22] and became an industrial centre like near-by Ekron. Beth-Shemesh, assuming that its site is Tell er-Rumēle, was destroyed in 701 BCE and totally abandoned after 670 BCE while Zorah and Eshtaol, two small dependencies of Beth-Shemesh, survived. The Assyrian policy of urbanization and centralization was put in effect in Shephelah. Not all of the population was deported or, if it was, not all the deportees were sent to faraway destinations. They were simply sent a few miles away to build and fill the new cities like Timnah and Ekron, while medium towns like Beth-shemesh died out. Parallel to urbanization, villages like Zorah and Eshtaol remained active, to till the land around the cities. In the seventh century BCE, Judg. 18 would necessarily be related either to the events of 701 BCE or to the Judaean recovery of the area. Both hypotheses may even be working together, any reasserting of Judaean power over the Shephelah would require an explanation of why it was lost in the first place. And rather than blaming Hezekiah's foolhardy rebellion, Josiah, himself about to disregard Assyrian rule, would prefer to conceal the painful reality of 701 BCE with a tale of the voluntary departure of 'Danites'.

Why was Dan selected as the new home of those Judaeans? Dan was not the only thriving city at the time.[23] But Dan was the northernmost city that could be considered as once belonging to Israel. Choosing Dan for their new abode thus delineates the northern limits of Israel streching from Dan to Beer-sheba. A summary of the migration of the Danites was later added in Josh. 19.47 to legitimize a Danite allotment that well exceeds the modest Danite area delineated in Judges.[24] If Josh. 19 also belongs to the Josianic era,[25] it conveniently justified the re-conquest and extension of the Judaean Shephelah.

21. Already under Manasseh according to H.L. Ginsberg, 'Judah and the Transjordan States from 734 to 582 B.C.E.' in *Alexander Marx Jubilee Volume* (New York: Jewish Theological Seminary of America, 1950), pp. 349-65; or during Josiah's reign: Finkelstein, 'Manasseh', p. 181.

22. Kelm, *Timnah*, p. 160.

23. A. Biran, *Biblical Dan* (Jerusalem: Israel Exploration Society, 1994).

24. Niemann, 'Zorah', p. 36.

25. Niemann, 'Zorah', p. 35; J. Strange, 'The Inheritance of Dan', *ST* 20 (1966), pp. 120-39.

This hypothesis has the advantage of remaining closer to the text than Niemann's proposal and it accounts for a well-attested 'migration'. Judges 18 explains away a painful episode and justifies the recovery of the area lost in 701 BCE, but a closer look to the text will reveal that more is at stake within Judg. 17–18.

Further Critiques against the Book of Saviours
Two fundamental elements of the BS reappear: זעק 'to cry' (Judg. 18.22-23) and שקט 'to be at rest' (Judg. 18.7, 27), a root already encountered in the saviour narratives. Here, these words are used to further defuse the BS.

The cries of the BS are used in v. 22 to call out Micah's neighbours to oppose the Danites who have just robbed the silver image and taken the Levite with them. In the next verse, it is the Danites who ask Micah for the reason of his crying, although here, crying brings no salvation. On the contrary, the marauding Danites warn Micah that, in addition to his cultic paraphernalia, he will also lose his life if he does not stop crying (Judg. 18.25).

The tranquility the land enjoyed after each deliverance wrought by the saviours (Judg. 3.11, 30; 5.31; 8.28) is now the direct cause of the downfall of Laish. Precisely because its inhabitants lived in a quiet and unsuspecting way (שקט ובטח), they have become an easy prey for the Danites who slaughter them and burn the city.

The basic principles of the book of Saviours are again ridiculed: no salvation is to be expected from crying. But the critique is going a step further: the very tranquillity promised by the saviours is deceitful, it turns out to be a false security leading those who rely on it to utter destruction.

The Danite Paradigm

Si Vis Pacem, Para Bellum
This assault on the tranquillity of the BS reveals the militarism of the editors of Judg. 18 who warn that confidence in Yhwh should not prevent serious military preparation.

If Judg. 18.7, 22-23, 27 refer polemically to the book of Saviours in the same way that the schema did (Judg. 2.11-19), the anonymous prophet (Judg. 6.7-10) and the bargaining episode with Yhwh (Judg. 10.6-16), all of which were attributed to Josiah in Chapter 3, Judg. 17–18 too are likely to belong to the Josianic edition of the book of Judges. The militarism of Judg. 18 is best understood during Josiah. Indeed, the kings after him did try to resist Egyptian and Babylonian interventions in the political affairs of the kingdom. However, Jehoiachin and Zedekiah's military activities appear to have been rather limited: they merely locked themselves behind Jerusalem's walls, to no avail. Josiah alone benefited from an international context favourable to consistent military ventures that went beyond feeble tactics that merely delayed an inescapable fate.

If Josiah invented the ideal Israel 'from Dan to Beer-sheba', he is likely to be also involved in the story of the conquest of Dan. In fact, Judg. 18 does not end with the departure of the Danites from Zorah and Eshtaol. The second half of the chapter describes with biting irony the robbing of Micah's divine image, made of silver he himself had stolen, the kidnapping of Micah's Levite and the founding of the cult of Dan. Apart from Judg. 18.27 which reports the actual conquest of the city, the bulk of chs. 17–18 (44 verses in all) is devoted to the tragi-comedy of the origin of Micah's image and how it ended up in Dan. That the story's aim is to establish the illegitimacy of the cult practised in Dan is obvious.

Interestingly, the Danites are not accused of worshipping foreign or other gods. In fact, the image is never named, nor is the god served by the Levite.[26] In spite of the lack of typically Deuteronomistic expressions, the whole narrative coheres with the Josianic period. One can infer from 2 Kgs 22–23 that Josiah robed his expansionist ambitions in religious guise, presenting himself as righteous servant of Yhwh, eager to purify his cult. The enemy this time does not come from foreign influences, but from a suspiciously vague 'mountain of Ephraim' (Judg. 17.1, 8; 18.2, 13), the hideout of Micah's mother, the idol maker and her idol worshipping son. These are the real villains of the story, they also are in the weakest position. The Danites, even if their doings are never heroic and although they set up Micah's image in Dan, are going in the right direction.[27] The narrators put in their mouths some striking words to convince the Levite to abandon Micah and follow them to Dan: 'Is it better for you to be priest to the house of one man, or to be priest of a tribe and family in Israel?' (Judg. 18.19). With this question, the Danites themselves announce the Josianic programme of cultic centralization. Moreover, the Danites are exemplary conquerors, the report of the spies is received with enthusiasm and a troop is sent immediately, in sharp contrast to the reaction of the Israelites when

26. A striking parallel with the bilingual inscription found at Dan, in honour of the god 'which is in Dan': A. Biran, 'Dan', *NEAEHL*, 1, pp. 323-32 (331).

27. Against U.F.W. Bauer, 'A Metaphorical Etiology in Judges 18.12', *JHebS* 3 (2001), pp. 37-47 who understands the Danites as anti-Yahwist desperados.

Caleb, Joshua and the other spies came back from the Valley of Eshcol (Num. 13–14).[28]

The Camp of Dan מחנה־דן at Kiriath-jearim is in Judah (Judg. 18.12), which indicates that the narrative presupposes the annexation of Benjamin by Josiah. The single brigade of 600 fighters (Judg. 18.11, 16), compared to the 1000 brigades aligned by Israel during the Exodus (Exod. 12.37) underlines the ease of the conquest.[29] Josiah has every reason to insist on the fact that the Assyrian provinces are ripe for a trouble-free take over.

Of course, the exemplary nature of Judg. 18 stops when the Danites set up Micah's idol in Dan. This counter-example allows Josiah to justify his own conquest as a religious crusade.

The Danites could then be understood as forerunners, albeit imperfect, of Josiah's programme. They are pointing the way, from Jerusalem or near-by, right up to Dan, plundering illegitimate cultic centres on the way, in order to purify them and to fill the meriting soldier's pockets. A fine harangue to motivate the troops before setting off on a promising looting campaign against rich and defenceless cities in the North. Judges 18 is not an anti-conquest story simply because Dan falls like an overripe fruit into Danites hands.[30] This leisurely stroll across Israel right up to Dan is an example to be followed by daring Judaeans who should take this unique opportunity to set up Solomon's 'Greater Israel'. At the same time, they will clean up the sanctuaries, appease Yhwh's wrath against Israel and re-establish kingly rule. Who could resist such an offer?

No King, No Peace
The ease with which the Danites conquered Dan is explained with a rather complicated verse. The people of Laish 'dwelt in security, after the manner of the Sidonians, quiet and unsuspecting, lacking nothing that is in the land, and possessing wealth, far from the Sidonians and having no dealings with any one' (Judg. 18.7). However, during Josiah's reign, Sidon does not exist any more. It has been destroyed by Esarhaddon (680–669 BCE) and replaced by Kar-Esarhaddon, the capital of an Assyrian province. Tyre is still standing on its island, but all its continental territory has been given over to Kar-Esarhaddon around 640 BCE, about the time when Josiah becomes king at Jerusalem (see Chapter 3).

---

28. A. Malamat, 'The Danite Migration and the Pan-Israelite Exodus-Conquest: A Biblical Narrative Pattern', *Biblica* 51 (1970), pp. 1-16 (7).
29. Malamat, 'Danite Migration', pp. 9-10.
30. Against Bauer, 'Anti-Spy Story', pp. 37-47.

The Sidonians of Josiah's days had therefore no king, no army, they lived within the Assyrian provincial system like Israel and Dan. Although the Sidonians did not officially bear the name of Sidonians any more, this description fits well with v. 7. The general prosperity and relative tranquillity are characteristics of seventh century BCE Palestine. The strange lesson אֵין־מַכְלִים 'there was no one speaking with authority' (v. 7) from a root *klm* attested in Akkadian and Arabic, does not need to be explained as a corruption of אֵין־מֶלֶךְ 'there was no king'.[31] It is a kind of pun that amounts to the same result since it is usually a king that speaks with authority. Once again, Josiah ignores the Assyrian king, and he uses a rare word in Hebrew *mklym* to suggest that the Assyrians kings are no proper kings *mlkym*, Dan is in the same situation than Israel during the days of the Judges, there is no king in charge.

However, how could the fact that Laish was far from Sidon רְחוֹקָה־הִיא מִצִּידוֹן explain the absence of deliverance אֵין־מַצִּיל if Sidon had no army anymore? Well, simply by the fact that the ranks of the Assyrian troops garrisoned in Kar-Esarhaddon and in the rest of Palestine at the end of Josiah's reign must have been much depleted, most contingents were then concentrated in Babylonia and in Assyria proper. This fact explains how Josiah was able to annex Benjamin without provoking any reaction before 609 BCE (Neko's execution of Josiah). Strengthened by this first success, Josiah could confidently affirm that no one would bat an eyelid if Judah invaded Israel as far as Dan.

The manner of the Sidonians (מִשְׁפָּט צִדֹנִים) therefore describes a kingless type of government as was already encountered in Tyre (Chapter 3). The promonarchical refrain (Judg. 17.6; 18.1) makes the same assertion for Israel: 'in those days there was no king in Israel'. Israelite and Sidonian kings had been replaced by governors, judges may have run Tyre, but as the Assyrian king and his troops were busy on other fronts, 'each one did what was right in his own eyes' (Judg. 17.6).

The Pro-monarchical Refrain
There is therefore good ground to follow Noth and keep the refrain within the first edition of Judg. 17–18.[32] The refrain not only explains the

31. A.A. Macintosh, 'The Meaning of *MKLYM* in Judges xviii 7', *VT* 35 (1985), pp. 68-77.

32. M. Noth, 'The Background of Judges 17-18', in B. Anderson and W. Harrelson (eds.), *Israel's Prophetic Heritage: Essays in Honor of James Muilenburg* (New York: Harper, 1962), pp. 68-85 (79): 'The formulas in Judges 17–18, unlike those in Judges 19–21, are located in places which are not so much exposed to redactional additions as

vulnerability of Dan and of the rest of Israel, but also calls for the re-establishment of kingship to avoid such aberrant behaviour as Micah's and the Danites'. The refrain regrets the absence of a king but does not indicate where the throne of this king should be. According to the hypothesis of a Josianic edition of Judg. 17–18, Josiah is deploring the fact that he is not ruling over the whole of Israel. He is promising that his royal supervision over the cults will be a blessing for all.[33]

These two chapters are therefore more programmatic than polemical. Bethel is not mentioned because it has already been annexed and purified (2 Kgs 23.15). There is no need to postulate any hidden polemics,[34] Josiah is simply preaching in favour of the second phase of his operation כל־ישראל 'all Israel' under one king.

Secondary Additions

Accepting a Josianic date for Judg. 17–18 does not exclude later additions. Becker believes that the small phrase telling Micah's return of the stolen silver ועתה אשיבנו לך (17.3bß) is secondary because it seems to belongs to Micah's speech but is inserted into the mother's reply.[35] The *BHS* editor suggests to transfer it at the end of v. 2a, without textual backing. But this is unnecessary as the words 'now therefore I will return it to you' can also mean that the mother is giving back to Micah what he just returned to her.

The notice concerning the patriarch Dan is not necessarily later than Josiah as Dan was probably already present in the Song of Deborah (Judg. 5.17), well before the formation of the twelve tribes system.

Micah's 'house of god' בית־אלהים (Judg. 17.5) is too well attested as baethylos[36] to need to be understood as a later polemic against Bethel.[37]

---

are the beginning and the end of narrative units. In Judges 17–18, they are found, rather, in the midst of the narrative and at conspicuous places: at the junctures between the beginning of the chief theme and the first subsidiary theme, and between the introductions of the two subsidiary themes. This means that they have been placed in their present locations by someone who comprehended the interior structure of the narrative, and most probably this was the author himself.'

33. Noth, 'Background', pp. 80-82 understands Judg. 17–18 as a critique of the tribal cult in Dan by the priests set in Dan by Jeroboam I.

34. Y. Amit, 'Hidden Polemics in the Conquest of Dan', *VT* 40 (1990), pp. 4-20 (12-19).

35. Becker, *Richterzeit*, p. 230.

36. A. de Pury, *Promesse divine et légende cultuelle dans le cycle de Jacob* (EB; Paris: J. Gabalda, 1975), pp. 425-28.

37. Against Becker, *Richterzeit*, p. 231.

The ephod and the teraphim (Judg. 18.14, 17, 18.20) could be later additions as these elements play no role in the story,[38] although nothing permits us to affirm it.

The only definitely secondary element within Judg. 17–18 is therefore in the last verses, namely the chronological note concerning Gershom, the captivity of the land and Shiloh (Judg. 18.30-31). This notice involves issues opposing different priestly groups that probably belong to the second temple period, when Jerusalem finally managed to replace Bethel, but one can hardly be more precise.[39]

Reading Judg. 17–18 as a Josianic manifesto for the annexation of Israel simplifies the literary history of these chapters.[40] Their pro-monarchical stance is quite natural when Josiah is preparing to replace the governors of the Israelite Assyrian provinces. That Josiah was executed before he could realize his plan is of no consequence because the migration as such is fictitious,[41] the only historically attested Danites are the inhabitants of the city of Dan. The choice of Dan as the destination of the Shephelah migrants was dictated by Josiah's ambition to establish a united kingdom of Israel from Dan to Beer-sheba. That the new dwellers of the city of Dan were descendants of a patriarch called Dan provided Josiah with immediate legitimacy over Israelite territory as far as Dan since the inhabitants of the Judaean Shefela and those of the city of Dan were from the same stock.

The artificial character of this Danite migration from the Shefela to Dan did not escape the scrutiny of the redactors of the books of Chronicles where Dan designates the city (1 Chron. 21.2; 2 Chron. 16.4; 30.5) or one of Israel's sons (1 Chron. 2.2). Interestingly, no offspring nor any inheritance is attributed to Dan in 1 Chron. 7. On the contrary, Kiriath-jearim, Manoah,[42] Zorah and Eshtaol appear as clanic designations within Judah's

---

38. Becker, *Richterzeit*, p. 231.

39. J. Blenkinsopp, 'The Judean Priesthood during the Neo-Babylonian and Achaemenid Periods: A Hypothetical Reconstruction', *CBQ* 60 (1998), pp. 25-43 (34-39).

40. According to Noth, 'Background', p. 82, the original pro-monarchical story behind Judg. 17–18 which he dates during the reign of Jeroboam I was not integrated within DH because DtrG could not accept Jeroboam's golden calf, nor Jeroboam's pro-monarchical stance. Judges 17–18 had therefore to be integrated later. Noth does not commit himself on the questions of why and where it was preserved, or why it was finally integrated into Judges.

41. Bauer, *Warum?*, p. 445.

42. Without presuming on the reality of Manahath as being a toponym or clan designation in 1 Chron. 2.52-54 (on which see E.A. Knauf, 'Manahath' and

descent and inheritance (4.2; 2 Chron. 11.10).[43] Zorah and Eshtaol are listed as Calebite clan belonging to Judah (1 Chron. 2.54-55), thus cutting short further speculations about Danite territories west of Jerusalem.

Finally, Judg. 17–18 are not the first appendix to the book of Judges, but the last part of its Josianic edition. This editorial stage is by far the largest one. Manasseh first added Judg. 1* and possibly Othniel to Bethel's book of Saviours. Then Josiah inserted his own introduction in Judg. 2* (the schema), critical material with the anonymous prophet in Judg. 6*, the judges and the Danites at the end of what became the book of Judges extending from Judg. 1* to Judg. 18* (the Jephthah and Samson narratives excluded). The death of Josiah marks the end of the long period of stability and prosperity that sustained a rich literary activity. The political situation during the reigns of the last kings of Judah was not so favourable. These kings were puppets installed and removed by Egypt and then by Babylon at a fast rate. Jerusalem was split by internecine fights that prevented the court from following a coherent political line. These factors do not preclude a post-Josianic date for Judg. 17–18: the defeat of the Babylonian troops in Egypt (601 BCE) could have been understood in Jerusalem as indicating that times were ripe to complete Josiah's plan for the conquest of Israel as far as Dan.[44] This would account for the position of Judg. 17–18 after the judges, and conveniently fill the gap between Josiah and Jerusalem's destruction. An early sixth century BCE date for Judg. 17–18 is therefore possible, although, for simplicity's sake, this 'deutero-Josianic' edition is kept under Josiah's reign. In any case, after 609 BCE, Judaean literature had entered post-classical times, the maturity of the long reign of Manasseh and the euphoria of Josiah's days had given way to turmoil leading to the 586 BCE conflagration.

However, the destruction of Jerusalem did not mark the end of the Judaean State, nor of the literary activity on the book of Judges. Chapter 5 is devoted to the Jephthah and Samson narrative that constitute the next editorial stage in Judges.

'Manahathites', in *ABD* 4 (New York: Doubleday, 1992), pp. 493-94), Manahath may simply refer to Manoah, Samson's father (Judges 13).

43. Niemann, 'Zorah', pp. 30-35.

44. As suggested orally by E.A. Knauf.

Chapter 5

DEMYTHOLOGIZING IN BETHEL, THE LOSERS: JUDGES 10–16

Jephthah and *Samson* are considered together as their heroes are neither saviours nor judges. Although both narratives begin like all saviour narratives with the phrase 'And the sons of Israel did what was evil in the eyes of Yhwh' (Judg. 10.6; 13.1), the two cycles do not end with an era of peace. Neither Jephthah nor Samson deliver Israel like the saviours did. Jephthah subdued the Ammonites (Judg. 11.33), but his victory inaugurates an annual grieving ritual in memory of his daughter (Judg. 11.40) and the massacre of forty-two thousand Ephraimites (Judg. 12.6). Samson was, right from the start, only expected to begin to save Israel (Judg. 13.5) and he ended up dying with his enemies (Judg. 16). Moreover, the place of Jephthah and Samson in Judg. 10–16 clearly indicates that they were not part of the book of Saviours.[1]

As for judging, Judg. 12.7; 15.20 and 16.31 do note that Jephthah and Samson judged Israel. However, they did not produce the large offsprings that characterized the judges. Jephthah sacrifices his only daughter and Samson is never depicted as a father. These fundamental differences render Noth's hypothesis that Jephthah belonged both to the saviours and to the judges rather unlikely.[2] Indeed, Jephthah's story is set right in the middle of the list of judges which it cuts across (Judg. 10.6–12.8). This insertion can be understood as a clue to the secondary character of Jephthah and Samson. Due to the difference of nature of their narratives, compared with either the saviours or the judges stories, *Jephthah* was inserted within the list of judges and not simply after the list, in order precisely to ensure that *Jephthah* and *Samson* would not risk being removed from the book of Judges by later editors. Of course, it is not theoretically impossible that Jephthah belonged originally to the judges, but since no charac-

---

1. W. Richter, 'Die Überlieferungen um Jephtah, Ri 10, 17-12, 6', *Biblica* 47 (1966), pp. 485-556.
2. Noth, *ÜS*, pp. 48-49.

teristics of the judges are now visible in the Jephthah narrative, one would have to postulate that what made Jephthah a judge (children, donkeys, towns) was edited out. It is therefore preferable to avoid such an unnecessary hypothesis and consider *Jephthah* and *Samson* for what they now stand: heroes who arose like saviours but ended in tragedy. They can only be anti-saviours, losers.[3]

Judges 10.6-16: Introduction to the Losers

There is also a literary reason to lump Jephthah and Samson together into a particular category. Judges 10.6aα copies the first element of the frames of saviour narratives (ויספו בני ישראל לעשות הרע בעיני יהוה 'The sons of Israel continued to do what was evil in the sight of Yhwh') but the evil is immediately qualified as serving the Baals and the Ashtaroth, the gods of Aram, of Sidon, of Moab, of the sons of Ammon and of the Philistines, in a manner similar to the schema and the anonymous prophet. The apostasy provokes Yhwh's wrath (Judg. 10.7//2.14; 3.8) who delivers Israel into the hands of the Philistines and of the sons of Ammon. Philistines and sons of Ammon are precisely the last enemies mentioned in v. 6, and they will be Samson and Jephthah's adversaries respectively. It is therefore clear that this passage introduces both narratives and they should be considered together.

The Ammonite oppression (Judg. 10.8-9) is directed against Gilead and even (גם) against Judah, Benjamin and the house of Ephraim, a clue to the Judaean origin of the stories. When the Israelites (not Judah!) cry to Yhwh (v. 10), Yhwh refuses to deliver and suggests rather ironically that Israel should go and cry (לכו זעקו) to the other gods (vv. 11-14), although Israel's cries are immediately followed by a confession of sin (v. 10) in which Israel spontaneously accuses itself of apostasy. Israel readily admits its sin again (v. 15) and puts away the foreign gods to serve Yhwh (v. 16). However, in spite of this show of good will, Yhwh does not send any saviour, he merely tempers his anger (ותקצר נפשו) in the face of the suffering of his people (v. 16).

This passage is therefore similar to the sermon of the anonymous prophet (Judg. 6.7-10): it is an editorial stitch joining *Jephthah* and *Samson* to the end of the book of Saviours and to the judges' list.

---

3.   Thanks to Denise Stephanus (Geneva, 1999) for the suggestion.

Judges 10.17–12.7: Jephthah the First Loser

Judges 10.17–11.11: A Cadi Instead of a Saviour
The Ammonites call up their troops (וַיִּצָּעֲקוּ) and invade Gilead. As Yhwh
sends no saviour, the elders seek a chief (רֹאשׁ vv. 17-18). A biographical
note tells of Jephthah's previous expulsion from his father's house.[4] As the
son of a *zonah*, he is not entitled to a share of the paternal heritage because
his father fostered other sons with his primary wives.[5] Jephthah survives at
the head of a gang of good-for-nothings (אֲנָשִׁים רֵיקִים Judg. 11.1-3).

The Gilead elders offer him the position of champion (קָצִין) to fight the
Ammonites and promise to place him at the head of Gilead in case of victory, thus giving him a chance to recover his lost status (Judg. 11.5-10).[6]

The story is interrupted by a long speech by Jephthah proving the
legitimacy of Israelite Transjordan possessions (Judg. 11.12-28). This will
be examined in Chapter 7 as it seems related to the Maccabaean campaigns in Transjordan.

Judges 11.29-40: Jephthah's Vow
Interrupted in v. 11, the Jephthah narrative now continues with the coming
of Yhwh's spirit on Jephthah (v. 29) and his immediate departure across
Ammonite territory. Geographical indications are as vague here as they are
for the Ammonite attack (v. 17). In spite of the ambiguity of the term
Gilead,[7] the story is clearly set in Northern Gilead. Jephthah leaves Tob
for Mizpah on the Jabbok (v. 11) and crosses over (v. 29) to rout the

---

4.   Jephthah is a toponym in Josh. 15.43 (in Judah) and 19.14 (in Zebulun). In
Judges, Jephthah √פתח 'to open' is the man who opened his mouth (see Judg. 11.35,
36): B. Webb, *The Book of Judges: An Integrated Reading* (JSOTSup, 46; Sheffield:
JSOT Press, 1987), p. 74. J. Classeens, 'Notes on Characterisation in the Jephthah Narrative', *JNES* 22 (1996), pp. 107-115 (111), counted 129 words for Jephthah's actions
against 360 words for his speeches.
5.   M.C. Astour, 'Tamar the Hierodule: An Essay in the Method of Vestigal
Motifs', *JBL* 85 (1966), pp. 185-96 (187); and Lipit-Ishtar Code: M.T. Roth, *Laws Collections from Mesopotamia and Asia Minor* (Atlanta: Scholars Press, 1994), pp. 23-35.
6.   For the difference between קָצִין and רֹאשׁ see H.N. Rösel, 'Jephthah und das
Problem der Richter', *Biblica* 61 (1980), pp. 251-556.
7.   Gilead sometimes also designates territory south of the Jabbok: B. MacDonald,
'Ammonite Territory and Sites', in B. MacDonald and R.W. Younker (eds.), *Ancient
Ammon* (Studies in the History and Culture of the Ancient Near East, 17; Leiden: E.J.
Brill, 1999), pp. 30-66 (35).

Ammonites near Rabbat-Ammon as indicated by the three locations in v. 33: Abel-keramim is SE of Rabbat-Ammon,[8] Aroer is Moabite (Ḥirbet 'Arā'ir 4 km S of Dibon) and Minnith is probably Tel el-'Umēri between Aroer and Abel-keramim near the Ammonite city.[9] Jephthah's victory pushes back the Ammonites into their territory while their city remains impregnable. It is therefore unnecessary to remove v. 33a from the original story.[10]

Before the attack, Jephthah pronounces the famous vow (v. 31) that turns his victory into a family tragedy. Jephthah is no saviour, in spite of the use of elements from the saviour frame (evil, divine wrath, oppression, cries, spirit and subduing of the enemy, see Figure 1). This is highlighted by the fact that the consequences of the vow are much more developed (vv. 34-40) than the battle itself which is related in very broad terms (vv. 32-33).

The Folklorization of the Tammuz Ritual

Jephthah is only a pale imitation of the saviours, and the vow makes sure that the hero is robbed of his victory. Nevertheless, the Jephthah story is still a victory tale, but the vanquished enemy is found at the end, in vv. 37-40. The narrative has nothing to teach about human sacrifices, nor about vows. Although these matters come to mind immediately, they are in no way thematized. The sacrifice of the girl is discreetly brushed over: ויעש לה את־נדרו אשר נדר 'Jephthah did to her his vow that he had vowed' (v. 39). Before that, the father readily admits that he spoke inconsiderately (פציתי־פי v. 35) and it is the daughter herself who summons him to do as he said (עשה לי כאשר יצא מפיך v. 36). Both actors are in full agreement, no narrative tension is built. The daughter asks for one favour only, to be able to 'go down on' the mountains (ירדתי על־ההרים)[11] to cry (בכה) over her childless condition (בתולה)[12] with her companions (v. 37). This is the

8. Saḥāb: E.A. Knauf, 'Abel Keramim', *ABD* 1, pp. 10-11; for other suggestions: MacDonald, 'Ammonite Territory', p. 34.

9. S. Mittmann, 'Aroer, Minnith und Abel Keramim (Jdc 11, 33)', *ZDPV* 85 (1969), pp. 63-75 (66); E.A. Knauf, 'Aroer', *RGG*, 1 (Tübingen: J.C.B. Mohr, 1998), p. 795.

10. Against M. Wüst, 'Die Einschaltung in die Jiftachgeschichte', *Biblica* 56 (1975), pp. 464-79.

11. Possible link with the first day of the Greek festival of Thesmophoria (ἄνοδος: N.M.P. Nilsson and M.H. Jameson, 'Thesmophoria', *OCD*, p. 1509.

12. Rather than 'virginity', a concept that has evolved too far from its original meaning of the absence of pregnancy (indicated by the last menstruation before

point of the whole Jephthah narrative: the ritual lament seemingly established in memory of her untimely death that prevented her to produce an offspring (v. 38). As is often the case with etiological narratives, the described reality precedes the narrative but the narrative offers a new meaning for it. The text alludes to a well-established custom (חק) in Israel, recorded elsewhere in the Bible (Ezek. 8.14; Isa. 17.10-11), namely, the laments of women over the young Dumuzi/Tammuz.

Dumuzi/Tammuz was a young Mesopotamian bridegroom who died without heir and therefore he had no time to establish a dynasty. This myth was an important element of the original sacred marriage cult, but as from the Old Babylonian period (c. 1500 BCE), the myth was not used any more in this context and Dumuzi remained as a tragic hero victim of the goddess Inanna.

Inanna decides to go down to the Underworld, probably to enlarge her dominion.[13] Several mythological compositions tell how she manages to come back from the kingdom from which no one comes back.[14] Inanna has to negotiate her return by promising to offer a substitute. Followed on her way back by demons charged to bring the substitute back to the Underworld, Innana barely manages to avoid that her associates be taken. Finally, it is the shepherd Dumuzi who is caught.[15] But Dumuzi and his sister Geshtinna protest bitterly and Inanna yields to their cries: 'You (Dumuzi will spend) one half of the year and your sister (will spend one half of the year in the Netherworld)'.[16]

Dumuzi must take Inanna's place in the Underworld but for half of the year he can go back and his sister replaces him.

marriage) towards intact hymen: E. Cassin, 'Virginité et stratégie du sexe', in *idem* (ed.), *Le semblable et le différent: symbolismes du pouvoir dans le Proche-Orient ancien* (Paris, La découverte, 1987), pp. 338-57.

13. J. Bottéro and S.N. Kramer, *Lorsque les dieux faisaient l'homme* (Paris: Gallimard, 1989), p. 290.

14. *Inanna's Descent to the Nether World*: S.N. Kramer, *Sumerian Mythology* (Philadelphia: University of Pennsylvania Press, 2nd edn, 1972), pp. 83-96; and *Dumuzi's dream*: B. Alster, *Dumuzi's Dream: Aspects of Oral Poetry in a Sumerian Myth* (Mesopotamia, 1; Copenhagen: Akademisk Forlag, 1972). F. Bruschweiler, *Inanna: La déesse triomphante et vaincue dans la cosmologie sumérienne* (Cahiers du CEPOA, 4; Leuven: Peeters, 1987).

15. Bottéro and Kramer, *Lorsque les dieux*, pp. 288-310.

16. W.R. Sladek, *Inanna's Descent to the Nether World* (J. Hopkins University Dissertation 1974, Ann Arbor, MI: University Microfilms, 1979), p. 181; Bottéro and Kramer, *Lorsque les dieux*, pp. 290, 388-304.

The descent of the hero was lamented each year by women,[17] in early summer when the vegetation dies and Dumuzi is mourned.[18] The Assyrians celebrated the *Taklimtu*, an annual ceremony in which the statue of Dumuzi was bathed and anointed for the solemn lying in state before his departure to the Nether World.[19]

Judges 11 may be aimed at diverting the laments of Israelite women for Dumuzi towards an Israelite hero and towards Yhwh his god. The goddess Inanna is replaced by Yhwh, brother and sister Dumuzi and Geshtinna become father and daughter. Nevertheless, Jephthah bears Dumuzi's tragic traits of the sympathetic human hero, the innocent victim embroiled into some nasty scuffles between the gods, but eventually the only one to foot the bill. As will become clearer in *Samson,* the theomachy is not as obvious in *Jephthah* than it is in *Samson*. But their common introduction indicates that they have to be understood together. And *Jephthah* does lead to the transfer of the benefits of a ritual offered to one god (or divinized hero) onto another god (Yhwh).

Jephthah's daughter steps in like Geshtinna to partly relieve her father from his fateful lot. That her father's vow brings about her premature death establishes the parallel with Dumuzi as it cuts short Jephthah's hopes of establishing a dynasty. But Jephthah's daughter's death also off-sets any glory the 'saviour' could have derived from his victory over the Ammonites. This point reveals the agenda of the creators of the Losers. The Assyrian-friendly heroes of the book of Saviours are bygones, the hopes they fostered proved unfounded, a more sober outlook is required to cope with a new situation. The details of this new context are not yet apparent, suffice now to underline the fact that what is at stake here goes far beyond the straight-forward dressing up of a mythological hero with Yahwistic garb. The wailing women who used to mourn the death of a mythological hero or of a vegetation god at the door of Yhwh's house (Ezek. 8.14), should not simply transfer their devotion to Jephthah. They

17. Rite practiced until the Middle Ages among Sabaean women in Harran: D. Chwolson, *Die Ssabier und der Ssabismus* (Amsterdam: Oriental Press, reprint of St. Petersburg 1856 edn, 1965), p. 27.

18. R. Kutscher, 'The Cult of Dumuzi/Tammuz', in J. Klein and A. Skaist (eds.), *Bar-Ilan Studies in Assyriology: Dedicated to Pinhas Artzi* (Ramat Gan: Bar-Ilan Univ. Press, 1990), pp. 29-44.

19. J. Lassøe, *Studies on the Assyrian Ritual and Series Bît Rimki* (Copenhagen: 1955), p. 13.

should rather repeat (תנה[20] Judg. 11.40) the story of the untimely death of Jephthah's daughter. Year after year, the daughters of Israel will literally repeat the sad tale of the Gileadite daughter instead of celebrating the feat of an Israelite saviour. A page has been turned. Israel, where are your heroes?

The Demythizing Process
Myths change,[21] myths die[22] but rites survive. It is improbable that this sad story put an end to the summer wailing and established a new ritual: no Jewish tradition preserved a festival or a rite connected with Jephthah's daughter. On the contrary, Jephthah is abhorred, lest people think that human sacrifices were practised in Israel.[23] However, *Jephthah* was probably never meant to found any actual ceremony or ritual. It is destructive rather than constructive. Israelite heroes and Assyrian mythology are to be forsaken since events have proved that they are delusory. This frontal attack against mythology, one of the cultural hallmarks of the Assyrian power, has certainly transformed the religion of Israel and Judah and turned it into Deuteronomistic Yahwism.

This process could be termed demythization[24] and has often been alluded to but understood in quite different ways. G. von Rad[25] and W.H. Schmidt[26] saw it as the absorption of Canaanite traditions into Yhwh's cult.[27] The 'pure' Israelite religion was then understood to have been 'canaanized' when the nomadic tribes settled in the land.[28] J. Heller applied this concept to the Ugaritic pantheon: Israel would have taken over

---

20. תנה is Aramaic for Hebrew שנה to repeat, a direct quote of Judg. 5.11, by the authors of the Jephthah's story.

21. G. Didi-Huberman, 'Celui par qui s'ouvre la terre', in G. Didi-Huberman, R. Garbetta and M. Morgaine (eds.), *Saint Georges et le dragon* (Paris: Adam Biro, 1994), pp. 19-124 (20).

22. C. Lévi-Strauss, 'Comment meurent les mythes', in *idem* (ed.), *Anthropologie structurale deux* (Paris: Plon, 1973), pp. 301-318.

23. H.L. Ginsberg and N.M. Sarna, 'Jephthah', in C. Roth (ed.), *Encyclopaedia Judaica* (Jerusalem: Keter, 1971), 9.1341-1344.

24. Not to be confused with Bultmann's demythologization.

25. G. von Rad, *Theologie des Alten Testaments* (München: Chr. Kaiser Verlag, 1957), 1.32.36-37; 2.351.355.361.

26. W.H. Schmidt, *Königtum Gottes in Ugarit und Israel: Zur Herkunft der Königsprädikation Jahwes* (BZAW, 80; Berlin: Töpelmann, 1961), pp. 75-76.

27. Von Rad, *Theologie,* 1.31.

28. Von Rad, *Theologie,* 1.33.

some Baalic attributes (nature and vegetation) for Yhwh, originally an El type of creator god, too distant to be manipulated in the cult. Demythization consists in transforming links between gods into links between gods and humans; Yhwh becomes creator and king of humans rather than of other gods. Demythization is an anthropologizing process.[29]

W. Herrmann also sees demythization at work in the context of Josiah's reign;[30] he speaks of folklorization of myths[31] when myths are considered dangerous or unacceptable by the ruling party, in particular during reformation upheavals. Rites need to be dealt with as they manifestly reinforce resistance to change. Ritual gestures are reoriented to foster new attitudes and new beliefs, supported by the authorities. Lelièvre believes that this process was reversed after the defeat in 586 BCE and that mythology was then taken up again to contradict events:[32] 'Yhwh victorious over Yam' as an answer to 'Yhwh defeated by Marduk'! Lelièvre's description of alternating attitudes towards myths following the vagaries of political fortunes is extremely interesting, although its sequence may be improved upon.

A Post-Assyrian Demythizing Process
The exaltation of Josiah by the books of Kings tends to concentrate most on reforming endeavours during Josiah's reign at the exclusion of other periods. It is important to note that Josiah's reign still belongs to the Assyrian period, even if he rebelled against his Assyrian lord. The end of the Assyrian Empire may have eventually left deeper marks on Judaean theology than Josiah's death in Megiddo. Obviously, the Bible is not too explicit on the shock experienced in Judah by the fall of an Empire considered as evil, although Habakkuk remains a fine example of the fear that the 'Chaldeans' (Hab. 1.6) inspired on the Assyrian vassals: they were not overjoyed by the fall of Niniveh. The western parts of the Empire (the

29. J. Heller, 'Die Entmythisierung des ugaritischen Pantheons im AT', in *idem* (ed.), *An der Quelle des Lebens* (Frankfurt am Main: Lang, 1988), pp. 173-83.

30. W. Herrmann, 'Das Aufleben des Mythos unter den Judäern während des babylonischen Zeitalters', *BN* 40 (1987), pp. 97-129 (127-28).

31. Folklore was long identified with oral traditions: P.G. Kilpatrick, *The Old Testament and Folklore Study* (JSOTSup, 62; Sheffield: JSOT Press, 1988), pp. 13-72, 116-17. See Knauf, *Umwelt*, pp. 269-72, *idem*, 'Der Exodus zwischen Mythos und Geschichte: Zur priesterschriftlichen Rezeption der Schilfmeer-Geschichte in Ex 14', in R.G. Kratz, T. Krüger and K. Schmid (eds.), *Schriftauslegung in der Schrift* (BZAW, 300; Berlin: W. de Gruyter, 2000), pp. 73-84.

32. A. Lelièvre, 'YHWH et la mer dans les Psaumes', *RHPR* 56 (1976), p. 275.

situation was obviously very different in Babylonia and in Elam), had bene-fited from an extraordinary long and prosperous era. Everyone realized that they had much to lose. The fate of Palestine under Babylonian rule confirmed those fears: Philistia and Judah were devastated, Jerusalem was razed, and the whole of Palestine was marginalized. Time was ripe in Babylonian Mizpah and Bethel to rethink the whole concept of Israel's position in the world and vis-à-vis its god.

The importance of Bethel. Bethel, the cradle of the book of Saviours according to Knauf's hypothesis tested in the present work, seems to have been an important centre from the early Israelite history throughout the royal period (1 Kgs 12-13) and into Assyrian rule (2 Kgs 17). There is no indication that the place was destroyed when Josiah took over the Ben-jamin area.

As from 590 BCE, the pro-Babylonian party (the Shafan family) set up a provisional government in Mizpah to anticipate the fall of Jerusalem and collaborate with the Babylonians (Jer. 6.1; 7; 21.9; 22; 26–29; 32; 34; 38). Mizpah replaced Jerusalem as the Judaean capital even before 586 BCE (Jer. 38.19) which explains why Benjaminite territory suffered no harm from Nebuchadnezzar's troops.[33] Located a few kilometres north of Miz-pah, Bethel served as the official cultic centre for the Babylonian province, and the Bethel traditions continued to be transmitted (Jacob,[34] Saul, Hosea, Amos, Jeremiah and, of course, the book of Saviours). It is probably in Bethel that most, if not all, of the Judaean traditions now in the Bible were preserved between 586 BCE and the restoration of Jerusalem in the Persian period. The date and the circumstances of the reconstruction of Jerusalem are impossible to determine.[35] However, the books of Ezra and Nehemiah do not hide the fact that it was a long and difficult process. Mizpah was probably no happier than Samaria to see the recovery of the 'rebellious city' קריתא מרדתא (Ezra 4). The consecration of the Jerusalem sanctuary did not cause the immediate closure of Bethel's temple. Its temple school

---

33. O. Lipschits, 'Benjamin Region under the Babylonian Rule', *TA* 26 (1999), pp. 155-90 (159-65).

34. A. de Pury, 'Situer le cycle de Jacob: Quelques réflexions, vingt-cinq ans plus tard', in A. Wénin (ed.), *Studies in the Book of Genesis: Literature, Redaction and History* (BETL, 155; Leuven: University Press, 2001), pp. 213-41.

35. L.L. Grabbe, *Judaism from Cyrus to Hadrian* 1 (Minneapolis: Fortress, 1992), pp. 126-29.

may have continued to operate as late as 450 BCE.[36] Archaeology is so far unable to provide more indications pertaining to the end of Bethel.

It is therefore unnecessary to wait for the Persian or even the Hellenistic period to find a suitable historical context for the story of Jephthah's vow. The Bethel priests had all the necessary information at hand since the seventh century BCE. They certainly did not have to read Euripides' Iphygenia to imagine Jephthah's vow.[37] But Josiah's Deuteronomists are not the most likely authors of such an all-out onslaught on Mesopotamian culture. They lacked the necessary hindsight to go beyond 'idol-smashing'. Babylonian Bethel provides a more convincing background for the mournful and heart-searching reconsideration of both the book of Saviours and of the book of Judges. Taking up the Josianic critique of the BS's cries that were supposed to bring about immediate deliverance from enemies, the conclusion of *Jephthah* invites Israel to mourn rather than cry (בכה instead of זעק Judg. 12.38). But here, the critique goes further, it is also directed against the judges whose glory resided in over abundant offspring: Jephthah's only daughter is to be mourned yearly for ever. No actual ritual but a kind of literary mourning process is intended here. Alongside the heirless daughter, it is Jephthah, and with him all the saviours and all the judges, that are deprived of successors. Jephthah, already in the middle of the list of Judges, forecasts the end of the period of the Saviours and that of the Judges. The great hopes born in 720 (the Bethel book of Saviours), in 700 (Manasseh's book of Saviours) and 640 BCE (Josiah's book of Judges) have to be forsaken. Weep Israel, lament Judah, Jephthah's daughter is dead, your hopes are gone! Gone are the days of the blessed Assyrian Empire.

However, we have not yet reached the end of the losers' narratives, not even of Jephthah's story. A strange murderous encounter between Gilead and Ephraim at the end of the Jephthah narrative has to be considered.

Judges 12.1-6: Cries and Cries, but no Saviour!
This passage starts with the BS' motto: 'they cried' ויצעק but used in the sense of mobilizing an army as in Judg. 10.17. It is a large Ephraimite troop that comes against Jephthah. His victory against the Ammonites, already overshadowed by his vow, is now a pretext for civil war. Jephthah

36. Blenkinsopp, 'Judean Priesthood', p. 34 n. 26 dates the destruction between 540 and 450 BCE! See literature in Lipschits, 'Benjamin Region', pp. 171-72 n. 31.
37. Against Th. Römer, 'Why Would the Deuteronomists Tell about the Sacrifice of Jephtah's Daughter?', *JSOT* 77 (1998), pp. 27-38.

is accused of having refused to call (קְרֹא) Ephraim in an episode reminiscent of Judg. 8.1-3 (against Gideon), and he is threatened with having his house burned on top of him (v. 1), a punishment that will be endured by Samson's wife in Judg. 15.6. Jephthah overturns the accusation and claims that he was forced to attack the Ammonites alone when he realized that Ephraim would not save (יֹשֵׁעַ) him (vv. 2-3).

Jephthah's answer is puzzling, as no Gileadite call for help towards Ephraim is recorded in Judg. 10–12. One is tempted to find an answer in 1 Sam. 11 where the town of Jabesh-gilead is sending messengers in the hope to rally rescuers to deliver it from the Ammonites. Ephraim appears nowhere in that story and it is Saul the Benjaminite who brings salvation. It may therefore be safer to look for an explanation within the book of Judges: as has been seen in the book of Saviours, no saviour comes from Ephraim! The passage of Judg. 12.1-6 has therefore been added, together with its parallel in Judg. 8.1-3, to show that nothing but trouble comes from Ephraim!

Jephthah then gathers all the men of Gilead and strikes 42,000 Ephraimites. The fugitives of Ephraim are slaughtered at the Jordan fords when they betray their origin by being unable to pronounce 'shibboleth' the way the Gileadites do, saying 'sibboleth' instead. The pronunciation difference between Gilead and Ephraim was not between ס and שׁ as suggested by the Massoretic text of Judg. 12.6 but between [s] and [th] like the name of King Baalis in Jer. 40.14.[38]

A tentative suggestion can be offered for such a puzzling passage. Mizpah's new status as centre of Babylonian Judah may have created friction with Ephraim, designating here what was left of the Assyrian province of Samaria after Nebuchadnezzar's destructions. This problem, certainly not a new one, would deepen during the following periods and led to the final rupture with the Samaritans. Still today, Nablus' claims on Jerusalem have not abated.

Judges 12.7: Conclusion
Contrary to its introduction which imitates the saviours (Judg. 10.6) the conclusion of the Jephthah narrative closes upon a note imitating the judges, mentioning the length of jurisdiction and the burial place.

---

38. E.A. Knauf and S. Maáni, 'On the Phonemes of Fringe Canaanite: The Cases of Zerah-Udruh and "Kamashalta"', *UF* 19 (1987), pp. 91-94; G.A. Rendsburg, 'The Ammonite Phoneme /Ṯ/', *BASOR* 269 (1988), pp. 74-75 postulates the existence of a √tbl but admits that it is nowhere attested.

Two distinct editorial stages have been discerned within the Jephthah narrative. The story of the loser Jephthah, provisionally dated in the Babylonian period, is cut across by a long defence of Israelite territorial rights over Perea in Judg. 11.12-28, dating to the third century at the earliest. This passage will be considered in Chapter 7.

Judges 13–16: Samson, the Loser Who Began To Save

The Samson narrative is the longest and the most complete cycle of the book of Judges, covering the entire life of the hero, from conception to burial. Samson is a fascinating character, his feats, amorous and others, render the Biblical Obelix most attaching, so much so that in spite of his blatant heterodoxy, he even seems to have the sympathies of the editors of the book. He is never blamed, possibly because he expresses the protest of farmers against Philistine cities that exploit them:[39] like the brave ones in the Song of Deborah (Judg. 5.11), he goes down to the city to pull out its gates (Judg. 16.3).

Judges 14–15 form the core of the story and refer to a vast array of very ancient figures like the wild and hairy man (Enkidu, Laḥmu), the master of animals (lion and foxes) who fights bare-handed and ignores the refinements of civilisation (alcohol, razor).[40] Women initiate him and introduce him to city life.[41] Samson also presents similarities with Heracles[42] and the riddle-telling Sphinx.

With its four chapters, the Samson cycle presents itself as a self-sufficient composition and is thus often considered independent from the rest of the book. Richter follows Noth and considers that the Samson narrative was added with those of Jephthah and Eli by DtrG in order to create a

39. S. Niditch, 'Samson as Culture Hero, Trickster and Bandit: The Empowerment of the Weak', *CBQ* 52 (1990), pp. 608-624.

40. H. Gese, 'Die ältere Simsonüberlieferung (Richter c. 14-15)', in *idem* (ed.), *Alttestamentliche Studien* (Tübingen: J.C.B. Mohr, 1991), pp. 52-71.

41. G. Mobley, 'The Wild Man in the Bible and the Ancient Near-East', *JBL* 41 (1997), pp. 217-33.

42. O. Margalith, 'Samson's Foxes', *VT* 35 (1985), pp. 224-28; *idem,* 'More Samson's Legends', *VT* 36 (1986), pp. 397-405; *idem,* 'Samson's Riddles and Samson's Magic Locks', *VT* 36 (1986), pp. 225-34; *idem,* 'The Legends of Samson/Heracles', *VT* 37 (1987), pp. 63-70; and A. Meissner, 'Alles oder Nichts. Die Tragik des Helden Simson (Richter 13-16)', in D. Bauer and A. Meissner (eds.), *Männer weinen heimlich: Geschichten aus dem Alten Testament* (Stuttgart: Katholisches Bibelwerk, 1993), pp. 59-75.

period of the Judges spanning from Judg. 10 to 1 Sam. 12.[43] Becker skips over the whole Samson story and goes directly from the end of Jephthah's story onto Judg. 17.

Synchronist exegetes have reacted strongly against this lack of interest for Samson and have stressed the unity of the cycle. Moreover, because Judg. 13 was often considered secondary to the rest of the cycle by diachronists, it has been studied alongside the other chapters as a single literary programme. Much is here at stake: if Judg. 13 does not belong to it, the original story tends to reduce *Samson* to the rogue story of a libertine, later glossed over with the religious veneer of that secondary chapter.[44]

In order not to lose itself in the bulk of the Samson story, the present study will follow the path opened by H. Gese who perceived in Judg. 13–16 a vast programme of religious deconstruction in favour of radical Yahwism.[45] This programme is in fact similar to what was found in Judg. 11 with the sacrifice of Jephthah's daughter; demythization will therefore be the Ariadne thread that will lead the following enquiry through the labyrinth of Judg. 13–16.

No history of research will be presented as the recent monograph by Kim offers an excellent analysis of the research pertaining to the Samson cycle.[46] Again, the analysis will draw on as much historical data as possible, and a small presentation of the geographical framework of Samson's adventures should first set the scene.

Geographical Framework
Samson's adventures take place in Philistia (Zorah, Timnah, Ashkelon, Gaza) and Judah (Etam, Ramat-Lehi, Hebron). The frame sets Samson's family in Zorah (Judg. 13.2, 25; 16.31), at Tel Ṣar'a (Iron II) 3 km N of Beth-Shemesh (Ḥirbet er-Rumēle, MB-LB-Iron I-II). Samson is buried in the family vault between Zorah and Eshtaol (Išwa', Iron II). Samson loved Delilah 'in the Sorek valley' (Judg. 16.4), in the deep canyon dug by naḥal śorēq in the buffer zone between Judah and Philistia. The Bible preserves the memory of repeated fighting in this crucial area for the defence of

---

43. Richter, 'Jephtah', pp. 555-56; *idem, Bearbeitungen*, pp. 129, 131.
44. J.L. Crenshaw, *Samson: A Secret Betrayed, a Vow Ignored* (Atlanta: John Knox Press, 1978), p. 64.
45. Gese, 'Simsonüberlieferung', pp. 279-80.
46. Kim, *Structure*, pp. 1-114.

Jerusalem's access.[47] Tribal lists reveal the political complexity of this area: Beth-Shemesh and Eshtaol belong sometimes to Dan (Ir-Shemesh Josh. 19.41), sometimes to Judah (Josh. 15.33; 21.16).

Samson is therefore moving across borders, within a complicated and disputed area.

The Shephelah under the Assyrians and the Babylonians
Samson's life is a deadly fight against the Philistines, generally understood as the Iron I Sea-people who settled in the coastal area and threatened the very existence of Israel, even killing King Saul. However, according to the historical framework of this study, it is necessary to put Samson's enemies in the context of the seventh and sixth centuries BCE.

In retaliation for Hezekiah's involvement in the 705 BCE uprising, Sennacherib razed 46 towns and villages of the Judaean Shephelah, exiled 200,000 inhabitants and turned the area over to the Philistines. This deportation is the first and the most severe one ever experienced in Judah,[48] but it is generally forgotten.[49] This huge negative migratory flux is coherent with the overall Assyrian picture: compared to the other great deporting kings (Tiglath-pileser III and Sargon II), Sennacherib has the highest score with a grand total of 469,000 deportees.[50] The 200,000 exiles in 701 BCE[51] are comparable to the 208,000 from Babylonia in 705 BCE.[52] From the city of Samaria in 720 BCE, Sargon II counts 27,000 deportees.[53] There is therefore no reason to reject these figures as totally unrealistic,[54] although

---

47. 2 Kgs 14.11; 2 Chron. 11.10.

48. Compared to 3023 Judaeans in 597 BCE, 832 Jerusalemites in 586 BCE and 745 Judaeans in 582 BCE: see Jer. 52.28-30 and Knauf, 'Exil'.

49. S. Stohlmann, 'The Judean Exile after 701 B.C.E.', in W.W. Hallo, J.C. Moyer and L.G. Perdue (eds.), *Scripture in Context. II. More Essays on the Comparative Method* (Winona Lake: Eisenbrauns, 1983), pp. 147-75.

50. 393,000 for Tiglath-pileser and 239,000 for Sargon: B. Oded, *Mass Deportations and Deportees in the Neo-Assyrian Empire* (Wiesbaden: L. Reichert, 1979), p. 21. These numbers are likely to be below reality as some recorded deportations give no numbers. For the 157 military campaigns recorded over three centuries of Neo-Assyrian Empire, only 43 give numbers of deportees, which add up to 1, 2 million exiles. Oded believes that they would amount to 4, 5 millions.

51. Luckenbill, *Sennacherib*, p. 33.

52. Luckenbill, *Sennacherib*, p. 25.

53. Fuchs, *Inschriften Sargons*, pp. 197, 344 (Prunk 23-24).

54. Millard, 'Large Numbers', pp. 213-22 against Ungnad, 'Zahl' who thinks that

it is unlikely that the 200,000 of 701 BCE all came from the Shephelah. The text of Sennacherib's third campaign simply provides the total of deportees at the end of the report of the campaign that closed in Judah. Among the 200,000 were also people from other rebellious kingdoms, Sidonians, Byblians, etc.

However, the Assyrians reorganized the area. Large Assyrian investments turned Philistia into a vast 'industrial' area; Ekron and Timnah became centres of oil production while Ashkelon concentrated on wine. The seventh century BCE was a most prosperous one for the Philistine kingdoms (Ps. 60.10) and for Judah.

On the contrary, the Babylonian period was marked by sharp decline and even widespread destruction as the Babylonians ruined the area once they realized that they would not be able to conquer Egypt.

Judges 13.1; 15.20; 16.31: Frame of Samson's Cycle
As it was the case for Jephthah, the Samson narrative begins with the introduction formula of the saviour narratives: 'The sons of Israel did again what was evil in the sight of Yhwh and Yhwh gave them into the hands of the Philistines for 40 years' (Judg. 13.1). However, it has two conclusions imitating the judges' formula:

וישפט את־ישראל בימי פלשתים עשרים שנה

He judged Israel in the days of the Philistines 20 years (Judg. 15.20).

והוא שפט את־ישראל עשרים שנה

And he had judged Israel 20 years (Judg. 16.31b).

The narrative and the chronological note in Judg. 15.20 are not taken over in Judg. 16.31. Grammatically, Judg. 16.31 is not adding 20 years to the narrative but simply repeating the first conclusion. Kim notes that the formula בימי־פלשתים is most unusual and suggests that Judg. 15.20 read originally וימשל ישראל בפלשתים 'Israel was ruled by the Philistines' corresponding to Judg. 15.11b משלים בנו פלשתים 'the Philistines are ruling among us'.[55] The author of the frame would have modified Judg.

the figure of 200,150 deportees in 701 BCE is one hundred times too high. The Jerusalem Prism records the same number: P. Ling-Israel, 'The Sennakerib Prism in the Israel Museum', in J. Klein and A. Skaist (eds.), *Bar-Ilan Studies in Assyriology: Dedicated to Pinhas Artzi* (Ramat Gan: Bar-Ilan Univ. Press, 1990), pp. 213-48 (228).

55. Kim, *Structure*, p. 300.

15.20 when the Samson narrative was integrated into the book of Judges in order to make it fit with Judg. 16.31.

It is also possible to understand the second conclusion as the mark of a register shift that sets ch. 16 in a totally different kind of reality from the previous chapters. Thanks to the demythizing process, Judg. 16 is not the sequel of Judg. 13–15 but its image mirrored onto a higher plane, an indication that what is going on is happening in a kind of simultaneity or a different temporality. This point will come to light in Judg. 16.

Before that, the chronological framework structuring the book of Judges should be examined.

Chronology of the Book of Judges
The book of Saviours mentions lengths of foreign oppressions and lengths of peaceful intervals between each deliverance. The judges also have an indication of the length of their office. These years have been computed with other indications in the books of Joshua, Samuel and Kings in such a way as to reach the 480 years separating the Exodus from the beginning of the building of Solomon's temple according to 1 Kgs 6.1.

The majority of scholars who attempted to piece together the 480 years have included the 70 years of the judges' terms of office. Wellhausen is apparently the only one who did not include these 70 years in his calculation because he believed that Judg. 10.1-5 and 12.8-15 had been added on by a postexilic editor, well after the Deuteronomistic edition of the Historical books, which, according to him, was responsible for the chronology.[56] Wellhausen also noted that the 70 years of Tola, Jair, Ibzan, Elon and Abdon correspond to the sum of the Kushite (8), Moabite (18), Canaanite (20), Midianite (7) and Ammonite (18) years of oppressions. To reach the fateful 480 years, Wellhausen excludes Samson but attributes 50 years to Saul (for whom only two remain in 1 Sam. 13.1 since the rest of the number has dropped out) and to Samuel (who has none).

Another half-dozen attempts can be found in exegetical literature, all reaching 480 years in spite of the fact that they all consider different figures.[57] There are enough temporal indications scattered about in the

---

56. J. Wellhausen, 'Einleitung in das Alte Testament von Friedrich Bleek', in J. Bleek and A. Kamphausen (eds.), *Einleitung in das Alte Testament von Friedrich Bleek* (Berlin: G. Reimer, 1878), pp. 183-86: Moses 40 years + Joshua 30 (see Nöldeke) + peace 200 + oppression 71 + Jephthah 6 + Philistine rule in Samson's days 40 + from Saul to Samuel 50 + David 40 + Salomon 3 = 480 years.

57. Nöldeke, *Untersuchungen zur Kritik*, pp. 173-98, counts only reigns without

Former Prophets to afford a large number of possibilities. However, the incomplete lesson of 1 Sam. 13.1 for the length of Saul's reign prevents the recovery of all the components for the compute. Each author thus supplies a given number of years for Saul and for Samuel in order to reach 480 years. In fact, these 480 years could be nothing else than 12 generations of 40 years, although the indication of Solomon's fourth year when work on the temple began tends to indicate a more elaborate calculation.[58]

No attempt will be made here to offer yet another compute for this doomed enterprise. However, it is worth toying with these years for a while because something can be learnt from it. A cursory look at Figure 6 shows that the sum of all the chronological indications available between the Exodus and Solomon's fourth year amounts to 554 years and that it is necessary to exclude some dates to reach 480 years.

Without the judges, 14 years are missing, and these could be the ones that were lost for Saul's reign. The 40 years of Eli's judging could be reduced to 20 years according to the LXX which would leave 34 years for Saul. The lacuna in 1 Sam. 13.1 (x + 2 years) could be filled with either 12 or 32 years since both the Egyptian and the Phoenician-Aramaic systems (the use of letters of the alphabet as numerals is not attested before the

periods of oppression. He therefore makes up time periods for Joshua and Samuel and adds 2 years to Saul's reign. Noth, *ÜS*, pp. 18-27, adds the saviours, the first 3 judges, 20 years for Samson, 0 for Eli, 40 years for Samuel, 45 years for the desert and the conquest, 46 years from Saul to the forth year of Salomon = 481 years rounded off to 480 because the last year of David overlaps with Salomon's first year. W. Vollborn, 'Die Chronologie des Richterbuches', in J. Herrmann (ed.), *Festschrift Friedrich Baumgärtel* (EF A, 10; Erlangen: Universitätsbund, 1959), pp. 192-96, adds all figures and substracts 20 years for Eli (according to LXX), 20 years for Samson and 20 years for the ark in Kiriath-jearim to reach 481 years. Richter, *Bearbeitungen*, pp. 132-41 calculates so: from the coming out of Egypt to Caleb's reception of Hebron: 45 years (Josh. 14.10 but Num. 14.33; 32.13; Deut. 1.3 = 40 years or Deut. 2.14 = 38 years). Reigns: Saul 2 years + David 40 years + Salomon 4 years = 46 years. Judges: Eli 40 + Samson 20 + Abdon 8 + Elon 10 + Ibzan 7 + Jephthah 6 + Jair 22 + Tola 23 = 136 years. Saviours (oppression + peace): Gideon 47 + Barak 60 + Ehud 98 + Othniel 48 = 253 years. Total 480 years. Richter does not include the 2 years of Eshbaal, 3 years of Abimelech, 20 years of the ark in Kiriath-jearim, 18 years of Ammonite oppression in the Galaad (Judg. 10.8), 40 years of Philistine oppression in Samson's days, 300 years of Israelite rule in Hesbon (Judg. 11.26) altogether 383 years. Richter does not mention the 7 months during which the ark stayed in Philistia.

58. Based on an Egyptian model: W.J. Chapman, 'Zum Ursprung der chronologischen Angabe I Reg 6, 1', *ZAW* 12 (1935), pp. 185-89.

	Oppression	Peace	Judges	Reign
Josh. 14.10 Exodus + Conquest				45
Judg. 3.7-11 Othniel	08	40		
Judg. 3.14, 30 Ehud	18	80		
Judg. 3.31 Shamgar	00	00		
Judg. 4.1–5.31 Barak	20	40		
Judg. 6.1–8.28 Gideon	07	40		
Judg. 9.22 Abimelech		0		03
Judg. 10.2 Tola			23	
Judg. 10.3 Jair			22	
Judg. 10.8; 12.7 Jephthah	01[59]	0	06	
Judg. 12.9 Ibzan			07	
Judg. 12.11 Elon			10	
Judg. 12.14 Abdon			08	
Judg. 13.1; 16.31 Samson	40	0	20[60]	
1 Sam. 4.18 Eli			40 MT	
1 Sam. 6.1 Ark in Philistia	01[61]			
1 Sam. 7.1 At Kiriath-jearim	20			
1 Sam. 13.1 Saul				02+?
2 Sam. 4.4 David				40
1 Kgs 6.1 Solomon				04
Total	115	200	136	94

Figure 6. *The Chronology of Judges and the 480 Years of 1 Kgs 6.1*

If the the judges' terms of office are not included in the calculation, the sum is 466 years:

Exodus	040 years
Conquest	005 years
Oppression	111 years
Peace	200 years
Eli	040 years
Ark in Philistia	001 years
Ark at Kiriath-jearim	020 years
Reigns	049 years (without Saul)
Total	466 years, 14 years missing

59. The 18 years of Ammonite oppression beyond the Jordan are excluded as they do not concern Israel.
60. The 20 years in Judg. 15.20 are not added to the 20 years in Judg. 16.31.
61. 7 months.

Hellenistic period), record the units after the tens: $\backslash///$ ⌐ or $\backslash///$ —(14) and $\backslash///$⌐™ or $\backslash///$ + (34).[62] This is enough to affirm that the 480 years that separate the coming out of Egypt to Solomon's fourth year can be reached without the judges.

This conclusion coheres with the suggestion put forward in Chapter 3, namely that the terms of the judges are not to be equated with the peaceful periods of the book of Saviours, but with the times of oppression. According to the Phoenician model, the judges rule temporarily, replacing the king during times of hardship due to foreign pressure. The Israelite *shofet* would be an Israelite local magistrate working under Assyrian supervision or assuming responsibilities in the absence of any legitimate central government. The 70 years of the period of the judges, a standard duration of punishment (Jer. 29.10), therefore do not refer to any Iron I pre-royal government but to the period after 720 BCE. However, this period of the judges can also be termed 'pre-royal' in the sense that it is meant to cover the interim between the end of Israelite monarchy and the future restoration of the kingdom of Israel. The pre-royal understanding of the period of the judges finally prevailed over its post-royal focus when the book of Judges was inserted between those of Joshua and 1 Samuel (see Chapter 7).

Judges 13.2-14: The Nazirite

Judges 13 is often considered secondary to the rest of the Samson story, it is for an obvious reason: the nazirite theme is central in ch. 13 but plays practically no role in the others,[63] if one excepts a very short passage in Judg. 16.17aα where Samson confides to Delilah: כי־נזיר אלהים אני מבטן אמי 'for I have been a Nazirite to God from my mother's womb'.

---

62. See the useful chart in Lemaire, *Inscriptions hébraïques* I, p. 281; for graphic exemples B. Porten and A. Yardeni, *Textbook of Aramaic Documents from Ancient Egypt* (Jerusalem: 1986), p. 72 (Cowley 31.19) and p. 84 (Cowley 16.6); studies by Y. Aharoni, 'The Use of Hieratic Numerals in Hebrew Ostraca and the Shekel Weights', *BASOR* 184 (1966), pp. 13-19; A.R. Millard, 'The Signs for Numbers in Early Hebrew', in K. van Lerberghe and A. Schoors (eds.), *Immigration and Emigration within the Ancient Near East: Festschrift E. Lipinski* (OLA, 65; Leuven: Peeters, 1995), pp. 189-94.

63. L.C. Jonker, 'Samson in Double Vision: Judges 13-16 from Historical-Critical and Narrative Perspectives', *JNSL* 18 (1992), pp. 49-66 (51-55); Gese, 'Simsonüberlieferung', pp. 261-80. Already Nowack, *Richter*, pp. 116-17 identified different conceptions for the Nazir status: a type of hairy fighter consecrated for the war (Judg. 13.5); late developments were introduced (prohibition of alcohol, of impure food and of contact with corpses) in Judg. 13.3b-4, 7, 13-14 for the Nazir and his mother.

This note could have been added at the same time than ch. 13. Moreover, the textual problems of Judg. 13 reveal the puzzlement of scribes and translators over the ambiguous stipulations relative to the Nazirite. Was Samson submitted to the same dietary restrictions than his mother?[64]

Kim has devoted a large part of his work to demonstrate the unity and the coherence of Judg. 13–16. He spots a number of refrains that appear regularly throughout the composition and a list of parallels between ch. 13 and chs. 14–16.[65] While Richter had used the opposition 'to know/not to know' that structures Judg. 13 to claim its secondary nature,[66] Kim shows that ידע 'to know' appears six times, twice in each part of the cycle (Judg. 13.16 and 21; 14.4 and 15.11; 16.9 and 20). Against Richter who affirms that the repetition of the Nazirite prescriptions prove that the Nazirite is the sole preoccupation of Judg. 13, Kim claims that the opposition between the Nazirite in ch. 13 and the libertine in the following chapters produces a tension holding the four chapters together. The reader is deliberately lead astray, expecting Samson to behave according to his Nazirite status. The repeated transgressions produce a critical distance of the narrator, and the real hero is Yhwh who does not forsake his people, in spite of Israel's transgressions.

Did Kim really prove that Judg. 13 was composed at the same time as Judg. 14–16? Is it impossible to imagine that the parallelisms, far from being the expression of the consummate genius of the first narrator, can reveal just as well the art of the editors who would have appended ch. 13 to an earlier composition starting in Judg. 14? Or are we condemned to carry on believing that Biblical texts were written by sublime poets and muddled up by incompetent editors? A relatively new issue could be introduced into an older text using the device of literary parallels to hold heterogeneous elements together, and thus offering a wonderful playground for subsequent interpreters. The sheer abundance of parallelisms proves nothing. A more convincing argument would be to show that Judg. 13 provides one crucial element that is presupposed by the other chapters. Such is not the case: the Nazirite theme remains a foreign body throughout Judg. 14–16.

64. See Jonker, 'Samson', pp. 52-53.
65. Kim, *Structure*, pp. 412-15. The most striking one is the word-play between ברך and חלל in Judg. 13.24-25 and 16.19: Yhwh blesses Samson and his spirit stirs Samson, while in ch. 16 Yhwh leaves Samson when is asleep on her lap ברכיה and she starts to humiliate him.
66. Richter, *TU*, pp. 140-41.

On the other hand, is it plausible that Judg. 13 would have been added in order to illustrate the Nazirite status? Samson hardly appears as an ideal figure for the kind of special religious consecration that Nazirites are supposed to practice. Could Samson have been chosen to found Nazirite vows while he is bent on transgressing all prescriptions laid out in ch. 13? Römheld's solution to this dilemma is classical as he postulates heroic traditions integrated by a Deuteronomistic editor who, through the addition of Judg. 13, wishes to denigrate the hero by having him transgress the obligations of the Nazirite.[67] Synchronists and Diachronists finally agree that Judg. 13 is a Deuteronomistic introduction radically undermining a profane heroic narrative, the aim being to make out of Samson the incarnation of impious Israel squandering Yhwh's grace.

However, the Nazirite theme cannot be understood without reference to Num. 6.1-21,[68] which poses a major problem if one postulates a Josianic date for Judg. 13. Even more devastating, Stipp picked out a point that is so obvious that it has blinded many an exegete: apart from the razor in v. 5, the obligations concern the mother only![69] This crucial point is confirmed in vv. 13-14 when the messenger repeats to Manoah what he has already told his wife in v. 5, that the *woman* האשה must abstain from all what comes from the vine and from impure food. Stipp asserts that the imposition of food restrictions on the mother is the work of later editiors, who turned the mother into the main actor.[70] Such an upsurge of feminism would be difficult to account for, but what matters here is that Samson's so-called transgressions are limited to the razor,[71] and it could be secondary.[72] In fact, v. 5 is rather overloaded by the words ומורה לא־יעלה על־ראשו 'and the razor shall not go over his head' and those words are absent from vv. 7, 13-14.

Two possibilities remain: either the razor prohibition in v. 5 is secondary, or it is original and thus implied in כל אשר־צויתיה 'all I have

---

67. K.F.D. Römheld, 'Von den Quellen der Kraft (Jdc 13)', *ZAW* 104 (1992), pp. 28-52 (47-52). For the date of Num. 6 and the other texts about Nazirites see H.-J. Stipp, 'Simson, der Naziräer', *VT* 45 (1995), pp. 337-69 (343-44, 355-63).

68. Römheld, 'Quellen', p. 44.

69. Stipp, 'Simson', pp. 364-65; T.W Cartledge, 'Were Nazarite Vows Unconditional?', *CBQ* 51 (1989), pp. 409-422 (411).

70. Stipp, 'Simson', p. 365.

71. Samson cannot be blamed for pushing his mother to break her vow when he offered her honey (Judg. 14.9) as food taboos would end at the birth of the child: Stipp, 'Simson', p. 349.

72. So Römheld, 'Quellen', pp. 44-47.

ordered her' in v. 14b. If there is a place where the razor would have been expected, it is at v. 12 in the messenger's reply to Manoah who asked him specifically about the boy's manner of life. It is therefore more likely that the razor was added on later, in v. 5 only, a hypothesis that leads Stipp to conclude that Samson cannot be accused of breaking regulations relative to Nazarites.[73] If the prohibition of the razor is not original, but was inferred later from Judg. 16 in order to aggravate Samson's case, there is no reason to exclude the whole of Judg. 13 (razor apart) from the rest of the original Samson narrative. In that perspective, Judg. 13 is no Deuteronomistic aggravation of a hero of Danite folklore, but is part of the cycle from its inception.[74] Why would the Josianic Deuteronomists denigrate Samson who, as will soon be seen, is going to serve their purpose so well? In fact, he serves them so well that one wonders whether Samson is not a pure Deuteronomistic creature, and if one should not search for Samson's prototype in Mesopotamian mythology rather than in Danite folklore.

If the Nazirite status is not the central theme of Judg. 13, the problem of Samson's paternity certainly is. Judges 13 is so close to the literary genre of Gospel annunciations that Samson used to be considered as a type of Christ.[75] Contrary to the birth narratives of Samuel, of Moses and others, all the stress is on the identity of the genitor. At this point, Samson is very close to Jesus, more so than John the Baptist since Manoah's role as sire is almost as openly denied as Joseph's. In fact, Judg. 13 systematically plays wife against husband, much to the pleasure of some feminist scholars.[76] Yhwh's messenger speaks to her first (v. 3) and when he finally does speak to Manoah, he emphasizes that he has already explained everything to the woman (v. 13). The most remarkable fact is that both encounters happen when Mrs Manoah is alone (vv. 3, 9) and she takes the initiative to fetch her husband. Manoah then walks behind his wife מנוח אחרי וילך אשתו (v. 11) and it is she again who explains that the divine appearance does not put their lives in danger (v. 23). This game may express Judaean derision of the Danites, but a more crucial point is at stake. The angel is a

73. Stipp, 'Simson', p. 369.

74. Stipp, 'Simson', pp. 348-49, considers that Judg. 13 was produced when the Samson cycle (then limited to Judg. 14–15 or 14–16) was integrated into DH slightly before 586 BCE. Judges 13.1 would be older, belonging to the original introduction of the cycle. During or after the exile were added Judg. 13.5, 25.

75. A. Calmet, *Commentarius literalis in librum Judicum, latinis literis traditus a J.D. Manci* (Wirceburgi: 1790), pp. 465-66.

76. See A. Reinhartz, 'Samson's Mother: An Unnamed Protagonist', in A. Brenner (ed.), *A Feminist Companion to Judges* (Sheffield: JSOT Press, 1993), pp. 157-71.

Waiting for Josiah

מַלְאָך 'messenger' for the narrator (vv. 3, 9, 13, 15, 16, 17, 18, 20, 21), but he is called אִישׁ הָאֱלֹהִים 'man of the god' by the woman (v. 6) and by Manoah (v. 7). In the centre of the story, he simply becomes a man: אֵלַי הָאִישׁ אֲשֶׁר־בָּא בַיּוֹם 'the man who entered today towards me' (woman v. 10), וַיָּבֹא אֶל־הָאִישׁ 'he entered towards the man' (narrator v. 11), and in Manoah's open accusation הַאַתָּה הָאִישׁ 'are you the man' (v. 11). Three times the text hints that a man entered towards a woman while she was alone (v. 9) in the fields, where she would be automatically washed from any suspicion.[77] A smart way to indicate that the encounter was most fruitful.[78] The lack of the usual formula 'he knew or entered his wife and she conceived'[79] should convince the last sceptics that Samson did not spring from Manoah's seed. The identity of Samson's real father prepares the son for a most exceptional life. Manoah plays his role perfectly as his insistence on hearing directly from the mouth of the 'man' what to do with the child would have been interpreted by a reader versed in law as pardon for the woman and legal recognition of the child to come.[80]

Judges 13 is therefore a meticulous plot for a perfect crime, each actor is exculpated, all ends well, and the Evangelists will have no other choice but claiming virginity for Mary in order to set Jesus above Samson. This proximity with the Gospel would indicate a late date for Judg. 13 if the ancient Near East was not teeming with heroes of ambiguous birth, millennia before the advent of Christ.

Judges 13.15-25: Manoah's Offering and Gideon's
Stipp takes over an old idea from the beginning of the century, that the sacrifice offered by Manoah in Judg. 13.15-20 has been elaborated from

---

77. Deut. 22.24-27 and Middle Assyrian laws §12.14.15.16.56: M. Roth, 'The Middle Assyrian Laws', *CoS* 2, pp. 353-60.

78. Reinhartz, 'Samson's mother', pp. 166-68; L.R. Klein, *The Triumph of Irony in the Book of Judges* (JSOTSup, 68; Sheffield: JSOT Press, 1988), p. 114. But Stipp, 'Simson', p. 366 n. 79 refuses the sexual interpretation of בוא because, according to him, Manoah's request to the man of god to enter once again towards us יָבֹא־נָא עוֹד אֵלֵינוּ 'wäre kurios'!

79. Gen 4.1; 16.4; 29.23, 30; 30.3-4.16; 38.2; 1 Sam. 1.19.

80. In Mesopotamia, the pardon granted by a cuckolded husband to his wife extended automatically to the other adulterous partner: Hammurabi Code §129, Hittite Code §198. The Bible does not offer any possibility of pardon of adulterous women, Prov. 6.35 and *Sot.* 6.1 even expressly forbid it. This interdiction probably indicates that husbands did, once the first anger had cooled off, calculate that the death of the two culprits was a rather expensive way to save morality.

Gideon's in Judg. 6.11-24.[81]

Figure 7 shows that Judg. 13 summarizes Judg. 6 and adds two developments in vv. 16-18 and 21-23. Judges 13 is also devoid of the sceptical elements found in the Gideon story (see Chapter 1). Manoah's sacrifice is not aimed at checking the provenance of the messenger as it was the case for Gideon because the magic wand episode (Judg. 6.19-21) is replaced by the demonstration of Manoah's inability to transcend his traditional understanding of sacrifices and cult. Although the angel had warned him that he would not eat from the offering, Manoah does not yet understand who the messenger is (v. 16): in the next verse Manoah is still asking for his name, and the angel reprimands him for this question in v. 18. As from v. 19, Judg. 13 is shorter than Judg. 6, culinary details (6.19-21) are omitted, and Manoah directly raises the offering onto the rock. The miracle is not the fire lit without wood (Judg. 6.21) but the messenger disappearing in the flame (Judg. 13.20).

These texts are linked and Judg. 13 is probably based on Judg. 6, although each story follows its own logic. Judges 6 multiplies signs in order to prove the lack of faith of Israel's saviours and to illustrate their tendency to build altars everywhere. Judges 13, for its part, demonstrates the divine origin of the messenger in order to suggest Samson's partly divine nature and raise him to the rank of Oriental heroes. The sharpness of the mother disqualifies Manoah as possible sire, but the fruit of her entrails is doomed to die at the end of the story alongside Dagon's worshippers. Rather than being the relics of old Canaanite *Altarätiologien*,[82] Judg. 6 should be understood as a critique of the book of Saviours, and Judg. 13 as the preparation of the great Yahwistic bonfire of Judg. 16.

---

81. B.R. Kittel, *Studien zur hebräischen Archäologie und Religionsgeschichte* (Leipzig: 1908), p. 106; H. Greßmann, *Die Anfänge Israels* (Göttingen: 1922), p. 240; P. Kübel, 'Epiphanie und Altarbau', *ZAW* 83 (1971), pp. 225-31; Y. Zakovitch, 'The Sacrifice of Gideon and the Sacrifice of Manoah', *Shnaton* 1 (1975), pp. 151-54, English summary in Y. Zakovitch, 'Assimilation in Biblical Narratives', in J.H. Tigay (ed.), *Empirical Models for Biblical Criticism* (Philadelphia: University of Pennsylvania Press, 1985), pp. 175-96.

82. Kübel, 'Epiphanie', p. 229, bibliography in D. Grimm, 'Name des Gottesboten in Richter 13', *Biblica* 62 (1981), pp. 92-98 (93-94).

Judg. 6.17-23	*Judg. 13.15-25*
17 ויאמר אליו אם־נא מצאתי חן בעיניך ועשית לי אות שאתה מדבר עמי 18 אל־נא תמש מזה עד באי אליך והצאתי את־מנחתי והנחתי לפניך ויאמר אנכי אשב עד שובך	15 ויאמר מנוח אל־מלאך יהוה נעצרה־נא אותך ונעשה לפניך גדי־עזים 16 ויאמר מלאך יהוה אל־מנוח אם־תעצרני לא־אכל בלחמך ואם־תעשה עלה ליהוה תעלנה כי לא־ידע מנוח כי־מלאך יהוה הוא 17 ויאמר מנוח אל־מלאך יהוה מי שמך כי־יבא דבריך וכבדנוך 18 ויאמר לו מלאך יהוה למה זה תשאל לשמי והוא־פלאי
19 וגדעון בא ויעש גדי־גזים ואיפת־קמח מצות הבשר שם בסל והמרק שם בפרור ויוצא אליו אל־תחת האלה ויגש 20 ויאמר אליו מלאך האלהים קח את־הבשר ואת־המצות והנח אל־הסלע הלז ואת־המרק שפוך ויעש כן 21 וישלח מלאך יהוה את־קצה המשענת אשר בידו ויגע בבשר ובמצות ותעל האש מן־הצור ותאכל את־הבשר ואת־המצות ומלאך יהוה הלך מעיניו. 22 וירא גדעון כי־מלאך יהוה הוא	19 ויקח את־גדי העזים ואת־המנחה ויעל על־הצור ליהוה ומפלא לעשות ומנוח ואשתו ראים 20 ויהי בעלות הלהב מעל המזבח השמימה ויעל מלאך־יהוה בלהב המזבח ומנוח ואשתו ראים ויפלו על־פניהם ארצה 21 ולא־יסף עוד מלאך יהוה להראה אל־מנוח ואל־אשתו אז ידע מנוח כי־מלאך יהוה הוא 22 ויאמר מנוח אל־אשתו מות נמות כי אלהים ראינו
ויאמר גדעון אהה אדני יהוה כי־על־כן ראיתי מלאך יהוה פנים אל־פנים 23 ויאמר לו יהוה שלום לך אל־תירא לא תמות	23 ותאמר לו אשתו לו חפץ יהוה להמיתנו לא־לקח מידנו עלה ומנחה ולא הראנו את־כל־אלה וכאת לא השמיענו כזאת

Figure 7. *Gideon and Manoah's Sacrifices*

Judges 14.1-7: Samson and the Lion
Unlike his conception, Samson's childhood is skipped over, the story
moves on directly to the youth who goes down to Timnah with his parents
to organize his marriage to a daughter of the Philistines. At the Timnah
vineyards, the family is attacked by a young lion, but Samson, hit (צלח)
by the spirit of Yhwh,[83] rips up the unsuspecting animal as one tears a kid,
bare-handed (vv. 5-6). This first feat is going to provide the substance of
the enigma presented to Samson's wedding guests. The lion's carcass is
set up as a trap that will eventually destroy the marriage, the bride, her
father and the guests, presuming their presence in the Dagon temple when
Samson will pull it down. The parallelism with the carcass of the wild ox
stricked by Shamash to set up a trap for the eagle in the Etana Epic can
hardly be accidental.[84]

Samson, 'little sun' (from שמש 'sun') inaugurates his ministry with the
slaughter of a lion, thus reflecting what goes on in the celestial plane: at
dawn the sun arises through the sky's doors,[85] his radiance turns Venus
dim and it is said that a lion, symbol of the morning star, is sacrificed.[86]

The lion is also a universal royal symbol since times immemorial. From
Sumer to the Neo-Assyrians kings, 'lion' was a royal epithet.[87] This
symbolism was also sustained by assiduous practice, the Sargonide kings
practised lion hunting on foot, boat or chariot, and killing lions were royal
privileges and duties.[88] Killing a lion, the animal holding the highest rank
in the chaotic wilds, the *erṣetu*, allowed the king to don the power of the

---

83. √פעם R. Alter, 'Simson without Folklore', in S. Niditch (ed.), *Text and
Tradition* (Atlanta: Scholars Press, 1990), pp. 47-56 (49).

84. This eagle had destroyed the brood of a snake in spite of an oath of a friendship
sworn in the presence of the divine judge with this very snake. Shamash strikes down a
wild ox and advises the serpent to hide in the carcass until the eagle comes to feed on
its flesh. The serpent then easily avenges his offspring by seizing his enemy: see J.R.
Novotny, *The Standard Babylonian Etana Epic* (SAACT, 2; Helsinki: The Neo-
Assyrian Text Corpus Project, 2001), p. xii and M. Haul, *Das Etana-Epos* (GAAL, 1;
Göttingen: Seminar für Keilschriftforschung, 2000).

85. R. du Mesnil du Buisson, *Etudes sur les dieux phéniciens hérités par l'Empire
romain* (EPR, 14; Leiden: E.J. Brill, 1970), p. 26.

86. At sunset the lion kills the bull symbolizing the heat of the day: du Mesnil du
Buisson, *Etudes,* pp. 7-29.

87. Cassin, 'Lion', pp. 167-73.

88. In a letter, a servant presents his excuses as the lioness he captured died before
the king could kill it himself: A 263 in G. Dossin, 'Documents de Mari', *Syria* 48
(1971), pp. 1-19.

king of animals and push back the limits of the uncivilized realm, thus extending the socialized space, the *mātu*.[89] Leonine images are often used in royal annals, Sennacherib rages against Merodach-Baladan king of Babylon: 'I raged like a lion, I stormed like a tempest, with my merciless warriors I set my face against Merodach-baladan (who was) in Kish'.[90] Reliefs show Assurbanipal hunting lions within a kind of arena fenced off by a line of soldiers,[91] but inscriptions close by indicate that the king also went to hunt lions in their natural habitat.[92]

Beside the prestige of lion hunting, more trivial security questions were also at stake: lions were a real danger for cattle and farmers.[93] It was therefore the king's duty to maintain order by war and hunt.

The Timnah lion is a precious clue for the date of the Samson cycle. Timnah is mentioned explicitly as taken by Sennacherib alongside Elte-keh,[94] the town survived and thrived during the Assyrian period.[95] The area between Ekron and Beth-Shemesh, in which Timnah is situated, was not affected by the destructions of 701 BCE and was not depopulated.[96] The situation did not change before the Babylonian campaigns that ravaged Philistia and Judah between 597 and 586 BCE. As a result, empty stretches of land soon covered themselves with brushwood teeming with wild animals, among them lions that endangered the lives of farmers and travellers.[97] Archaeology tends to confirm the increase of lion population in this period as, apart from a twelfth-century BCE skull found in Jaffo, the few lion bones identified in excavations have so far all been dated to the Iron II

89. Cassin, 'Lion', p. 212.

90. Cassin, 'Lion', p. 181, citing Luckenbill, *Sennacherib*, p. 51 l. 25.

91. Illustrations in E. Wissert, 'Royal Hunt and Royal Triumph in a Prism Fragment of Ashurbanipal', in S. Parpola and R.M. Whiting (eds.), *Assyria 1995* (Helsinki: The Neo-Assyrian Text Corpus Project, 1995), pp. 354-55.

92. Cassin, 'Lion', pp. 195-96.

93. Dossin, 'Documents', pp. 2-19, A 717 explains the capture of a marauding lion in a pit.

94. 'Altakû and Tamnâ I besieged, I captured and took away their spoil. I drew near to Ekron and slew the governors and nobles who had commited sin...' Luckenbill, *Sennacherib*, p. 32.

95. G.L. Kelm, *Timnah: A Biblical City in the Soreq Valley* (Winona Lake: Eisenbrauns, 1995).

96. Bunimovitz and Lederman, 'Beth-Shemesh', pp. 42-49, 75-77.

97. For this phenomena in Babylonia under Sargon: Oded, 'Mass Deportation', p. 69; under Assurbanipal: Cassin, 'Lion', p. 193.

period.[98] 2 Kgs 17.25 reports the same phenomenon in Samaria after the 722–720 BCE campaigns. The inhabitants of the area suffered from a lion plague attributed to Yhwh's anger, until a Bethel priest came back to appease him, and probably also until Sargon settled Arab exiles in the area to boost local demography.[99]

The Timnah lion is therefore the unfortunate witness of the aftermath of the Babylonian destructions. Doing bare-handed what Nebuchadnezzar and his descendants should have been achieving, Samson is clearly presented as a royal figure, not as a rustic.[100] On the mythical plane, Samson sets out, right from the beginning of his 'ministry', onto a vast theomachy, like the hero, whose name has disappeared in a lacuna in a tale from Assurbanipal's library (668–627 BCE), who killed Labbu, a mythical lion which decimated humans.[101]

Judges 14.8-9: Honey
On the way to his next visit to his Philistine 'sunshine', Samson finds a swarm of bees in the carcass of the lion and eats some honey. This episode has been related to bugonia,[102] a myth first alluded to by Eumelos of Corinth in the eighth century BCE.[103] However, it is not described before Virgil presents it as a way for farmers to get new colonies of bees when hives have been decimated by disease: a calf is choked in an open shed, the body beaten to activate putrefaction. The carcass is laid on a bed of fresh thyme and laurel branches. Larvae soon appear and develop into full-grown bees.[104] The idea was that bees were naturally born out of decaying meat. However, in the myth, it is out of the carcass of bull[105] or of a calf that the bees come from. The bull was, like the lion, another epithet of

---

98. P. Wapnish, 'Lions', in E.M. Meyers (ed.), *The Oxford Encyclopedia of Archeology in the Near East* (New York: Oxford University Press, 1997), pp. 361-62.

99. Fuchs, *Inschriften Sargons*, 110.320 (715 BCE, seventh year, ll. 120-23).

100. Mobley, 'Wild Man', n. 41.

101. Bottéro and Kramer, *Lorsque les dieux*, pp. 464-69.

102. Gese, 'Simsonüberlieferung', p. 61.

103. G.L. Huxley, *Greek Epic Poetry from Eulemos to Panyassis* (London: 1969), pp. 62.67.79. Herodotus, *History* 5.114 reports a similar episode, but the bees sprang from out of the head of a beheaded king.

104. Virgil, *Georgics,* 4.198-9. This tradition was taken over from Archelaos: M. Détienne, 'Orphée au miel', in J. Le Goff and P. Nora (eds.), *Faire de l'histoire* 3 (Paris: Gallimard, 1974), pp. 56-75 (56).

105. J. Chornarat, 'L'initiation d'Aristée', *Rel* 52 (1974), pp. 185-207 (207) connects it with the burial of the Apis bull in Memphis. A good word-play in any case.

Assyrian kings. The bovine metaphor is reserved to Samson's wife called a heifer and accused by Samson of ploughing for the guests, nagging Samson until he reveals the solution of the enigma (Judg. 14.18).

The discovery of the symbol of resurrection implied by the bugonia myth is attributed to an Israelite hero[106] in order to be folklorized. Mythical honey, joy of the heart and sign of victory of life over death will turn very bitter in the mouths of all those who tasted it. The story of honey coming out of the lion's carcass inaugurates a cycle of carnage. A kind of resurrection will not take place before the end of the cycle, when Samson's hair grows back, and then only with the aim of allowing the hero to offer himself for the ultimate sacrifice. This apotheosis will only be another opportunity to kill more enemies, more than during his whole life (Judg. 16.30).

Judges 14.15-20: Bitter Honeymoon

The dead lion flowing with honey is the key to the enigma presented by Samson to trick the Philistine guests at his wedding. The wording of the enigma, particularly the second part 'Out of the strong came something sweet' belongs to the sexual metaphores that pepper marriage revelries.[107]

The guests soon realize that they have been invited to fall into a trap. They force the bride to betray her groom in order to save her life (v. 15) and the answer is provided through a proverb:[108] 'What is sweeter than honey? What is stronger than a lion?' (v. 18).

To his guests who wrung out of his bride the answer of the enigma, Samson replies: 'If you had not plowed with my heifer, you would not have found out my riddle'. A link is thus established between marriage and ploughing, two activities which were traditionally accompanied by the same obscene allusions, understood as fostering fertility in both cases.[109]

The treacherous discovery of the answer to the riddle provides only a temporary respite for the Philistines. Yhwh's spirit activates the trap all the same (v. 19), and then Samson kills thirty Ashkelonites to 'reward' his guests and returns to his parents' home. Samson's bride is given to his best man, further confrontation is inevitable.

---

106. Gese, 'Simsonüberlieferung', p. 63: 'Das, was der Heros Aristäus erst durch Proteus mit Hilfe seiner göttlichen Mutter Kyrene erfährt, findet Simson selbst heraus!'

107. C.V. Camp and C.R. Fontaine, 'The Words of the Wise and their Riddles', in S. Niditch (ed.), *Text and Tradition* (Atlanta: Scholars Press, 1990), pp. 127-51.

108. See the first Ahiqar proverb: מ[ה]חסי[ן הו מן חמר נער בן [תא 'What is stronger than a braying ass…?' Lindenberger, *Proverbs*, p. 43.

109. Servier, *Portes*, pp. 114-15.

Judges 15.1-3: Aborted Reconciliation

Samson brings a kid to Timnah in order to visit his wife, but her father offers his younger daughter instead. This kid has been understood as indicating that Samson had contracted a *Sadīqa* type of marriage, according to which the wife remains in her father's house and is visited occasionally by the husband.[110] However, this kind of relation, attested among pre-Islamic Arabs, is not a marriage but a temporary arrangement.[111] In Samson's case, *errêbu* marriage (from a √ערב 'to enter') would be a more fitting explanation:[112] a man of modest origin enters the family of a man who has no son by marrying one of his daughters. No bride price is due as the son-in-law is adopted and the girl stays in the father's home, under the father's authority. Children born to the couple remain the property of their grandfather.[113]

However, Judg. 14 does not present such a situation. Samson has simply left the wedding feast, betrayed and furious, and he then comes back to fetch his wife.[114] The kid is mentioned just as a token of good will: the purpose is to present Samson under the best possible light, as a man willing to forget the betrayal and get on with married life. The aim is not to describe any particular type of marriage but to make sure that the fight continues: Samson's good will, indeed, is met by the grave blunder of his father-in-law who has to admit that he has given Samson's wife to his companion מרע. This was probably a kind of best man, charged by the groom to organize the marriage. Mesopotamian laws expressly forbade him to marry the girl if the marriage failed.[115] It is difficult to determine whether these laws were applied there and then in Palestine. Samson's answer tends to favour a positive answer as he immediately refuses the offer of the younger daughter to replace his wife (v. 2) and declares that he will be innocent when he takes revenge from the Philistines (v. 3). No

110. S.A. Cook, *The Laws of Moses and the Laws of Hammurabi* (London: 1903), pp. 76-77.

111. E. Neufeld, *Ancient Hebrew Marriage Laws: With Special References to General Semitic Laws and Customs* (London: Longman, 1935), pp. 63-64.

112. G.R. Driver and J.C. Miles, *The Assyrian Laws* (Oxford: 1935), §25.26.27.30. 32.33.36.38.

113. Neufeld, *Marriage Laws*, pp. 61-67.

114. A. Schulz, *Das Buch der Richter und das Buch Ruth* (HSAT, 2, 4/5; Bonn: Peter Hanstein, 1926), see Judg. 14.8.

115. See Hammurabi Code §161 and Lipit-Ishtar Code: A. Van Selms, 'The Best Man and Bride—From Sumer to St John with a New Interpretation of Judges 14-15', *JNES* 9 (1950), pp. 65-75 (74); Roth, *Laws Collections*.

replacement could possibly make up for this offence, even if here it seems to have been committed in good faith.

Judges 15.4-5: Foxes Spark off Trouble

Samson burns off Philistine fields and orchards by letting off foxes tied two by two with a lit torch on their tails in retaliation for the loss of his wife. Burning standing grain at the approach of the harvest is a well-known war practice.[116] Classicists have also proposed to relate the foxes with rituals destined to protect crops, in particular with the festival of the *Cerialia* related by Ovid, practised in Rome besides chariot racing.[117] Foxes were let loose in the hippodrome with lit torches fastened to their tails. Ovid then tells an anecdote that he heard from a friend but that has obviously nothing to do with the original meaning of the ritual:

> A boy once caught a vixen fox which had carried off many farmyard fowls. The captive brute he wrapped in straw and hay, and set a light to her; she escaped the hands that would have burnt her. While she fled, she set fire to the crops that clothed the fields and a breeze fanned the devouring flames.[118]

The meaning of the fox race seems to have been forgotten in Rome by the time Ovid wrote, a vivid demonstration of the ability of rituals to survive long after the myth that was connected to it has fallen into oblivion.

Wissowa believed that the fox race during the *Cerialia* symbolized the scorching sun, enemy of the grain during the dog days,[119] but Bömer considers that Ovid confused the *Cerialia* with another festival, the *Robigalia* over which he transmits some much more precise information:

> When April shall have six days left, the season of spring will be in mid course, and in vain will you look for the ram in Helle, daughter of Athamas; the rains will be your sign, and the constellation of the Dog will rise. On that day, as I was returning from Nomentum to Rome, a white-robed crowd blocked the middle of the road. A flamen was on his way to the grove of ancient Mildew (*Robigo*), to throw the entrails of a dog and the entrails of a sheep into the flames. Straightway I went to him to inform myself of the rite. Thy flamen, O Quirinus, pronounced these words: 'Thou scaly Mildew, spare the sprouting corn, and let the smooth top quiver on the surface of the

---

116. Hannibal had used oxen (Livy 22.16-17), the Mamelouks used dogs and foxes: Gese, 'Simsonüberlieferung', p. 64 see also 2 Sam. 14.30; Jdt. 2.27.

117. H. Le Bonniec, *Le culte de Cérès à Rome* (Paris: Klincksieck, 1958), p. 122.

118. Ovid, *Fasts* (trans. J.G. Frazer; LCL, London: Heinemann, 1959), 4.704-708.

119. G. Wissowa, 'Cerialia', PW III.2, pp. 1980-81.

ground. O let the crops, nursed by the heaven's propitious stars, grow till they are ripe for the sickle. No feeble power is thine: the corn on which thou hast set thy mark, the sad husbandman gives up for lost. Nor winds, nor showers, nor glistening frost, that nips the sallow corn, harm it so much as when the sun warms the wet stalks; then, dread goddess, is the hour to wreak thy wrath. O spare, I pray, and take thy scabby hands off the harvest! Harm not the tilth; 'tis enough that thou hast the power to harm. Grip not the tender crops, but rather grip the hard iron. Forstall the destroyer. Better that thou shouldst gnaw at swords and baneful weapons. There is no need of them: the world is at peace. Now let the rustic gear, the rakes, and the hard hoe, and the curved share be burnished bright; but let rust defile the arms, and when one essays to draw the sword from the scabbard, let him feel it stick from long disuse. But do not thou profane the corn, and ever may the husbandman be able to pay his vows to thee in thine absence'. So he spoke. On his right hand hung a napkin with a loose nap, and he had a bowl of wine and a casket of incense. The incense, and wine, and sheep's guts, and the fool entrails of a filthy dog, he put upon the hearth—we saw him do it. Then to me he said, 'Thou askest why an unwonted victim is assigned to these rites?' Indeed I had asked the question. 'Learn the cause,' the flamen said. 'There is a Dog (they call it the Icarian dog), and when that constellation rises, the earth is parched and dry, and the crop ripens too soon. This dog is put on the altar instead of the starry dog, and the only reason for killing him is his name'.[120]

Ovid tells of a sacrifice offered to Robigo, goddess of rust, in order to protect crops from this disease developing at springtime in a warm and moist environment. Both sacrificial victims, the dog and the ram, indicate that the rite was understood as referring to astral realities. The dog is Sirius whose rise corresponds very approximately to the vesperal setting of the Ram.[121] It is therefore possible that the bitch sacrificed for *Robigalia* (April 25th) was originally connected with the movable feast of *Augurium canarium* celebrated between the end of April and mid July.[122] During this festival, russet bitches were sacrificed in order to preserve harvests from

120. Ovid, *Fasts*, 4.901-943; Gese, 'Simsonüberlieferung', pp. 63-67; T.H. Gaster, *Myth: Legend and Custom in the Old Testament* (New York: Harper & Row, 1969), pp. 535-36. F. Bömer, 'Die Römischen Ernteopfer und die Füchse im Philisterlande', *WS* 69 (1956), pp. 372-84.

121. See notes by R. Schelling on Ovid, *Fasts*, p. 133 n. 287-88 and Bömer, 'Ernteopfer', p. 380. The Romans borrowed rituals concerning the dog days from Egypt where they were meant to coincide with the beginning of the year and the Nile floods: C. Desroches-Noblecourt, *Amours et fureurs de la Lointaine* (Paris: Stock/ Pernoud, 1995).

122. Bömer, 'Ernteopfer', p. 380.

the hardships of the dog days.[123] The *Augurium canarium* was named after the sacrificial victim killed on the occasion and it is only through a secondary development that it became associated with Sirius, the largest star of the Dog constellation.[124] Ovid's confusion is understandable as a canine sacrifice was effected during a grain protection rite. But equating *Robigalia* with *Augurium canarium* is problematic because the two festivals refer to two different stages of growth of the grain, and also because foxes were never sacrificial victims at Rome.[125] Specialists agree nevertheless to attribute a Greek origin to the rituals dedicated to Ceres.[126] Bayet suggests a parallel with the *kernophoria* celebrating fire and heat during rituals associated with plant growth.[127] These rites are well attested in Carthage and the Punic connection could allow them to move away from Imperial Rome and go back to Phoenicia and to sixth century BCE Palestine. Unfortunately, the *kernophoria* were clearly introduced in Carthage from Sicily at the beginning of the fourth century BCE.[128] There is therefore no way to establish a direct link with Phoenicia. A connection between the foxes that were let loose in the Roman hippodrome and Samson's is thus impossible to establish. The only thing the two examples have in common is the lit torches fastened at the tails of the foxes. Moreover, Ovid is of no help in understanding Judg. 15 because, when he wrote, the original significance of the ritual had long been forgotten. It is therefore necessary to turn back to the Levant.

Two Oriental connections are open, one of them through pre-Islamic Arabs who practised a ritual against drought. Saelanthus and aselepias branches were tied to the tails of cattle that were then pushed off a cliff.[129] However, this ritual is not shedding much light on Judg. 15.5. The inquiry should therefore turn to Mesopotamia where crop-protecting rituals are better known.

123. Bömer, 'Ernteopfer', pp. 374-83.
124. Bömer, 'Ernteopfer', pp. 380-81.
125. See critical remarks by Le Bonniec, *Cérès*, p. 119.
126. Bömer, 'Ernteopfer', pp. 381-82; Le Bonniec, *Cérès*, pp. 379-455.
127. J. Bayet, 'Les Cerialia', *RBPH* 29 (1951), pp. 5-32 (22-23). The participants carried a clay crown with a small hearth surrounded with small offering cups.
128. M. Le Glay, 'Déméter et Koré', *DCPP*, pp. 128-29.
129. I. Goldziher, *Muhammedanische Studien* (Halle: Max Niemeyer, 1888), pp. 34-35.

Mesopotamian ritual field prophylaxis. The *Sumerian Georgics* (eighteenth century BCE) entreat farmers to accomplish the proper rites for each stage of the growth of the grain.[130] Some of those rites are known and will offer a possible context against which Judg. 15.4-5 could be read. One ritual catalogue mentions an incantation formula to prevent caterpillars from devouring crops.[131] Other texts prescribe the setting of offering tables at the four corners of the field to be protected.[132] Some tablets from Assurbanipal's library explain the procedure to be followed against crickets: the ritual requires burning part of the field.[133] Among other divinities, Ninurta, Enlil's ploughman is evoked in this text, and this Ninurta will be encountered again as Samson's prototype.[134] But here, Ninkilim, a kind of deified mongoose, plays the main role, and apparently has the power to repel a list of pests answering to the general designation of 'dogs of Ninkilim': caterpillars, crickets and various rodents.[135]

It is clear, therefore, that in Mesopotamia rituals involving the burning of plants were practised in or near fields in order to protect them. The pests were designated as dogs. In the light of this evidence, the question arises whether Samson's setting fire to fields with the help of foxes should not be understood as a hint to these widespread rituals. The reference would obviously be ironic, since the angry Danite inverts the logic of the rituals: instead of burning a symbolic part of the crop to avert the pests (the dogs), Samson uses foxes (dogs) to destroy the whole of the Philistines crops.

Foxes. If Samson's destruction of the Philistine harvest is clearly related to his final onslaught against Dagon, the Philistine god of grain (Judg. 16), a satisfying explanation for Samson's use of foxes is yet to be found. It seems therefore worth trying to see how foxes were considered in the ancient Orient.

---

130. M. Civil, *The Farmer's Instructions: A Sumerian Agricultural Manual* (AOSup, 5; Sabadell Barcelona: AUSA, 1994).

131. K 2389 R. Caplice, 'Namburbi Texts in the British Museum 1', *Orientalia* 34 (1965), pp. 105-131 (109).

132. S.M. Maul, *Zukunftsbewältigung* (BF, 18; Mainz: Ph. von Zabern, 1994), pp. 366-72.

133. A. Georges, 'The Dogs of Ninkilim', in H. Klengel and J. Renger (eds.), *Landwirtschaft im Alten Orient. Ausgewählte Vorträge der XLI. RAI* (BBVO, 18; Berlin: D. Reimer, 1999), pp. 291-99 (295).

134. Georges, 'Ninkilim', p. 296.

135. Georges, 'Ninkilim', p. 297.

Margalith suggests that Samson's use of foxes is meant to supply an etymology for the popular Greek word for fox λάμπουρις 'lamp-tail' to Semites who only knew grey foxes (*Canis aureus*). Samson would be providing an explanation of this strange designation that was obvious in Greece where it applied to red foxes but incomprehensible for Palestinians accustomed to grey foxes only.[136] However, the study of bone remains has now revealed the presence of red foxes (*Vulpes vulpes*) in the Levant since the Palaeolithic period.[137] It is therefore safer to abandon naturalistic explanations and turn again to mythology.

Foxes were also considered as harbingers of doom. Once, a fox entered the Assyrian capital and fell into a well, this was significant enough to have prompted the sending of a letter to inform the king.[138] In Sumerian texts, the fox is compared to demons sneaking into sleeping towns at night and dragging their tails on the ground.[139] Lists of divination signs designate foxes specifically.[140]

Foxes were also renowned for their cunning and our Medieval *Roman de Renart* derives from the Sumerian *Tale of the Fox*, a composition well attested through Neo-Assyrian tablets.[141] In spite of its fragmentary state, the general outlook of that story is clear. During a severe drought, Enlil is inspecting worldly affairs and a dog accuses a wolf and a fox of decimating flocks. The fox exculpates himself by putting all the blame of the wolf.[142] Fire is mentioned several times,[143] alluding to mythical compo-

136. A. Vincent, *Le livre des Juges: Le livre de Ruth* (Paris: Cerf, 1952), p. 107; Margalith, 'Samson's Foxes', pp. 224-28.

137. E. Tchernov (Jerusalem), E-mail 11th October 2000, through Brian Hesse, thank you.

138. ABL 142 = K 551: S. Parpola, *Letters from Assyrian and Babylonian scholars* (SAA, 10; Helsinki: University of Helsinki Press, 1993), p. 105. Maul, *Zukunfts-bewältigung*, p. 21; A.L. Oppenheim, 'A New Prayer to the Gods of the Night', *Studia biblica et orientalia* 3 (AnBib, 12; Roma: Pontifico Istituto Biblico, 1959), pp. 282-301 (285, 288).

139. W. Heimpel, *Tierbilder in der Sumerischen Literatur* (StPo, 2; Roma: Pontificium Institutum Biblicum, 1968), pp. 349-50: 'Du bist der bose *Alû*-Daemon, der wie ein Fuchs in der Nacht lautlos durch die Stadt streifet' (CT 16, 28, 44-45); 'Unter diesen sieben [Daemonen] ist der Erste ein Fuchs, der den Schwanz (ueber den Boden) schleifen laesst' (TMHNF 3, 22 II 8 (A) = UM 29.15.219, 11' (B).

140. E. von Weiher, *Spätbabylonische Texte aus Uruk*, II (ADFU, 10; Berlin: Mann, 1983), pp. 146-48.

141. Lambert, *Babylonian Wisdom*, pp. 186-212.

142. Lambert, *Babylonian Wisdom*, p. 188.

143. Lambert, *Babylonian Wisdom*, pp. 195-97: VAT 10349 obverse 19-20.

sitions now lost.[144] A torch appears at the end of the story:

> Reverse Col B 7 [...] open for me! 8 [...] let me bring a torch and pitcher into the temple. 9 [...] let it be expelled behind you, 10 [And I] will sacrifice to my lord Enlil [with] my assembled family. 11 [...] the Fox prayed to Enlil.[145]

This torch (*gizillû*) is always used in cult and serves in purification contexts.[146] The fox is seemingly promising to sacrifice to Enlil, which suggests that he manages to play the stupidity of the wolf against the dog's conceit,[147] and finally managed to buy the supreme judge's favour.[148] This would indicate that the Tale of the Fox is a fierce satire of society. In this case, the choice of foxes where one would have expected dogs to intervene signales the ironic turn of the story.

A mythological fox appears in conjunction with a torch in a Babylonian fertility ritual that the Assyrians were promoting. The tablet is broken and its reading is not assured, but it seems that the fox is used as a symbol for a torch brandished in an unknown mythical episode: 'The fox which comes out howling, is Nergal [...when] Nusku lifted a bright torch in front of Bêl'.[149] This is so far the closest Mesopotamian parallel to Samson's foxes and torches. The fox is clearly associated with Nusku, son and attendant of Enlil, connected with light and fire. Nusku plays a central role in Šurpu and Maqlû rituals[150] against unknown evils and black magic. The

---

144. Lambert, *Babylonian Wisdom*, p. 189.

145. Lambert, *Babylonian Wisdom*, p. 209.

146. Used to purify Bel's new year temple. *'gizillâ ina libbi bîti ushbat'*, F. Thureau-Dangin, *Rituels accadiens* (Paris: E. Leroux, 1921), p. 140 l. 343; A.L. Oppenheim, 'Analysis of an Assyrian Ritual', *HR* 5 (1966), pp. 250-65 (251-52). A supplicant stands in front of the *pū u lišanu* (dKA.EME 'mouth and tong') of the great *Bît eqi* of Kar-Tukulti-Ninurta sanctuary. He holds a torch in the left hand and offers cakes, incense and beer with the other. The Ishtar priest blesses him, assuring that the *pū u lišanu* will intercede in his favour and that the goddess will provide him with health and happiness as bright as this torch. A similar torch is used in a ritual to heal a person stung by a scorpion: K 5944 reverse l.3, Caplice, 'Namburbi Texts', pp. 121-23.

147. H. Vanstiphout, 'The Importance of "The Tale of the Fox"', *AS* 10 (1988), pp. 191-228 (199).

148. Vanstiphout, 'Tale of the Fox', p. 198 n. 36.

149. The rites of Egashankalamma no 38 lignes 37-38: A. Livingstone, *Court Poetry and Literary Miscellanea* (SAA, 3; Helsinki: University of Helsinki Press, 1989), p. 97 STT 243.

150. G. Meier, *Die assyrische Beschwörungssammlung Maqlû* (AfO Beiheft, 2; Osnabrück: Biblioverlag, 1967), pp. 11 (1.122-24) and 13 (2.1-17).

priest lights a *Gizzilu* in Šurpu ritual and gives it to the patient while reciting 'I hold the torch, release from the evil'.[151] To exorcise a dreamt evil, a patient must call on Nusku with a bunch of reeds. He breaks one, rolls it in a piece of material taken from his clothing and burns it on the Nusku torch.[152] Nusku was in vogue in Haran during the Neo-Assyrian period and became the son of Sîn.[153] Assurbanipal addresses him as pure dispenser of justice and companion of Shamash the judge.[154] At Ugarit, Shapash himself is described as torchbearer, an obvious epithet for the god of justice who must reveal to light what is hidden.[155] Nusku's torches are therefore extremely well qualified to carry out Samson's vengeance. In Maqlû rituals, Nusku is called 'burning Nusku, who strikes the enemies'.[156]

One may doubt the ability of scholars in peripheral areas like Bethel to have access to the vast corpus of Sumero-Babylonian compositions and their capacity to use it for their own purpose. However, this literature was sufficiently well-known in the seventh century BCE to be quoted regularly by Neo-Assyrian kings. Sennacherib's account of the battle of Halule (691 BCE, against a large Elamo-Babylonian coalition), a summit of Assyrian literature,[157] quotes the Tale of the Fox and Enuma Elish several times.[158] This process was not new as it appears already in Sargon's annals.[159] But Sennacherib's example is more interesting as it is more likely to have been known in Judah. It proves that the *Tale of the Fox* and *Enuma Elish* were

---

151. E. Reiner, *Surpu, a Collection of Sumerian and Akkadian Incantations* (AfO Beihefte, 11; Graz: Biblioverlag, 1958), p. 11 (1.8).

152. M.-J. Seux, *Hymnes et prières aux dieux de Babylone et d'Assyrie* (LAPO, 8; Paris: Cerf, 1976), p. 373.

153. J. Black and A. Green, *Gods, Demons and Symbols of Ancient Mesopotamia* (London: British Museum Press, 1992), p. 145.

154. T. Bauer, *Das Inschriftenwerk Assurbanipals* II (Leipzig: 1933), p. 38.

155. 1 AB 13 A. Caquot, M. Sznycer and A. Herdner, *Textes ougaritiques, mythes et légendes* (LAPO, 7; Paris: Cerf, 1974), p. 253; KTU 1.6.11.13.

156. Meier, *Maqlû*, p. 13 (2.8).

157. Luckenbill, *Sennacherib*, p. 17.

158. E. Weissert, 'Creating a Political Climate: Literary Allusions to Enuma Elish in Sennacherib's Account of the Battle of Halule', in H. Waetzoldt and H. Hauptmann (eds.), *Assyrien im Wandel der Zeiten. XXXIXe RAI* (HSAO, 6; Heidelberg: Heidelberger Orientverlag, 1997), pp. 191-202.

159. J. Renger, 'Neuassyrische Königsinschriften als Genre der Keilschriftliteratur. Zum Style und zur Kompositionstechnik der Inschriften Sargons II. von Assyrien', in K. Hecker and W. Sommerfeld (eds.), *Keilschriftliche Literaturen: Ausgewählte Vorträge der XXXII. RAI* (BBVO, 6; Berlin: D. Reimer, 1986), pp. 109-128.

known to large audiences otherwise their use in royal propaganda would have been useless. There is no need to affirm that every Judaean farmer read cuneiform, but it is very likely that court officials were acquainted with Mesopotamian culture and texts in the seventh and sixth centuries BCE just as their predecessors already were in the Late Bronze Age.[160] The Bible itself supplies ample proof of this knowledge,[161] so the re-use of some of those mythological motives within the Samson cycle is in no way surprising.

Tying up torches to foxes' tails may therefore be more than a simple war technique. This episode refers to crop protecting rituals and to mythological motives involving divine foxes and torches. In a demythizing process similar to the one at work in the story of Jephthah's daughter, the rites that were supposed to protect crops are mimicked to utterly destroy harvest and orchards, and avenge Little Shamash.

If the Samson cycle was produced in Bethel during the Babylonian period, the foxes episode could be understood as a literary attempt at purifying Palestine of Assyrian mythology. Indeed, the source of most of Assyrian religion sprang from Babylonia, and it seems doubtful that Babylonian vassals would take the risk to launch an attack against Mesopotamian, that is mainly Babylonian mythology. However, since archaeology indicates that the Babylonians abandoned Southern Palestine after destroying Philistia, Jerusalem and probably also Galilee,[162] it can be affirmed that Bethel and Mizpah were much more free to criticize their nominal suzerain than they had been under the Assyrian administration. With the book of Saviours, Bethel had endorsed the Assyrian imperial programme. The sudden disappearance of Assyria left Bethel with a kind of intellectual hangover. The administration it had faithfully served had vanished, what was to be done with the facinating culture it had brought with it? Abandoned in their mountains with little resources, Bethel realized that it had been intoxicated by the Mesopotamian culture, with its venerable compositions going back to Sumerian originals a millennium older, and with all the scientific expertise than went with it: astrology, mathematics, magic, medicine, omina… Bethel then reacted with a resounding 'Never again!' and launched on a detoxification programme. Samson's setting ablaze the

160. A. Goetze and S. Levy, 'Fragment of the Gilgamesh Epic from Megiddo', *Atiqot (English series)* 2 (1959), pp. 121-28.

161. For example, the creation accounts, Moses' birth, the Uriah letter: B. Alster, 'A Note on the Uriah Letter', *ZA* 77 (1987), pp. 169-73.

162. E. Stern, 'The Babylonian Gap', *BARev* 26/6 (2000), pp. 45-51.

whole of the Philistine harvest, and even the barns and the olive groves (v. 5) is a fitting description of Nebuchadnezzar's obliteration of Assyrian achievements in Palestine. Using foxes and torches for that purpose provided the military campaign with a religious gloss to present it as a kind of ritual purification from all traces of the abhorred Assyrian rule. Bethel, once the spiritual centre of pro-Assyrian thinking, needs to work overtime to present itself as an eager promoter of Babylonian rule.

In the light of the following episode that deals with the consequences of Samson's arson, Samson's destructive foxes may also refer to Gula, the goddess of healing. Gula is always identified on seals by her dog and she was particularily popular in Assyria in the seventh century BCE as Ninurta's consort.[163] Considering that the foxes episode leads to the burning alive of Samson's wife by her own people (see next paragraph), it is terribly ironic to use foxes (standing for Gula's dog) to set fire to Philistia because the Assyrians revered Ninurta's consort as the goddess of healing!

To conclude, this episode appears as a learned composition drawing on several mythological motives which are not at present sufficiently understood: the goddess of healing, foxes replacing Gula's dog and torches to reinforce the purification motive. This midrashic work describes Nebuchadnezzar's campaigns of destruction in Palestine.

Judges 15.6-8: Tit for Tat
The Philistines seem well aware of the Mesopotamian laws mentioned for Judg. 15.3: they burn Samson's wife and father-in-law upon hearing that Samson burned the harvest because his wife had been given to his best man (v. 6). They thus recognize that Samson's anger was justified, just as he had claimed himself in v. 3. However, Samson uses the burning of his wife to justify a new round of violence: אם־תעשון כזאת כי אם־נקמתי בכם 'if this is what you do I will avenge myself' (v. 7). He then claims that after one last act of revenge, they will be even and that he will cease his rampage ואחר אחדל (v. 7). Samson strikes a great blow and retires to the rock of Etam (v. 8).

---

163. D. Collon, *Catalogue of the Western Asiatic Seals in the British Museum: Cylinder Seals IV* (London: British Museum Press, 2001), p. 122 and plates 232-39. *idem*, 'Neo-Assyrian Gula in the British Museum', in N. Cholidis, M. Krafeld-Daugherty and E. Rehm (eds.), *Beschreiben und Deuten in der Archäologie des Alten Orients* (AVO, 4; Münster: Ugarit-Verlag, 1994), pp. 43-48. F.R. Kraus, 'Die Göttin Nin-Isina', *JCS* 3 (1949), pp. 62-86; W.H. Römer, 'Einige Beobachtungen zur Göttin Nininsina', in W. Röllig (ed.), *Lišān mitḫurti* (AOAT, 1; Neukirchen-Vluyn: Butzon & Bercker Kevelaer, 1969), pp. 279-305. Black & Green, *Gods*, pp. 101-102.

Judges 15.9-17: Samson Invents the Sickle

Samson has no more reason to fight, but the cycle of vendetta is too well engaged to come to a halt.[164] The family drama now takes on international dimensions as Samson is hiding in Judaean territory. The rock of Etam is sited between Bethlehem and Teqoa ('Ain 'Aṭān) or at 'Araq Ismā'īn SW of Jerusalem. The second identification is preferable as it remains within the geographical frame of the cycle.[165] Wādī Ismā'īn, a few kilometres long, joins the Soreq 4 km upstream from Beth-Shemesh. Eshtaol sits on a hill between Wādī Ismā'īn and Wādī el-ğirab. As for Lehi (v. 14), this term could be a wordplay between לחי 'jawbone' and Akkadian *lītu/lētum* 'jawbone' or 'topographical limit, border'. Hence the vocalization לחי indicating the article and at the same time that Lehi is not a proper noun but a general designation. Therefore, the Philistines are deployed (נטשׁ√ niphal) along the Judaean border (v. 9) and not against a particular town (see 2 Sam. 5.17, 22).[166] Negotiations are engaged until Judah accepts to deliver Samson to fend off a Philistine attack. Three thousand Judaeans fetch Samson from the rock of Etam.[167] They reproach him to put everyone in danger as they are under Philistine domination: 'Do you not know that the Philistines are rulers over us' הלא ידעת כי־משׁלים בנו פלשׁתים (v. 11). Kim notes the strange use of ידע√[168] attested only here in a question and in the negative. It would therefore be a rhetorical question with the implied meaning: 'You know like everyone else that the Philistines are dominating us!' However, the question could also be an editorial device addressed at the audience: are we really still under foreign domination? Indeed, since 586 BCE, what is left of the kingdom of Judah (i.e. the Benjamin region) is not subserviant to the Philistine lowland anymore because Nebuchadnezzar has turned it into a no man's land.

Samson accepts to be bound with two new ropes and handed over to the Philistines, he is then struck (צלח see Judg. 14.6) once more by the spirit of Yhwh who melts the ropes as under the action of fire (v. 14). Samson

164. Gese, 'Simsonüberlieferung', pp. 57-59.

165. C.S. Ehrlich, 'Etam', *ABD* 2, p. 644. Niemann, *Daniten*, pp. 183-83.

166. See also 2 Sam. 5.17, 22 and M. Lubetski, 'Lehi', *ABD* 4, p. 275.

167. Rock of the screamer (a kind of kestrel?) from עיט√ 'to scream' a possible wordplay on the shouts of Philistines when they saw Samson arriving: ופלשׁתים הריעו לקראתו (Judg. 15.14): S. Segert, 'Paronomasia in the Samson Narrative', *VT* 34 (1984), pp. 254-461 (458).

168. Kim, *Structure*, p. 413.

takes hold of a fresh donkey jawbone[169] and knocks down a thousand
Philistines. Samson then sings a celebration of the jawbone:

בלחי החמור חמור חמרתים

By a jawbone of the ass: one heap, two heaps.

בלחי החמור הכיתי אלף איש

By a jawbone of the ass, I struck a thousand men.

The first part plays on the word חמור 'donkey' or 'heap', and suggests a
kind of harvesting song, as sickles were commonly made, still in the Iron
I, with jawbones fitted with flint blades at the place of the teeth.[170] Any
kind of jawbone would do: the ass is chosen here for its homonymy with
the heap[171] (Hab. 3.15) and possibly with the grain measuring unit חֹמֶר
'homer'. The second part refers to the same jawbone but applies to its
second use, as a weapon. Gese provides an illustration at the end of his
article showing the similarity of shape between a donkey's jawbone and
the sickle-sword, the כידון in Goliath's hand in 1 Sam. 17.6, used as a
weapon in the Bronze age and as a symbol of royal power in the Iron
age.[172] The sickle-sword is a feature of Ninurta on seals, particularly when
it is hanging from the elbow of the warrior.[173]

In this passage, a kind of proto-evhemerism is at work. It is Samson, a
'mere' Israelite hero, who discovers both the sickle and the sickle-sword.
He uses Ninurta's weapon (the sickle-sword) for his gory harvest, whereas
mythology claimed that the sickle was invented by Kronos,[174] in the same

169. לחי חמור טריה wordplay on the other meaning of √לחח 'to be fresh, humid'.
See Judg. 16.7-8.
170. The Megiddo 2000 excavations found over fifty of these blades in an Iron I
farm (area K) next to a goat jaw waiting to be equipped. See also E. Coqueugniot,
'Outillage de pierre taillée au Bronze récent', in M. Yon (ed.), *Arts et industries de la
pierre à Ras Shamra-Ougarit* (Paris: Recherches sur les civilisations, 1991), pp. 127-
202.
171. Segert, 'Paronomasia', p. 456.
172. Gese, 'Simsonüberlieferung', p. 69; O. Keel, *Studien zu den Stempelsiegeln aus
Palästina/Israël* (OBO, 67/88/100/135; Fribourg/Göttingen: Universitätsverlag/
Vandenhoeck and Ruprecht, 1985-94), I 62, 77, 82-3, 105; II 253-4; III 31, 36, 40.
173. Collon, *Catalogue*, p. 148 and plates 232.292; U. Moorgat-Correns, 'Ein
Kultbild Ninurtas aus neuassyrischer Zeit', *AfO* 35 (1988), pp. 117-35.
174. H.W. Attridge and R.A. Oden, *Philo of Byblos, the Phoenician History:
Introduction, Critical Text, Translation, Notes* (CBQMS, 9; Washington: Catholic
Biblical Association, 1981), p. 49 Frag. 2: ...κατεσκεύασεν Κρόνος ἐκ σιδήρου

way that the hoe was supposedly invented by Enlil in a second millennium BCE Sumerian text[175] or the plough by Dagon in Philo's *Phoenician History*.[176] These are reduced to folklore and lose much of their religious drive.

Judges 15.18-20: Death Knell for the Saviours

Dead thirsty, Samson calls on Yhwh who splits the rock to let water out and to revive his servant. The wording of the invocation is premonitory:

אתה נתת ביד־עבדך את־התשועה הגדלה הזאת

You gave by the hand of your servant this great salvation

ועתה אמות בצמא ונפלתי ביד הערלים

but now I will die of thirst and fall into the hand of the uncircumcised.

This phrase is usually translated as a rhetorical question: 'You gave into the hand of your servant this great salvation, but now will I die of thirst and fall in the hand of the uncircumcised?', the implied answer being 'of course I will not let you die in the hands of the Philistines!' However, this mistranslation misses the point of the phrase. The absence of an interrogative particle renders the presence of an interrogative sentence unlikely, as Hebrew makes a very extensive use of the interrogative form, even when the sentence is not conveying a question.[177] The transformation

---

ἄρπην καὶ δόρυ. 'Kronos made a sickle and spear of iron'. In Hesiod, *Theog.*, pp. 161-62, 175, it is Ge who devices the sickle by which Kronos is castrated: Attridge & Oden, *Philo of Byblos,* p. 88 n. 91. See also A.I. Baumgartner, *The Phoenician History of Philo of Byblos* (EPR, 89; Leiden: E.J. Brill, 1981).

175. See *The Creation of the Pickax* in Kramer, *Sumerian Mythology,* pp. 51-53; G. Farber, 'The Song of the Hoe', *CoS* 1, pp. 511-13.

176. Attridge and Oden, *Philo of Byblos,* p. 53: Fragment 2: Ὁ δὲ Δαγών, ἐπειδὴ εὑρεν σῖτον καὶ ἄροτρόν, ἐκλήθη Ζεὺς Ἀρότριος 'Dagon, since he discovered grain and plough, was called Zeus' Ploughman' (l. 25).

177. Joüon and Muraoka, *Grammar*, §161a n. 1. In Hebrew like in most European languages, it is possible to imply a question without any interrogative particle or pronoun, the context and the intonation suffice to convey the interrogation. Rhetorical questions differ from these unexpressed questions in the way that what is implied in rhetorical questions is the answer itself, and that answer is deemed so obvious that it is not provided. However, translating phrases like Judg. 15.18 as rhetorical questions would require to go one step further in abstraction: a straight affirmation would have first to be understood as an unexpressed question, and then the answer to this implicit question would also be implied and considered obvious. This rather extreme level of abstraction overstresses the capacity of any normal reader or listener to get the point.

of this affirmative sentence into a rhetorical question is therefore even less likely.[178] The text skillfully places in Samson's mouth the announcement of his own death thus introducing the central theme of the next chapter. The rest of the story is therefore overcast by a sense of foreboding, the hearer must be aware that these will be the last feats of the hero, his stature is enhanced by the inescapable nature of his destiny. But according to the editors, Samson stands also at the end of Israel's collection of heroes, he is Israel's last and least saviour as he only began to save Israel (Judg. 13.5). In spite of 'this great salvation' (v. 18), Samson must die, and with him must end the era of the saviours and that of the judges. The hope raised by integration within the Assyrian Empire (the book of Saviours) as much as those of a liberation of Israel and the restoration of an Israelite monarchy under Josiah (the book of Judges) have proved unfounded. Sobered up by Babylonian operations, Bethel takes the cynical outlook of the survivors who know that they were not more deserving than those who died.

Before the curtain opens for the last act, a first conclusion imitating the judges' notice is closing the central part of the cycle: 'He judged Israel in the days of the Philistines 20 years'. One can almost hear the old Bethel priests, those who had the privilege to be trained during the blessed days of Assurbanipal: 'Yes, those were the days, the days when there still were Philistines in Philistia to fight with'. What came next on the plane of politics, and what comes next in the Samson story, is of a very different nature, it is not the vindication of an Israelite hero any more.

Judges 16.1-3: Samson through the Gates of the Sun
A dancer of Gaza sees her client get up in the middle of the night. He carries the town gates to Hebron, under the very nose of the guards who were laying in wait for him, not expecting him to get up before sunrise. The real nature of Little Sun is revealed, being able to strike right in the

However, this kind of labyrinthine interpretation is nevertheless used more than once in Biblical translation in particular to evade doctrinal difficulties (see Job 2.10 and Jon. 4.11, P. Guillaume, 'Caution: Rhetorical Questions!', *BN* 103 (2000), pp. 11-16). Among the texts cited by Joüon and Muraoka, *Grammar*, §161a, Judg. 11.23 is the only one that cannot be rendered otherwise than by a rhetorical question. In Judg. 14.16, Samson is affirming to his nagging wife that he will soon be telling her the solution of the enigma, which he does in the next verse. 2 Sam. 11.11; Jer. 25.29; 49.12; Ezek. 20.31 are followed by an answer which clearly indicates that the preceding phrase is a unexpressed question; Isa. 37.11 is voluntarily ambiguous compared to ch. 36; Jer. 45.5 is a straight forward exclamation.

178. LXX (A + B) translated Judg. 15.18 correctly as affirmation.

middle of the night, forcing his way through the gate in spite of the guards. The sheer excess of the story (several tons being hauled over dozens of kilometres uphill!) marks a radical change of plane, Samson is entering cosmic realities through the mythical gate crossed over every morning by Shamash.[179] The sun then follows his heavenly course through the day, to mysteriously enter the Underworld in the evening. A kind of vessel then carries him during the night to reappear in the opposite direction.[180]

Samson needs no such device. He himself carries the doors of the evening from Gaza (West) back to Hebron (East), where the sun seems to rise from, when one is observing sunrise from Gaza. Speaking here of demythization would not do justice to the violence of the scene. Samson is literally overthrowing cosmic order. But since the sun probably carried on raising and setting at the same place and at the same time before and after Nebuchadnezzar, Samson's displacing of the gates of the sun has a political meaning. Since the desolation of the Philistine kingdoms, Gaza has lost its status of gateway to Egypt. Gaza had remained an Egyptian outpost until Esarhaddon succesfully conquered Egypt.[181] After the Assyrian conquest of Egypt, Gaza carried on fulfilling the same function. However, once the Babylonians failed to conquer Egypt, the destruction of Philistia, Jerusalem and Southern Judah was designed to sever all ties with Egypt. Gaza was not any more the gateway to the kingdom of the sun-god Re (all the 26th dynasty pharaohs bore a Re compound name. For instance, Neferibrê 'Beautiful is the heart of Re' was the Egyptian name of Psammetichus II). The centre has shifted back to the mountains, back to the old tribal oligarchies that duly reappear as soon as state or imperial power wanes. The mention of Hebron may thus be a tribute of the official Babylonian capital Mizpah to the traditional centre of Judah. Although the lack of sources curtails the reconstitution of the political situation, one may affirm that Mizpah's control over Hebron and Southern Judah was nominal if at all it existed. What was left of the area after the passage of

179. Iconography for Shahar and Shalim, the guardians of the door: R. du Mesnil du Buisson, *Nouvelles études sur les dieux et les mythes de Canaan* (EPR, 33; Leiden: E.J. Brill, 1973), pp. 110-25.

180. J. Bottéro, *Mésopotamie: L'écriture, la raison et les dieux* (Paris: Gallimard, 1987), p. 330 n. 1. See also the Egyptian *Amduat* and the *Book of the Night* that deal with the sun's nocturnal passage: E. Hornung, *Aegyptische Unterweltsbücher* (Zürich / München: Artemis, 1972), pp. 59-194, 489-93.

181. A share of the Judaean Shephelah was attributed to Gaza at the Assyrio-Kushite peace conference in 701 BCE: Knauf, 'Beersheba II', pp. 181-95.

the troups that besieged and destroyed Jerusalem was apparently controlled by the Edomites.[182] Was Mizpah trying to establish links with the
descendants of Absalom's supporters (1 Sam. 15.7-10)? It is hard to tell,
but Mizpah certainly needed all the support it could find to reorganize
Judah after the traumatic events it went through.

Judges 16.4-23: Binding the Sun

A woman will finally succeed where guards have failed. Delilah (from
√דלל 'to weaken'?) finds a way to reduce the destructive force of the sun.
Obviously, no ligature of any kind (ropes Judg. 15.13; 16.12, fresh sinews
Judg. 16.7) can bind fire, apart from bonds of love (v. 4). The story builds
a skilful tension by focusing the scope on the hair locks in v. 13, only to
mislead Delilah again. In the end, Delilah shaves the seven locks,[183]
Samson is blinded and usefully grinds grain in prison (v. 21) instead of
burning harvests.[184]

Delilah, from traitress to priestess. The Biblical text remains amazingly
neutral concerning Delilah.[185] She does not belong to either side, nothing
proves that she is Philistine,[186] she simply comes from wadi Soreq (v. 4).
Although she accepts the offer of the Philistine tyrants, she never lies nor
plays a double game.[187] In spite of the Philistine order to seduce (פתי)
Samson (v. 5),[188] Delilah remains astonishingly straight forward. She asks
Samson three times how to bind him (vv. 6, 10, 13), even adding the first
time 'in order to oppress you' לענותך. Verse 16 does use the same nagging words than the Timnite used in Judg. 14.17, but as four times she

---

182. J.R. Bartlett, 'Edom and the Fall of Jerusalem', *PEQ* 114 (1982), pp. 13-24.

183. C. Grottanelli, 'Motivi escatologici nell'iconografia di un rasoio cartaginese',
RSF 5 (1977), pp. 18-22; R. Meyer-Opificius, 'Simson, der sechslockige Held?', *UF*
14 (1982), pp. 149-51; R. Wenning and E. Zenger, 'Der siebenlockige Held Simson.
Literarische und ikonographische Beobartungen zu Ri 13-16', *BN* 17 (1982), pp. 43-
55.

184. K. Van der Toorn, 'Judges xvi 21 in the Light of the Akkadian Sources', *VT* 36
(1986), pp. 248-51.

185. 'Qualified neutrality': C. Smith, 'Samson and Delilah: A Parable of Power?',
JSOT 76 (1997), pp. 45-57 (48).

186. Against L.R. Klein, 'The Book of Judges: Paradigm and Deviation in Images of
Women', in A. Brenner (ed.), *A Feminist Companion to Judges* (Sheffield: JSOT Press,
1993), pp. 55-71 (66).

187. Against Smith, 'Samson and Delilah', p. 46.

188. √פתה 'to convince' is not always negative in spite of Judg. 14.15.

applies exactly the same procedure, Samson could not ignore the outcome after the third time. Mata Hari would not have had much success with such methods. If there is a liar here, Samson is the one. Is Samson a downright womanizer losing himself to women, or are they both serving a higher cause? Delilah is a heroine in her own right, she sets the fox to mind the geese, corresponding to the first woman of the cycle, Samson's own mother. The following verses will show that her accomplishment goes far beyond that of a seductress out for pillow talk. She quite simply turns a mythological figure into a man, in order to sacrifice him.

Delilah the demythizer. Three times Samson tells Delilah that he will become 'like one of (the) Adam' וְהָיִיתִי כְּאַחַד הָאָדָם (vv. 7, 11, 17), and this even before she shaves his locks. As soon as Samson is asleep on her lap she calls *the* man וַתִּקְרָא לָאִישׁ, not an attendant waiting to bring the razor, but Samson himself, who told her all his heart (v. 18).[189] There is no magical power in Samson's hair, his power comes from Yhwh and he is like any other man as soon as Yhwh turns away from him (v. 20). Like the courtesan in the Gilgamesh Epic,[190] Delilah humanizes Samson, a demigod becomes a normal man, and the end of every man is to die. This is precisely where the narrative is leading. In the Babylonian context, the leaders of the remnants of the Judaean kingdom in Bethel and Mizpah are seeking to disprove Mesopotamian mythology, suggesting that it is a human construct and that it was therefore bound to disappear.

But Samson's hair began to grow again (v. 22)…

Judges 16.23-31: Yhwh's Triumph

Samson is called out of prison to amuse the Philistines assembled for a festival in honour of Dagon. Samson grasps two columns and the house collapses on him and on the revellers: through his death, he killed more enemies than he had killed during his life (v. 30).[191]

189. J. Sasson, 'Who Cut Samson's Hair? (And Other Trifling Issues Raised by Judg. 16?)', *Prooftexts* 8 (1988), pp. 330-39 (338).

190. Copied in a Late Bronze school at Megiddo: I. Finkelstein and D. Ussishkin, 'Back to Megiddo', *BARev* 20 (1994), pp. 30-43 (33).

191. Herodotus (2.44-45) had heard a similar story about Heracles which he refers as foolish: while in Egypt, Heracles was garlanded as a victim and led in procession. On reaching the altar, he broke his bonds and killed the Egyptians: see M.L. West, *The East Face of Helicon* (Oxford: Clarendon Press, 1997), pp. 464-65.

Dagon. This god is well attested at Mari and then at Ugarit.[192] The Eshmunasar inscription (fifth century BCE) calls the Sharon plain *'rṣt dgn h'drt* 'the rich land of Dagon'.[193] Philo of Byblos attributes to Dagon an important role in his speculative reconstitution of Phoenician religion: Dagon (or Siton) is the discoverer of grain and the inventor of the plough.[194] The return of the ark on a cart drawn by two heifers in 1 Sam. 6 is probably mimicking a ritual procession in honour of Dagon, celebrating both ploughing and harvesting.[195] Golden rats, certainly one of the worst enemy of the grain, replace the original image of Dagon! The Samson cycle presents another one of the grain's enemy: the scorching sun that regularly dries up the ears before the full development of the grain.

In spite of the ark narrative in 1 Samuel and of the Samson cycle, Dagon seems more at home in the Phoenician realm than among the Philistines as no indication of Dagon worship have so far been revealed in Philistia[196] apart from the toponyms Beth-dagon.[197] This indicates that these Biblical texts may be using the Philistines as a code name to designate the whole range of Palestinian, Syrian and Mesopotamian mythology.

Shemesh. Philo of Byblos reports that Aeon and Protogonos, the first human settlers in Phoenicia, used to raise their hands towards the sun during droughts because they considered him, the lord of the sky, as the only god and called him Beelsamen.[198] This is a precious witness to a process of identification that must have taken place at Byblos between Baal Shamim and Shemesh. This process could have started in the seventh century BCE, as Esarhaddon's treaty with Baal of Tyre evokes Baal-

---

192. J.F. Healey, 'Dagon', *DDD*, pp. 407-413 (408); N. Wyatt, 'Relationship of the Deities Dagan and Hadad', *UF* 12 (1980), pp. 375-79 (378).

193. P.K McCarter, 'Eshmunasar Inscription', *CoS* 2, pp. 182-83.

194. Healey, 'Dagon', p. 410; Attridge and Oden, *Philo of Byblos,* p. 53 Frag. 2.25.

195. See Argos who had an image and a mobile altar drawn by a pair of animals (ναòν ζυγοφορούμενον): Attridge and Oden, *Philo of Byblos,* p. 45: *Fragment* 2.13 and bibliography p. 85 n. 71.

196. See the temple of the goddess at Ekron: S. Gitin and M. Cogan, 'A New Type of Dedicatory Inscription from Ekron', *IEJ* 49 (1999), pp. 193-202; M. Görg, 'Die Göttin der Ekron-Inschrift', *BN* 93 (1998), pp. 9-10.

197. One in the Shephelah and the other one in Asher, but both of uncertain location: W.R. Kotter, *ABD* 1, p. 683.

198. Attridge and Oden, *Philo of Byblos,* p. 41: *Fragment* 2.7 and Eusebius of Caesarea, *Preparation for the Gospel* (trans. E.H. Gifford, Oxford: Clarendon Press, 1903), 1, p. 10.8.

Shamem at the very beginning of the list of divinities:[199] However, sun worship was no Phoenician speciality, it was also practised in Jerusalem,[200] 2 Kgs 23.11 and Ezek. 8.16 indicate that Yhwh's cult was influenced by the general solarization of the seventh century BCE.[201]

The Samson story is therefore an onslaught against the two main divinities in Phoenicia, and possibly also in Philistia, namely Dagon and Shamash. Samson becomes a man on Delilah's lap in order to die with Dagon's worshippers. Various myths relative to Shamash and Dagon are turned into folklore and not the other way round. The Samson cycle is not a collection of picturesque tales but the folklorization of mythological compositions aiming at emptying them of their power.[202] Shemesh and Dagon are both supplanted by Yhwh who pulled the strings from the beginning (Judg. 13.25; 14.4, 19).

At first sight, this deconstruction of myths seems to fit better in the reign of Josiah: a process of elimination of the 'other' gods in order to make room for the accession of Yhwh to the rank of supreme creator god. However, as was already said previously, this may be ascribing to Josiah's court more than could have been done then. Judah lacked the hindsight Babylonian Benjamin had, Josiah's days still belonged to the high tide of the Assyrian world, and Josiah merely tried to imitate the Assyrians. He would have been more likely to dress Yhwh with Mesopotamian mythological garb than launching on the heart-rending demythization visible in the Jephthah and Simson's cycles. There is a tragic depth to these two characters that prevents the reader from considering them simply as fools. The bewilderment of their authors transpires throughout their narratives.

---

199. M. Lidzbarski, 'Balsamem', *EsE* 2 (1915), pp. 122.

200. Two scarabs bearing Ra and Sedeq inscriptions were found in the Rephaim valley near Jerusalem: O. Keel and C. Uehlinger 'Jahwe und die Sonnengottheit', pp. 279-81. A local solar cult could have been practised in Jerusalem in the Bronze Age. Joshua 10.1-15 indicates such a cult in Gibeon, 1 Kgs 8.12-13 mentions the replacement of the solar god by the storm god in Jerusalem: Keel and Uehlinger, 'Jahwe', pp. 283-87; H.P. Stähli, *Solare Elemente im Jahweglauben des Alten Testaments* (OBO, 66; Freiburg/Göttingen: Universitätsverlag/Vandenhoeck & Ruprecht, 1985), pp. 5-12.

201. E. Lipinski, 'Shemesh', *DDD*, pp. 1445-1452 (1447); Keel and Uehlinger, 'Jahwe', pp. 298-99; J.G. Taylor, 'A Response to Steve A. Wiggins, "Yahweh: The God of Sun?"', *JSOT* 71 (1996), pp. 107-119.

202. See U. Simon, 'Samson and the Heroic', in M. Wadsworth (ed.), *Ways of Reading the Bible* (London: Sussex, 1981), pp. 154-67 (158): 'The Samson story has indeed an earthiness...which removes it from mythology'!

Samson and Mesopotamian Mythology
Samson is often compared to Heracles in the presupposition that this will favour a Hellenistic date for the Samson cycle.[203] However, there is no need to wait for such a late period: both Samson and Heracles are based on their Mesopotamian ancestor, Ninurta, Enlil's ploughman, who was already providing advice in the *Sumerian Georgics* in the eighteenth century BCE.[204] Seals and reliefs, some going as far back as the third millennium, depict several achievements that will later be attributed to Heracles.[205] Although the importance of Ninurta for the origin of Heracles' works is now well documented,[206] the same is not so true for Samson's feats.[207] Since Ninurta is not as well known as his Greek and Roman counterparts, a few pages should be devoted to his presentation.

Ninurta in Palestine. Ninurta is known as the victorious hunter of mythical enemies[208] and found his way in the Bible as Nimrod, the 'mighty hunter

---

203. F. Siegert, 'L'Héraclès des Juifs', in M.-M. Mactoux and E. Geny (eds.), *Discours religieux dans l'Antiquité: actes du colloque—Besançon 27-28 janvier 1995* (Paris: Belles Lettres, 1995), pp. 151-76 (152-53). Already: Augustine, *The City of God* (trans. Matthews Sanford and Green; LCL, Cambridge MA: Heinemann, 1965), 18, p. 19.

204. Civil, *Instructions*, 32-33.50.56: v. 109.

205. H. Frankfort, *Cylinder Seals: A Documentary Essay on the Art and Religion of the Ancient Near East* (Farnborough: Gregg Press, 1939), p. 115 pl. XXe, pp. 132-37 pl. XXIIIc-g, p. 198 pl. XXXIVc. M. von Oppenheim, *Tell Halaf: A New Culture in Oldest Mesopotamia* (London: Putnam's Sons, 1937), pp. 178-79 pl. xxxviiB, xxxiB.

206. H. Stahn, *Die Simsonsage* (Göttingen: Vandenhoeck & Ruprecht, 1922), pp. 57-58; G.R. Levy, 'The Oriental Origin of Herakles', *JHS* 54 (1934), pp. 10-53. M. Oka, 'An Enquiry into the Prehistory of Herakles in the light of the Near Eastern Literature', *JCS* (Kyoto) 7 (1959), pp. 48-64. J. van Dijk, *Lugal ud me-lám-bi nir-gál* (Leiden: E.J. Brill, 1983), pp. 11-19. W. Burkert, 'Oriental and Greek Mythology: the Meeting of Parallels', in J. Bremmer (ed.), *Interpretations of Greek Mythology* (London: Croom Helm, 1987), pp. 10-40, idem, 'Eracle e gli altri eroi culturali del Vicino Oriente', in C. Bonnet and C. Jourdain-Annequin (eds.), *Héraclès: D'une rive à l'autre de la Méditerranée* (Bruxelles/Rome: Institut historique belge de Rome, 1992), pp. 111-27. F.E. Brenk, 'The Herakles Myth and the Literary Texts Relating to the Myth of Ninurta', in D. Musti (ed.), *La Transizione dal miceneo all'alto arcaismo* (Roma: Consiglio nazionale delle ricerche, 1991), pp. 507-526. J. Boardman, 'Herakles' Monsters: Indigenous or Oriental?', in C. Bonnet and C. Jourdain-Annequin (eds.), *Le bestiaire d'Héraclès* (Kernos Sup., 7; Liège: Centre international d'étude de la religion grecque antique, 1998), pp. 27-35.

207. In spite of West, *Helicon*, pp. 458-72.

208. Van Dijk, *Lugal*, p. 68, updated translation in Bottéro and Kramer, *Lorsque les*

before Yhwh' (Gen. 10.8-12) after a folklorization process similar to evhemerism.[209] Ninurta/Nimrod's feats were known in Palestine: eighth to seventh century BCE seals are illustrated with some of them, in particular Ninurta's fight against the lion.[210] This ancient Sumerian figure did not wait for the Neo-Assyrian period to appear in Palestine. In the Late Bronze age, Ninurta is attested in Ugarit, in the el-Amarna letters,[211] and in the Gilgamesh fragment from Megiddo,[212] where he plays the role of chief of forced labour.[213] Ninurta was even attested by Bronze age Palestinian orthography of toponymy in [URU]Bît-[d]NIN-URTA (EA 290.16), probably the city of Beth-Horon[214] or Beth-Anat. Ninurta was in vogue west of the Euphrates in the Late Bronze because he played a major role with Anat in the overthrow of Egyptian rule and the establishment of the kingdom of Amurru.[215] Within the couple Ninurta-Anat, Anat represents aggressive aspirations for 'national' liberation while Ninurta catalyzes poor people's yearnings for land and stability necessary for cultivation.[216]

At Emar, Ninurta became son of Dagan, the northern counterpart of Enlil.[217] Chronologically, this process is rather far from our seventh century BCE Samson, but the link Dagan-Ninurta could indicate that the connection Dagon-Samson in Judg. 16 draws on an ancient mythological

dieux, p. 345: 'Voici, Ninurta, la liste des braves que tu as abattus: le Kuli-anna, le Dragon, le Gypse (?), le Cuivre-résistant, le soudard, le Mouflon-à-sept têtes, le Magilum, sire Saman-anna, le bison, le Roi-palmier, l'Anzû, le serpent-à-sept-têtes' (ll. 128-33). *Return of Ninurta,* comparative study by J.S. Cooper, *The Return of Ninurta to Nippur* (AnOr, 52; Rome: Institut Biblique Pontifical, 1978), pp. 141-54.

209. C. Uehlinger, 'Nimrod', *DDD*, pp. 1181-1186 (1183-1184).

210. O. Keel and C. Uehlinger, *Göttinnen, Götter und Gottessymbole* (QD, 134; Freiburg: Herder, 4th. edn, 1998), §§169-70.

211. EA 74.84.170.290.374; RS 16.170. KTU IV, 78. RS 17.123.

212. Finkelstein and Ussishkin, 'Back to Megiddo', p. 33.

213. Tablet 11, 1.17. D. Ferry, *Gilgamesh, a New Rendering in English Verse* (New York: Noonday Press, 1993).

214. W.F. Albright, 'The Canaanite God Haurôn', *AJSL* 53 (1936), pp. 1-12; Z. Kallaï & H. Tadmor, 'On the History of the Kingdom of Jerusalem in the Amarna Period (Ivrit)', *Eretz-Israel* 9 (1969), pp. 138-47.

215. EA 74 and P. Artzi, 'Ninurta in the mid-Second Millenium "West"', in H. Klengel and J. Renger (eds.), *Landwirtschaft im Alten Orient* (Berlin: Reimer, 1999), pp. 361-67.

216. Artzi, 'Ninurta', pp. 366-67; Lambert, *Babylonian Wisdom,* 118, ll. 11.17.

217. Artzi, 'Ninurta', p. 363; D.E. Fleming, 'The Rituals from Emar', in M.W. Chavalas and J.L. Hayes (eds.), *New Horizons in the Study of Ancient Syria* (Malibu: Undena Publications, 1992), pp. 51-61 (56).

pattern. Between the fourteenth and the sixth century BCE, Ninurta did not fall into oblivion in Syro-Palestine: he is cited in Sfire among the divinities witnessing a treaty between Barga'yah and Mati'el around 755 BCE.[218] To claim that Judaean scholars knew about Ninurta mythology and used it to create the figure of Samson is not far-fetched. It is therefore worth looking into a few of the Mesopotamian compositions about Ninurta.

Ninurta and the stones or LUGAL-E. This is one of the most widespread works, with over 200 witnesses spreading from the beginning of the second millennium BCE to the Seleucid period, and most probably the source of the works of Heracles.[219] After vanquishing his enemies, Ninurta founded civilization by introducing royalty, cities, irrigation,[220] ploughing[221] and commerce: he is NIN.URTA, 'lord of the arable land'. Before accomplishing these noble civilizing tasks, Ninurta designates 42 kinds of stones, attributing to each a function, an aetiology and a blessing or a curse. With this long inventory (a third of the 730 lines), Ninurta takes over the traits of NIN.GIRSU, the warrior god of Eastern and North-western Mesopotamia, mountainous areas whose populations frequently threatened the plain.[222] In Assyria, Ninurta reached a rank equal to Ashur during the reign of Ashurnasirpal II (883–859 BCE) who moved his capital from Ashur to Kalḫu and built a temple and a ziggurat for Ninurta. It is probably in this temple that Sennacherib was murdered (2 Kgs 19.37).[223]

218. Gibson, *Textbook*, p. 33 Sfiré iA38 אנרת Inurta = Ninurta see N. Avigad, 'Seals of Exiles', *IEJ* 15 (1965), pp. 222-32 (224); H. Tadmor, 'A Note on the Seal of Mannu-ki-Inurta', *IEJ* 15 (1965), pp. 233-34.

219. Van Dijk, *Lugal*, pp. 17-18.

220. Van Dijk, *Lugal*, pp. 95-96; updated translation in Bottéro and Kramer, *Lorsque les dieux*, pp. 353-54: 'Au bout de l'horizon, il installa un barrage. Avec l'habileté la plus grande, il endigua pareillement toutes les villes, bloquant de parois en rochers les eaux puissantes: désormais elles ne monteraient plus du plat-pays sur les hauteurs! Il rassembla ce qui se trouvait dispersé: les eaux disséminées en lacs, dans la montagne, il les mêla toutes ensembles, les abouchant au Tigre, pour arroser, en inondations printanières, la terre arable' (ll. 353-59).

221. 'La charrue, source de prospérité qu'il avait inventée, les sillons rectilignes qu'il avait enseigné à creuser, et les monceaux de grains qu'il avait entassés, et les silos qu'il avait remplis' ll. 706-708: Bottéro and Kramer, *Lorsque les dieux*, p. 367.

222. Bottéro and Kramer, *Lorsque les dieux,* p. 338.

223. W. von Soden, 'Gibt es Hinweise auf die Ermordung Sanheribs in Ninurta-Tempel (wohl) in Kalah in Texten aus Assyria?', *NABU* (1990), pp. 16-17. Or in the temple of Nisrok (2 Kgs 19.37), a distortion of Nimrod: Uehlinger, 'Nimrod', p. 1184: מ > ס, ד > ר, or a distortion of Marduk: E. Lipinski, 'Nimrod and Assur', *RB* 73

ANZU myth. The myth of ᵈZU is transmitted in Akkadian in a short version (1600 BCE, one witness) and a long one dated before the end of the second millennium (a dozen witnesses).[224] This composition tells how Ninurta vanquished ANZU, 'the Mountaineer', a frightful bird expressing again the threat of the mountains over Mesopotamia. After a short recollection of Ninurta's mighty works, the circumstances that led Ninurta to fight with ANZU are presented: ANZU, servant of ENLIL, steals the tablet of destinies and paralyzes the universe. As no one dares to confront ANZU, Ninurta's mother is approached and flattered until she convinces her son to tackle ANZU. The hero's mother plays an essential role, like in the Samson cycle.[225]

When Ninurta meets ANZU with bow and arrows, ANZU uses magic formula to protect himself:

> O reed-arrow that has come against me, return to your canebrake! Frame of the bow, to your forests! Return, o thong, to the sheep's rump, (and) feathering to the birds![226]

Ea finally suggests the way to victory: the monster has to be worn out with strong winds, his wings severed as soon as he lands to rest. The loss of his wings so disturbs ANZU that he forgets to pronounce the magic spell and the arrow reaches its target. Samson's use of formulaic speech may be alluding to the same pattern, although Samson avoids magic and replaces it with enigmas and proverbs.

Temptation and Punishment of Victorious Ninurta. A short text from Ur (second millennium BCE) seems to be the sequel of Ninurta's victory over ANZU, so it was named Temptation and Punishment of Victorious Ninurta. In spite of the fact that his victory has allowed Ninurta to receive praise among the great gods, Ninurta regrets bitterly having handed over the tablet of destinies to Enlil. Had he kept it, he would have dominated all the gods. Enki, lord of the Apsû, creates a turtle, perfect antithesis of ANZU, who drags Ninurta into a hole to punish his hubris. Likewise, Yhwh abandons Samson when he may become too sure of himself.[227]

(1966), pp. 77-93 (79) and J.P. Lettinga, 'A note on 2 Kings xix 37', *VT* 7 (1957), pp. 105-106.

224. Bottéro and Kramer, *Lorsque les dieux,* pp. 389-418.

225. Bottéro and Kramer, *Lorsque les dieux,* p. 14.

226. H.W.F. Saggs, 'Additions to Anzû', *AfO* 33 (1986), pp. 1-29 (15 ll. 62-65).

227. B. Alster, 'Ninurta and the Turtle', *JCS* 24 (1972), pp. 120-25; updated french translation in Bottéro and Kramer, *Lorsque les dieux,* pp. 418-20.

Nergal and Ereshkigal. The Akkadian myth of Nergal and Ereshkigal is known through a short version from el-Amarna (85 lines) and a long one from Sultantepe (seventh century BCE) and from Uruk (fifth century BCE). Nergal had refused to pay homage to Namtar, the delegate of Ereshkigal, the terrible goddess of the underworld. Nergal shaves his head so as not to be recognized by Namtar who roams around to avenge Ereshkigal. Fearing that one day his growing hair may betray him, Nergal goes down to the Underworld with fourteen demons for reprisals. He must accept nothing if he is to come back, but he falls under Ereshkigal's charm and agrees to marry her. She who wanted to kill him (*ana mûti*), accepts him as husband (*ana muti*). After six nights of passion (the seventh might have proved fatal), Nergal escapes Ereshkigal's embrace and manages to come home to the realm of the living. Finally, Nergal is sent back to Ereshkigal and becomes the ruler of the Underworld with her. Once again, we find elements of the Samson cycle in a venerable and widespread myth. Of course the motive of the shaving of the hair does not play the same function for Samson and for Nergal. But the getting up in the middle of the night to escape an ambush is rather similar in both stories.[228]

Samson as mythological patchwork. It is therefore unlikely that an exact Mesopotamian parallel to Samson can be found. Although Ninurta is Samson's prototype and although the whole of Samson story shows an extensive familiarity with Mesopotamian culture, Samson's creators drew their motives from a vast array of sources to tailor an original figure. The Assyrians contributed to keep the great Sumero-Babylonian mythological tradition alive and used it to their own ends. That tradition was alive in Palestine in the sixth century BCE. It is therefore not necessary to wait for Heracles and his canonical works to account for the presence of the Samson cycle in the book of Judges. By the seventh century, Judah had all the knowledge and the expertise to craft elaborate figures like Jephthah and Samson.

However, the Assyrian Empire was wiped out in the two decades that followed the death of Assurbanipal. The end of the Assyrians as masters of the world came so rapidly and so soon after the reign of their most brilliant king, that this event took everyone unprepared. The book of Habakkuk expresses the utter shock felt in Judah as the stability and the prosperity of the seventh century BCE gave way to the destruction of all the economical

228. O.R. Gurney, 'The Myth of Nergal and Ereshkigal', *AnSt* 10 (1960), pp. 105-131; S. Dalley, 'Nergal and Ereshkigal', *CoS* 1, pp. 384-90.

centres of Southern Palestine. The war damages were not offset by immediate reconstruction efforts as it had been the case with the Assyrians.
Mizpah and Benjamin became the centre of Babylonian Judah but
slumped into a prolonged period of recession, in spite of the fact that it
was the only part of the kingdom of Judah that escaped unscathed from the
Babylonian burnt-earth policy.

Bethel had been a staunch believer and upholder of Assyrian integration. Bethel and Mizpah remained faithful to the Babylonians, but the returns for their faithfulness was very meagre compared to what they had
known under the Assyrian rule. Disillusion was looming large. The Assyrians had vanished when they seemed unshakeable and the Chaldeans
proved disappointing. The natural reaction was to come back to the
fundamentals of ancestral traditions and to deem all the Mesopotamian
mythological niceties deceitful in order to face a new reality. Both Mesopotamian mythology and Israelite saviours and losers had to be disavowed.
But the Bethel scholars were probably too educated to simply adopt the
basic anti-baal rhetoric typical of the books of Kings. Motives from the
mythological arsenal of the dominant culture were selected to model two
pathetic figures that nevertheless call for the sympathy of their audience as
they reflect the position of the weak in a world that does not make sense
anymore. Attributing peripheral identities (Galaadite and Danite) to the
Losers maintains a safe distance for the readers. But Jephthah conveys the
bewilderment of the faithful who has been cheated. Samson's inability to
go beyond the beginning of a saving act may be reminiscent of Josiah's
early death. His rampage in Philistia probably reflects Nebuchadnezzar's
destructive campaigns. Indeed, Yhwh wins in the end, but the victory has a
bitter taste. His people are struggling in the difficult situation revealed by
Jer. 40–44. Gedaliah and his successors have to cope with untended fields,
abandoned farmsteads and roaming bands. And not a word is uttered about
Jerusalem, the old rival, now erased from the map.

Chapter 6

JERUSALEM VERSUS MIZPAH IN THE PERSIAN PERIOD: JUDGES 1.22-26; 19–21

Jerusalem survived Niniveh, but the Judaean leaders did not realize that behind an Empire often lurks another Empire. This is precisely what happened, the destroyers of Niniveh duly destroyed Jerusalem, Southern Judah and Philistia, and the Edomites took control of what was left of Judah in the South. Nothing significant would happen again in Jerusalem before a century. Life went on, albeit on a much lower level, a few kilometres to the north, where traditions were preserved. Among others, the book of Judges was saved from the flames, and its saviours came, again, from Bethel.

Judges 1.22-26: Conquest of Bethel

Judges 1.22-26, the episode that relates the conquest of Bethel by the House of Joseph, has not yet been considered. That 'House of Joseph' reappears in v. 35b, suggesting that the conquest of Bethel, just as v. 35a, belongs to the Josianic edition (see Chapter 3). Such a date would set the story of the conquest of Bethel within the context of Josiah's incursion into the Bethel region during his purification spree (2 Kgs 23.15). However, in spite of its Yahwist zeal, 2 Kgs 23 does not go as far as affirming that Josiah actually closed down Bethel's sanctuary. The text simply claims that he defiled the high places where the priests had been burning incense, from Geba to Beer-sheba (v. 8). In Bethel however, the royal zeal is restricted to Jeroboam's high place, its altar and the Asherah. If there were other cultic installations at Bethel, which is a likely assumption for such a venerable centre, they were left unscathed. Diplomatic considerations towards the newly conquered Benjaminites probably prevented Josiah from accomplishing other destructions in Bethel. There are therefore not many chances that Josiah has been the model for the story of the conquest of Bethel by the House of Joseph.

In fact, Judg. 1.22-26 does not present the conquest of Bethel as a military feat. The city is stormed by surprise, by the way of a postern treacherously indicated by a Bethel resident who was promised safety in exchange for the information (v. 24). This man was then allowed to leave the city with all his family and he built another city called Luz (v. 26//Gen. 28.19), Luz being presented as the former name of Bethel (v. 23). This story is as obscure as it is short, much information seems presupposed. Its obvious aim is to explain the foundation of another Luz, in the Land of the Hittites. No such city has yet been revealed,[1] but since almond trees thrive around Bīr Zēt today, Luz 'almond' is likely to describe the Benjaminite almond-growing district around Bethel (Gen. 23; 26.34; Num. 13.29). This narrative is closer to the sparing of Rahab at Jericho than to the triumphal conquest narratives of Josh. 10–12. It is therefore necessary to turn to a period after Josiah to find a historical context for Judg. 1.22-26.

The date and the circumstances of the reconstruction of Jerusalem are impossible to determine.[2] However, the books of Ezra and Nehemiah do not hide the fact that it was a long and difficult process. Mizpah was probably no happier than Samaria to witness the recovery of the 'rebellious city' קריתא מרדתא (Ezra 4). The consecration of the Jerusalem sanctuary did not cause the immediate closure of Bethel and its temple school, which may have continued to operate as late as 450 BCE.[3] Archaeology is so far incapable of providing more indications pertaining the end of Bethel. Nevertheless, the rivalry that opposed Bethel and Jerusalem in the first half of the Persian period has left traces in postexilic literature.[4]

It is in the context of this rivalry that the story of the conquest of Bethel by the house of Joseph in Judg. 1.22-26 makes the most sense. Jerusalem heaped opprobrium on Bethel (1 Kgs 12, see Exod. 32),[5] and Bethel may have defended itself with a narrative explaining that Bethel was conquered at the same time as Jerusalem and was therefore no less qualified to serve as the sanctuary. The position of this passage within Judg. 1, just after the narrative of the conquest of Jerusalem and of the rest of Judah (Judg. 1.4-

---

1.   W.I. Toews, 'Luz', *ABD* 4, p. 420.
2.   Grabbe, *Judaism*, pp. 126-29.
3.   Blenkinsopp, 'Judean Priesthood', p. 34 n. 26 dates the destruction between 540 and 450 BCE! See literature in Lipschits, 'Benjamin Region', pp. 171-72 n. 31.
4.   Blenkinsopp, 'Judean Priesthood', pp. 32-43.
5.   Blenkinsopp, 'Judean Priesthood', pp. 37-38.

19), favours such an explanation of the function of Judg. 1.22-26. The fairness of the House of Joseph towards its informant is emphasized to contrast with Judaean barbarism in the previous verses. Contrarily to Judah who had cut off Adonibezek's thumbs (Judg. 1.7), the House of Joseph saved the life of the Luzite and his family just as the Ephraimite Joshua had done in Jericho with Rahab (Josh. 6.22-25//Judg. 1.25). Apart from this generous gesture (חסד Judg. 1.24), the text indicates that Bethel was purified by conquest as much as Jerusalem was: 'they smote the city with the edge of the sword' (Judg. 1.25), ready to serve as a good Israelite sanctuary.

The Identity of the House of Joseph
There is no indication concerning the identity of the House of Joseph in Judg. 1. The text apparently presupposes that this group means Ephraim and Manasseh taken together (Num. 13.12; 26.28; 34.23; 36.5; Deut. 33.17; Josh. 14.4; 16.1; 17.14; 18.11; 1 Kgs 11.28). Joseph has been considered as an old designation of a tribal league,[6] but without external evidence.[7] The fact that Ephraim is coupled with Manasseh (rather than with Machir like in Judg. 5.14) renders dates before the ninth century BCE improbable. The pairing of Ephraim and Manasseh as a separate political entity is more likely to reflect the Assyrian provincial system, particularly after Josiah had amputated the province of Samaria of Benjamin, its southernmost part. Since that division was taken over by the Babylonian and Persian Empires, the implied reality endured from the late seventh century until at least the fourth century BCE, a time-span too wide to provide much help for dating Judg. 1.22-26. Although Joseph clearly plays a secondary role in the twelve tribe system, the origin and the date of the designation 'House of Joseph' remains unknown.[8]

Some Greek witnesses read 'sons of Joseph' בני־יוסף instead of 'House of Joseph' בית־יוסף in v. 22, thus showing that the translators were influenced by the opposition between Judah and the Sons of Judah in the previous passage (Judg. 1.3-18 see Chapter 2). However, in v. 23 all the

6. E. Cortese, *Josua 13-21: Ein priesterschriftlicher Abschnitt im deuteronomistischen Geschichtswerk* (OBO, 94; Freiburg/Göttingen: Universitäts-verlag/Vandenhoeck & Ruprecht, 1990), pp. 51-52.
7. H. Donner, *Geschichte des Volkes Israel und seiner Nachbarn in Grundzügen*. I. *Von den Anfängen bis zur Staatenbildungszeit* (GAT. Ergänzungsreihe, 4, 1; Göttingen: Vandenhoeck & Ruprecht, 2000), p. 136.
8. J. Wehrle, 'Josef', *NBL* 2, pp. 385-87.

versions agree with MT's בית־יוסף, so there is no doubt that the 'House' of Joseph is original. The basic meaning of the passage is probably that the House of Joseph (Manasseh and Ephraim) conquered Luz and then re-named it 'House of El' בית־אל. The change of name underlines the change of nature of the cultic place, attributing to Israel the foundation of Bethel. This is in clear opposition to the conquest of Jerusalem which is attributed to the Sons of Judah in v. 8. In the context of the Persian period, that opposition can only stem from Bethel itself, the obvious aim being to resist growing Jerusalemite control and interference. Bethel is insisting on its antiquity and its fundamental Israelite nature, in the clash that is looming ahead between the Judaean and the Benjaminite elements within the Persian province of *Yehud* since Jerusalem's restoration.

Jerusalem against Benjamin

The Persian administration took over the Babylonian layout of the north-ern Judaean border, thus ratifying Josiah's annexation of Benjamin by Judah. Bethel and Benjamin inevitably resented the gradual but irresistible recovery of Jerusalem as the capital, which meant that Mizpah was losing its leading political role. The rebuilding of the Jerusalem temple put Jeru-salem in direct competition with Bethel, situated less than twenty kilo-metres to the north of Jerusalem and the threat of a transfer of Bethel's cultic role to Jerusalem was looming large. Facing such a challenge, the Bethel priests would seek every argument to shore up their position. The antiquity of the Bethel cult, added to the fact that Bethel had not only survived but even replaced Jerusalem during the Babylonian and the beginning of the Persian periods, would certainly plead for Bethel, but it could not convince upstart Jerusalem, which benefited from official Persian backing. Under such conditions, Judg. 1.22-26 would insist on Benjaminite specifics, establishing a 'Benjaminite exception' to resist the ever-increasing centripetal attraction towards Jerusalem. Unable to prevent Jerusalem from reasserting itself as the main Judaean cultic centre, Bethel claimed that Jerusalem could not replace Bethel for Benjaminites and the other Israelite populations of the area. This strategy most probably failed. In the end, under unknown circumstances, Bethel was destroyed and its cult was discontinued for 'good', sometime during the Persian period.[9]

---

9.   Lipschits, 'Benjamin Region', pp. 171-72.

Backwards and Forwards between Bethel and Jerusalem

The recovery of Jerusalem in the Persian period marks the end of the book's peregrinations between Bethel and Jerusalem.

There is no way to tell whether or not these movements concerned the actual material scroll of the book. This or these rolls may have simply remained all the while at the temple school of Bethel. The Manassic additions could have been introduced in order to take into account the situation in nearby Judah since Judaean students such as Jeremiah were trained in Bethel. Once Bethel came under direct Judaean rule, during Josiah's reign, Bethel simply continued to integrate official propaganda into its own traditions. However, even if the roll of the book of Judges did not actually move several times between Bethel and Jerusalem, it seems useful to carry on speaking as though it did, since the successive shifts of ideologies and interests are thus more graphically depicted.

As was seen in Chapter 1, the original book of Saviours (Judges 3*–9) originated in Bethel around 720 BCE, and it is Manasseh who brought it to Jerusalem. There, Josiah greatly enlarged it and turned it into a book of Judges, which was then saved from the flames when the capital was transferred to Mizpah. Bethel preserved Judaean traditions with its own, and the Judaean additions to Bethel's book of Saviours were integrated, preserved, taught and transmitted, in spite of the fact that Josiah's edition was a passionate refutation of the message of the BS. Events had since proven Josiah wrong and the BS right, Jerusalem laid in ruins, the situation had changed radically but the texts remained. They had lost their primary relevance, they had suddenly become traditions and it was Bethel's duty to preserve what could be preserved. In 586 BCE, Josiah's additions to the BS became part and parcel of the heritage, or Josiah had already imposed upon Bethel his enlarged version of the BS when he had taken over Benjamin. In any case, the BS had returned to Bethel after its first sojourn in Jerusalem during the seventh century BCE. However, this was not the last act, for Bethel finally yielded to Jerusalem's pressure and the book of Judges returned to Jerusalem with most, if not all, the traditions preserved in Bethel. Bethel would never rise again as a cultic and literary centre. Moreover, it would take another century before *Judges* was included into the Prophetic collection, later to enter world literature by means of the Greek translations. This process will be examined in Chapter 7, but before that, the struggle between Jerusalem and Bethel, between Benjamin and Judah raged on and left a dreadful scar at the end of the canonical book of Judges.

Judges 19–21: Jerusalem's Revenge

Why does the book of Judges closes on the near annihilation of the tribe of Benjamin (Judg. 20)? Why is that episode followed by the story of two most dubious women-hunts (Judg. 21) with the avowed purpose to allow the Benjaminite survivors to foster descendants and prevent the disappearance of an Israelite tribe? The murderous campaign against Benjamin is triggered by the collective rape of the Judaean concubine of a Levite in Gibeah (Judg. 19). While Judah is clearly designated by Yhwh as the leader of the punitive campaign against Benjamin (Judg. 20.18), Judaean responsibility seems to be diluted into the general designation of the 'Sons of Israel' throughout the rest of Judg. 20. These sons of Israel suffer two humiliating setbacks (Judg. 20.20-25) before they manage to storm Gibeah by means of an ambush. They scorch the town (Judg. 20.40) and the disaster then spreads to all Benjaminite towns and villages. Their inhabitants and the cattle are all slaughtered (Judg. 20.48), apart from 600 soldiers who found refuge at the Rock of Rimmon (Judg. 20.45; 21.13). Due to the polysemy of Rimmon, 'thunder' or 'pomegranate', this Rock of Rimmon (possibly located 5 km E of Bethel)[10] could be a demythizing note. A local toponym connected to Baal Rimmon (2 Kgs 5.18 'Lord of Thunder') may have been reinterpreted as the Rock of the pomegranate, symbol of fertility, an obvious place to find refuge in order to remarry and produce offspring.

A Local Affair
The pan-Israelite frame of Judg. 19–21 should not hide the fact that what is at stake here is an internal settling of scores between Judah and Benjamin: the other tribes are never mentioned by name. The pan-Israelite scope is a mere ploy to add extra legitimacy to the genocide of the Benjaminites. The repetition of the promonarchical refrain from Judg. 17.6; 18.1 in Judg. 19.1 links the narrative to Josiah's book of Judges, but obviously, the understanding of the 'period when there was no king in Israel' has changed: from its original setting in the Josianic period when it referred back to the Assyrian era (see Chapter 3), it now has evolved to designate the Babylonian and Persian period as the implied reference of

---

10. Rammûn: J. Simons, *Geographical and Topographical Texts of the Old Testament* (SFS, 2; Leiden: E.J. Brill, 1959), §638.

the narrative. However, at this point the pre-monarchical 'period of the Judges' as it is now understood, has not yet been conceived (Chapter 7).

Date of Judges 19–20

The scale of the Benjaminite genocide is baffling. The slaughter of the 50,000 Benjaminite warriors (Judg. 20.35, 44, 47), the massacre of the entire Benjaminite population, all this mayhem to avenge the murder of a Judaean concubine! Counting one wife and two children per soldier, the total of Benjaminite casualties amounts to a minimum of 200,000 people, and that is equivalent to the total number of deportees during Sennacherib's third campaign! Such a demographic density was never reached in Benjaminite territory before the twentieth century CE. These numbers are therefore historically unreliable, but they clearly convey the rage and hatred of the editors against their Benjaminite neighbours.

A wide range of dates has been suggested for Judg. 19–21. H. Jüngling and J. Unterman understand these chapters as a plea for kingship at the onset of the institution,[11] while J.E. Tollington suggests a link with the so-called Syro-Ephraimite war: the Northern kingdom is presented as a danger for Judah because it is a Judaean woman who dies after being delivered to Benjaminites by an Ephraimite.[12] For obvious reasons, Becker rejects all pre-exilic dates[13] and favours exilic or postexilic dates. Blenkinsopp's early Persian proposal is backed up with the most convincing evidence: rather than considering the clear distinction of Bethel's and Mizpah's functions as the result of the conflation of two separate sources, Blenkinsopp takes it as a key dating indicator.[14] The Levite lodges his legal complaint in Mizpah (Judg. 20.1, 3), the decision to punish Gibeah is taken in Mizpah (Judg. 20.8), so is the promise not to marry Israelite maidens to Benjaminites (Judg. 21.1). Bethel is set apart as the appropriate place for consulting Yhwh, for fasting and for sacrifices (Judg. 20.18, 26; 21.2).[15] The five kilometres that separate Bethel from Mizpah contradict

11. H.-W. Jüngling, *Richter 19—Ein Plaidoyer für das Königtum: Stilistische Analyse der Tendenzerzählung Ri 19, 1-30a; 21, 5* (AnBib, 84; Rome: Biblical Institute Press, 1981), p. 291. J. Unterman, 'The Literary Influence of "the Binding of Isaac" (Genesis 22) on "the Outrage at Gibeah" (Judges 19)', *HAR* 4 (1980), pp. 161-66.

12. J.E. Tollington, 'The Book of Judges: The Result of Post-Exilic Exegesis?', in J.C. de Moor (ed.), *Intertextuality in Ugarit and Israel* (OTS, 40; Leiden: E.J. Brill, 1998), pp. 186-96 (193).

13. Becker, *Richterzeit*, pp. 262, 297.

14. Blenkinsopp, 'Judean Priesthood', pp. 30-31.

15. Judg. 20.1 does say that the congregation was assembled in Mizpah, but all

the wide pan-Israelite scope of the story and reveal a political set-up that corresponds to the period between 586 BCE and the first half of the Persian era, as long as Jerusalem was in ruins. Mizpah was then the province's capital and Bethel served as the main cultic centre. Blenkinsopp notes that the cultic vocabulary used in Judg. 19–21 bears distinct Persian traits.[16]

Blenkinsopp's Persian date is confirmed by research done under the supervision of Professor Na'aman at the University of Tel Aviv. Cynthia Edenburg is currently showing that Judg. 19–21 is strewn with terms, idioms and grammatical usage characteristic of the language of late first millennium Hebrew sources. The distribution of these indicators seems to exclude their explanation as later glosses. There are therefore two possibilities: either an ancient text was edited after the exilic period (but in that case, the edition process was so large that it would be more appropriate to term it rewriting), or as Edenburg suggests, Judg. 19–21 represent the conscious attempt of a postexilic author to write classical Hebrew. Literary analysis of the intertextual allusions within the text seems to indicate that the author was familiar with the Pentateuch and the Deuteronomistic literature in their final or almost final forms.[17] In addition to these philological remarks, Edenburg is using the results of another Tel Aviv University study dealing with the archaeological analysis of Benjamin during the Babylonian period.[18] She thus concludes that the last three chapters of Judges stem from an early Persian context, expressing a Judaean reaction against Benjamin when Jerusalem was beginning to recover.

Against such a date, the 'days of Gibeah' (Hos. 9.9; 10.9) could militate in favour of an earlier date for Judg. 19–21, as Hos. 9–10 would seem to presuppose Judg. 19.[19] However, Becker has argued convincingly that these passages in Hosea do not refer to the rape of the Levite's concubine.[20] The ambiguity of the name Gibeah does not help to clarify the matter,[21] and nothing proves that Hosea is referring to a town: the word

religious functions are held in Bethel apart from Judg. 20.23 that gives no geographical indication.

16. Blenkinsopp, 'Judean Priesthood', p. 31: עדה (Judg. 20.1; 21.10, 13, 16) and קהל (Judg. 20.2; 21.5, 8) are characteristic of the Priestly writer.

17. C. Edenburg, email June 11th 2000.

18. Lipschits, 'Benjamin Region', pp. 155-90.

19. J. Joosten, 'Les Benjaminites au milieu de Jérusalem: Jérémie vi 1ss et Juges xix–xx', *VT* 49 (1999), pp. 65-72 (71).

20. Becker, *Richterzeit*, pp. 263-64.

21. A. Demsky, 'Geba, Gibeah and Gibeon, an Historical-Geographical Riddle', *BASOR* 212 (1973), pp. 26-31.

'Gibeah' is always used with the article (הגבעה Hos. 9.9; 10.9a and בגבעה Hos. 10.9b). Moreover, Hosea mentions 'days' of Gibeah while Judg. 19 relates events that happened in a single night. In spite of all the uncertainty, Judg. 19 could still be illustrating what went on, at night, on one of the proverbial 'days of Gibeah'. Moreover, as Hosea and the book of Saviours both originate from Bethel, Jerusalem would be using a Benjaminite proverb to legitimize the destruction or the discontinuation of Bethel's cultic functions.

The Benjaminites probably made use of the Saul traditions to resist the restoration of Jerusalem. They would have stressed that Saul was king before David and that David was a servant of Saul. Against such claims, Judg. 19 stresses the discrepancy between two symbols of Judaean and Benjaminite rule: Bethlehem, the home of both David and the Levite's concubine (1 Sam. 17.12; Judg. 19.1-2), stands for Judah, while Gibeah/ Gibeon, Saul's capital and the scene of the rape (1 Sam. 11.4; Judg. 19.15), stands for Benjamin. In Bethlehem, the concubine's father is so overwhelmingly hospitable that it takes the Levite two days to extricate himself and take leave (Judg. 19.5-9). In Gibeah, local Benjaminites leave the travellers on the open square and deny them the most elementary hospitality (Judg. 19.15). The choice of these two towns is significant: Bethlehem marks the southern limit of Judaean territory after 586 BCE, as Hebron and the rest of Southern Judah then came under Edomite control.[22]

Parallelisms with Saul's Traditions

In Judg. 19, all decisions are taken in Mizpah because, at the time of writing, Mizpah is the capital of Judah. This situation is also reflected in 1 Sam. 10.17 where Samuel calls Israel together in Mizpah to draw lots for a king. That a Benjaminite would be chosen to become the first king of Israel, an entity traditionally centred around Shechem, Tirzah and then Samaria, can be explained by the proximity of Benjamin with the Philistine core in the tenth century BCE.[23] That this king should be 'elected' in Mizpah rather than in Gibeon, Saul's capital, is intriguing, unless this passage has in mind, like Judg. 20, the Judaean political situation at the end of the sixth century BCE.[24] Several disparaging references to Saul are manifestly aimed at countering the Benjaminites' use of the Saul traditions

22. Bartlett, 'Edom', pp. 13-24.
23. E.A. Knauf, 'David, Saul, and the Philistines: From Geography to History', *BN* 109 (2001), pp. 15-18.
24. Mathys, 'Saul'.

to justify Jerusalem's replacement by Mizpah: the dismembering of the concubine (Judg. 19.29) is the most obvious of these references. To the same aim, Saul's oxen are replaced by a Judaean woman to call out Israel (1 Sam. 11.7), this time, not to save Jabesh-gilead but to slaughter the whole of Benjamin. In Judg. 19.16, it is not the dashing young Saul who returns from the fields (1 Sam. 11.5), but an old Ephraimite whose house is to become a trap for the Levite and his concubine. All this amounts to a literary war, a war over Mizpah's dignity and ability to remain the province's capital.

Secondary Additions

The ark. The ark of the covenant appears in Judg. 20.27b-28a. This note presupposes the end of the Priestly narrative in Josh. 18.1: 'Then the whole assembly of the people of Israel assembled at Shiloh, and set up the tent of meeting there; the land laid subdued before them'. If the Priestly writer accomplished his work around 515 BCE,[25] the note about the ark in Judg. 20 could be original. However, because the ark plays no role in the story, it was more probably added later in order to harmonize Judges with the other books, once the collection of 'historical books' was appended to the Torah (see Chapter 7). This note does not betray the original leanings of the text. It just makes Bethel's divinatory faculties subservient to the presence of the ark, a presence that seems exceptional and short-lived if one takes into account that the books of Samuel duly record how the ark was lost before being brought in Jerusalem by David. By setting the scene of Yhwh's order for the final onslaught against Gibeah in front of the ark at Bethel, the editors are foretelling Benjamin's demise and the replacement of Bethel by Jerusalem.

The Levite. The mention of Phinehas son of Eleazar son of Aaron in the same note (Judg. 20.28) is more difficult to evaluate. According to Blenkinsopp, that element reflects struggles among priestly factions, between Jerusalem and Bethel before Jerusalem supplanted Bethel for good.[26] In

25. E.A. Knauf, 'Die Priesterschrift und die Geschichten der Deuteronomisten' in Th. Römer (ed.), *The Future of the Deuteronomistic History* (BETL, 147; Leuven: Peteers, 2000), pp. 101-118 (114-15). Or around 530 BCE according to A. de Pury, 'Der priesterschriftliche Umgang mit der Jakobsgeschichte', in R.G. Kratz, T. Krüger and K. Schmid (eds.), *Schriftauslegung in der Schrift* (BZAW, 300; Berlin: W. de Gruyter, 2001), pp. 33-60 (39-40).

26. Blenkinsopp, 'Judean Priesthood', p. 42.

fact, Phinehas is not totally isolated in Judg. 19–20: the main figure in Judg. 19 is a Levite, and Levites (Aaronites or not) are clearly linked to the sanctuary of Bethel.[27] In a society that evaluated women's actions according to their impact on men's fortune and prestige, the flight of the concubine back to her father's home was harmful to the Levite's reputation.[28] Whatever the exact status of the concubine and the reason of her departure,[29] the fact is that the Levite was unable to prevent her flight. Moreover, his xenophobic insistence to spend the night in Israelite territory rather than in the city of the Jebusites (Judg. 19.11-13) is the primary cause for the death of his Judaean concubine. Worse, Judg. 19.29 suggests that his dismembering of the woman was a human sacrifice.[30] If the Levite is victim of the Benjaminites, he is also victim of his own stubbornness. Levites do not come out of Judg. 19 any better than they did in Judg. 17–18. In other words, Judaean women are warned to keep away from Levites as well as from Benjaminites.

Whether or not Phinehas is original here is of little consequence. What matters is to understand that Judg. 19–20 is situated literally at the exact opposite from the story of the conquest of Bethel (Judg. 1.22-26), which was considered at the beginning of this chapter. In Judg. 1.22-26, Bethel asserts its credentials against Jerusalem. Judges 19–20 is Jerusalem's reply in the form of narrative slander, heaping opprobrium on Benjaminite traditions (Saul) and Benjaminite clergy (Levites). Judges 20 illustrates the consequences for despising Jerusalem and considering it as a foreign city.[31] Such adamant rejection of Jerusalem leads to the total destruction of Benjamin save for a few hundred men. Whether this destruction records a civil war that actually took place is difficult to say, but the end result is clear: the future of Benjamin is now in Judaean hands, and the power has shifted from Mizpah and Bethel back to Jerusalem. Judges 21 delineates the conditions for a Benjaminite revival.

27. Blenkinsopp, 'Judean Priesthood', pp. 34-43.

28. K. Stone, *Sex, Honor and Power in the Deuteronomist History* (JSOTSup, 234; Sheffield: Sheffield Academic Press, 1996), pp. 72-73.

29. In Judg. 19.2, the Hebrew lesson 'She played the harlot' is not well attested in the versions.

30. מאכלת 'knife' in Judg. 19.29 is a *terminus technicus* for sacrifice (see Gen. 22.6, 10): Jüngling, *Richter 19*, p. 254; Unterman 'Binding', pp. 161-66.

31. That the Levite considers Jerusalem as foreign expresses Benjaminites feelings at the beginning of the Persian period rather than the fact that David had not yet conquered Jerusalem.

Judges 21: Women for Benjamin

Is Judges 21 Later than Judges 19–20?

The last chapter of Judges explains how 600 women were found for the Benjaminite warriors who had escaped the genocide of Judg. 20. Judah is never mentioned. A vague group called 'man of Israel' (איש ישראל) is said to have sworn in Mizpah not to give daughters in marriage to Benjaminites (Judg. 21.1), but such a oath, vital for the developments of the whole chapter, is not recorded in the previous chapters. Judges 21 could therefore be suspected to have been appended secondarily to Judg. 20. The 'people' or the 'militia' (Judg. 21.2-12) go up to Bethel and shed tears over the annihilation of Benjamin which has just been accomplished so thoroughly. The change of attitude is so radical and sudden that it adds to the suspicions about the secondary character of Judg. 21. The annihilation of Benjamin would have offered a satisfactory conclusion for Judg. 19–20 for the benefit of Jerusalem, thus providing an etiological tale for the steady decline of the Benjamin region in the Persian period. This decline has been explained as the consequence of a civil war,[32] and Judg. 19–20 could well mirror such events. A later edition, more favourable to Benjamin, would have criticized the genocide and added a story about the rehabilitation of the lost tribe of Israel.

However, the loud cries (בכי גדול) at Bethel (Judg. 21.2) may actually be crocodile tears. The origin of the first lot of maidens, obtained through the slaughter of the rest of the population of Jabesh-gilead (Judg. 21.8-12), favours this impression. The ban on Jabesh is justified by the fact that the Jabeshites did not turn up at the Mizpah assembly, thus exposing themselves to the sanction of another oath that supposedly had been taken in Mizpah, but over which Judg. 19–20 remain silent. It is difficult to avoid the conclusion that the choice of Jabesh is meant to refer to Saul's rescue of the same Jabesh in 1 Sam. 11. The story of Jabesh-gilead's massacre appears then to be preoccupied more with staining Saul's heroic deed than with offering a realistic solution to the near extinction of Benjamin. That impression is confirmed by the fact that the 400 maidens from Jabesh did not suffice to provide a spouse for each Benjaminite survivor (Judg. 21.14). A question therefore arises: is the Jabesh episode to be understood as a serious attempt to find a solution to the Benjaminite problem or is it

---

32. Grabbe, *Judaism* 1, pp. 93-94, 99-100.

yet another way to cover Israel with ridicule? A historical evaluation is therefore necessary.

What would the invitation to marry Jabeshites mean to Benjaminites at the end of the sixth century or at the beginning of the fifth century BCE? Gilead had in fact been controlled by Damascus since Jehu's days (841–814 BCE) and was then integrated into the Assyrian Empire.[33] This obviously did not prevent the survival of blood ties across the Jordan. Ties were still strong when the Tobiads, based just opposite Benjamin in Philadelphia and Iraq el-Amir, played an important role in Judaean politics during the Persian and Hellenistic periods. Links across the Jordan valley are therefore structural and survived political fluctuations.[34] Looking for wives in Gilead could then be a realistic option for Benjaminites during the Persian period. However, the method used in Judg. 21, through the banning of the rest of the town, is much more dubious. Heavy doubts remain over the real intentions of the narrators.

Benjamin in the Fifth and Fourth Centuries BCE
The slow decline of the Benjamin region is well attested by the Benjamin survey,[35] in spite of the fact that Benjamin was spared Babylonian destruction around 586 BCE, and in spite of the installation of the province's administrative centre in Mizpah. The eastern and western fringes (Shephelah and Jordan valley) were soon deserted, but all the population did not go down to Egypt (against Jer. 43; 2 Kgs 25.11, 26). The population concentrated itself on the Benjaminite plateau, around Mizpah. The high tide of the seventh century BCE demography had receded, these were difficult times. The economical situation was depressed since the Babylonians had ravaged Jerusalem, Southern Judah and Philistia once they realized that Egypt could not be conquered. This scorched earth policy created a deserted buffer zone between Syria and Egypt. Benjamin and the

33. M. Ottoson, *Gilead: Tradition and History* (ConBOT, 3; Lund: C.W.K. Gleerup, 1969), pp. 232-35; N. Na'aman, 'Rezin of Damascus and the Land of Gilead', *ZDPV* 111 (1995), pp. 105-17.
34. E.A. Knauf, 'Berg und Tal, Stadt und Stamm: Grundzüge der Geschichte Palästinas in den letzen fünftausend Jahren' in G. Völger, K. von Welck and K. Hackstein (eds.), *Pracht und Geheimnis: Kleidung und Schmuck aus Palästina und Jordanien. Katalog der Sammlung Widad Kawar anlässlich einer Ausstellung des Rautenstrauch-Joest-Museums in Zusammenarbeit mit dem Institute of Archaeology and Anthropology der Yarmuk Universität Irbid vom 3. Oktober 1987 bis 27. März 1988* (Ethnologica, 13; Köln: Rautenstrauch-Joest-Museum, 1987), pp. 26-35, 417-18.
35. Lipschits, 'Benjamin Region'.

Mountain of Ephraim remained as islands, isolated from the economical centres of the northern Phoenician harbours.

The slow recovery of Jerusalem, once the Persians had conquered Egypt, did not drastically improve the situation in Benjamin. With renewed foreign investments, Jerusalem soon became Benjamin's competitor, gradually taking over all the official functions that had kept Mizpah and Bethel alive through the Babylonian period. The story of Benjamin's destruction and the desperate search for women could be a distorted reflection of the economical crisis that prolonged itself in Benjamin in the Persian period.

The books of Ezra and Nehemiah reflect in their own way the great odds faced by the restorers of Jerusalem. To repopulate the city, they even had to revert to coercive measures (Neh. 11.1). Opposition came from all sides and the oath against giving women in marriage to Benjaminites (Judg. 21.1) bears similarities with the one in Neh. 10.30, although this last one is directed against 'the peoples of the land' עמי־הארץ rather than directly against Benjamin. However, in the eyes of the new masters of Jerusalem, Benjamin was certainly included among these abhorred peoples of the land, alongside Edomites in the South and other Israelites in the North. It is noteworthy that Neh. 11 considers Judah and Benjamin as two separate entities within *Yehud* (Neh. 11.4, 7, 25, 31) and the Benjaminite leaders were probably just as keen to keep the distinction in order to preserve as much autonomy from Judah as possible. Jerusalem even appears as another separate area, a kind of free zone, subjected to particular rules. The holy city עיר־הקדש (Neh. 11.1, 18) is thus peopled in equal parts by sons of Judah, sons of Benjamin, priests, Levites and gatekeepers. The rest of 'Israel' lives in all the towns in Judah (Neh. 11.20) while the people of Benjamin live in Benjamin (Neh. 11.31). But this neat arrangement is disturbed by some Levites who belong to Benjamin but possess property in Judah: ומן־הלוים מחלקות יהודה לבנימין 'And certain divisions of the Levites in Judah were joined to Benjamin' (v. 36). Persian *Yehud* is made up of three separate constituencies, Benjamin, Judah and neutral Jerusalem in between; it is no melting pot, rancour is running high between the different factions. This situation should have repercussions on the understanding of Judg. 21.

Slaughtering Jabesh to Make up for the Slaughter of Benjamin
How should the massacre of the population of Jabesh, carried out to provide wives for Benjamin, be interpreted? In the context of the Persian

period, it is obvious that the exiles that came back from Babylonia with Persian official backing would not accept the authority of Mizpah and that tensions would readily come to a head. From the returnees' vantage point, Mizpah and Bethel were traitors, lackeys of Nebuchadnezzar who had ruined Jerusalem and deported them, servants of a power that was now defeated. The Benjaminites were just as likely to resist the authority of these freshly arrived upstarts who were eager to wipe out all traces of the Babylonian period and return Jerusalem to its former status. The returnees had to affirm their position over a hostile local population by standing apart from the people of the land, at least at the beginning. Hence the oath to forbid *conubium* and to stay pure from involvement with the Babylonian collaborators. In such a context, the weird solutions for the Benjaminite survival recommended by Judg. 21 may not be solutions at all. Coming from the new masters of Jerusalem, Judg. 21 would amount to a point-blank refusal of alliances with the former Benjaminite elite of the province. Power had shifted back into Judaean hands, and the Judaeans wanted no Benjaminite allies. Benjaminites should follow the example of their ancestor and seek women in Gilead (Gen. 28). Judah reaches the height of irony by offering to the Benjaminites to slaughter their Benjaminite cousins in Gilead, precisely the descendants of those who were saved by Saul. The point is clear enough, no one among the Benjaminites would take the advice literally.

Abduction of the Shiloh Dancers

Can the same be said about the second solution, the recommendation of the elders of the congregation to kidnap maidens from the dancers at the Shiloh festival? Is this also a tongue-in-cheek offer or is it a serious proposal that could indicate the presence of a Benjaminite-friendly edition? It is possible that this episode has been appended later because the negative particle in Judg. 21.14b ולא־מצאו להם כן 'and they did (not) find so' indicating that the Jabesh maidens did not suffice, is unattested by most Greek versions. An earlier draft would have moved directly from v. 14 onto v. 24, concluding that the Jabesh maidens were given to the Benjaminite survivors and that it had been the way the Benjaminites had found their women before the people of Israel went back home, every man to his inheritance. Adding the negation in v. 14 and the number 400 in v. 12 made way for the introduction of a second episode explaining how the 200 missing women were found. Compared to the first part of the chapter, the tone seems to have changed, a solution is found without further massacre in sharp contrast with the previous episode. The text even seems to underline the fairness of the deal, as the Benjaminites took women according to their numbers נשים למספרם (Judg. 21.23). Of course, the text is aware that the anger of the dancers' families would have to be placated. The elders have a solution ready at hand in v. 22: 'And when their fathers or their brothers come to complain to us, we will say to them, "Grant them graciously to us; because we did not take for each man of them his wife in battle, neither did you give them to them, else you would be guilty".' A rather complicated argument indeed, but the understanding of the Shiloh episode hangs on the understanding of this verse. It is therefore necessary to give it a closer look.

Translated literally, Judg. 21.22 says:

והיה כי־יבאו אבותם או אחיהם לרוב אלינו

It will happen that their fathers or their brothers will come to complain to us

ואמרנו אליהם חנונו אותם

we will tell them: 'grant them graciously

כי לא לקחנו איש אשתו במלחמה

because we did not take each his wife in the war

כי לא אתם נתתם להם

because it is not you who gave to them

כעת תאשמו

now you are guilty'.

A first problem appears in the identity of the fathers and brothers that will come to complain to the elders. According to the context, they are obviously the relatives of the Shiloh dancers who are bound to require compensation and redress for the offence they suffered. However, in this case the text should read אבותן או אחיהן, (plural feminine suffixes) instead of אבותם או אחיהם (plural masculine suffixes) since women and women only are referred to. The masculine suffixes make no sense because after the ban on Benjamin, the Benjaminite raptors would have no surviving fathers or brothers who could come to complain. And if some were still alive, they would have no reason to complain if their sons or brothers got some wives for free. However, since the gradual supplentation of the plural feminine suffix by its masculine counterpart is a mark of late

Biblical Hebrew,[36] the masculine suffixes can be understood as referring to the stolen women's relatives.

A second problem arises with the reason invoked by the elders to placate the kidnapped maidens relatives: they should be compassionate towards the Benjaminite survivors because 'we' did not take each his woman in the war. This 'we' must refer to those who were presented as the speakers at the beginning of the episode (v. 16): the elders, speaking presumably in the name of the whole congregation and of all the participants in the war against Benjamin in Judg. 20. Whether or not these complaining fathers and brothers are included in the 'we' is open to question. The idea is that the women were not captured during the war, although this would have been a normal war procedure. The only way to make sense of the argument is that, unlike the other Israelites, these fathers and brothers had indeed taken for themselves Benjaminite women as captives instead of killing them all as Judg. 20 seemed to presuppose. The reason that they should grant their daughters for free is thus that they themselves had taken some Benjaminite female prisoners as wives, contrarily to the 'we' who is speaking. In fact, a close reading of Judg. 20 shows that the slaughter of Benjaminite women is inferred but never made explicit.[37] It is therefore possible that some Benjaminite women were taken by Israelites instead of being killed and that their new owners happened to be the ones who had lost their daughters in Shiloh.

Moreover, the elders provide a second reason to convince the fathers and brothers: they would not actually *give* the women. This is usually understood as a ruse to circumvent the oath forbidding to give daughters to Benjamin: indeed the girls were to be stolen rather than given.[38] In that case, the last words כעת תאשׁמו 'now you are guilty' have to be rended as 'else you would now be guilty', a rather twisted translation. Another problem arises with the understanding of the clause introduced by the second כ: is it introducing a second reason or is it part of the same argument? The elders seem to reproach the fathers and brothers the fact that they were prevented by these very fathers and brothers to take women captives for themselves because they did not give them. This reading presents two difficulties: in apposition, אתם should be placed before

---

36. Joüon and Muraoka, *Grammar,* §149b.

37. Judg. 20.35 mentions soldiers, v. 37 the whole population of Gibeah. Verses 44-46 count only the warriors and v. 48 has a strange lesson מתם before the beasts in the Benjaminite towns.

38. Becker, *Richterzeit,* p. 290 understands this solution as a 'raffinierte Lösung'.

the negation: כי אתם לא נתתם 'because you, you did not give' instead of
כי לא אתם נתתם להם 'because it is not you who gave to them'. The object
of the verb is clearly indirect: נתתם להם 'gave to them' referring to the
Benjaminites and not to the 'we' as suggested by *BHK*. Two ideas seem to
be entangled: firstly, the families whose girls were abducted by the Benjaminite survivors happen to be the ones who kept some Benjaminite
female prisoners alive, they are therefore guilty and should not claim compensation. Secondly, the oath was not broken because the Shiloh girls
were taken and not given.

As a whole, the verse that is supposed to provide the solution for the
Benjaminite problem remains rather unclear. Either it was damaged through
transmission or it was meant to be tortuous from the start, expressing
mumbo jumbo bargaining between rogues, rather than a convincing argument to afford protection to the Benjaminite survivors. In this case, the
editor's disdain for Benjamin is conveyed in a more convincing way than
the reason why the offended brothers should not seek revenge on the last
Benjaminites who raped their sisters. This brings us back to the question:
are the editors really looking for solutions? Are they genuinely caring for
the Benjaminites' fate? More than ever, the answer is no.

Another element to reverse this impression could come from extra-
biblical confirmation of the feasibility of matrimonial solutions such as the
one recommended by the elders.

Oriental Marriage Custom

Oriental customs pertaining to marriage procedures are rather strict. The
obscure reasons put forward by the elders are unlikely to be very persua-
sive, even if the fathers of the girls were guilty of keeping some captives
and even if the rape was a convenient way to circumvent a solemn oath.
Nevertheless, some elements do indicate that rape was an option to acquire
wives.

Attested practices of abduction of wives. Ethnological studies have shown
that certain groups perform the ritual capture of the bride during the marriage ceremonies.[39] These rites used to be understood as remnants of
primitive practices[40] but they are now interpreted as expressions of the
pain induced by separation in exogamic marriages, the grief of the bride

39. Neufeld, *Marriage Laws*, pp. 84-85; R.H. Barnes, 'Marriage by Capture', *JRAI*
46 (1999), pp. 57-73 (57-68).
40. Neufeld, *Marriage Laws*, p. 77.

who is being uprooted and the resistance of her mother and brothers to letting her go.[41] These mock abductions, sometimes performed with such eagerness that they cause serious injuries, are rites of passage rather than survivals of ancient practices.

However, real rapes and abductions aiming at procuring wives are still attested today, in particular where fathers or brothers are granted unchallenged authority over the marriage of the women of the family. The enquiry will begin with contemporary Turkish examples.

Oriental marriages are the result of a long negotiating process to reach agreement over bride price, date of the ceremony and dowry payment. Certain preliminary conditions are necessary before negotiations can even start. The groom's family should represent the best offer available to the bride's family, both families should therefore have equivalent social standing. In practice, many obstacles can prevent marriage: the presence of other suitors is likely to push up the bidding. Abduction then becomes an option for a keen but not so well off party.

One has to act quickly, before marriage is settled with another suitor. Often helped by a few friends and with the complicity of one of the girl's relatives, usually a woman herself married through abduction, the young man kidnaps the girl and rapes her. Once she has lost her virginity, her most precious asset in the eyes of her family, she is not likely to file a legal complaint against her rapist, her best interest is to side with her new husband. The new couple is taken into the family of the rapist, morally bound to look after them both even if it objects to the marriage, or it would commit an even graver offence towards the girl's family.[42] Compensation is paid, but the groom ought not to meet his brothers-in-law. It is not before at least a year, or better, after the birth of the first child, that the couple will visit the girl's family to make peace. On that occasion, a mock ambush is set and the man is hung by the feet until his mother-in-law redeems him by offering a drink to the avengers. Relations may nevertheless remain very tense between the two families for years.[43]

---

41. M. Burrows, *The Basis of Israelite Marriage* (AOS, New Haven: 1938), pp. 51-52; E. Grosse, *Die Formen der Familie und die Formen der Wirtschaft* (Freiburg: 1896), pp. 105-106; Barnes, 'Marriage by capture', p. 69; Neufeld, *Marriage Laws*, p. 85.

42. A. Kudat, 'Institutional Rigidity and Individual Initiative in Marriages of Turkish Peasants', *AQ* 47 (1974), pp. 288-303 (291-99).

43. D.G. Bates, 'Normative and Alternative Systems of Marriages among the Yörük of Southeastern Turkey', *AQ* 47 (1974), pp. 270-87 (278).

This Turkish example shows that, parallel to the preferred mode of cousin marriage arranged by the family, a large proportion of marriages (around 20%) are contracted through rape. This deviant and frowned upon practice allows adaptation to economical reality while, at the same time, preserving the ideological basis of the society.[44] But it should be noted that some elopments are covered up as rapes in order to preserve the girl's reputation vis-à-vis her family and village.

It is therefore clear that abduction and rape are a viable option to get a wife today in Turkey and that it can be inferred that a similar situation could have existed in Israel during the Persian period. However, it remains a dangerous method, engendering serious and lasting social trauma.

A second example, this time from Jordan, shows that the social trauma engendered by the abduction of maidens has been used to heal an even worse trauma: the trauma of unending blood feuds between Bedouin tribes. In this case, the rapes were organized by King Abdullah to put an end to the vendetta that tore his people. Having a young man, from the wronged tribe, abduct and marry a maiden from the guilty tribe, the king apparently managed to break the cycle of violence because the blood of the raped girl put an end to the shedding of blood in both groups.[45] These modern practices can be compared to ancient law codes to look for evidence of abduction practices closer to the Persian period.

Ancient laws punishing rape and abduction of women. Biblical laws are silent over the abduction of women, apart from defining the status of war captives (Deut. 21.10-14). A decree edicted by Ptolemy II around 260 BCE deals specifically with captured wives: 'Whoever of the soldiers on active duty and the other military settlers in Syria and Phoenicia are living with native wives whom they have captured need not declare them.'[46] The captors are exonerated from taxes on this category of slave, on condition that they live with them. Once again, these women were captured in war or in the anarchic aftermath of the conquest of Palestine by Ptolemy. This military context suits the Jabesh episode but not that of Shiloh. Hittite laws are the most lenient towards the man who abducted his wife to overcome family refusal.[47] On the other hand, Assyrian laws tolerate no marriage

44. Bates, 'Yörük', p. 284.

45. M. Assad, *Le chemin de la Mecque* (Paris: Fayard, 1976), pp. 106-107.

46. R.S. Bagnall and P. Derow, *Greek Historical Documents: The Hellenistic Period* (SBLSBS, 16; Atlanta: Scholars Press, 1981), p. 96.

47. H.A. Hoffner, 'Hittite Laws', *CoS* 2, pp. 106-119: §28a 'If a daughter has been

following abduction once the bride price has been paid (A §26).[48] Prior to such payment, rape (A §55) is clearly distinguished from elopement and consent (A §56) but both practices are discouraged, the price is higher than for a normal marriage and the offended father retains the right to receive compensation without granting his daughter to the rapist. A §55 mentions the case of rape during the city festival, a situation similar to the Shiloh episode. However, festivals are no excuse for rape, Assyrian laws allow no mitigating circumstances during feasts. Until contrary evidence can be found, the Shiloh festival cannot be considered as a particular time of sexual license providing special relaxation of rules in order to facilitate matrimonial endeavours.

In spite of differing attitudes, Hittite and Mesopotamian codes prove that some marriages were the result of abduction. Although it is impossible to ascertain how close these laws are to the ones practised in Persian Israel and Judah, one has to admit that, in regard to the desperate situation of the Benjaminite survivors, the solution recommended by the elders is realistic, or at least more realistic than the ban on Jabesh. It could be added that the abduction of the Shiloh dancers is the best possible option for men

promised to a man, but another man runs off with her, he who runs off with her shall give to the first man whatever he paid and shall compensate him'. §35 'If a herdsman elopes with a free woman and does not pay a brideprice for her, she will become a slave for (only) 3 years'. §37 'If anyone elopes with a woman, and a group of supporters goes after them, if 3 or 2 men are killed, there shall be no compensation: you (singular) have become a wolf'.

48. M. Roth, 'The Laws of Eshnunna', *CoS* 2, pp. 332-35: §26 'If a man brings the bridewealth for the daughter of a man, but another, without the consent of her father and mother, abducts her and then deflowers her, it is indeed a capital offense, he shall die'. Roth, 'Assyrian Laws', pp. 353-60: A §55 'If a man forcibly seizes and rapes a maiden who is residing in her father's house…whether in the city or in the countryside, or at night whether in the main thoroughfare, or in a granary, or during the city festival, the father of the maiden shall take the wife of the fornicator of the maiden and hand her over to be raped; he shall not return her to her husband, but he shall take (and keep?) her; the father shall give his daughter who is the victim of fornication into the protection of the household of her fornicator. If he (the fornicator) has no wife, the fornicator shall give triple the silver as the value of the maiden to her father; her fornicator shall marry her; he shall not reject(?) her. If the father does not desire it so, he shall give triple silver for the maiden, and he shall give his daughter in marriage to whomever he chooses'. A §56 'If a maiden should willingly give herself to a man, the man shall so swear; they shall have no claim to his wife; the fornicator shall pay triple the silver as the value of the maiden; the father shall treat his daughter in whatever manner he chooses'.

who lost everything in the war, in spite of the obvious dangers incurred by them. As it is the case today in Turkey, abduction of a woman in order to marry her was probably better than what the Turks call *iç güveyilik*. According to this type of marriage, a poor and landless man enters the wife's family that is in need of manpower. In this case, the groom admits his social inferiority and his cowardice, compared to the man who has proved his courage and his passion by daring to abduct his wife.[49] Judges 21 is therefore based on two kinds of practices, marriage of war captives and abduction of maidens during period of peace.

But, as we saw that the Shiloh episode could have been added on later, it is also possible that Judg. 21.14-24 does not refer so much to an actual practice as to mythological rapes since these are well attested in the Mediterranean world.[50]

Mythological Abduction and Rape
The rape of the Shiloh dancers has many parallels in classical mythology,[51] a few of which are now reviewed, starting from the Phoenician coast westwards.

Europa. The daughter of a Tyrian legendary king, Europa is abducted by Greeks. Her brother Kadmos searches Greece for her and, on the way, founds cults in Thera, Rhodes and Lindos. He transmits the alphabet and bronze metallurgy to the Greeks. The Greek origin of the myth is admitted because it conveys the Greek vantage point on Phoenician colonization of the Mediterranean, and because Europa does not appear on Tyrian coinage before the Roman period.[52]

Hippolyte. The earliest attestation of the Amazons in Attica is found in connection with Heracles who seized the girdle of Hippolyte their queen. The introduction of the Amazons within the Heracles traditions is attributed to the tyrant Pisistratus who consolidated his rule in Athens by identifying himself to Heracles. After Pisistratus (his tyranny ended in 510 BCE), the Amazons are integrated into the *Theseis*, the epic of the king who abdicated in favour of his people. Traditionally known as Helen and

---

49. Exactly what Hos. 12.12 reproaches to Jacob!
50. B. Lincoln, 'The Rape of Persephone: A Greek Scenario of Women's Initiation', *HTR* 72 (1979), pp. 223-35.
51. Gaster, *Myth*, p. 445.
52. C. Bonnet, 'Kadmos', *DCPP*, p. 241.

Ariadne's abductor,[53] Theseus also became Hippolyte's whom he married and brought to Athens. The Amazons retaliated by invading Attica and attacking Athens. A treaty was arranged thanks to Hippolyte's intervention. Hippolyte probably became the mother of Theseus' successor in Athens, but it is not sure since the *Theseis* is now fragmentary.[54] However, the rape of Hippolyte is attested on a Athenian bas relief around 510 BCE[55] and in a fragment from the mythographer Pherecydes around 475 BCE.[56] The rape motive was purged from the *Theseis* when the Athenian victories over the Persians turned Athens into the champion of anti-Persian resistance and centre of a counter-empire.[57] Amazons then became the symbol of the Persian aggressor, and the rape was unsuitable as it put Athens in the role of the aggressor, the invasion of Attica being the result of the rape of Hippolyte by Theseus. Moreover, Hippolyte's conciliatory role would have deprived Athens of the ideological basis for its imperialistic ventures over the other Greek cities.[58]

The rape of Hippolyte was therefore well known throughout the Greek world in the fifth century BCE,[59] when, according to the working hypothesis of this chapter, Judg. 21 was composed. Though it involves only one woman, it justified the synoecism that allowed the young city of Athens to extend its dominion.[60]

Greek myths record other rapes, Persephone or Kore by Hades,[61] Anymone by Poseidon, Polyxena by Achilles, Oreithyia by Boreus, Auge by Heracles, Hermione by Orestes, the Leucippides by the Dioscuri and

53. Attested from the seventh century BCE: M. Robertson, *History of Greek Art* (Cambridge: Cambridge University Press, 1975), fig. 125.441.535.579.596.

54. Huxley, *Epic Poetry*, pp. 116-18.

55. D. von Bothmer, *Amazons in Greek Art* (Oxford: Oxford University Press, 1957), pp. 117-119; W.B. Dinsmoor, 'The Athenian Treasury as Dated by its Ornaments', *AJA* 50 (1946), pp. 111-13.

56. F. Jacoby, *Die Fragmente der Griechischen Historiker* (Leiden: E.J. Brill, 1968), 1 A 64 fr. 15; 1 A 98 fr. 152.

57. J.H. Blok, *The Early Amazons* (Leiden: E.J. Brill, 1995), p. 441.

58. W.B. Tyrrell, *Amazons: A Study in Athenian Mythmaking* (Baltimore: John Hopkins, 1984), p. 15.

59. J.G. Préaux, 'La sacralité du pouvoir royal à Rome', *ACERB* 1 (1962), pp. 108-135 (117).

60. R. Parker, *Athenian Religion: A History* (Oxford: Clarendon Press, 1996), pp. 10-17.

61. N.J. Richardson, *The Homeric Hymn to Demeter* (Oxford: Clarendon Press, 1974), pp. 10-11.

many others. These were spread across the Mediterranean world through graphic representation on Attic ware attested in Palestine since the sixth century BCE.[62]

The Messenians. Soggin claims that this episode is the most interesting parallel for Judg. 21 because it takes place during a religious festival:[63]

> On the border of Messenia there is a sanctuary, who is called the Lady of the Lake; and the only Dorians who shared the possession of the sanctuary were the Messenians and Lacedaemonians. The Lacedaemonians say that some of their maidens who went to the festival were violated by men of Messenia... Further they say that the violated maidens destroyed themselves from shame.[64]

The outcome of the Messenian event is very different from the one in Shiloh. The girls commit suicide and a grievous war ensues.

Pausanias reports another case of abduction of maidens who were dancing at Caryae in honour of Artemis. The wealthiest and noblest ones were picked up and taken for ransom, not for marriage. Here, like in the previous episode, it is clear that the abduction of young women during ritual dances or during festivals is not accepted practice and provokes extremely violent reactions. In this case, some of the men who were guarding the girls during the night tried to rape them, but the misbehaving guards were put to death by the abductors themselves.[65]

Judging from the Greek evidence, it seems doubtful that festivals offered any particular relaxing of laws concerning abduction and rape. Judges 21 would be advising the Benjaminites to follow a most dangerous path. The trouble-free accomplishment of the advice in v. 23 remains baffling and it is hard to accept this conclusion of a happy ending without wondering if this is not another instance of Judaean derision of the Benjaminites.

62. J.Y. Perreault, 'Céramique et échanges: les importations attiques au Proche Orient du VIème au milieu du Vème s. av. J.C.', *BCH* 110 (1986), pp. 145-75; A. Cohen, 'Portrayals of Abduction in Greek Art', in N. Boymel Kampen (ed.), *Sexuality in Ancient Art* (Cambridge: 1996), pp. 117-35.

63. J.A. Soggin, *Judges* (London: SCM Press, 1981), p. 304 citing Gaster *Myth*, p. 445.

64. Pausanias, *Description of Greece* (trans. W.H.S. Jones; LCL; London: Heinemann, 1940), 4.4.2.

65. Pausanias, 4.16.9.

Persian women according to Herodotus. In the introduction to his *Histories*, Herodotus discusses the guilt of Persians, Phoenicians and Greeks concerning the rapes of Io, Europa and Helen:

> We think, say they [the Persians] that it is wrong to carry women off: but to be zealous to avenge the rape is foolish: wise men take no account of such things: for plainly, the women would have never been carried away had they not themselves wished it (Herodotus 1.4).

This passage cannot be used to found a comparison of attitudes to rape between Greeks and Persians, as Herodotus is merely building an argument on hearsay without pronouncing himself on the matter. However, this imaginary discussion shows that in the ancient Orient, the rape of 200 dancers from Shiloh would have been a very serious matter. It would have required much more than the somewhat jumbled argument in Judg. 21.22 to end up as happily as it does in Judg. 21.23-24.

The Sabines. The tale of the rape of the Sabines, by far the closest parallel to the Shiloh episode, recounts the abduction of several hundred young women by the founders of Rome. The oldest versions do not limit the abduction to the daughters of the Sabines, one of the most powerful people around Rome.[66] It is only after a 'sabinization' process of the pre-republican traditions that the episode became known as *Sabinae raptae*.[67]

A few years after its founding by Romulus, Rome was suffering from a grave shortage of women that compromised the future of the city. The king sent serious matrimonial proposals to the nearby people but his envoys were turned away. Romulus then organized games attended by many guests from the surrounding cities. At the king's signal, the young Romans threw themselves on the young women and carried them off. Strict orders had been given in order to protect the honour of the women, and the next day they were presented to the king and duly married to their abductors according to the rituals of their place of origin. In spite of these precautions, the offended people attacked Rome but the women, who had become mothers in the meantime, intervened between their husbands and

---

66. Livy, *Roman History* (trans. B.O. Foster; LCL; London: Heinemann, 1961), 1.9; Dionysius of Halicarnassus, *Roman Antiquities* (trans. E. Cary; LCL; London: Heinemann, 1960), 2.30.

67. J. Poucet, *Recherches sur la légende sabine des origines de Rome* (Bruxelles/Kinshasa: Publications universitaires/Université Lovanium, 1967), p. 164.

their brothers to impose reconciliation.[68] Rome thus assured its survival thanks to the birth of a new generation, but also affirmed its hegemony over the area by sealing alliances with its most powerful neighbours, offering citizenship and honours to the relatives of the raped women. The conciliatory role of the women, even if it was not necessarily part of the earliest forms of the story,[69] is nevertheless a powerful motive of the narrative. Nubile women are the only ones who could provide the city with three generations in less than a year (ascendants, collaterals and children), while reducing to a minimum the dangers of reprisals.

The rape of the Sabines was not integrated into the Romulus cycle before the end of the third century BCE.[70] Roman biographers used Greek models (the Amazon Hippolyte) to explain the integration of important Sabine groups by the city in the fifth century BCE.[71] The aim of both the Hippolyte and the Sabines narratives is to explain the origin of synoecism that prevails between the group who is telling the story and another group, considered up to then as the enemy.

Strangely, this element is lacking in Judg. 21. No centre like Jerusalem is telling how it managed to integrate its powerful neighbours. Instead of mingling Judaeans and Benjaminites to found the city, the rape of the Shiloh girls strengthens the *conubium* interdict and pushes Benjamin into the opposite direction, towards Shiloh, explicitly sited in the land of Canaan (Judg. 21.12).[72] The festival is outside the confines of Judah, in Israelite territory, a fact that excludes the presence of many Judaean dancers. It is therefore clear that Judg. 21 is not refering to any mythological composition. On the contrary, the Jordanian practice mentioned above shows that the abduction of maidens would have been a realistic way to end the conflict, but the fact that the Benjaminites are sent to Shiloh in

---

68. According to G. Dumézil, *Mariages indo-européens* (Bibliothèque historique; Paris: Payot, 1979), p. 75, this episode illustrates the three types of Roman marriages: abduction considered as the highest form of marriage; marriage ceremonies the next day establishing the *confarreatio* (marriage before the gods). A full year of cohabitation establishes the *manus* of the husband on his wife as she has not made use of her right of *usurpatio trinoctii* which would have invalidated the *usus*.

69. Poucet, *Recherches*, p. 239.

70. Poucet, *Recherches*, p. 433.

71. Poucet, *Recherches*, p. 427.

72. This mention of Canaan is not necessarily disparaging because the Priestly writer uses it to designate the promised land (Gen. 33.18; 35.6) see de Pury, 'Umgang', p. 42 n. 43 (read Gen. 33.18 instead of Gen. 33.28). But it clearly indicates that Shiloh is outside of *Yehud*.

Canaan, appears, from the Judaean vantage point, to lead to the opposite conclusion. Judah, the leader of the punitive campaign against Benjamin, makes sure of minimizing the number of Judaean maidens at risk of falling into Benjaminite hands.

Fake Solutions to the Benjaminite Problem: Judaean Apartheid

Both parts of Judg. 21, the slaughter of Jabesh and the rape of the Shiloh dancers convey the same anti-Benjaminite ideology, in spite of the fact that the Shiloh episode may be somewhat later than the Jabesh slaughter. Even if Judg. 21.14-23 is secondary and is simply designed to produce an Israelite counter-part to Hellenistic mythological references, anti-Benjaminite leanings remain strong throughout Judg. 21.

The differences between Judg. 21.1-14a and 14b-23 are therefore not enough to postulate very different origins and dates.[73] The reference to Jabesh is hostile to the Saul traditions cherished in Bethel and Benjamin. The rape in Shiloh may seem more neutral, but the sheer number of abducted girls would sooner start another civil war than resolve the near extinction of the seed of Benjamin. In any case, Judg. 21 keeps Benjamin at arms length from Judah and Jerusalem.

Historically, both solutions to the Benjaminite crisis are theoretically possible. The massacre of Jabesh under Judaean leadership is historically unthinkable before the Hasmonaean period and the campaigns of Alexander Jannaeus (103–76 BCE) in Transjordan. However, there is no need to wait for such a late date for the Jabesh episode as it is a literary reference to Saul's cycle. Matrimonial links between both sides of the Jordan are attested in the Persian period: a Jerusalem priest, son of 'Barzillai' had taken a wife from the daughters of Barzillai the Gileadite and was called by their name (Neh. 7.63-64). Moreover, as the Greek rape stories are attested in Palestine in the fifth century BCE, Judg. 21 can originate at this date. In spite of the great uncertainties pertaining to this period,[74] Neh. 11 clearly indicates the tensions prevailing between Judah and Benjamin during the restoration of Jerusalem. The number of Benjaminites deported by Nebuchadnezzar was negligible contrarily to those from Judah (Neh. 7.6-38) and, as Benjamin was spared devastation by the Babylonians,[75] the Benjaminites provided the largest contingents of masons and carpenters for rebuilding the city (Neh. 3 and 11). The Persian date suggested by

---

73. Against Becker, *Richterzeit*, pp. 290-91.
74. Grabbe, *Judaism* 1, pp. 119-22.
75. Lipschits, 'Benjamin Region', pp. 155-90.

Edenburg for Judg. 19–21 is therefore convincing. These chapters reflect the struggle of Jerusalem's new masters against Benjamin until the hegemony of the new capital was firmly established, until Mizpah and Bethel were pushed into the background, in spite of Bethel's self-defence in Judg. 1.22-26. The pro-monarchical refrain from Judg. 17.6; 18.1 was taken over to append these three new chapters to Josiah's book of Judges. It was split and the first part ('In those days there was no king in Israel') was placed in Judg. 19.1 as introduction. The second part ('every man did what was right in his own eyes') was inserted at the darkest moment of the story, in the middle of the night when the Ephraimite host is offering his daughter and the Levite's concubine to the Benjaminite mob: 'Do with them what seems good in your eyes' עשו להם הטוב בעיניכם (Judg. 19.24). These words thus receive a sinister meaning that they had not in the Josianic period (see Chapter 4).[76] Judges 19–21 are not meant, as Judg. 17–18 were, to justify the annexation of the Israelite provinces but to illustrate the behaviour of Benjaminites when they are given a free hand, and this, of course, with the purpose to justify the rule of Jerusalem over Benjamin. It has even been conjectured that the re-use of the refrain could reflect Zerubbabel's aborted attempt to restore David's throne.[77]

As Judg. 17–18 are part of the Josianic edition, Judg. 19–21 constitute therefore the only appendix proprer to Judges. Amit is right: there is a polemic against Bethel at the end of Judges, but it reaches its greatest virulence in Judg. 19–21 and it is hardly hidden.[78]

Judges 19 and Genesis 19
Before closing this chapter, it may be useful to review the relationship between the parallel rape stories in Judg. 19 and Gen. 19 (the rape attempt of the guests in Lot's home in Sodom). Most exegetes who pronounced themselves on the literary order of dependency of these two chapters are in

---

76. F.E. Greenspahn, 'An Egyptian parallel to Judges 17, 6 and 21, 25', *JBL* 101 (1982), pp. 129-30 has shown the parallels of the refrain with a formula used by Ramesses IV to describe the chaos which preceded the accession of Setnakhte (1184–1182 BCE): 'The land of Egypt had been overthrown with every man being his own standard of right since they had no leader for many years in the times of others'. See W. Erichsen, *Papyrus Harris* 1 (BAe, 5; Bruxelles: Fondation égyptologique Reine Elisabeth, 1933), p. 91.

77. Grabbe, *Judaism* 1, pp. 77-79; on Davidic restoration see W.H. Rose, *Zemah and Zerubbabel* (JSOTSup, 304; Sheffield: Sheffield Academic Press, 2000).

78. Amit, 'Hidden Polemics'.

favour of the antecedence of Gen. 19 over Judg. 19.[79] S. Niditch stands out in believing that Judg. 19 is older because the rape is essential for the development of the narrative in the following chapters while in Gen. 19 it has no link with the context.[80] It can also be noted that both texts correspond to canonical logic: in the blessed times of the patriarchs, Yhwh intervened to prevent heinous crimes but during the time of the judges, Israel had reached such a degree of perversion that God did not intervene any more. If Judg. 19–21 belong to the beginning of the Persian period, before or during the composition of the Torah, Gen. 19 should be considered as a Midrash of Judg. 19, anticipating it and deepening the contrast to darken the 'period of the Judges' which is gradually being conceptualized. Based on their probable dates of composition, Judg. 19 is probably slightly older than Gen. 19, as Niditch suggests.

79. Becker, *Richterzeit*, p. 262 n. 139.

80. S. Niditch, 'The "Sodomite" Theme in Judges 19-20: Family, Community and Social Desintegration', *CBQ* 44 (1982), pp. 365-78 (376-77).

Chapter 7

THE BOOK OF JUDGES WITHIN JEWISH HISTORIOGRAPHY:
JUDGES 1.1-3, 19-21, 36; 2.6-10, 20-3.6;
4.5, 11, 17, 21; 11.12-28; 21.25

The end of the book of Judges has been reached in the previous chapter but a few scattered passages remain to be considered. These have been kept for the end as they belong to the very last editorial stage of the book before its canonization, the period when it was inserted between the books of Joshua and 1 Samuel in order to become one chapter of the so-called Deuteronomistic History or better, one scroll of the Prophetic collection.

The transition between *Joshua* and *Judges* has given rise to contradictory hypotheses, which have been presented in Chapter 2. Schmid is not dealing directly with this issue since his main concern is the way the patriarchs' narratives were connected with the Mosaic story of the Exodus. Although he appears to still be working within the Nothian hypothesis, Schmid is insisting on the fact that within Genesis–2 Kings, the two main caesuras are found between *Genesis* and *Exodus* and between *Joshua* and *Judges*.

The first caesura, between *Genesis* and *Exodus* results from the assembling of the Patriarchal story and the Moses-Exodus story which were, up to then, independant literary blocks.

The second caesura, between *Joshua* and *Judges*, results from the formation of a collection of historical books. The complicated transition between *Joshua* and *Judges* may indicate that *Judges* was independant both from Joshua and from *Samuel-King*.[1]

Schmid remains very cautious and dates the fusion of the Patriarchs with the Exodus-Conquest and with the Judges-Kings narratives during the

---

1. Schmid, *Erzväter*, p. 374, also R.G. Kratz, *Die Komposition der erzählenden Bücher des AT* (Uni-Taschenbücher, 2157; Göttingen: Vandenhoeck & Ruprecht, 2000), p. 198.

early Persian era.[2] However, Schmid's second caesura reveals the weakness of the Nothian Deuteronomistic History that had postulated links between the three books as early as the exilic period. The puzzle of the relation of *Judges* to *Joshua* and *Samuel* is resolved by shifting the process from the Babylonian to the early Persian period. Indeed, this is a small step forward, but another novelty is that Schmid is working with the concept of books and not any more with volatile traditions.[3] Schmid has demonstrated the particularity of *Judges* that does not readily belong to any of the literary blocks within the Genesis–Kings complex. His work therefore legitimizes what has been done here, namely to read *Judges* independently from the other Prophetic books. Moreover, since Schmid has effected the small time shift from the Babylonian to the Persian period, it will be easier to let this first move carry on into the Ptolemaic era, but before we get to problems of date, the transitional material that was inserted into *Judges* in order to fit this so-far independent book between *Joshua* and *1 Samuel* should first be examined.

Transition between Joshua and Judges

Judges 1.1-3: Introducing Joshua Son of Nun into Judges

Judges 1.1. The book of Judges is set after the book of Joshua with the simple words 'After the death of Joshua', thus repeating the device used in Josh. 1.1 to append the book of Joshua to the Moses-Exodus story.[4] The artificial nature of the transition is obvious as, contrarily to Moses (Num. 27.18-23), no successor was ever promised to Joshua. So, rather than introducing a successor, the next words introduce the conquest theme with a question by the sons of Israel to Yhwh: 'Who will go up for us towards the Canaanites in the beginning to fight them (by him)?' מי יעלה־לנו אל־הכנעני בתחלה להלחם בו (Judg. 1.1b). This question reproduces the one asked in Bethel to determine who should go up first against Benjamin מי יעלה־לנו בתחלה למלחמה עם־בני בנימן (Judg. 20.18). All the material between Judg. 1 and 20, that is the whole book of Judges, is thus branded with the mark of catastrophic progression, as the Canaanites of Judg. 1.1 are replaced by Benjaminites in Judg. 20.18, the original conquest ending up in civil war.

---

2.   Schmid, *Erzväter*, p. 373.
3.   Schmid, *Erzväter*, p. 32.
4.   Schmid, *Erzväter*, pp. 30-31.

This characterization of the judges narratives as a catastrophic progression is in blatant contradiction to the original message of Bethel's book of Saviours and even to Josiah's book of Judges, but it suitably allowed for the introduction of the four books of Kings after Judges.

That Judah should be first to go up against the Canaanites would be very puzzling if Joshua and Judges were part of the same continuous narrative: Judges starts as though nothing had ever happened in the book of Joshua, as if the conquest was yet to be undertaken. This fact is a thorn in the flesh of Noth's disciples who insist that the Deuteronomistic History was first designed as an unbroken presentation of the history of Israel. That such a neat and convincing masterpiece came to be hacked up by inconsiderate scribes who stuffed so many loose traditions into it that they were finally forced to split it into separate books remains difficult to account for. A cold comparison with Blum's attempt, however subtle and masterly,[5] with the sheer straight-forwardness of Schmid's system is in itself an argument in favour of the superiority of the independent-books model over the Nothian theory.

The book of Judges was not originally written to relate the events that took place in Israel and Judah after the period of the conquest. That Judg. 1.1 reverts the action back to the beginning of the conquest of Canaan was not a matter of concern for the librarians who shelved the Judges scroll between Joshua and 1 Samuel. Reintroducing the mention of Joshua's death at the beginning of Judges simply provided a reading order that set Judges into a definite chronological sequence. Rather than blaming the editors for a failed transition,[6] one should recognize how judicious their choice was, considering the difficulties incurred by the insertion of the self-sufficient book of Judges into a sequence that had initially no room for it.

Judges 1.2. The divine answer from Judg. 20.18 'Judah shall go first' is reproduced with the addition of a few words: 'since I have given *the* land into his hand' הנה נתתי את־הארץ בידו. Which land and how much of it Judah should conquer is not said. What matters is to introduce the Adonibezek episode (vv. 4-7) and to affirm that it was Judah's mission from the very beginning to conquer the whole of *Eretz Israel*. That the House of Joseph and the other Israelite tribes had very little success in conquering Israel in vv. 22-34 makes perfect sense. Had Israel let Judah conquer Eretz

5.   Blum, 'Knoten', see Chapter 3.
6.   Lindars, *Judges 1–5*, p. 92; see Chapter 3.

Israel, Israel would have lived in peace ever since. Such an argument fits the second century BCE when the Maccabaeans were setting off into a new conquest that would lead to place the whole of Palestine under Judah's rule.

Judges 1.3. Once Judah has received Yhwh's order to go up first, Judah invites Simeon to join him in conquering their lots together and thus introduces the allotment concept (גורל) from Josh. 13–21.[7] The association of Simeon with Judah is taken over from Judg. 1.18 where it justified Judah's conquest of the Negeb (see Chapter 2), but neither v. 18 nor the rest of Judg. 1 mentioned lots before vv. 1-3 had become the new introduction to the book.

These three verses intertwine two very different conceptions of the conquest at the junction between Joshua and Judges. They may have replaced the previous introductory verses of Josiah's book of Judges because the beginning and the end of narrative units are most exposed to editorial activity,[8] but it is of course impossible to prove anything from silence. Judges 1.4 'Judah arose, Yhwh gave the Canaanites and the Perizzites into his[9] hands' could possibly suffice to introduce the independent book of Judges.

Although the first form of the book of Joshua was probably drafted by Josiah's ideologists at the same time that these same ideologists transformed Manasseh's book of Saviours into a book of Judges, that does not imply that the two works were meant to be serialized at that time. Each book had its own logic and both were still connected with seventh century realities rather than supposed to refer to pre-monarchical times.

The latest introduction to Judges is to be found neither in Judg. 1.1–2.5 nor in Judg. 2.6–3.6[10] but in Judg. 1.1-3. These three verses connect Judges with Joshua without solving the chronological problem because chronology was not the main concern. It was nevertheless a feat to put these books together as both had almost reached their canonical form

---

7. Josh. 14.2; 18.11; 19.51; 21.4-20.

8. Noth, 'Background', p. 79.

9. MT reads בידם ויכום '…in their hands. They defeated…' but LXXA's …ἐν χειρὶ αὐτοῦ, καὶ ἐπάταξεν… may still preserve the original lesson of the first verse of Judges before the addition of vv. 1-3. Judah was then the sole subject as Simeon only appeared in v. 17. LXXB and MT later harmonized with the plural to take into account Simeon who, according to v. 3, went to war with Judah.

10. See discussion in Chapter 3 and Schmid, *Erzväter*, p. 219.

when the collection was created.[11] It therefore required some adjustments, which will now be considered.

Judges 1.19-21: Harmonizing Judges with Joshua
Judg. 1.19-21 smooth out some of the most blatant contradictions between Joshua and Judges that arose once the two books were linked to one another.[12]

Judges 1.19. The scribe warns his readers that his additions do not in any way call into question Yhwh's gift of the land to Judah in Judg. 1.4. Judges 1.18 had claimed for Judah the taking of Gaza, Ashkelon and Ekron, thus closing King Manasseh's account of the Judaean conquest during the reign of his father Hezekiah (see Chapter 2). So, in Judg. 1.19, the scribe adds that Yhwh was with Judah (ויהי יהוה את־יהודה) and that Judah took the mountain in order not to dispossess the inhabitants of the plain (כי לא להוריש את־ישבי העמק) because they had chariots of iron (Judg. 1.19). The versions 'improved' the argument by adding that Judah *could* not take, but most Hebrew manuscripts only attest יכלו in the margin. In fact, the Hebrew is probably carefully avoiding the conclusion that Judah did not take the plain because it *could* not do so! The chariots of iron are borrowed from Josh. 17.16, 18 where they had served to justify the attribution of a double lot to Joseph.

The need for this correction arose when Judges was severed from its original seventh century BCE context to represent the days before King Saul. Manasseh was able to claim that Hezekiah had taken part of Philistia, but the David narratives would not make sense after such a claim.

Judges 1.20. Then, v. 20 corrects Judg. 1.10, which had attributed the conquest of Hebron to Judah, in order to conform it to the word of Moses in Josh. 14.14-15; 15.13-14 and to give the honour of the conquest of Hebron back to Caleb.

In Josh. 11.21 it was Joshua who wiped out the Anakim from Hebron; Judg. 1.20 follows Josh. 15.14 in presenting Caleb as the liberator of Hebron. However, Josh. 15.13-19 and Judg. 1.11-15 are almost identical (conquest of Debir by Othniel and Achsah episode). It therefore becomes very difficult to decide which text copied the other. The only certainty is that these parallels form an extra link between the two books in order to

11. Schmid, *Erzväter*, pp. 214-24.
12. Lindars, *Judges 1–5*, p. 42.

overcome their fundamental incompatibility. On closer inspection, it
appears that the passage is anchored more solidly in Judg. 1 than in Josh.
15. The conquest of Debir and the Achsah episodes are part and parcel of a
careful presentation aimed at contrasting the fairness of Judah against the
barbarian Sons of Judah whereas, in Josh. 15, these episodes interrupt a
border description and a town list. Judges 1.4-18 is entirely devoted to
presenting Judah's accomplishments: Judah catches Adoni-bezek (v. 8),
defeats Sheshai, Ahiman and Talmai in Hebron (v. 10), and goes against
Debir (v. 11). Caleb intervenes as a member of Judah and gives his daughter Achsah to Othniel as a reward for the conquest of Debir (vv. 12-15).
Finally, Judah takes Hormah with the help of Simeon (v. 17-18) plus
Gaza, Ashkelon and Ekron (v. 18). King Manasseh's Judah needed no
Joshua!

The Joshua narrative follows a different logic: in Josh. 11, the Ephraimite Joshua is leading the conquest and, logically, he is the one who
wipes out the Anakim from Hebron, Debir, Anab and from all the hill
country. Then, in Josh. 14.6-14 Caleb recalls Num. 13–14 and asks for his
share, which he receives from Joshua's hands. But Josh. 14.12 is in
tension with the rest of Josh. 11–14 as Caleb implies that the Anakim are
still in Hebron when he asks for it: 'maybe Yhwh will be with me and I
will conquer...' אולי יהוה אותי והורשתים. This tension anticipates the
rectification in Josh. 15.13-14: Joshua gave Hebron to Caleb (//Josh. 14)
and Caleb drove out from there the Anakim (≠ Josh. 11.21 but //Josh. 14)
named Sheshai, Ahiman and Talmai (//Judg. 1.10 where they are never
called Anakim). Then Josh. 15.15-19 repeats Judg. 1.11-15, the implied
subject of the first verse changing from Judah to Caleb.

The harmonizing function of Josh. 15.13-19 is carried on in Judg. 1.20
that offers a convenient summary of the final version: *they* (Judah and
Joshua) gave Hebron to Caleb and Caleb drove out the three sons of Anak
(their number comes from Judg. 1.10 and their father comes from Josh.
11.21).

This fascinating process started with two separate texts: under Manasseh's reign, Judg. 1* attributed to Judah the conquest of all the kingdom's
realm. Caleb appeared as a Judaean general in front of Debir, but not in
Hebron. Under Josiah's reign, Josh. 11–14* claimed that Joshua had conquered everything and then gave Hebron to Caleb according to the word
of Moses.

When Joshua and Judges were put together, the words 'maybe Yhwh
will be with me and I will conquer them as Yhwh said' were added at the

end of Josh. 14.12. Joshua's granting of Hebron to Caleb was then repeated in Josh. 15.13. Caleb's need to drive the Anakim out of Hebron,
first suggested in Josh. 14.12b, was then reaffirmed in Josh. 15.14. Judges
1.11-15 was then repeated in Josh. 15.15-19. At the same time, these
cross-references were completed by a summary of the conquest of Hebron
in Judg. 1.20: 'Hebron was given to Caleb, as Moses had said, and he
drove out from it the three sons of Anak', a perfect synthesis of the whole
Hebron question.

Judges 1.21. Finally, the last verse of this harmonizing note is concerned
with Jerusalem. The same note is also found in Josh. 15.63: Josh. 15
claims that the sons of *Judah could* not dispossess the Jebusites living in
Jerusalem, while in Judg. 1 it is the sons of *Benjamin* who *did* not dispossess them. However, both agree that the Jebusites reside with either
Judah or Benjamin in Jerusalem until this day. The vocabulary is taken
from the progressive conquest (ישב, לא־הוריש Judg. 1.27-34) and makes
sense only in the context of Judg. 1: v. 21 corrects v. 19 and explains that
in fact Judah was not only prevented from taking the plain but that
Jerusalem too escaped its hold, in spite of its location in the mountains.
This lesson is still transmitted at the end of Josh. 15. However, it was
modified in Judg. 1, Judah being replaced by Benjamin as these two
limitations of Judah's success were felt to be contrary to the presentation
of Judah's prowess in Judg. 1.4-18.

Judges 1.36: Harmonizing Judges with Joshua 19
In Chapter 4, consideration was given to the geographical transfer
operated by Judg. 1.35. The Danites living around the city of Dan in v. 34
had been settled west of Jerusalem by the simple translocation of the
Amorites into the Shephelah in order to set the scene for their migration, a
migration that was supposed to serve as a model for Josiah's conquest of
Israel as far as Dan. Verse 36 then seems to describe the Amorite territory
starting from one point on the southern border of Judah's territory in Josh.
15.1-4: 'And the border of the Amorites ran from the ascent of Akrabbim,
from Sela and from the ascent' (וגבול האמרי ממעלה עקרבים מהסלע
ומעלה), but the description ends abruptly without indicating any point of
arrival for these three starting points. Such a description starting with
'from' should logically end up on a last toponym introduced by 'until'

עַד.[13] The end of this verse was therefore lost, but it may have located Amorite territory south of Judah in order to reconcile Judg. 1.35, that attributes Har-heres, Aijalon and Shaalbim to the Amorites, with Josh. 19.41, that gives those towns to Dan. In the same effort, the Danites' loss of their lot from Judg. 18.27-31 was copied after Dan's town list in Josh. 19.47.

Judges 2.6-10: Inserting Joshua 24.29-31 and Exodus 1.6, 8

In spite of the great debt owed to Schmid for liberating the book of Judges from the shackles of Noth's Deuteronomistic History, the present study cannot follow him completely on the relation between Josh. 24 and what he calls *das sogenannte deuteronomistische Richterschema.* According to Schmid, this 'schema of the judges' (which is not deuteronomistic) pre-supposes Josh. 24.[14] Schmid seems to include in this schema most of the materials within Judg. 1.1–3.6[15] that turn the stories of the saviours into a transitional period after the end of salvation history in Josh. 24.[16] In the light of what has been seen so far, in particular the distinction that was established between the schema and the frames of the saviour narratives (Chapter 1), the introductory function of Judg. 1.4-18, 27-34 for Manasseh's book of Saviours (Chapter 2) and the critique of the book of Saviours operated by Judg. 2.1-5, 11-19 under Josiah (Chapter 3), Schmid's hypothesis is unsuitable if what he means by *Richterschema* covers the whole of Judg. 1.1–3.6. However, he mentions Judg. 2.10 specifically, and his argument is acceptable if it is limited to Judg. 2.6-10.

In fact, Judg. 2.6-10 is a compound: vv. 6-9 are an almost *verbatim* repetition of Joshua's death notice in Josh. 24.29-31,[17] while v. 10 draws its inspiration from Exod. 1.6, 8:[18]

(Judg. 2.10a) וְגַם כָּל־הַדּוֹר הַהוּא נֶאֶסְפוּ אֶל־אֲבוֹתָיו

(Exod. 1.6) וַיָּמָת יוֹסֵף וְכָל־אֶחָיו וְכֹל הַדּוֹר הַהוּא

(Judg. 2.10b) וַיָּקָם דּוֹר אַחֵר אַחֲרֵיהֶם אֲשֶׁר לֹא־יָדְעוּ אֶת־יְהוָה

(Exod. 1.8) וַיָּקָם מֶלֶךְ־חָדָשׁ עַל־מִצְרָיִם אֲשֶׁר לֹא־יָדַע אֶת־יוֹסֵף

Joshua 24 and Judg. 2.6-10 belong to the same editorial stage, the one that links the book of Judges to the book of Joshua (with Judg. 2.6-9) and

---

13. Josh. 15.5; 19.33; Lindars, *Judges 1–5*, pp. 72-73.
14. Schmid, *Erzväter*, pp. 220, 235.
15. Schmid, *Erzväter*, p. 219.
16. Schmid, *Erzväter*, p. 220.
17. Rösel, 'Überleitung', pp. 342-50.
18. Schmid, *Erzväter*, p. 38.

to the Moses-Exodus-Joshua narrative as a whole (with Judg. 2.10).

Judges 2.6-10 must not be considered as part of the schema which is limited to Judg. 2.11-19, in spite of the similarity between the generation (דור) mentioned in v. 10 and the fathers mentioned in vv. 17, 19. In his study of Israel's fathers, Th. Römer did analyze v. 10 at the same time as the schema,[19] but he had to refute Beyerlin who had expressed strong doubts over the attribution of v. 10 to the same hand as the one who wrote the schema.[20] Beyerlin's suggestions are based on more convincing evidence (see discussion in Chapter 1) than Römer's discussion of whether or not the transition between vv. 10 and 11 is really *störend.*

One may still wonder why Joshua's death was repeated in Judges and why it was inserted in Judg. 2.5 rather than at the very outset of the book. The answer can only be tentative as it is impossible to enquire into the motives of the editors. However, it is instructive to examine how these editors worked. In spite of the insertion of the Bokim incident that cast a disapproving light over Israel's progressive conquest, Judg. 1 carried on offering a very different understanding of Israel and Judah's rise to power in the land. The editors chose a surrounding strategy to encrust {sandwich, enclose?} Judg. 1 between two mentions of Joshua's death. In this way, the strange conquest account of Judg. 1 (compared to Joshua's) is set within the range of Joshua's days with a minimum of textual interference. The 'days of the judges' (Judg. 2.18) start in Judg. 2.11 and Josiah's 'second burial'[21] pushes Judg. 1 back into the period of Joshua's conquest.

The straight-forward repetition of Josh. 24.29-31 in Judg. 2.6-9 is therefore another strong argument in favour of the very late date of the insertion of Judges after Joshua. At that time, both books had existed independently for so long, that editorial interventions or changes had to be kept to a minimum. This repetition by no means indicates that what is comprised between Josh. 24.29 and Judg. 2.9 is secondary[22] or that Judg. 1.1-2.5 was originally an appendix of the book of Joshua.[23] On the con-

---

19. Th. Römer, *Israels Väter* (OBO, 99; Freiburg/Göttingen: Universitätsverlag/ Vandenhoeck & Ruprecht, 1990), pp. 296-97.

20. Beyerlin, *Gattung*, p. 8.

21. Smyth-Florentin, F., 'When Josiah Has Done his Work or the King Is Properly Buried: A Synchronic Reading of 2 Kings 22.1–23.28', in A. de Pury and Th. Römer (eds.), *Israel Constructs its History* (JSOTSup, 306, Sheffield: Sheffield Academic Press, 2000), pp. 343-58.

22. Rofé, 'End of Joshua', pp. 217-27.

23. M.Z. Brettler, 'Jud 1, 1-2, 10: from Appendix to Prologue', *ZAW* 101 (1989),

trary, Josh. 24.28-31 and Exod. 1.6, 8 are inserted into Judges 2.6-10, and
the foreign character of these elements is not meant to be hidden: the
thread of the seam remains visible to the reader who is thus made aware of
the process. No delusion is attempted, the scrolls are simply ordered according to a rough classification that provides a convenient reading order
rather than a strict chronological thread.

Judges 2.20–3.6: Military Training

This strange passage appears as an outgrowth of the schema (Judg. 2.11-
19). Judges 2.20 begins like v. 14 'Yhwh's anger was kindled against
Israel' (ויחר אף יהוה בישראל) and adds comments on the consequences of
divine wrath (v. 21). However, Joshua is mentioned twice (Judg. 2.21, 23),
which indicates that the whole passage belongs to the editorial stage that
introduced the figure of Joshua into the book of Judges (Judg. 1.1-3; 2.6-
10).

Judah is now one *Ethnos* (גוי) among others (Judg. 2.20), and the danger
does not come from outside plunderers (שסים), intruders from round about
(מסביב Judg. 2.14), but from within, from nations that Joshua left when he
died (Judg. 2.21). From the time of Josiah's failure to take control of the
whole of Israel, Palestine has gradually become a mosaic of ethnic groups.

Judges 2.22 offers a first theodicy for this situation: Yhwh himself
decided to leave those nations in place in order to test (נסות) Israel and to
check whether or not they would observe the commandments (...השמרים
אם־לא). The status of the enemies has evolved from snares (Judg. 2.3) to
military instructors in the hands of Yhwh. The massive condemnations of
the schema are turned into an open question because a new dawn is rising.
The rest (נוח) that Yhwh gave to the nations was not meant to be final,
Yhwh simply did not drive them out quickly (מהר Judg. 2.23): new
conquest opportunities are now at hand.

Judges 3.1-6 introduces a second explanation for the persistence of the
nations: it was not just to punish Israel's disobedience but also to teach
war (ללמדם מלחמה) to the generations that had not known the wars of
Canaan (Judg. 3.1-2). The moral explanation does not suffice any more,
past failures are also attributed to a lack of military preparation. The
descendants of Josiah claim that in war, however holy it may be, faith is
not enough.

Judges 3.3, 5 then present two conventional lists of enemies: Philistines,

pp. 433-35 (435) and now Brettler, *Book of Judges*.

Canaanites, Sidonians and Hivites (v. 3), Canaanites, Hittites, Amorites, Perizzites, Hivites and Jebusites (v. 5), concluded by the traditional litany over Israelite *conubium* with these cousins and worship of their gods (///Joshua 23).

Judges 2.22 is repeated in Judg. 3.4 in a most revealing manner:

v. 22b השמרים הם את־דרך יהוה ללכת בם כאשר שמרו אבותם אם־לא

Would they observe the way of Yhwh to go according to them as had observed their fathers, or not.

v. 4b לדעת הישמעו את־מצות יהוה אשר־צוה את אבותם ביד־משה

To know if they would listen to the commandments of Yhwh, which he commanded their fathers by the hand of Moses

The test does not determine any more whether or not Israel observes the ways of Yhwh as their fathers did. The uncertain model of fathers is re-placed by commandments transmitted to the fathers by the lawmaker Moses. The Torah is now a well established code, but as the Samaritans boast of being its 'keepers', observing שמר is replaced by listening שמע to avoid granting any legitimacy to these disturbing cousins.

Judges 2.20-3.6 presents a careful chiastic structure[24] that further links Judges not only to Joshua but also to the Torah. The first canon is receiv-ing a second part with the *Nebiim*, which will mark once for all the differ-ence between Jews and Samaritans. This is probably the most pressing motive behind the constitution of the Deuteronomistic History and the whole Prophetic collection. It produced the religious basis for Hasmonaean campaigns, in particular against the House of Joseph that resulted in the destruction of the Samaritan temple. Judges 2.20-3.6 witnesses the gradual recovery of Jerusalem and the growing tensions with Neapolis, the new Samaria. It is moving to see how Josiah's schema is re-worked to prepare for a new uprising.[25] The fact that the ancestors failed does not lead to a new approach. The past simply shows that military preparation needs to be better. The Romans are now providing logistical support to help overthrow the remains of Seleucid rule. Observant Jews, often fanaticized by the conflict, are getting ready to offer their blood to liberate their land.

However, the Romans, as everyone knows, soon became their execu-tioners and purged Palestine of Deuteronomism for a good 17 centuries.

24. See Becker, *Richterzeit*, p. 103, attributed to DtrN.
25. See J. Kampen, *The Hasideans and the Origin of Pharisaism: A Study in 1 and 2 Maccabees* (SCS, 24; Atlanta: Scholars Press, 1989).

However, they did not eradicate it for good because it survived in the text. So Deuteronomistic theology is still setting Levantine tribes one against the other in the name of a merciful god.

Judges 4.11, 17, 21; 5.24: Heber the Kenite and Jael's Hammer
It is possible to accept, with A. Bendenberger, the presence of Maccabaean editorial activity in Judg. 4–5.[26]

Heber the Kenite. Jael's husband, Heber ('associate') the Kenite (Judg. 4.11, 17; 5.24) could have been introduced in Judg. 4–5 by the Maccabaeans to seal an alliance with the Jewish group linked with the book of Enoch. The Maccabaeans would have thus recognized that their insurrection needed the support of others, like the Kenites and the Rechabites (1 Chron. 2.55).

The maqevet. The Maccabaeans who may derive their name from the surname of their leader Judas Maccabeus 'Hammer' may have also changed the name of Jael's tool in Judg. 4. In Judg. 4.21, Jael takes hold of a Maccabaean hammer מקבת in order to crush Sisera, while the parallel in Judg. 5.26 uses a different term for the fatal tool: הלמות העמלים 'workmen's mallet'. The LXX confirms that Judg. 4 and 5 use two different terms for 'hammer'.[27] It is therefore possible that the *maqevet* was introduced in Judg. 4 to honour the Maccabaeans by comparing their rebellion to Jael's daring feat.

These two points are only minute points in the mass of the book of Judges, but they show how here and there the text could still receive small additions and modifications as late as the middle of the second century BCE.

Judges 11.12-28: Justifying the Annexation of Perea
If the Maccabaean's editorial activity in Judges is very limited, their Hasmonaean successors seem to have left a more substantial mark in Judg. 11.

In a long monologue, Jephthah addresses an Ammonite king to substantiate Israel's rightful claim to some Transjordanian territory. The argument

---

26. A. Bendenbender, 'Biene, Fackel, Blitz: Zur Metaphorik der Namen in der Deborageschichte', *TuK* 76 (1997), pp. 43-55.

27. A. Bendenbender, 'Theologie im Widerstand: Die Antiochoskrise und ihre Bewältigung im Spiegel der Bücher Exodus und Richter', *TeKon* 23 (2000), pp. 3-39 (21).

is based on Exodus itineraries in Num. 21 (Num. 21.11-13//Judg. 11.18; Num. 21.24//Judg. 11.13; Num. 21.26//Judg. 11.15). This eastern itinerary differs from the simpler one in Num. 33 that takes the lower route through the Arabah. Numbers 32 follows the same route and has the Reubenite and Gadite shepherds contemplate the Moabite plateau and Gilead (Num. 32.1). Numbers 21, also based on the lower route (Num. 21.10-13), diverts the people of Israel to the East on the Moabite plateau in order to meet Sihon and the Amorites north of Edom and of the river Arnon. The conquest of the Hesbon region is justified by Sihon's refusal to let Israel cross his kingdom. The conquered Amorite territory spreads from the Arnon in the South to the lower part of the Jabbok in the North, while the Ammonite territory is left unscathed (Num. 21.24). Judges 11.12-28 takes over the information from Num. 33[28] and introduces a new element. The land of Sihon (south of Ammon) is now claimed by the Ammonites (Judg. 11.13). The unnamed king of the Ammonites justifies his present attack of Gilead (north of Ammon) as retaliation against the Israelite annexation of the area comprised between the Arnon and the Jabbok (Sihon's territory according to Numbers). Jephthah argues from the data in Numbers to show that this land was Sihon's and that its annexation caused no harm, neither to Moab nor to Ammon (Judg. 11.18-22). Ammon is sited north east of the contested zone, an area corresponding to the latter province of Perea, south and west of Ammon. Judges 11.12-28 is justifying Judaean claims on Perea while the rest of Jephthah's story stages an Ammonite aggression against northern Gilead (Tob[29] Judg. 11.3). Judges 11.12-28 is therefore much later than 598 BCE,[30] and since it presupposes Num. 33, it is likely to

---

28. J.M. Miller, 'The Israelite Journey through (around) Moab and Moabite Territory', *JBL* 108 (1989), pp. 577-95 (585-87). Numbers 21.10-13 combines the perspectives of Num. 33 and Judg. 11: G.I. Davies, 'The Wilderness Itineraries and Recent Archaeological Research', in J.A. Adney (ed.), *Studies in the Pentateuch* (VTSup, 41; Leiden: E.J. Brill, 1990), pp. 161-75. Numbers 21 is one of the latest chapters of the book: Wüst, 'Einschaltung', pp. 464-79; E.A. Knauf, 'Supplementa Ismaelitica 14: Mount Hor and Kadesh Barnea', *BN* 61 (1992), pp. 22-26.

29. Located at eṭ-Ṭayibeh S-E of Der'a (Edreï): P.L. Redditt, 'Tob', *ABD* 6, p. 583.

30. In 600-597 BCE, Ammon provided troops to the Babylonians against Judah (2 Kgs 24.1-2 and E.A. Knauf, 'Psalm lx und Psalm cviii', *VT* 50 [2000], pp. 55-61). Ammon may have then extended its territory towards the Jordan like Edom who invaded Southern Judah. But at the end of the Hellenistic period, the Hasmonaeans and the Herodians recovered the lost territories. The mention of Kemosh as god of the Ammonites (Judg. 11.24) could indicate that the Ammonites are entitled to the northern part of Moab (Deut. 32.8-9 LXX). In this case, the text is Persian as it is only

be late Hellenistic. This involvement with Transjordan points towards the Hasmonaean conquests when Perea was controlled by Jerusalem (128–88 BCE).[31] This seems too late a date for Judg. 11.12-28 as all the LXX tradition transmits this passage while the first Greek translation of Judges were already completed by the time of the Maccabaeans.[32] However, territorial claims could have been expressed before the opportunity to realize them arose; Judg. 11.12-28 could therefore be dated before 200 BCE, slightly before the first Greek versions of Judges, or at the beginning of the Hasmonaean period.

Smaller Links between Joshua and Judges

Some of the elements of the negative conquest of Judg. 1 were introduced into the tribal lots in Josh. 16–19:[33] Judg. 1.27-28 into Josh. 17.11-13 and Judg. 1.29 into Josh. 16.10.

Jabin, the king of Hazor (Judg. 4.2, 7, 17, 23-24) for whom Sisera served as general (see Chapter 1) was copied from Judg. 4–5 into Josh. 11.1.

Transition between Judges and Samuel

Judges 4.5: Deborah's Palm and 1 Samuel 7

Deborah and Samuel are the only figures in the books of Judges and Samuel to present a description of a judge in the process of judging. In Judg. 4.5, Deborah is sitting under Deborah's palm tree between Ramah and Bethel in the hill country of Ephraim, and the people of Israel come to her for judgment לְמִשְׁפָּט.

then that Heshbon would have belonged to Ammon: Jer. 49.1; E.A. Knauf, 'Hesbon, Sihons Stadt', *ZDPV* 106 (1990), pp. 135-44 (137); H.-C. Schmitt, 'Das Hesbonlied Num 21, 27ab-30 und die Geschichte der Stadt Hesbon', *ZDPV* 104 (1988), pp. 26-45 (35). But this Ammonite extension to the South is not sure as Jer. 49.1-5, on which it is based, may have first concerned Rabbat Moab rather than Rabbat Ammon. This second Moab oracle (the first one is in Jer. 48) would have been turned against Ammon following Jer. 25.21 (and Amos 1.13-15; Ezek. 40.13; 41.10.15), although the Jeremiah traditions had no grievance against Ammon: E.A. Knauf, 'Jeremia xlix 1-5: Ein zweites Moab-Orakel in Jeremia-Buch', *VT* 52 (1992), pp. 124-27. According to U. Hübner, *Die Ammoniter* (ADPV, 16; Wiesbaden: Otto Harrassowitz, 1992), p. 167 n. 55, Judg. 10–11 is more concerned with Moab than with Ammon, hence the mention of Kemosh. A Persian date is therefore quite uncertain.

31. D.I. Treacey-Cole, 'Perea', *ABD* 5, pp. 224-25 (224); 1 Macc. 5.

32. Harlé, *Bible d'Alexandrie*, p. 47.

33. See Becker, *Richterzeit*, p. 23.

In 1 Sam. 7.16-17, Samuel follows a yearly judging tour that leads him to Bethel, Gilgal and Mizpah and back home to Ramah. In the following verses, Samuel installs his sons as judges in Beer-sheba, but as they pervert justice, the Israelites ask him to give them a king instead (1 Sam. 8.1-5). As king-maker, Samuel has to be the last judge. These verses mark the end of the period of the Judges and introduce the royal era, but they are secondary to the rest of the Samuel traditions, which do not present Samuel as judge. In fact, this characterization of the role of the judge as dispenser of justice marks a clear evolution from the model of Phoenicians *suffets* which had inspired the judges of Judg. 10 and 12 (see Chapter 3). The 'judges' that Josiah had integrated among the saviours were substitutes for the Israelite king during the Assyrian rule. But Deborah under her palm tree and Samuel on his circuit have a different function: they establish a connection between Judges and 1 Samuel. They mark the boundaries of a period before Saul and David. The mention of Bethel and Ramah in both passages is a literary device to reinforce the geographical and chronological framing of the period of the judges rather than the factual description of a particular judicial system.

The transition between the books of Judges and 1 Samuel is also effected by the whole of 1 Sam. 7, which can be read as a summary of the book of Judges. Samuel preaches repentance and the giving up of the Baals and of the Astartes in a very similar way to the schema (Judg. 2.11-19//1 Sam. 7.2-4). Then Israel is gathered at Mizpah for fasting (Judg. 20!) and confession of sins (Judg. 10.10, 15//1 Sam. 7.5-6). Samuel judges Israel, the Philistines come up and Israel is afraid (v. 6). The Israelites ask Samuel not to cease crying (זעק) to Yhwh so that he would save (ישע) them from the hands of the Philistines (v. 8). The authors of 1 Sam. 7 obviously have taken note of Judg. 10.14 where Yhwh refuses to answer the cries of Israel, so they put Samuel in the role of mediator. Samuel cries (זעק) to Yhwh (v. 9) who thunders instead of sending a saviour (v. 10). The Philistines are subdued (כנע Judg. 3.30; 4.23; 8.28//1 Sam. 7.13), and the peace formula of the saviour narratives is partially taken over. This patch-work of references to Judges is describing Samuel both as saviour and as judge, thus attempting to reconcile two functions that were merely juxtaposed in Judges. This is not meant to describe the work of a charismatic war leader (see rather 1 Samuel 11), but to work out the transition between Judges and Samuel.

Judges 20.27-28: Ark

The ark of the covenant is introduced through a parenthesis in order to connect Judges with 1 Samuel and to disqualify Bethel's oraculary potential once the ark has left for Jerusalem (2 Sam. 6).

Judges 21.25: Final Note

Noth's argument that the pro-monarchical refrain is original in Judg. 17-18 is still valid[34] (see Chapter 4). This refrain was copied in Judg. 19.1 in order to connect the Persian polemic against Benjamin (Judg. 19–21) at the end of Josiah's book of Judges (see Chapter 6). The situation is less clear concerning the fourth and last occurrence of the refrain as the last verse of the book in Judg. 21.25. There are two ways to explain it. Judges 21.25 could have been added at the end of Judg. 21 in order to frame Judg. 19–21 during the Persian period when these anti-Benjaminite chapters were added to Josiah's book of Judges. However, Judg. 21.24 would also be fit as a conclusion for an independant book of Judges: 'The sons of Israel departed from there at that time, every man to his tribe and family, and they went out from there every man to his inheritance'. It is therefore more likely that the refrain was added on as a second conclusion when the 'period of the judges' was instituted as a designation for the time elapsing from Joshua's conquest and the rise of King Saul. Repeating that in those days 'there was no king in Israel' in the last verse of Judges just before the beginning of 1 Samuel defined once for all those days as the ones before Saul.

With Judg. 4.5; 21.25 and 1 Sam. 7, the Judges–Samuel transition is therefore as carefully tailored as the one between Joshua and Judges. The designers of the Biblical historiography (Genesis to 2 Kings) were not content to copy the pro-monarchical refrain in Judg. 21.25. They worked out a large inclusion between Judg. 4.5 and 1 Sam. 7 to consolidate the awkward transition between Judg. 21 and 1 Sam. 1 with a period of the judges. The reader is thus guided through the intricate literary maze of saviours, judges, losers, Danites, Benjaminites, Samuel and wandering ark by the thread of the 'judges', who are now defined as arbitrators like Deborah under her palm tree and Samuel on his circuit.

---

34. Noth, 'Background', p. 80.

The Period of the Judges

The transition between the books of Joshua, Judges and Samuel has been presented in this chapter. It is now time to discuss the all-too-famous period of the Judges.

2 Kings 23.22

The locution 'days of the judges' appears in 2 Kgs 23.22, to indicate that no such Passover as Josiah's had been celebrated since the days of the judges that judged Israel and the days of the kings of Israel and of the kings of Judah:

מימי השפטים אשר שפטו את־ישראל
וכל ימי מלכי ישראל ומלכי יהודה

It therefore seems that the period of the Judges was conceptualized well before the third century BCE.[35] However, the antiquity of vv. 21-23 has often been doubted due to the dependence of v. 21 on Deut. 16.1. A note in *BHK* gives weight to the secondary character of part of these verses since it indicates that the whole of וכל ימי מלכי ישראל ומלכי יהודה 'and all the days of the kings of Israel and of the kings of Judah' were placed under asterisk in Origen's system of Syrohexaplarian text, one of the most reliable witness for asterisks and obeli. The words 'and the days of the kings of Israel and the days of the kings of Judah' are almost certainly a MT plus compared to the original LXX. Origen borrowed it from Aquila's version.[36] This means that these words were added to MT after the completion of the first Greek versions of Judges. These translations were done before the end of the second century BCE, since Ben Sirach's grandson seems to indicate that in his days, the Prophets and the other books have been translated in Greek (Sir. prologue 24).[37]

---

35. See bibliography in M. Delcor, 'Réflexions sur la Pâque du temps de Josiah d'après 2 Rois 23, 21-23', in *idem* (ed.), *Environnement de l'Ancien Testament* (AOAT, 228; Kevelaer: Butzon & Bercker, 1990), pp. 90-104 and M. Delcor, 'Le récit de la célébration de la Pâque au temps d'Ezékias d'après 1 Chr 30 et ses problèmes' in A. Schenker (ed.), *Studien zu Opfer und Kult im Alten Testament* (FAT, 3; Tübingen: J.C.B. Mohr, 1992), pp. 93-106.

36. G.J. Brooke and N. McLean, *The Old Testament in Greek. II.2. The later historical books, 1 and 2 Kings* (Cambridge: Cambridge University Press, 1930), p. 381. I am endebted to Professor Adrian Schenker of the University of Fribourg (CH) for these indications.

37. Harl, Dorival and Munnich, *La Bible grecque,* pp. 96-98; E. Tov, 'The

The parallel in 2 Chron. 35.18 mentions the 'days of Samuel the prophet and all the kings of Israel'. Neither 'days' of the kings nor 'kings of Judah' appear. No period of the judges was known to the writers. The 'days of Samuel the prophet' (he was not yet judge because 1 Sam. 7 had not yet been written) described the time prior to King Saul, an obvious conclusion for anyone who reads *1 Samuel*. The writers do not equate the days of the kings of Judah with those of Israel, for they follow their source in attributing an Israelite origin to the Passover.

The following evolution can thus be reconstituted:

מימי השפטים אשר שפטו את־ישראל (2 Kgs 23.22*)

מימי שמואל הנביא וכל ימי מלכי ישראל (2 Chron. 35.18)

מימי השפטים אשר שפטו את־ישראל וכל ימי מלכי ישראל ומלכי יהודה
(2 Kgs 23.22)

מימי נגודצא דדנו ית ישראל [ו]כל ימי מלכי ישראל ומלכי דבית יהודה
(Targ. 2 Kgs 23.22)

Because the Judaeans writers of 2 Kings passed an overall negative judgment on the Israelite monarchy, they referred to the days of the judges in order not to mention the Israelite kings. These days of the judges probably described the same reality than Josiah's judges: the days when there was no (more) kings in Israel. Unless 2 Chron. 35.18 attest an older form of the text than the one transmitted by 2 Kgs 23.22, the writers of 2 Chron. 35.18 preferred to refer to the 'days of the prophet Samuel and all the kings of Israel' because, in their eyes, it better described the days before Saul since the period of the judges was not yet conceptualized. The discrepancy between 2 Kgs 23.22 and 2 Chron. 35.18 was never harmonized as these books were not part of the same collection.

The Aramaic versions, less influenced by Greek historiographical traditions, do not attest the copula between the days of the judges and those of the kings. The Targum reads כל ימי מלכי ישראל for MT's וכל ימי מלכי ישראל, thus placing the days of the kings in apposition to those of the judges. The Peshitta also disconnects the judges who saved Israel from the days of the kings by adding the masculine plural suffix to כל. It thus reads '...since the day (singular) of the judges who judged Israel, all them ܒܠܗܘܢ namely the days (plural) of the kings of Israel and the kings of

Judah'. To a reader who had never heard of the period of the judges, the days of the judges in 2 Kgs 23.22 could be equated to the days of the reigns of the kings of Israel and of the kings of Judah rather than presented as two separate and successive eras. The Aramaic tradition indicates that the structuring of Israel's past in successive epochs remained a strange concept to Semitic readers even after the organization of the scrolls of the Former Prophets according to periods.

In any case, the days of the judges in 2 Kgs 23.22 cannot be used to prove that the period of the judges was invented in exilic times. The judges of this formula originally were the judges who had come after the Israelite monarchy. In a second stage, these judges were understood as those who officiated during the days of Samuel (as indicated by 2 Chronicles). Finally, they ended up designating the period before Saul (see below).

Ruth 1.1
The book of Ruth is set 'in the days when judged the judges' (בימי שפט השפטים). This formula, contrarily to 2 Kgs 23.22, constitutes an unmistakable reference to the period of the Judges understood as a particular era in Israel's past. The context of the period of the Judges corresponds to the last verses of the book that insert Ruth in David's genealogy (Ruth 4.17b-22).

Apart from this time-setting, provided by the first and last verses of the book, the narrative could fit any other context. Setting the book in the days of the judges allowed the Greek canon to append Ruth to Judges. The fact that the Hebrew tradition kept Ruth within the Writings is a weighty argument in favour of the late construction of the period of the Judges.

The Days of the Judges from Josiah to Alexandria
Contrarily to the Nothian credo, the period of the Judges, understood as the period between the conquest and the 'united monarchy' was not conceptualized from the early days of writing of the book of Judges. The days of the judges had different meanings at different times.

The days when there was no (more) king in Israel. The days of the judges first designated the rule of the judges of Judg. 10 and 12 who were heroes replacing Bethel's saviours but describing happy and prosperous times, with hosts of gambolling children around them. Those judges were meant as substitutes, ruling Israel until Josiah would come and restore Solomon's kingdom. In the Josianic understanding of Israel's past, the days of the

judges were an interim period between 720 BCE and Josiah, designed on
the model of the Phoenician *suffets* (see Chapter 3). However, the nice
postcard-presentation of those prolific judges from the landed aristocracy
of Israelite fringes would have defeated Josiah's point had they not been
completed by a description of the dangers inherent to the prolonged
absence of a king. The concept of 'days when was no king in Israel' was
first made explicit as leitmotiv in Judg. 17–18 to show the religious
dangers of a kingless government but also the great opportunities offered
to Judah by such a power vacuum. The judges had done a good job at
ruling Israel after 720 BCE, now the Danite example should be followed
and Israel should be conquered as far as Dan.

The days when there was no (more) king in Israel (nor in Judah). However, Josiah's programme fizzled out, Judaean rule only managed to reach
as far as Bethel. This northern expansion of Judaean territory had a most
unexpected result half a century later. In 586 BCE, or even slightly before,
Benjamin became the centre of what was left of Judah! This situation produced fierce competition a century later, when the new Persian Jerusalem
tried to recover its seventh century BCE status. The 'days when there was
no king in Israel' were taken over in Judg. 19–21 from Judg. 17–18 to
describe Benjamin's rule, the days when Mizpah dared to replace Jerusalem until Jerusalem managed to reaffirm itself and put an end to this
appalling situation. Judges 19–21 did not describe the dangers of decentralized cults as Judg. 17–18 did, but the Benjaminite devious ways when
they are not curbed by Jerusalem's control. The days when there was no
king characterized the Darkest Ages ever experienced by Jerusalem, when
there still was no king in Israel but nor in Judah either (Judg. 19–21).

This conception of post-monarchical period of the Judges is illustrated
by Obad. 21:

ועלו מושעים בהר ציון לשפט את־הר עשו והיתה ליהוה המלוכה

And saviours will go up in Mount Zion to judge Mount Esau and it will be
the kingship for Yhwh.

This is not the appropriate place to deal with the problems involved with
this verse.[38] However, it is worth noting that the LXX translators did not
translate מושעים by a straightforward σωτῆρες (used in Judges) but by

---

38. See E. Ben Zvi, *A Historical-Critical Study of the Book of Obadiah* (BZAW,
242; Berlin: W. de Gruyter, 1996), pp. 223-26.

the complicated ἄνδρες σεσωσμένοι. In sharp contradiction to MT that bears no trace of scribal unease with the fact that saviours à la book of Judges would avenge Zion after 586 BCE, the Alexandrian translators obviously avoided too direct a reference to the book of Judges. Their unease is another indicator of the location and date of the conceptualization of the pre-monarchical period of the Judges. The translators were almost certainly associated with the literary milieu which was responsible for the organization of the prophetic books into 'Historical' books after the fashion of Greek Histories. Everything points towards Alexandria for the formation of a specific chronographical period characterized by judges before the days of the kings. It is no accident that it is also the Greek canon that links the book of Ruth to Judges in order to give some consistancy to its brand new pre-monarchichal period of the judges. The qualms of the translators with the saviours of Obad. 21 are therefore understandable since this verse clearly announces the arrival of saviours and judges in post-monarchical times. Obadiah 21 nevertheless indicates that someone (in Bethel or Mizpah during the Babylonian era?) understood saviours and judges as a post-royal type of rule that would punish the Edomites for their exactions commited against Judah *after* 586 BCE.

The days when there was no king (yet) in Israel. Finally, the period of the judges was pushed back into the so-called pre-monarchical, pre-Saul days. The crucial issue is when this last stage was performed. One possibility is to rely on the obvious insistence at the end of the book of Judges that a kingless society leads to anarchy in order to postulate an early date, at the end of the fifth century BCE.[39] The aim would be to legitimize the restoration of a new Judaean dynasty during Zerubbabel's failed attempt at restoring David's throne. A more promising episode would be the successful restoration of the Judaean monarchy by the Hasmonaeans. However, this date is obviously too late because Sir. 46.11 is mentionning judges after Joshua and Caleb and before Samuel, thus attesting the pre-monarchical period of the judges. Since the book of Sirach was written around 200 BCE,[40] it is necessary to date the conception of the pre-monarchical period of the judges before the second century. Are we condemned to go back as far as the fifth century BCE to find a suitable historical setting for the invention of the pro-monarchical period of the judges? Most scholars answer positively to this question because, consciously or not, they are

---

39. Schmid, *Erzväter*, p. 273.
40. G. Sauer, *Jesus ben Sirach* (JSHRZ, 3.5; Gütersloh: G. Mohn, 1981), p. 483.

influenced by the Nothian dogma of an exilic Deuteronomistic History. In principle, the fact that Judaeans would have invented Historiography before Herodotus should not be an unsuperable obstacle for the acceptance of Noth's hypothesis. However, considering the fact that the all too famous Exilic period is the worst possible time[41] for such a vast enterprise as the collection and linear organization of the literary material contained within Josua and 2 Kings, this hypothesis should only be accepted as a last resort. Moreover, the third century BCE offers a much more convincing setting for the insertion of the book of Judges between those of Joshua and Samuel. Since only the Greek canon appends Ruth to Judges and since it is only the translators of Obad. 21 who were uneasy with post-monarchical saviours, Alexandria is the most obvious place not only for the translation, but also for the crafting of the collection of Jewish 'Historical books'. For that matter, Jerusalem had as much expertise as Alexandria, but Alexandria was in a better position to provide the resources and the political will required to support the writing of a Jewish historiography.[42] We are therefore left with a time span beginning in the reign of Ptolemy II (282– 246 BCE, earliest possible date for the translation of the Torah), to the redaction of the book of Sirach (200 BCE, the earliest evidence of the insertion of the book of Judges before 1 Samuel). According to this hypothesis, the pre-monarchical period of the Judges was first worked out by Egyptian Jews who translated and organized some of the books which

41. Exiles certainly had more immediate concerns than the composition of a vast theodicy, unless the Babylonian authorities sponsored a group of Judaean scribes to accomplish this task. As for the elite that took over in Mizpah, the severe economical crisis that prevailed in Palestine throughout the Babylonian period, plus the political problems with the Edomites were not conducive to intense redactional activity. Moreover, for Mizpah and its government, the destruction of Jerusalem and the execution or deportation of the leaders of the rebellion meant the elimination of the enemy. Neither Jeremiah nor the Shaffan family cried over Jerusalem, they therefore had no need for a theodicy meant to explain the destruction of Jerusalem.

42. No definite answer can be provided to the intricate question of the relation between the Greek and the Hebrew canonical orders, since both conceptions have probably influenced each other and that LXX and MT's orders as we have them now reflect this interaction. Sirach's prologue is a weighty argument in favour of the primacy of the Prophetic collection because it takes as a well established fact that the second part of the Canon is Prophetic. However, in spite of its clear non historical ordering, MT seems to have integrated LXX's historical scheme for Joshua–2 Kings, its Former Prophets. This is a weighty argument in favour of the existence of a Jewish historiography in Greek, prior to MT's order. Thanks owed to Professor Adrian Schenker (Fribourg).

were not included into the Torah in order to offer a comprehensive description of Israel's history. This process seems to have taken some time and at least two different attempts as the variant LXX reading for Josh. 24.33 shows.[43] This first historiography thus filled the lacuna that so puzzled Hecateaus of Abdera who exclaimed that 'the Jews never had a king'.[44] It is important to note that, writing during the reign of Ptolemy I (306–283 BCE), Hecateaus does know about judges, but they are those appointed by Moses 'to be judges in all major disputes' (Exod. 18), not pre-monarchical judges from the book of Judges. Either his informers did not know about a pre-monarchical period of the Judges, or they made a point not to reveal it to Hecateaus!

An Alexandrian setting and date for the composition of the first ever Jewish historiography is nevertheless unlikely to convince many Nothians. It is therefore worth enquiring into the few alleged proofs presented for a fifth century date for the Deuteronomistic history.

The first evidence of DH could be found in 2 Sam. 7.8-12. This passage can certainly be used as a clue for the existence of a pre-monarchical period of the Judges before the third century BCE since it clearly refers to a day or days (LXX) when Yhwh commanded judges on his people Israel, before the reign of David. Yhwh is answering David's offer to build a cedar temple by having Nathan recall David's career: he was taken from the sheepcote (v. 8) and Yhwh was with him to vanquish all his enemies (v. 9). Yhwh then promises to plant Israel in a place so that the children of wickedness will not afflict them as they did at the beginning (v. 10).[45] Which is the beginning is unclear, but the next verse appears as a clarification: since the day when Yhwh ordered judges for his people Israel (v. 11a). That the period of the Judges is meant here is possible but far from certain.[46] Not only the mention of judges is situated at the junction between two very different passages (vv. 1-7 and 11b-16),[47] a fact that

43. See Rofé, 'End of Joshua', pp. 217-27. This reading that jumps directly from Josh. 24 to the story of Ehud could either be a 'pocket edition' of the Jewish history or a first attempt that only included selected passages.

44. Diodorus of Sicily XL.3 (trans. F.R. Walton; LCL; London: Heinemann; 1967), p. 283.

45. D. Vanderhooft, 'Dwelling beneath the Sacred Place: A Proposal for Reading 2 Samuel 7.10', *JBL* 118 (1999), pp. 625-33.

46. D.F. Murray, *Divine Prerogative and Royal Pretention* (JSOTSup, 264; Sheffield: Sheffield Academic Press, 1998), p. 184.

47. See S.L. McKenzie, 'Why Didn't David Build the Temple? The History of a Biblical Tradition', in M.P. Graham, R.R. Marrs and S.L. McKenzie (eds.), *Worship*

already indicates its secondary nature, but also the verb צוה 'to order' is more likely to have first applied to משפטים 'judgments' rather than to the שפטים 'judges' as is the case in 1 Chron. 22.13, 28.7. This way, the text makes much more sense because it refers to the giving of the commandments at Mount Sinai just after the liberation from 'the children of wickedness who afflicted Israel' (v. 10b), that is in Egypt.[48] The מ of the participle would have simply been removed once the pre-monarchical period of the judges was created.

Nehemiah 9 appears to present a historical summary of Israel and Judah's past along clear chronological lines: Creation (v. 6), Patriarchs (vv. 7-8), Exodus (vv. 9-21), Conquest (vv. 22-25) and, according to Schmid, the times of the Judges and of the Kings (vv. 26-31).[49] Indeed this text is clearly following the sequence presented by the five books of Moses and Joshua. However, after the conquest, the narrative is not following the neat succession of judges and then kings that a Nothian scholar would expect. In fact, judges are not even mentioned. The book of Saviours is clearly alluded to (צעק and מושיעים v. 27, זעק v. 28), but where are the judges of the pre-monarchical period of the Judges invented during the exile? Nehemiah nowhere names any judges, not even in v. 28 where the author is citing the Schema (Judg. 2.11-19) which is precisely the section of the book of Judges that mentions judges instead of saviours (see Chapter 3). The obvious reason for such a omission is that the authors of Neh. 9 knew the book of Saviours in its Josianic version but they did not know that this book was called 'book of Judges' nor that it covered a specific period of the history of Israel. For them, the book of Saviours merely depicted Israelite disobedience rather than as the glorification of Israelite heroes, thus following the ideology of Josiah's use of the book of Saviours. However, the authors of Neh. 9 were not clear about the relation of the book of Saviours with the books of Samuel and Kings. Samuel is completely ignored, Judaean or Israelite kings are presented, not as

and the Hebrew Bible (JSOTSup, 284; Sheffield: Sheffield Academic Press, 1999), pp. 204-224.

48.　This solution was already hinted at by S.R. Driver, *Notes on the Hebrew Text and the Topography of the Books of Samuel* (Oxford: Clarendon Press, 1960), p. 275: 'As the text stands, the reference in 10b will be to the sufferings of Egypt, but this is a thought alien to the context in which rather the blessings secured by the settled government of David are contrasted with the attacks to which Israel was exposed during the period of the Judges'.

49.　Schmid, *Erzväter*, pp. 302-304.

representatives of a specific period, but alongside princes, priests, prophets, fathers and people (vv. 32 and 34). Moreover, the first verse of this passage (v. 26) is affirming that prophets were killed, while the book of Judges does not relate any such episode. Allusions to the murder of prophets are only found in the books of Kings (1 Kgs 13, 18–19, 2 Kgs 21). It is therefore clear that Neh. 9 presents the Torah (vv. 26, 29, 30, 34) and its sequel (the book of Joshua) in its firm chronological sequence that leads to the Conquest, but after the Conquest, there is no more chronological thread to follow because the Deuteronomistic History did not exist. Kings, prophets and saviours were lumped together because at the time the Torah was the only collection of books or scrolls. The other works, be they books of kings, of prophetic oracles or the book of Saviours, were still unconnected to each other.

Psalm 106 may provide evidence for a pre-monarchical period of the Judges. It refers to a time after the Exodus when Israel sacrificed to Canaanite idols (v. 38), was given over to to the hand of the heathens (v. 41), and was oppressed by its enemies (v. 42). The book of Saviours is probably refered to, although its most characteristic features are missing: vv. 43-44 use √צלל rather than ישע for the act of deliverance and רנן instead of צעק for the cries uttered by the people. Neither judges nor saviours nor kings appear, and v. 46 jumps directly to the exile, by-passing the monarchy, just as Ezek. 20 and Ps. 78 do. One can hardly talk about a systematic presentation of Israel's history. Psalms 105 and 106 show that the sequence of events narrated in the Hexateuch is fixed, but after the conquest, there is still no model to organize the various books along a neat chronological thread.

The earliest extra-Biblical evidence for a pre-monarchical period of the judges is found in Sir. 46.11 which has already been considered. More evidence is found in Bar. 2.1, in *1 En.* 89.42; *2 Bar.* 60. However, these passages are all younger than Sir. 46,[50] therefore they have no bearing on the third century BCE date offered here.

There is therefore no obstacle to date the invention of the pre-monarchical period of the judges in Alexandria at the end of the third century BCE. Chronographical reasons were behind such an enterprise.[51] The 'days

---

50. See Schmid, *Erzväter*, pp. 316-49, for dates and bibliography on these different works.

51. The chronography was probably continued with a post-monarchical period with Daniel, Ezra-Nehemiah, Esther: Josephus, *Apion*, 1.38-41; R. Beckwith, *The Old*

when there was no king in Israel' became, then and only then, the days *before* the kings (Ruth 1.1). The books of Judges and of Ruth were assigned the task of illustrating that particular period within a succession of periods leading up, from the origins of the world and of Israel, to the Persian era (Ezra, Nehemiah, Esther). The Hasmonaeans soon put this chronological sequence into use in order to establish a conscious link between the Maccabees and the judges: 'Jonathan took up residence in Michmash and began to judge the people, rooting the godless out of Israel' (1 Macc. 9.73). The Hasmonaeans used the Greek 'Historical books' to legitimize their dynasty! In spite of the paradox, this is probably one of the reasons that led the Pharisees to retain the Greek order for their 'Former Prophets' (except for Ruth).

The organization of the various books into periods of the Conquest, of the Judges and of the Monarchy belongs to the same process that created the category of Historical books in the Greek and then the Christian Bible. This chronographical concern bears the unmistakable seal of Alexandria[52] and should logically be attributed to the third century BCE. The chronological thread does not exactly fit the limits of the individual books. The period of the judges really starts after the second burial note of Joshua (Judg. 2.11)[53] and ends somewhere between 1 Sam. 8 (the rejection of Samuel's sons as judges) and 1 Sam. 11 (Saul's deliverance of Jabesh imitating the saviour accounts).

The period of the Judges is therefore a literary construct that should not be used as evidence for the reconstitution of the factual history of Israel before statehood.[54] The term should be definitively banned from serious Histories of Israel.

However, recognizing the fictitious character of the period of the Judges should not prevent Bible readers from noticing how carefully the periods were crafted and from marvelling at the sheer effectiveness of their construction: the period of the Judges is still believed historical by almost everybody, even by scholars who have long abandoned the idea of a historical Exodus and of a historical conquest under the leadership of Joshua.[55]

Testament Canon of the New Testament Church and its Background in Early Judaism (Grand Rapids, MI: Eerdmans, 1985), pp. 78-80, 118-27.

52. Schmid, *Erzväter*, p. 51.

53. Against Schmid, *Erzväter*, p. 218, who has the period of judges starting in Josh. 24.

54. Kratz, *Komposition*, p. 195.

55. W.G. Dever, 'What did the Biblical Writers Know, and When Did They Know

At this point, the book of Judges has been covered entirely. Its growth has been plotted approximately from 720 to 200 BCE when it was integrated into the Historical books of the Septuagint. It was then ready to enter world literature, although a few Maccabaeans additions were introduced around 150.

about It?', in J. Magness and S. Gitin (eds.), *Hesed ve-Emet: Studies in Honor of Ernest S. Frerichs* (Atlanta: Scholars Press, 1998), pp. 241-57 (244-45).

The Book of Judges in Seven Steps

The growth of the book of Judges has been presented in six stages related to crucial turning-points in the history of Israel and Judah. Each one will now be recapitulated.

Bethel's Book of Saviours (720 BCE): Judges 3*–9 (Chapter 1)

Richter's *Retterbuch* remains a most valid starting point if the aim is to identify the beginning of the editorial process that led to the canonical the book of Judges, Becker and Lindars' objections not withstanding. The outlines of Richter's *Retterbuch* have been confirmed (Judg. 3*–9) but the historical method applied to identify the secondary elements within these chapters has permitted a much simpler division of the secondary material than Richter himself has envisaged (see Figure 8 for details). Later editions did not introduce shreds of verses but coherent passages, apart from the few words added here and there by the Maccabaeans at the time of the canonization of the Former Prophets. Doubts remain over the beginning of the book of Saviours: it is not clear whether Judg. 3.7-11 was originally an anonymous *Beispielstück*, or whether the whole passage was added later, together with the figure of Othniel.

Richter's proposal of a date during the reign of Jehu has been abandoned in favour of Knauf's hypothesis: the book of Saviours can be located in Bethel around 720 BCE. This historical context has been put into sharper perspective since it has become manifest that the reconstitution of a history of Israel stands on firmer grounds for the Assyrian era than for the previous centuries. Cogan's work has been used to recover a more realistic view of Assyrian religious policies pursued by the Assyrians in their provinces. Beyerlin's contribution, too, has revealed itself to be crucial in its perception of the fundamental differences between the framework of the saviour narratives and the later critique of the book of Saviours (Schema of Judg. 2, anonymous prophet, and losers), thus cracking the axiom of an overall and all-pervasive 'Deuteronomistic redaction'

Ch.	720 BCE	700 BCE	620 BCE	580 BCE	500 BCE	200 BCE	150 BCE
1		4-18 Judah 27-34 Israel	35-36 Amorites		22-26 Bethel	1-3 Transition 19-21 Harmonization	
2			1-5 Bochim 11-19 Schema			1 Gilgal	6-10, 20-23 Theodicy
3	7-11 Beispielstück ? 12-30 Ehud	8, 9b Cushan? 10b Othniel?	7b Idols 10b Judge 31 Shamgar				1-6 Theodicy
4	1-24 Barak						
5	1-31 Song of Deborah		14a Amalek 15a Issachar 17b Asher				21 *maqevet*
6	1-3a, 4b-6.33, 34 Gideon		3b, 4a, 33b Amalek, Qedem 7-32 Prophet, call, altar 35-40 Manasseh…, fleece				
7	1-3 Release of shakers 9 Going down 16-21 Torchs		4-8 Dogs 10-15 Dream 22 Transjordan				

8	22-23 Crown refused 28 Frame	1-21 Transjordan 24-27 Ephod 29-35 Abimelech, Baal-Berith	
9	1-57 Abimelech		
10-12		10.1–11.6; 12.8-15 Jephthah Judges	11.12–28 Perea
13–16		Samson	
17–18		17.1–18.30a Danites	18.30b-31 Shiloh
19–21		19.1–21.24 20.27-28 Ark Benjamin 21.25 Refrain	

Figure 8. *General Overview*

that would have arisen out of the ashes of Jerusalem in 586 BCE.

The results of the work of Richter, Beyerlin, Cogan and Knauf have been simply articulated to reveal that the book of Saviours was expressing an Assyrian-friendly attitude rather than sounding a call to arms. This collection of heroic deeds was held together by a coherent message of trust in Yhwh, the god who had always answered the cries of his people and would continue to do so. The evil committed by Israel was unspecified and it only served to explain setbacks as the consequence of Yhwh's wrath. Setbacks were temporary, Yhwh would always answer and send a saviour who would deliver Israel in the most unexpected manner, but without any king or army. This collection of heroic tales was meant to help Israel accept the integration of the kingdom into the provincial system. Bethel, under Samaria's oversight, claimed that Assyrian occupation did not mark the end of Israel. More than ever, Israel remained the people of Yhwh. The Abimelech episode concluded the book of Saviours in order to underline the responsibility of the successive Israelite monarchs for the disasters that had befallen the kingdom. The Israelite kings broke the *berith* with the Assyrians and therefore rebelled against Yhwh. In this perspective, 720 BCE marked the end of the royal parenthesis and opened the way to Yhwh's direct intervention through saviours whenever the need would arise, in the distant past as well as again in the future! Sargon's conquest of Samaria could even be understood as a saving act, saving Israel from anarchy and rebellion. Compare Abimelech's miserable end with the glorious deeds of Ehud, Barak and Gideon!

Manasseh's Book of Saviours (700-642 BCE): Judges 1*; 3.9-11 (Chapter 2)
The blockade of Jerusalem and the loss of the Shephelah in 701 BCE forced Judah into closer co-operation with the Empire. The Assyrians favoured the city and its elite over the conservative tribal elite. King Manasseh became the symbol of the Assyrian-friendly policy that ushered the small kingdom into one of its most prosperous periods. Deportations and tax-pressure required the intensification of production and the reorganization of whole tracks of the countryside. Social upheavals caused resentment from the country elite which was losing its power to the city. But stability was the key to success and to survival: crops had to be produced and sold for the tribute to be paid in time, and all rebellious attempts were stifled to avoid Assyrian retaliations. In that context, the Assyrian-friendly book of Saviours was introduced from Bethel to Jerusalem with the aim of providing a religious basis to Manasseh's

scrupulous vassalage. The appeasement message of the book of Saviours was put to effect in Judah with a new introduction centred on the accomplishment of Judah in Judg. 1.4-18. With this passage, the Jerusalem elite proclaimed its superiority over the sons of Judah, depicted as a horde of raiders from the Negeb. Judah's success was put into perspective with Israel's gradual control over the cities of the plains (Judg. 1.27-34). The progressive conquest was not yet seen in a negative light. It served to downplay the gravity of the division of the Israelite kingdom into three provinces and the subsequent loss of control of Samaria over the territories of Dor and Megiddo. To the Judaeans who would be tempted to preach rebellion, Judg. 1 replied that Manasseh's court in Jerusalem was the only legitimate group to rule Judah. Moreover, the events in Israel between 735 and 720 BCE were nothing new for Israel: they did not jeopardize the future of either Israel or Judah. Since Othniel was able to defeat a formidable Assyro-kushite coalition (Judg. 3.7-11), Judah should not fear the Assyrians but willingly collaborate with them.

Josiah's Book of Judges (640-609 BCE): Judges 2.1-5, 11-19; 6.7-10; 10.1-3; 12.9-15; 17–18 (Chapters 3 and 4)
The stability of Manasseh's reign coincided with the apex of the Assyrian Empire. But at the first signs of weakness of the central power, Amon, Manasseh's successor was murdered and the Judaean people of the land took over the control of Judah. An ambitious programme of territorial expansion was prepared (the first draft of the book of Joshua) and partially effected (as far as Bethel). Manasseh's book of Saviours now stood in the way of this radical reversal of foreign politics. It was therefore 'improved' with the addition of a number of short but very critical passages inserted at regular intervals: the Bokim episode (Judg. 2.1-5) transformed Judg. 1* into a story of guilty non-conquest on the part of Israel, the aim being to legitimize Josiah's imperialistic ventures towards Israel. The schema (Judg. 2.11-19) and the notice of the anonymous prophet (Judg. 6.7-10) reduced to nought the immediate and unconditional salvation promised by the book of Saviours: Yhwh would only deliver those who came to him without Assyrian religious lore. The Gideon cycle received many additions with the obvious purpose to reduce Gideon's heroism and to depict Israel as idolatrous and cowardly. The story of Abimelech was left unscathed, its critique of Israelite kings being virulent enough as it stood. The Saviours were turned into Judges and reinforced by the addition of five colleagues (Judg. 10; 12) this having the effect of presenting the

Assyrian period as an interim, waiting for Josiah. Finally, the migration of the Danites (Judg. 17–18) illustrated the dangers incurred by a kingless people and the opportunities offered to Judah by the power vacuum left by the waning Assyrians. The date suggested by Niemann for the Danite migration (after 735 BCE) was simply lowered to be related with the aftermath of the 701 BCE deportation.

The book of Saviours thus became the book of Judges. However, Josiah had underestimated the Egyptian factor and he was executed in Megiddo. His successors followed his steps and pushed Judah into senseless cycle of rebellions that ended up in the devastation of Judah and the destruction of Jerusalem.

Demythization in Babylonian Bethel (586–515 BCE): Judges 10.6–11.11;
11.29–16.31 (Chapter 5)
Ironically, the only part of Israel that Josiah had managed to conquer (Benjamin) is the one which saved the Judaean heritage. Lipschits' work on the archaeology of Benjamin has confirmed the importance of Mizpah as the capital of the Babylonian province. Likewise, Bethel became the main cultic centre for what was left of Judah and saved the book of Saviours with its Josianic additions along all the other Judaean writings. The book of Saviours, by now the book of Judges, received the addition of two Losers who had the double task of bidding good-bye to Israel's heroes (saviours and judges) and disavowing Mesopotamian mythology. The story of Jephthah was inserted in the middle of the list of Judges and the Samson cycle was added after it (Judg. 10–16). The demythizing process, pointed out by Gese in the Samson cycle, has been applied to both Jephthah and Samson and has been understood as Bethel's effort to rid itself of its Assyrian heritage which had proved ineffective against the Babylonians.

Jerusalem versus Benjamin (515-450 BCE): Judges 1.22-26; 19–21*
(Chapter 6)
Tensions arose as soon as some Judaeans came back from Babylonia to restore Jerusalem to its former function. Bethel defended its position by claiming its antiquity and its legitimacy by inserting the Bethel conquest-account just after Jerusalem's self-glorification (Judg. 1.22-26). Edenburg's study of Judg. 19–21 has revealed how Jerusalem replied with an atrocious story depicting the chaos of Benjaminite rule (Judg. 19 against Saul's traditions), legitimizing the destruction of Benjamin (Judg. 20) and establishing apartheid between Persian Jerusalem and the remaining

Benjaminites. With Persian support, Jerusalem prevailed over Benjamin, the functions of Mizpah and Bethel were gradually taken over by the old capital built anew. The book of Judges came back to Jerusalem and its last three chapters were appended. Judges 19–21 forms the only appendix to the book, as Judg. 17–18 still belongs to the Josianic edition.

Period of the Judges and Greek Historiography (200 BCE): Judges 1.1-3, 19-21, 36; 2.6-10; 4.5; 21.25 (Chapter 7)

Schmid has demonstrated that the book of Judges was integrated between the books of Joshua and Samuel after the redaction of those books. The constitution of this 'Deuteronomistic History', very different from the one imagined by Noth, provided the Greek-speaking world with a historiography of the Jewish nation.

The figure of Joshua was inserted three times into Judges: in a new introduction (Judg. 1.1-3), in the repetition of Joshua's death notice from Josh. 24 (Judg. 2.6-10) and in the theodicy for the unfinished conquest (Judg. 2.20–3.6). Joshua's second burial in Judg. 2 effected the difficult transition between the two books and somehow severed the conquests accounts in Judg. 1 from the rest of the book to integrate them into the era of Joshua's conquest. The rest of Judges was presented as a particular period in Israel's past, demarcated by the parallels between Judg. 4.4-5 (Deborah under her palm) and 1 Sam. 7.16-17 (Samuel's circuit). The transition from the period of the judges to the period of the kings is effected by 1 Sam. 8 where Samuel recapitulates the main figures of the book of Judges.

Maccabaean and Hasmonaean additions (150 BCE): Judges 2.20–3.6; 4.11, 17, 21; 5.24; 11.12-28; (Chapter 7)

A few details were added during the Maccabaean and Hasmonaean times. Apart from two substancial passages (the call for better military training in Judg. 2.20–3.6 and the justification of the annexation of Perea in Judg. 11.12-28), the rest concerns only a few words added or changed in already existing verses: Heber the Kenite in Judg. 4.11, 17, 21 and Jael's maccabaean hammer in Judg. 5.24.

The scope of this study, devoted to the whole of Judges, has curtailed the possibility of going deeper into the details of the text. The aim was to provide an overview of the meaning of the book of Judges when read outside Noth's Deuteronomistic History hypothesis. It can be read, not as a patch-work of old traditions, but first as a treatise coming out of Bethel around 720 BCE, and then, as a book of traditions making sense at the various turning points of the history of Judah. However, the conclusions of this study rely heavily on the history of Israel as it is now possible to understand it.

Recapitulative Theses

The main results of this study can thus be summarized:

- The song of Deborah remains one of the oldest Biblical texts.
- The *Retterbuch* hypothesis is still valid.
- 701 BCE is a crucial date for Judah's history in general and the book of Judges in particular.
- The seventh century BCE is an important period of literary activity in Judah (Manasseh's reign as much as Josiah's), at least as important for Biblical texts aas for the Persian period.
- The categories of saviours, judges, losers are preferable to major/minor judges distinction.
- The demythizing process is the key to understanding the narratives of Jephthah and Samson.
- No Histories of Israel should present the Period of the Judges as an era in Israel's past.
- Noth's Deuteronomistic History should be abandoned since the removal of Judges from it destroys its coherence.

BIBLIOGRAPHY

Abel, F.-M., 'Le monastère de Beth-Shémesh', *RB* 45 (1936), pp. 538-42.

—*Géographie de la Palestine* (EB, Paris: Gabalda, 1938).

Ackerman, S., 'What If Judges Had Been Written by a Philistine?', in J.C. Exum (ed.), *Virtual History and the Bible* (Leiden: E.J. Brill, 2000), pp. 33-41.

Adinolfi, M., 'Originalità dell apologo di Jotham', *RB* 7 (1959), pp. 322-42.

Aharoni, Y., 'The Use of Hieratic Numerals in Hebrew Ostraca and the Shekel Weights', *BASOR* 184 (1966).

—*The Land of the Bible* (London: Burns and Oates, 1968).

Ahituv, S., *Canaanite Toponyms in Ancient Egyptian Documents* (Jerusalem/Leiden: Magnes Press/E.J. Brill, 1984).

Ahlström, G.W., *Royal Administration and National Religion in Ancient Palestine* (Leiden: E.J. Brill, 1982).

—*Who Were the Israelites?* (Winona Lake: Eisenbrauns, 1986).

—*The History of Ancient Palestine from the Paleolithic Period to Alexander's Conquest* (JSOTSup, 146; Sheffield: JSOT Press, 1993).

Albrektson, B., *History and the Gods: An Essay on the Idea of Historical Events as Divine Manifestations in the Ancient Near East and in Israel* (ConBOT, 1; Lund: C.W.K. Gleerup, 1967).

Albright, W.F., 'The Canaanite God Haurôn (Hôron)', *AJSL* 53 (1936), pp. 1-12.

—'Jethro, Hobab and Reuel in Early Hebrew Tradition', *CBQ* 25 (1952), pp. 1-11.

Alejandrino, M., *Deborah and Barak: A Literary-Historical Analysis of Judges 4 and 5* (Rome: Université Grégorienne, 1998).

Allen, A., *The Fragments of Mimnermus: Text and Commentary* (Palingenesia, 44; Stuttgart: F. Steiner, 1993).

Alonso-Schökel, L., 'Erzählkunst im Buche der Richter', *Bib* 42 (1961), pp. 143-72.

Alster, B., *Dumuzi's Dream: Aspects of Oral Poetry in a Sumerian Myth* (Mesopotamia, 1; Copenhagen: Akademisk Forlag, 1972).

—'Ninurta and the Turtle', *JCS* 24 (1972), pp. 120-25.

—'A Note on the Uriah Letter', *ZA* 77 (1987), pp. 169-73.

—'An Akkadian Animal Proverb and the Assyrian Letter ABL 555', *JCS* 41 (1989), pp. 187-93.

Alt, A., *Kleine Schriften* 1 (München: 1953).

—'The Formation of the Israelite State in Palestine', in *idem*, *Essays in Old Testament History and Religion* (Sheffield: JSOT Press, 1989), pp. 171-238.

Alter, R., 'Simson without Folklore', in S. Niditch (ed.), *Text and Tradition* (Atlanta: Scholars Press, 1990), pp. 47-56.

Alvarez Barredo, M., 'Aspectos literarios y lectura teológica de Jue 2, 6-3, 6', *Antonianum* 73 (1998), pp. 219-39.

—'Convergencias redaccionales sobre la conquista de la tierra prometida en Jue 1, 1-2, 5', *Carthaginensia* 14 (1998), pp. 1-42.

—'El Cántico de Débora (Jue 5, 1-31): Perfiles literarios y teológicos', *Verdad y vida* 56 (1998), pp. 327-70.

—'Los relatos sobre los Primeros Jueces (Jue 3, 7-4): Enfoques literarios y teológicos', *Antonianum* 73 (1998), pp. 407-57.

—'Perfiles literarios y teológicos de Jue 7', *Antonianum* 75 (2000), pp. 3-40.

—'Abimelec: Paradigma de una actitud autonoma ante Dios. Estudio literario de Jue 9', *Carthaginensia* 17 (2001), pp. 1-66.

Amit, Y., 'The Use of Analogy in the Study of the Book of Judges', in M. Augustin *et al.* (eds.), *'Wünschet Jerusalem Frieden': Collected Communications to the XIIth Co* (BEAT, 13; Frankfurt: P. Lang, 1986), pp. 387-94.

—'The End of the Book of Judges', in *Proceedings of the Ninth World Congress of Jewish Studies* (Jerusalem: World Union of Jewish Studies, 1986), pp. 73*-80*.

—'Judges 4: Its Content and Form', *JSOT* 39 (1987), pp. 89-111.

—'The Story of Ehud (Judges 3.12-30): The Form and the Message', in J.C. Exum (ed.), *Signs and Wonders: Biblical Texts in Literary Focus* (SBLSS, SBL, 1989), pp. 97-124.

—'Hidden Polemics in the Conquest of Dan', *VT* 40 (1990), pp. 4-20.

—*The Book of Judges: The Art of Editing (Hebrew)* (The Biblical Encyclopedia Library, 6; Jerusalem—Tel Aviv: Mosad Bialik & Chaim Rosenberg School of Jewish Studies, Tel Aviv University, 1992).

—'Literature in the Service of Politics: Studies in Judges 19-21', in H.G. Reventlow, Y. Hoffman and B. Uffenheimer (eds.), *Politics and Theopolitics in the Bible and Postbiblical Literature* (JSOTSup, 171; Sheffield: Sheffield Academic Press, 1994), pp. 28-40.

—*History and Ideology* (BS, 60; Sheffield: Sheffield Academic Press, 1999).

—*Hidden Polemics in Biblical Narrative* (BInt, 25; Leiden: E.J. Brill, 2000).

Ap-Thomas, D.R., 'Saul's "Uncle" ', *VT* 11 (1961), pp. 241-45.

Appolodore, *La bibliothèque d'Appolodore* (trans. J.C. Carrière and B. Massonie; Paris: Belles Lettres, 1991).

Arav, R., 'Bethsaida Preliminary Report', in R. Arav and R.A. Freund (eds.), *Bethsaida: A City by the North Shore of the Sea of Galilee* (Kirksville MI: Truman State University Press, 1999), pp. 3-114.

Arbeitman, Y.L., 'Iranian "Scribe", Anatolian "Ruler" or Neither', in *idem* (ed.), *Fucus* (Amsterdam: 1988), pp. 1-101.

Arnold, P.M., *Gibeah: The Search for a Biblical City* (JSOTSup, 79; Sheffield: Sheffield Academic Press, 1990).

—'Gibeah', in D.N. Freedman (ed.), *ABD* 2 (New York: Doubleday, 1992), pp. 1007-9.

Artzi, P., 'Ninurta in the Mid-Second Millennium "West" ', in H. Klengel and J. Renger (eds.), *Landwirtschaft im Alten Orient* (Berlin: Reimer, 1999), pp. 361-67.

Asen, B.A., 'Deborah, Barak and Bees: Apis Mellifera, Apiculture and Judges 4 and 5', *ZAW* 109 (1997), pp. 514-33.

Assad, M., *Le chemin de la Mecque* (Paris: Fayard, 1976).

Assmann, A., 'Schriftliche Folklore: Zur Entstehung und Funktion eines Überliefe-rungstyps', in A. Assmann and C. Hardmeier (eds.), *Schrift und Gedächtnis: Beiträge zur Archäologie der literarischen Kommunikation* (Archäologie der literarischen Kommunikation, 1; München: Wilhelm Fink, 1983), pp. 175-93.

Astour, M.C., 'Tamar the Hierodule: An Essay in the Method of Vestigal Motifs', *JBL* 85 (1966), pp. 185-96.

Athenaeus, *Deipnosophistae* (trans. C.A. Campbell; LCL, V; London: Heinemann, 1955).

Attridge, H.W., and R.A. Oden, *Philo of Byblos, the Phoenician History: Introduction, Critical Text, Translation, Notes* (CBQMS, 9; Washington: Catholic Biblical Association, 1981).

Auerbach, E., 'Untersuchungen zum Richterbuch II. Ehud', *ZAW* 51 (1933), pp. 47-51.

Augustine, *The City of God* (trans. Matthews Sanford and Green; LCL, Cambridge MA: Heinemann, 1965).

Auld, A.G., 'Judges 1 and History: A Reconsideration', *VT* 25 (1975), pp. 261-85.

—'Review of Boling's Judges: The Framework of Judges and the Deuteronomists', *JSOT* 1 (1976), pp. 41-46.

—'Textual and Literary Studies in the Book of Joshua', *ZAW* 90 (1978), pp. 412-17.

—'Tribal Terminology in Joshua and Judges', in Lincei (ed.), *Covegno sul tema: Le Origini di Israele* (Roma: Accademia Nazionale dei Lincei, 1987), pp. 87-98.

—'Gideon: Hacking at the Heart of the Old Testament', *VT* 39 (1989), pp. 257-67.

—'What Makes Judges Deuteronomistic?', in *idem* (ed.), *Joshua Retold* (Edinburgh: T. & T. Clark, 1998), pp. 120-26.

—'The Deuteronomists and the Former Prophets', in L.S. Schearing and S.L. McKenzie (eds.), *Those Elusive Deuteronomists* (JSOTSup, 268; Sheffield: Sheffield Academic Press, 1999), pp. 116-26.

—'What If the Chronicler Did Use the Deuteronomistic History?', in J.C. Exum (ed.), *Virtual History and the Bible* (Leiden: E.J. Brill, 2000), pp. 137-50.

Auzou, G., *La force de l'esprit: Etude du livre des Juges* (Connaissance de la Bible, 5; Paris: 1965).

Avigad, N., 'A Seal of Manasseh, Son of the King', *IEJ* 13 (1963), pp. 133-36.

—'Seals of Exiles', *IEJ* 15 (1965), pp. 222-32.

—'Chronique archéologique', *RB* 80 (1973), pp. 576-79.

—'The Priest of Dor', *IEJ* 25 (1975), pp. 101-105.

—*Bullae and Seals from a Post-Exilic Judean Archive* (Qedem, 4; Jerusalem: Institute of Archeology, 1976).

—*Hebrew Bullae from the Time of Jeremiah* (Jerusalem: Israel Exploration Society, 1986).

—'Samaria (city)', in E. Stern (ed.), *NEAEHL* 4 (Jerusalem: Israel Exploration Society and Carta, 1993), pp. 1300-10.

—'The Governor of the City Bulla', in H. Geva (ed.), *Ancient Jerusalem Revealed* (Jerusalem: Israel Exploration Society, 1994), pp. 138-40.

Babrius, *Babrius and Phaedrus* (trans. B.E. Parry; LCL, Cambridge MA: Heinemann, 1965).

Bach, A., 'Rereading the Body Politic: Women and Violence in Judges 21', *BibInt* 6 (1998), pp. 1-19.

Bagnall, R.S., and P. Derow, *Greek Historical Documents: The Hellenistic Period* (SBLSBS, 16; Atlanta: Scholars Press, 1981).

Bahat, D., 'The Wall of Manasseh in Jerusalem', *IEJ* 31 (1981), pp. 235-36.

Bal, M., *Lethal Love: Feminist Literary Readings of Biblical Love Stories* (Bloomington: Indiana University Press, 1987).

—'Dealing with Women: Daughters in the Book of Judges', in R.M. Schwartz (ed.), *The Book and the Text: The Bible and Literary Theory* (Oxford: Blackwell, 1990), pp. 16-39.

Balzer, H.R., 'My God and Your Idols: Political Rivalry between Human Representatives of the Divine in the Old Testament', *OTE* 4 (1991), pp. 257-71.

Barag, D., 'The Effects of the Tennes Rebellion on Palestine', *BASOR* 183 (1966), pp. 6-12.

Barkay, G., 'A Second "Governor of the City" Bulla', in H. Geva (ed.), *Ancient Jerusalem Revealed* (Jerusalem: Israel Exploration Society, 1994), pp. 141-6.

Barnes, R.H., 'Marriage by Capture', *JRAI* 46 (1999), pp. 57-73.

Barr, J., 'Mythical Monarch Unmasked? Mysterious Doings of Debir, King of Eglon', *JSOT* 48 (1990), pp. 55-68.

Barrett, W.S., *Euripides: Hyppolytus* (Oxford: Oxford University Press, 1964).

Barré, M.L., 'The Meaning of *pršdn* in Judges III 22', *VT* 41 (1991), pp. 1-11.

—'Lightning', in K. Van der Toorn, B. Becking and P.W. van der Horst (eds.), *DDD* (Leiden: E.J. Brill, 1995), pp. 970-73.

Bartelmus, R., 'Die sogenannte Jothamfabel: eine politisch-religiöse Parabeldich-tung', *TZ* 2 (1985), pp. 97-120.

—'Forschung am Richterbuch seit Martin Noth', *ThR* 56 (1991), pp. 221-59.

—'Menschlicher Misserfolg und Jahwes Initiative', *BN* 70 (1993), pp. 28-47.

Bartlett, J.R., 'Edom and the Fall of Jerusalem', *PEQ* 114 (1982), pp. 13-24.

Bates, D.G., 'Normative and Alternative Systems of Marriages among the Yörük of Southeastern Turkey', *AQ* 47 (1974), pp. 270-87.

Bauer, T., *Das Inschriftenwerk Assurbanipals* II (Leipzig: 1933).

Bauer, U.F.W., 'Eine synchrone Lesart von Ri 18, 13-18', in Talstra (ed.), *Narrative and comment* (Kampen: Kok Pharos, 1995), pp. 53-63.

—*Warum nur uebertretet ihr SEIN Geheis: Eine synchrone Exegese der Anti-Erzaehlung Ri 17-18* (BEAT, 45; Frankfurt: Lang, 1998).

—'Judges 18 as an Anti-Spy Story in the Context of an Anti-Conquest Story', *JSOT* 88 (2000), pp. 37-47.

—'A Metaphorical Etiology in Judges 18.12', *JHebS* 3 (2001), pp. 37-47.

Baumgartner, A.I., *The Phoenician History of Philo of Byblos* (EPR, 89; Leiden: E.J. Brill, 1981).

Bayet, J., 'Les Cerialia', *RBPH* 29 (1951), pp. 5-32.

Beal, T.K., 'Ideology and Intertextuality', in D.N. Fewell (ed.), *Reading Between Texts* (Louisville, KY: Westminster / John Knox Press, 1992), pp. 27-39.

Bechmann, U., *Das Deborahied zwischen Geschichte und Fiktion: Eine exegetische Untersuchung zu Richter 5* (DThR, 33; St. Ottilien: EOS Verlag, 1989).

Becker, U., *Richterzeit und Königtum: Redaktionsgeschichtliche Studien zum Richterbuch* (BZAW, 192; Berlin: W. de Gruyter, 1990).

—*Jesaja, von der Botschaft zum Buch* (FRLANT, 178; Göttingen: Vandenhoeck & Ruprecht, 1997).

Becker-Spörl, S., 'Krieg, Gewalt und die Rede von Gott im Deboralied (Ri 5).', *BK* 51 (1996), pp. 101-106.

—'*Und sang Debora an jenem Tag': Untersuchungen zu Sprache und Intention des Deboraliedes (Ri 5)* (Europäische Hochschulschriften, 620; Frankfurt am Main/Wien: Lang, 1998).

Becking, B., *The Fall of Samaria: An Historical and Archeological Study* (SHANE, 2; Leiden: E.J. Brill, 1992).

Beckwith, R., *The Old Testament Canon of the New Testament Church and its Background in Early Judaism* (Grand Rapids, Mi.: Eerdmans, 1985).

Beek, M.A., 'The Meaning of the Expression "the Chariots of Israel" (2 Kings ii 12)', in *idem et al.* (eds.), *The Witness of Tradition* (OTS, 17; Leiden: E.J. Brill, 1972), pp. 1-10.

Beem, B., 'The Minor Judges: A Literary Reading of Some Very Short Stories', in K.L. Younger (ed.), *The Biblical Canon in Comparative Perspective* (ANETS, 11; Lewiston: Edwin Mellen Press, 1991), pp. 147-72.

Begg, C., 'Hezekiah's Display: Another Parallel', *BN* 41 (1988), pp. 7-10.

Ben Zvi, E., 'The Account of the Reign of Manasseh in II Reg 21, 1-18 and the Redactional History of the Book of Kings', *ZAW* 103 (1991), pp. 355-74.

—'Isaiah 1, 4-9, Isaiah and the Events of 701 BCE in Judah', *SJOT* 1 (1991), pp. 95-111.

—'History and Prophetic Texts', in M.P. Graham, W.P. Brown and J.K. Kuan (eds.), *History and Interpretation: Essays in Honor of John H. Hayes* (JSOTSup, 173; Sheffield: JSOT Press, 1993), pp. 106-20.

—'Inclusion in and Exclusion from Israel as Conveyed by the Term "Israel" in Post-Monarchic Biblical Texts', in S.W. Holloway and L.K. Handy (eds.), *The Pitcher is Broken* (JSOTSup, 190; Sheffield: JSOT Press, 1995), pp. 95-149.

—'Prelude to a Reconstruction of the Historical Manassic Judah', *BN* 81 (1996), pp. 31-44.

—*A Historical-Critical Study of the Book of Obadiah* (BZAW, 242; Berlin: W. de Gruyter, 1996).

—'The Urban Center of Jerusalem and the Development of the Literature of the Hebrew Bible', in W.E. Aufrecht, N.A. Mirau and S.W. Gauley (eds.), *Urbanism in Antiquity : From Mesopotamia to Crete* (JSOTSup, 244; Sheffield: JSOT Press, 1997), pp. 194-209.

Ben-Barak, Z., 'The Queen Consort and the Struggle for Succession to the Throne', in J.-M. Durand (ed.), *La femme dans le Proche-Orient Ancien* (Paris: Recherche sur les civilisations, 1987), pp. 33-39.

Bendenbender, A., 'Biene, Fackel, Blitz: Zur Metaphorik der Namen in der Deborageschichte', *TuK* 76 (1997), pp. 43-55.

—'Theologie im Widerstand: Die Antiochoskrise und ihre Bewältigung im Spiegel der Bücher Exodus und Richter', *TeKon* 23 (2000), pp. 3-39.

Benz, F.L., *Personnal Names in the Phoenician and Punic Inscriptions* (Studia Pohl 8, Roma: 1972).

Beydon, F., 'Violence sous silence: Juges 19', *FVCb* 28 (1989), pp. 81-87.

Beyerle, S., 'Der Name Issachar', *BN* 62 (1992), pp. 51-60.

Beyerlin, W., 'Gattung und Herkunft des Rahmens im Richterbuch', in E. Würthwein and O. Kaiser (eds.), *Tradition and Situation, Studien zur alttestamentlichen Prophetie* (Göttingen: Vandenhoeck & Ruprecht, 1963), pp. 1-29.

—'Geschichte und heilsgechichtliche Traditionsbildung im Alten Testament: Ein Beitrag zur Traditionsgeschichte von Richter VI-VIII', *VT* 13 (1963), pp. 1-25.

Bietak, M., 'Une citadelle royale à Avaris de la première moitié de la XVIIIe dynastie et ses liens avec le monde minoen', in A. Caubet (ed.), *L'acrobate au taureau. Les découvertes de Tell el-Dab'a (Egypte) et l'archéologie de la Méditerranée orientale (1800-1400 av. J.-C.)* (Louvre conférences et colloques, Paris: La documentation française, 1999), pp. 29-81.

Billen, A.V., 'The Old Latin Version of Judges', *JTS* 43 (1942), pp. 140-49.

Biran, A., 'Dan', in E. Stern (ed.), *NEAEHL*, 1 (Jerusalem: Israel Exploration Society & Carta, 1993), pp. 323-32.

—*Biblical Dan* (Jerusalem: Israel Exploration Society, 1994).

Black, J.A., 'The New Year Ceremonies in Ancient Babylon: "Taking Bel by the Hand" and a Cultic Picnic', *Religion* 11 (1981), pp. 39-59.

Black, J. and A. Green, *Gods, Demons and Symbols of Ancient Mesopotamia* (London: British Museum Press, 1992).

Blau, J., *On Pseudo-Corrections in Some Semitic Languages* (Jerusalem: Israel Academy of Sciences and Humanities, 1976).

Bledstein, A.J., 'Is Judges a Woman's Satire on Men who Play God?', in A. Brenner (ed.), *A Feminist Companion to Judges* (Sheffield: JSOT Press, 1993), pp. 34-54.

Blenkinsopp, J., 'Some Notes on the Saga of Samson and the Heroic Milieu', *Scripture* 11 (1959), pp. 81-89.

—'Structure and Style in Judges 13-16', *JBL* 82 (1962), pp. 65-76.

—*Gibeon and Israel* (SOTSM, 2; Cambridge: Cambridge University Press, 1972).

—'Did Saul Make Gibeon his Capital?', *VT* 24 (1974), pp. 1-7.

—'The Judean Priesthood during the Neo-Babylonian and Achaemenid Periods: A Hypothetical Reconstruction', *CBQ* 60 (1998), pp. 25-43.

Block, D.I., 'Deborah among the Judges: the Perspective of the Hebrew Historian', in A.R. Millard, J. Hoffmeier and D.W. Baker (eds.), *Faith, Tradition, and History: Old Testament Historiography in its Near Eastern Context* (Winona Lake: Eisenbrauns, 1994), pp. 229-56.

Blok, J.H., *The Early Amazons* (Leiden: E.J. Brill, 1995).

Bluedorn, W., *Yahweh Versus Baalism: A Theological Reading of the Gideon-Abimelech Narrative* (JSOTSup, 329; Sheffield: Sheffield Academic Press, 2001).

Blum, E., *Die Komposition der Vätergeschichte* (WMANT, 57; Neukirchen-Vluyn: Neukirchener Verlag, 1984).

—*Studien zur Komposition des Pentateuch* (BZAW, 189; Berlin: W. de Gruyter, 1990).

—'Der kompositionelle Knoten am Übergang von Josua zu Richter: Ein Entflechtungsvorschlag', in M. Vervenne and J. Lust (eds.), *Deuteronomy and Deuteronomic Literature* (BETL, 133; Leuven: Peeters, 1997), pp. 181-212.

Boardman, J., 'Herakles' Monsters: Indegenous or Oriental?', in C. Bonnet and C. Jourdain-Annequin (eds.), *Le bestiaire d'Héraclès* (Kernos Sup., 7; Liège: Centre international d'étude de la religion grecque antique, 1998), pp. 27-35.

Bodine, W.R., *The Greek Text of Judges: Recensional Developments* (Chico, CA: Scholars Press, 1980).

Bohmbach, K.G., 'Conventions/Contraventions: The Meanings of Public and Private for the Judges 19 Concubine', *JSOT* 83 (1999), pp. 83-98.

Boling, R.G., 'In Those Days There Was no King in Israel', in H.N. Bream, R.D. Heim and C.A. Moore (eds.), *A Light unto my Path* (Philadelphia: Temple University Press, 1974), pp. 33-48.

—*Judges: A New Translation with Introduction and Comments* (AB; New York: Doubleday, 1975).

Boling, R.G., and G.E. Wright, *Joshua* (AB; New York: Doubleday, 1982).

Börner, F., 'Die Römischen Ernteopfer und die Füchse im Philisterlande', *WS* 69 (1956), pp. 372-84.

Bonnet, C., 'Kadmos', in E. Lipinski (ed.), *DCPP* (Louvain: Brepols, 1992), p. 241.

Bonnet, C., and C. Jourdain Annequin, 'Images et fonctions d'Héraclès: Les modèles orientaux et leurs interprétations', in S. Ribichini, M. Rocchi and P. Xella (eds.), *La questione delle influenze orientali sulla religione greca* (Roma: Consiglio Nazionale delle Ricerche, 2001), pp. 195-223.

Bordreuil, P. and A. Lemaire, 'Nouveaux sceaux hébreux, araméens et ammonites', *Semitica* 26 (1976), pp. 45-63.

—'Tanit du Liban', in E. Lipinski (ed.), *Phoenicia and the East mediterranean in the first Millennium B.C.* (SP, 5; Leuven: Peeters, 1987), pp. 79-85.

Borger, R., *Die Inschriften Asahaddons* (AfO Beihefte, 9; Graz: Selbstverlage des Herausgebers, 1956).

Borowski, O., 'Hezekiah's Reforms and the Revolt against Assyria', *BA* 58 (1995), pp. 148-55.

—*Agriculture in Iron Age Israel* (Winona Lake: Eisenbrauns, 1987).

Bothmer, D. von, *Amazons in Greek Art* (Oxford: Oxford University Press, 1957).

Bottéro, J., *Mésopotamie: L'écriture, la raison et les dieux* (Paris: Gallimard, 1987).

Bottéro, J., and S.N. Kramer, *Lorsque les dieux faisaient l'homme* (Paris: Gallimard, 1989).

Brandfon, F., 'Beth-Shemesh', in D.N. Freedman (ed.), *ABD* 1 (New York: Doubleday, 1992), pp. 696-98.

Braudel, F., *La Méditerranée et le monde méditerranéen à l'époque de Philippe II* (Paris: A. Colin, 1985).

Brenk, F.E., 'The Herakles Myth and the Literary Texts Relating to the Myth of Ninurta', in D. Musti (ed.), *La Transizione dal miceneo all'alto arcaismo* (Roma: Consiglio nazionale delle ricerche, 1991), pp. 507-526.

Brenner, A., 'Afterword', in *idem* (ed.), *A Feminist Companion to Judges* (Sheffield: JSOT Press, 1993), pp. 231-35.

Brettler, M.Z., 'Jud 1, 1-2, 10: From Appendix to Prologue', *ZAW* 101 (1989), pp. 433-35.

—'The Book of Judges: Literature as Politics', *JBL* 108 (1989), pp. 395-418.

—'Never the Twain Shall Meet? The Ehud Story as History and Literature', *HUCA* 62 (1991), pp. 285-304.

—*The Creation of History in Ancient Israel* (London: Routledge, 1995).

—'The Composition of 1 Samuel 1-2', *JBL* 116 (1997), pp. 601-12.

—*The Book of Judges* (London: Routledge, 2001).

Briant, P., *Histoire de l'Empire perse* (Paris: Fayard, 1996).

Briend, J., 'Israël et les Gabaonites', in Laperrousaz (ed.), *La protohistoire d'Israël* (Paris: Cerf, 1990), pp. 121-82.

Brooke, A.E. and N. McLean, *The Old Testament in Greek. II.2. The later historical books, 1 and 2 Kings* (Cambridge: Cambridge University Press, 1930).

Brooks, S.S., 'Saul and Samson Narratives', *JSOT* 71 (1996), pp. 19-25.

Broshi, M., 'The Expansion of Jerusalem in the Reigns of Hezekiah and Manasseh', *IEJ* 24 (1974), pp. 21-26.

Brown, F., S.R. Driver and C.A. Briggs, *A Hebrew and English Lexicon of the Old Testament* (Oxford: Clarendon Press, 1951).

Brueggemann, W., 'Social Criticism and Social Vision in the Deuteronomic Formula of the Judges', in J. Jeremias and L. Perlitt (eds.), *Die Botschaft und die Boten* (Neukirchen-Vluyn: Neukirchener Verlag, 1981), pp. 101-14.

Brunner, H., 'Die religiöse Antwort auf die Korruption in Ägypten', in W. Röllig (eds.), *Das Hörende Herz* (OBO, 80; Freiburg/Göttingen: Universitätsverlag/Vandenhoeck & Ruprecht, 1988), pp. 103-109.

Brunner-Traut, E., 'Ägyptische Tiermärchen', *ZÄS* 80 (1955), pp. 12-32.

Bruschweiler, F., *Inanna: La déesse triomphante et vaincue dans la cosmologie sumérienne* (Cahiers du CEPOA, 4; Leuven: Peeters, 1987).

Budde, K., *Das Buch der Richter* (KHAT, 7; Freiburg i. Br.: 1897).

—*Die Bücher Samuel erklärt* (KHAT, 8; 1902).

Bulbach, S., 'Judah in the Reign of Manasseh as Evidenced in Texts during the Neo-Assyrian Period and in the Archeology of the Iron Age' (PhD dissertation; Ann Arbor, MI: University Microfilms, 1981).

Bunimovitz, S., and Z. Lederman, 'Beth-Shemesh: Culture Conflict on Judah's Frontier', *BARev* 23 (1997), pp. 42-49, 75-77.

—*The Land of Israel in the Late Bronze Age: A Case Study of Socio-Cultural Change in a Complex Society* (Tel Aviv: Tel Aviv University Press, 1989).

—'The Problem of Human Resources in Late Bronze Age Palestine and its Socio-Economic Implications', *UF* 26 (1994), pp. 1-20.

Bunnens, G., 'Considérations géographiques sur la place occupée par la Phénicie dans l'expansion de l'empire assyrien', in E. Gubel, E. Lipinsky and B. Servais-Soyez (eds.), *Redt Tyrus/Sauvons Tyr* (SP, 1.2; Leuven: Peeters, 1983), pp. 169-94.

Burkert, W., 'Oriental and Greek Mythology: the Meeting of Parallels', in J. Bremmer (ed.), *Interpretations of Greek Mythology* (London / Sydney: Croom Helm, 1987), pp. 10-40.

—'Eracle e gli altri eroi culturali del Vicino Oriente', in C. Bonnet and C. Jourdain-Annequin (eds.), *Héraclès: D'une rive à l'autre de la Méditerranée* (Bruxelles/Rome: Institut historique belge de Rome, 1992), pp. 111-27.

—*The Orientalizing Revolution* (Cambridge, MA: Harvard University Press, 1992).

Burney, C.F., *The Book of Judges* (London: Rivingtons, 1918).

Burrows, M., *The Basis of Israelite Marriage* (AOS, New Haven: 1938).

Butts, J.R., *The Progymnasmata of Theon: A New Translation and Commentary* (Claremont: Microfilm edition, 1986).

Calder, N., 'The *sa'y* and *Jabîn*: Some notes on Qur'ân 37.102-3', *JSS* 31 (1986), pp. 17-26.

Callimachus, *Hymns and Epigrams* (trans. A.W. Mair; LCL, London: Heinemann, 1960).

Callimaque, *Iambes* (trans. E. Cahen; Belles Lettres, Paris: 1922).

Calmet, A., *Commentarius literalis in librum Judicum, latinis literis traditus a J.D. Manci* (Wirceburgi: 1790).

Camp, C.V., and C.R. Fontaine, 'The Words of the Wise and their Riddles', in S. Niditch (ed.), *Text and Tradition* (Atlanta: Scholars Press, 1990), pp. 127-51.

Campbell, E.F., 'Judges 9 and Biblical Archeology', in C.L. Meyers and M. O'Connor (eds.), *The Word of the Lord Shall Go Forth* (Winona Lake: 1983), pp. 263-71.

Caplice, R., 'Namburbi Texts in the British Museum I', *Orientalia* 34 (1965), pp. 105-31.

—'Namburbi Texts in the British Museum V*', *Orientalia* 40 (1971), pp. 133-83.

Caquot, A., M. Sznycer and A. Herdner, *Textes ougaritiques: mythes et légendes* (LAPO, 7; Paris: Cerf, 1974).

—'Les tribus d'Israël dans le cantique de Débora (Juges 5, 13-17)', *Semitica* XXXVI (1986), pp. 47-70.

Carden, M., 'Homophobia and Rape in Sodom and Gibeah: A Response to Ken Stone', *JSOT* 82 (1999), pp. 83-96.

Carter, C.E., *The Emergence of Yehud in the Persian Period: A Social and Demographic Study* (JSOTSup, 294, Sheffield: Sheffield Academic Press, 1999).

Cartledge, T.W., 'Were Nazirite Vows Unconditional?', *CBQ* 51 (1989), pp. 409-22.

Cassin, E., 'Forme et identité des homes et des dieux chez les Babyloniens', in C. Malamoud. and J.P. Vernant (eds.), *Corps des dieux* (*Le temps de la réflexion*, 7; Paris: Gallimard, 1986), pp. 63-76.

—'Le roi et le lion', in *idem* (ed.), *Le semblable et le différent: Symbolismes du pouvoir dans le Proche-Orient ancien* (Paris: La découverte, 1987), pp. 167-213.

—'Virginité et stratégie du sexe', in *idem* (ed.), *Le semblable et le différent: Symbolismes du pouvoir dans le Proche-Orient ancien* (Paris: La découverte, 1987), pp. 338-57.

Castatini, A., 'Samuele il nazireo', *Henoch* IX (1987), pp. 161-94.

Castelbajac, I. de, 'Histoire de la rédaction de Juges IX: une solution', *VT* 51 (2001), pp. 166-85.

Cathcart, K.J., 'The Trees, the Beasts and the Birds: Fables, Parables and Allegories in the Old Testament', in J. Day, R.P. Gordon and H.G.M. Williamson (eds.), *Wisdom in Ancient Israel: Essays in Honour of J. A. Emerton* (Cambridge / New York: Cambridge University Press, 1995), pp. 212-21.

Cazelles, H., 'Le livre des Juges', in *idem* (ed.), *DBSup* (Paris: Letouzey & Ané, 1949), pp. 1394-414.

—'Review of Jean-Robert Kupper, *Les nomades en Mésopotamie au temps des rois de Mari* (Paris: Belles Lettres, 1957)', *VT* 8 (1958), pp. 316-20.

Certeau, M. de, *La faiblesse de croire* (Paris: Seuil, 1987).

Chalcraft, D.J., 'Deviance and Legitimate Action in the Book of Judges', in D.J.A. Clines (ed.), *The Bible in Three Dimensions* (JSOTSup, 87; Sheffield: JSOT Press, 1990), pp. 177-201.

Chambry, E., *Fables/Esope* (Budé, Paris: Belles Lettres, 1996).

Chaney, M.L., 'Systemic Study of the Israelite Monarchy', *Semeia* 37 (1986), pp. 72-73.

—'Bitter Bounty: The Dynamics of Political Economy Critiqued by the Eighth-Century Prophets', in N.K. Gottwald (ed.), *The Bible and Liberation: Political and Social Hermeneutics* (New York: Maryknoll, 1993), pp. 250-63.

Chapman, W.J., 'Zum Ursprung der chronologischen Angabe I Reg 6, 1', *ZAW* 12 (1935), pp. 185-89.

Charpin, D., 'Compte rendu du CAD vol. Q', *AfO* 36-37 (1989-1990), pp. 93-124.

Chornarat, J., 'L'initiation d'Aristée', *Religion* 52 (1974), pp. 185-207.

Chwolson, D., *Die Ssabier und der Ssabismus* (Amsterdam: Oriental Press, 1965).

Cintas, P., *Céramique punique* (Bruxelles: 1950).

Civil, M., *The Farmer's Instructions: A Sumerian Agricultural Manual* (AOSup, 5; Sabadell [Barcelona]: AUSA, 1994).

Claassens, J., 'Notes on Characterisation in the Jephtah Narrative', *JNSL* 22 (1996), pp. 107-15.

—'Theme and Fonction in the Jephtah Narrative', *JNSL* 23 (1997), pp. 203-19.

Clines, D.J.A., 'Metacommenting Amos', in *idem* (ed.), *Interested Parties: The Ideology of Writers and Readers of the Hebrew Bible* (JSOTSup, 205; Sheffield: JSOT Press, 1995), pp. 76-93.

—'Psalm 2 and the MLF (Moabite Liberation Front)', in *idem* (ed.), *Interested Parties* (JSOTSup, 205; Sheffield: JSOT Press, 1995), pp. 244-75.

Coats, G.W., 'An Exposition for the Conquest Theme', *CBQ* 47 (1985), pp. 47-54.

—'The Book of Joshua: Heroic Saga or Conquest Theme?', *JSOT* 38 (1987), pp. 15-32.

Cogan, M., *Imperialism and Religion: Assyria, Judah and Israel in the Eighth and Seventh Centuries B.C.E.* (Missoula, MT: Scholars Press, 1974).

Cogan, M., and H. Tadmor, *II Kings: A New Translation with Introduction and Commentary* (AB, 11; New York: Doubleday, 1988).

Cohen, A., 'Portrayals of Abduction in Greek Art', in N. Boymel Kampen (ed.), *Sexuality in Ancient Art* (Cambridge: 1996), pp. 117-35.

Collon, D., 'Neo-Assyrian Gula in the British Museum', in N. Cholidis, M. Krafeld-Daugherty and E. Rehm (eds.), *Beschreiben und Deuten in der Archäologie des Alten Orients* (AVO, 4; Münster: Ugarit-Verlag, 1994), pp. 43-48.

—*Catalogue of the Western Asiatic Seals in the British Museum: Cylinder Seals V* (London: British Museum Press, 2001).

Coogan, M.D., *West Semitic Personnal Names in the Murašu Documents* (Missoula, MT: Scholars Press, 1976).

—'A Structural and Literary Analysis of the Song of Deborah', *CBQ* 40 (1978), pp. 143-66.

Cook, S.A., *The Laws of Moses and the Laws of Hammurabi* (London: 1903).

Cooper, J.S., *The Return of Ninurta to Nippur* (AnOr, 52; Rome: Institut Biblique Pontifical, 1978).

Cooper, J.S., and W. Heimpel, 'The Sumerian Sargon Legend', *JAOS* 103 (1983), pp. 67-82.

Coote, R.B., and M.P. Coote, *Power, Politics and the Making of the Bible* (Minneapolis: Augsburg Fortress, 1990).

Coqueugniot, E., 'Outillage de pierre taillée au Bronze Récent', in M. Yon (ed.), *Arts et industries de la pierre à Ras Shamra-Ougarit VI* (Paris: Recherches sur les civilisations, 1991), pp. 127-202.

Cortese, E., *Joshua 13-21: Ein priesterschriftlicher Abschnitt im deuteronomistischen Geschichtswerk* (OBO, 94; Freiburg/Göttingen: Universitätsverlag/Vandenhoeck & Ruprecht, 1990).

Craig, K.M.J., 'Bargaining in Tov (Judges 11, 4-11): The Many Directions of So-Called Direct Speech', *Biblica* 79 (1998), pp. 76-85.

Craigie, P.C., 'Deborah and Anat: A Study of Poetic Imagery (Jg 5)', *ZAW* 90 (1978), pp. 374-81.

Crenshaw, J.L., 'The Samson Saga: Filial Devotion or Erotic Attachment?', *ZAW* 86 (1974), pp. 470-504.

—*Samson: A Secret Betrayed, a Vow Ignored* (Atlanta: John Knox Press, 1978).

Cross, F.M., 'The Themes of the Book of Kings and the Structure of the Deuteronomic History', in *idem* (ed.), *Canaanite Myth and Hebrew Epic* (Cambridge, MA: Harvard University Press, 1973), pp. 274-89.

—'The Ammonite Oppression of the Tribe of Gad and Reuben: Missing Verses from 1 Sam 11 found in 4QSama', in E. Tov (ed.), *The Hebrew and Greek Texts of Samuel* (International Organisation for Septuagint and Cognate Studies. Proceedings; Jerusalem: Academon, 1980), pp. 105-19.

Crowford, J.W., K.M. Kenyon and E.L. Sukenik, *The Objects from Samaria* (London: 1957).

Crowley, A.E., *The Mystic Rose* (London: Mcmillan, 1902).

Crüsemann, F., *Der Widerstand gegen das Königtum: Die antiköniglichen Texte des Alten Testaments und der Kampf um den frühen israelitischen Staat* (WMANT, 49; Neukirchen-Vluyn: Neukirchener-Verlag, 1978).

Culley, R.C., *Themes and Variations: A Study of Action in Biblical Narrative* (SBLSS; Atlanta: Scholars Press, 1992).

Doherty, E., 'The Literary Problem of Judges I, 1-III, 6', *CBQ* 18 (1956), pp. 1-7.

Dahood, M., 'Scriptio Defectiva in Judges 1, 19', *Biblica* 60 (1979), p. 570.

Dalley, S., 'Chariotry and Cavalry of Tiglath-Pileser III and Sargon II', *Iraq* 47 (1985), pp. 33-41.

—'Nergal and Ereshkigak', in W.W. Hallo (ed.), *CoS* 1 (Leiden: E.J. Brill, 1997), pp. 384-90.

—'Yabâ, Atalyâ and the Foreign Policy of Late Assyrian Kings', *SAAB* 12/2 (1998), pp. 82-98.

Davies, G.I., 'Megiddo in the Period of the Judges', *OTS* 24 (1986), pp. 34-53.

—'The Wilderness Itineraries and Recent Archaeological Research', in J.A. Adney (ed.), *Studies in the Pentateuch* (VTSup, 41; Leiden: E.J. Brill, 1990), pp. 161-75.

Davis, D.R., *A Proposed Life-Setting for the Book of Judges* (Ann Arbor, MI: University Microfilms, 1978).

—'Comic Literature—Tragic Theology: A Study of Judges 17-18', *WTJ* 46 (1984), pp. 156-63.

Day, J., 'Bedan, Abdon or Barak in 1 Samuel XII 11?', *VT* 43 (1993), pp. 261-64.

De Moor, J.C., 'The Twelve Tribes in the Song of Deborah', *VT* XLIII (1993), pp. 483-93.

Dearman, J.A., *Property Rights in the Eighth-Century Prophets* (SBLDS, 106; Atlanta: Scholars Press, 1988).

Deist, F.E., '"By the Way, Hophni and Phinehas Were There"', *JNSL* 18 (1992), pp. 25-35.

—'The Prophets: Are We Heading for a Paradigm Switch?', in R.P. Gordon (ed.), *"The Place Is Too Small for Us": The Israelite Prophets in Recent Scholarship* (Sources for Biblical and Theological Studies 5, Winona Lake: Eisenbrauns, 1995), pp. 582-99.

—' "Murder in the toilet" (Judges 12.3-30): Translation and Transformation', *Scriptura (Stellenbosch)* 58 (1996), pp. 263-72.

Deixinger, F., 'Ein Plaidoyer für die Linkshänder im Richterbuch', *ZAW* 89 (1977), pp. 268-69.

Delcor, M., 'Reflexions sur la Pâque du temps de Josias selon 2 Rois 23, 21-23', in *idem* (ed.), *Environnement de l'Ancien Testament* (AOAT, 228; Kevaeler: Butzon & Bercker, 1990), pp. 90-104.

—'Le récit de la célébration de la Pâque au temps d'Ezékias d'après 1 Chr 30 et ses problèmes', in A. Schenker (ed.), *Studien zu Opfer und Kult im Alten Testament* (FAT, 3; Tübingen: J.C.B. Mohr, 1992), pp. 93-106.

Demsky, A., 'Geba, Gibeah and Gibeon—an Historical-Geographical Riddle', *BASOR* 212 (1973), pp. 26-31.

Desnoyers, L., *Histoire du peuple hébreu des Juges à la captivité* 1 (Paris: 1922).

Desroches-Noblecourt, C., *Amours et fureurs de la Lointaine* (Paris: Stock/Pernoud, 1995).

Détienne, M., 'Orphée au miel', in J. Le Goff and P. Nora (eds.), *Faire de l'histoire* 3 (Paris: Gallimard, 1974), pp. 56-75.

—*L'invention de la mythologie* (Paris: Gallimard, 1981).

Dever, W.G., 'What Did the Biblical Writers Know, and When Did They Know about It?', in J. Magness and S. Gitin (eds.), *Hesed ve-Emet: Studies in Honor of Ernest S. Frerichs* (Atlanta: Scholars Press, 1998), pp. 241-57.

Di Lella, A.A., 'The Book of Tobit and the Book of Judges', *Henoch* 22 (2000), pp. 197-206.

Didi-Huberman, G., 'Celui par qui s'ouvre la terre', in G. Didi-Huberman, R. Garbetta and M. Morgaine (eds.), *Saint Georges et le dragon* (Paris: Adam Biro, 1994), pp. 19-124.

—*Devant le temps* (Paris: Minuit, 2000).

Diebner, B.J., and H. Schult, 'Thesen zu nachexilischen Entwürfen der frühen Geschichte Israels im Alten Testament', *DBAT* 7 (1974), pp. 41-47.

—'Wann sang Debrora ihr Lied?', *AC* 14 (1995), pp. 106-30.

Dietrich, M., and O. Loretz, *Keilalphabetischen Texte aus Ugarit* (Kevaeler/Neukirchen-Vluyn: Butzon und Bercker/Neukirchener Verlag, 1976).

Dietrich, W., *Prophetie und Geschichte: Eine redaktionsgeschichtliche Untersuchung zum deuteronomistischen Geschichtswerk* (FRLANT, 108; Göttingen: Rüprecht, 1972).

—'Das harte Joch (1. Kön 12, 4): Fronarbeit in der Salomo-Überlieferung', *BN* 34 (1986), pp. 7-16.

Dihle, H., 'Zur Datierung des Mimnermos', *Hermes* 90 (1962), pp. 257-75.

Dinsmoor, W.B., 'The Athenian Treasury as Dated by its Ornaments', *AJA* 50 (1946), pp. 111-13.

Diodorus of Sicily, (trans. F.R. Walton; LCL; London: Heinemann; 1967).

Dion, P.E., 'Yhwh as Storm-God and Sun-God: The Double Legacy of Egypt and Canaan as Reflected in Psalm 104', *ZAW* 103 (1991), pp. 43-71.

Dionysius of Halicarnassus, *Roman Antiquities* (trans. E. Cary; LCL; London: Heinemann, 1960).

Dirksen, P.B., *Judges* (The Old Testament in Syriac, 2; Leiden: E.J. Brill, 1978).

Donner, H., *Geschichte des Volkes Israel und seiner Nachbarn in Grundzügen. I. Von den Anfängen bis zur Staatenbildungszeit* (GAT Ergänzungsreihe, 4, 1; Göttingen: Vandenhoeck und Ruprecht, 2000).

Donner, H., and W. Röllig, *Kanaanäische und Aramäische Inschriften* (Wiesbaden: O. Harrassowitz, 1962-1964).

Dornseiff, F., 'Das Buch der Richter. I. Die literarische Absicht', *AfO* 14 (1944), pp. 319-28.

Dossin, G., 'Documents de Mari', *Syria* 48 (1971), pp. 1-19.

Dothan, M., 'Ashdod', in D.N. Freedman (ed.), *ABD* 1 (New York: Doubleday, 1992), pp. 477-82.

Dragga, S., 'In the Shadow of the Judges: The Failure of Saul', *JSOT* 38 (1987), pp. 39-46.

Drews, R., 'The "Chariots of Iron" of Joshua and Judges', *JSOT* 45 (1989), pp. 15-23.

—'Canaanites and Philistines', *JSOT* 81 (1998), pp. 39-61.

—'Medinet Habu: Oxcarts, Ships and Migration Theories', *JNES* 59 (2000), pp. 161-90.

Driver, G.R., and J.C. Miles, *The Assyrian Laws* (Oxford: 1935).

Driver, S.R., *Notes on the Hebrew Text and the Topography of the Books of Samuel* (Oxford: Clarendon Press, 1960).

—*An Introduction to the Literature of the Old Testament* (International Theological Library, Edinburgh: T. & T. Clark, 1962).

du Mesnil du Buisson, R., *Etudes sur les dieux phéniciens hérités par l'Empire romain* (EPR, 14; Leiden: E.J. Brill, 1970).

—*Nouvelles études sur les dieux et les mythes de Canaan* (EPR, 33; Leiden: E.J. Brill, 1973).

Dumbrell, W.J., 'In those Days There Was No King in Israel; Every Man Did What Was Right in his Own Eyes', *JSOT* 25 (1983), pp. 23-33.

Dumézil, G., *Mariages indo-européens* (Paris: Payot, 1979).

Dus, J., 'Bethel und Mizpa in Jdc. 19-21 und Jdc. 10-12', *OrAnt* 3 (1964), pp. 227-43.

Dutcher-Walls, P., 'The Social Location of the Deuteronomists: A Sociological Study of Factional Politics in Late Pre-Exilic Judah', *JSOT* 52 (1991), pp. 77-94.

Easterlly, E., 'A Case of Mistaken Identity: The Judges in Judges Don't Judge', *BR* 13 (1997), pp. 40-43.

Ebach, J., and U. Rüterswörden, 'Pointen in der Jothamfabel', *BN* 31 (1986), pp. 11-18.

Edelman, D., 'Saul's Rescue of Yavesh-Gilead', *ZAW* 96 (1984), pp. 195-209.

—'Saul's Battle against Amaleq (1 Sam. 15)', *JSOT* 35 (1986), pp. 71-84.

—*The Rise of the Israelite State under Saul* (Chicago: Chicago University Press, 1987).

—'Saul's Journey through Mt. Ephraim and Samuel's Ramah (1 Sam 9, 4-5; 10, 2-5)', *ZDPV* 104 (1988), pp. 44-58.

—'Tel Masos, Gueshur and David', *JNES* 47 (1988), pp. 253-58.

—'The Deuteronomist Story of King Saul: Narrative Art or Editorial Product?', in C. Brekelmans and J. Lust (eds.), *Pentateuchal and Deuteronomistic Studies* (BETL, 94; Leuven: Leuven University Press, 1990), pp. 207-20.

—*King Saul in the Historiography of Judah* (JSOTSup, 119; Sheffield: Sheffield Academic Press, 1991).

Edenburg, C., *The Story of the Outrage of Gibeah (Jdg 17-21) its Composition, Sources and Historical Background* (Tel Aviv: Tel Aviv University, forthcoming).

Ehrlich, C.S., 'Etam, Rock of', in D.N. Freedman (ed.), *ABD* 2 (New York: Doubleday, 1992), p. 644.

Eisenstadt, S.N., *The Political Systems of Empires* (London: Collier-Macmillan, 1963).

Eissfeldt, O., 'Die Rätsel in Jdc 14.', *ZAW* 30 (1910), pp. 132-35.

—*Hexateuch-Synopse: Die Erzählung der fünf Bucher Moses und des Buches Josua mit dem Anfange des Richterbuches* (Leipzig: J.C. Hinrichs, 1922).

—*Die Quellen des Richterbuches* (Leipzig: J.C. Hinrichs, 1925).

—'Ba'alsamem und Jahwe', *ZAW* 57 (1939), pp. 1-31.

—'Der Gott des Tabor und seine Verbreitung', in R. Sellheim and F. Maass (eds.), *Kleine Schriften* (Tübingen: J.C.B. Mohr, 1963), pp. 29-54.

—*The Old Testament: An introduction* (Oxford: Basil Blackwell, 1965).

—'Renaming in the Old Testament', in P.R. Ackroyd and B. Lindars (eds.), *Words and Meanings: Essays Presented to David Winton Thomas* (Cambridge: 1968), pp. 68-80.

Eitam, D., 'Olive Presses of the Israelite Period', *TA* 4 (1979), pp. 146-54.

Elat, M., 'Phoenician Overland Trade within the Mesopotamian Empire', in M. Cogan and I. Eph'al (eds.), *Ah Assyria...* (SH, 23; Jerusalem: Magnes Press, 1991), pp. 21-35.

Elayi, J., 'The Phoenician Cities in the Persian Period', *JNES* 12 (1980), pp. 13-28.

—'Les cités phéniciennes et l'Empire assyrien à l'époque d'Assurbanipal', *RA* 77 (1983), pp. 45-54.

—'Les relations entre les cités phéniciennes et l'Empire assyrien sous le règne de Sennachérib', *Semitica* 35 (1986), pp. 19-26.

—*Recherches sur les cités phéniciennes à l'époque perse* (Napoli: Istituto Universitario Orientale, 1987).

—*Sidon, cité autonome de l'Empire perse* (Paris: Idéaphane, 1989).

—'Tripoli (Liban) à l'époque perse', *Transeuphratène* 2 (1990), pp. 59-72.

Elayi, J., and A. Cavigneaux, *Sargon II et les Ioniens* (OA, 18; Paris: 1979).

Elliger, K., 'Die Heimat des Propheten Micha', *ZDPV* 57 (1934), pp. 81-152.

Emerton, J.A., 'New Light on Israelite Religion: The Implications of the Inscriptions from Kuntillet 'Ajrud', *ZAW* 94 (1982), pp. 2-20.

—'Some Comments on the Shibboleth Incident (Judges XII 6)', in A. Caquot *et al.* (eds.), *Mélanges bibliques et orientaux* (AOAT, 215; Neukirchen: Butzon & Bercker, 1985), pp. 146-57.

Erichsen, W., *Harris Papyrus 1* (BAe, 5; Bruxelles: Fondation égyptologique Reine Elisabeth, 1933).

Eslinger, L.M., *Into the Hands of the Living God* (JSOTSup, 84; Sheffield: Almond Press, 1989).

Esope, *Fables* (trans. E. Chambry; Belles Lettres, Paris: 1927).

Eusebius, *Preparation for the Gospel* (trans. E.H. Gifford; Oxford: Clarendon, 1903).

Evans, A., 'Knossos Excavations', *ABSA* 9 (1902), pp. 1-153.

Evans, W.E., 'An Historical Reconstruction of the Emergence of Israelite Kingship and the Reign of Saul', in W.W. Hallo, J.C. Moyer and L.G. Perdue (eds.), *Scripture in Context* 2 (Winona Lake: Eisenbrauns, 1983), pp. 61-77.

Exum, J.C., 'Aspects of Symmetry and Balance in the Samson Saga', *JSOT* 19 (1981), pp. 3-29.

—'Isaac, Samson and Saül: Reflections on the Comic and Tragic Visions. Aspects of Symmetry and Balance in the Samson Saga', *Semeia* 32 (1981), pp. 5-40.

—'The Theological Dimension of the Samson Saga', *VT* 31 (1983), pp. 30-46.

—'The Centre Cannot Hold: Thematic and Textual Instabilities in Judges', *CBQ* 52 (1990), pp. 410-31.

—'On Judges 11', in A. Brenner (ed.), *A Feminist Companion to Judges* (Sheffield: Sheffield Academic Press, 1993), pp. 131-44.

—'Samson's Women', in *idem* (ed.), *Fragmented Women: Feminist (Sub)versions of Biblical Narrative* (Valley Forge: Trinity Press International, 1993), pp. 61-93.

—'Why, why, why, Delilah?', in *idem* (ed.), *Plotted, Shot and Painted: Cultural Representations of Biblical Women* (JSOTSup, 215; Sheffield: Sheffield Academic Press, 1996), pp. 175-237.

—'Harvesting the Biblical Narrator's Scanty Plot of Ground: A Holistic Approach to Judges 16, 4-22', in M. Cogan, B.L. Eichler, J.H. Tigay (eds.), *Tehillah le-Moshe* (Winona Lake: Eisenbrauns, 1997), pp. 39-46.

—*Was sagt das Richterbuch den Frauen?* (SBS, 169; Stuttgart: Katholisches Bibelwerk, 1997).

—'Lovis Corinth's Blinded Samson', *BibInt* 6 (1998), pp. 410-25.

Eynikel, E., 'The Portrait of Manasseh and the Deuteronomic History', in M. Vervenne and J. Lust (eds.), *Deuteronomy and Deuteronomic Literature* (Leuven: Leuven University Press, 1997), pp. 233-62.

Farber, G., 'The Song of the Hoe', in W.W. Hallo (ed.), *CoS* 1 (Leiden: E.J. Brill, 1997), pp. 511-13.

Faulkner, R.O., 'The Installation of the Vizier', *JEA* 41 (1955), pp. 18-29.

Feldman, L.H., 'Josephus's Portrait of Ehud', in J.C. Reeves and J. Kampen (eds.), *Pursuing the Text* (JSOTSup, 184; Sheffield: Sheffield Academic Press, 1994), pp. 177-201.

Fensham, F.C., 'Salt as Curse in the Old Testament and in the Ancient Near East', *BA* 25 (1962), pp. 48-50.

—'Did a Treaty between the Israelites and the Kenites Exist?', *BASOR* 175 (1964), pp. 51-54.

—'Literary Observations on Historical Narratives in Sections of Judges', in D. Garrone (ed.), *Storia e tradizioni di Israele: Scritti in onore di J. Alberto Soggin* (Brescia: Paideia, 1991), pp. 77-87.

Ferry, D., *Gilgamesh, a New Rendering in English Verse* (New York: Noonday Press, 1993).

Fewell, D.N., 'Judges', in C.A. Newsom (ed.), *The Women's Bible Commentary* (London: SPCK, 1992), pp. 67-77.

—'Deconstructive Criticism: Achsah and the (E)razed City of Writing.', in G.A. Yee (ed.), *Judges and Method: New Approaches in Biblical Studies* (Minneapolis: Fortress Press, 1995), pp. 119-45.

Finkelstein, I., *The Archeology of the Israelite Settlement* (Jerusalem: Israel Exploration Society, 1988).

—'Arabian Trade in the Negev', *JNES* 47 (1988), pp. 241-52.

—'The Archeology of the Days of Manasseh', in M.D. Coogan, J.C. Exum and L.E. Stager (eds.), *Scripture and Other Artifacts* (Louisville, KY: Westminster / John Knox Press, 1992), pp. 169-87.

—'Two Notes on Early Bronze Urbanization and Urbanism', *TA* 22 (1995), pp. 47-69.

—'Middle Bronze 'Fortifications': a Reflection of Social Organisation and Political Formations', *TA* 19 (1995), pp. 201-20.

—'The Territorial-Political System of Canaan in the Late Bronze Age', *UF* 28 (1996), pp. 221-58.

—'The Archeology of the United Monarchy', *Levant* XXVIII (1996), pp. 177-88.

—'State Formation in Israel and Judah: a Contrast in Context, a Contrast in Trajectory', *NEA* 62 (1999), pp. 35-52.

Finkelstein, I., and N.A. Silberman, *The Bible Unearthed: Archaeology's New Vision of Ancient Israel and the Origin of its Sacred Texts* (New York: Free Press, 2001).

Finkelstein, I., and D. Ussishkin, 'Back to Megiddo', *BARev* 20 (1994), pp. 30-43.

Fishelis, A., *Judges: A New English Translation, Translation of Text, Rashi and Commentary* (New York: Judaica Press, 1979).

Fleming, D.E., 'The Rituals from Emar', in M.W. Chavalas and J.L. Hayes (eds.), *New Horizons in the Study of Ancient Syria* (Malibu: Undena Publications, 1992), pp. 51-61.

—'The Mountain Dagan: KUR and (^{d})KUR.GAL', *NABU* (1994), pp. 17-18.

Fohrer, G., 'Altes Testament-"Amphictyonie" und "Bund"', *TZ* 91 (1966), pp. 893-904.

Fouet, P., *Gastro-entérologie* (Abrégés, Paris: Masson, 1983).

Fowler, J.D., *Theophoric Personnal Names in Ancient Hebrew* (JSOTSup, 49; Sheffield: Sheffield Academic Press, 1988).

Frahm, E., *Einleitung in die Sanherib-Inschriften* (AfO Beihefte, 26; Wien: 1997).

Frame, G., *Babylonia 689-627 B.C. a Political History* (Istanbul: Nederlands Hist.-Arch. Instituut, 1992).

Frankel, F., 'Aphek', in D.N. Freedman (ed.), *ABD* 1 (New York: Doubleday, 1992), pp. 275-77.

Frankena, R., *Takultu* (Leiden: E.J. Brill, 1954).

—'The Vassal Treaties of Esarhaddon and the Dating of Deuteronomy', *OTS* 14 (1965), pp. 150-54.

Frankenstein, S., 'The Phoenicians in the Far West: A Function of Neo-Assyrian Imperialism', in M.T. Larsen (ed.), *Power and Propaganda* (Mesopotamia, 7; Copenhagen: Akademisk Forlag, 1979), pp. 263-96.

Frankfort, H., *Cylinder Seals: A Documentary Essay on the Art and Religion of the Ancient Near East* (Farnborough: Gregg Press, 1965).

Freu, J., 'La fin d'Ugarit et de l'Empire hittite', *Semitica* 47 (1997), pp. 17-37.

Fritz, V., 'Abimelech und Sichem in Jdc ix', *VT* 32 (1982), pp. 129-44.

—*Kinneret: Ergebnisse der Ausgrabungen auf dem Tell el-`Orême am See Gennesaret 1982-1985* (ADPV, 15; Wiesbaden: Otto Harrassowitz, 1990).

Frolov, S., and V. Orel, 'Notes on 1 Samuel', *BN* (1994), pp. 15-23.

Fry, P., *Spirit of Protest* (Cambridge: Cambridge University Press, 1976).

Fuchs, A., *Die Inschriften Sargons II aus Khorsabad* (Göttingen: Cuvillier Verlag, 1993).

Gadd, C.J., 'Inscribed Prisms of Sargon II from Nimrud', *Iraq* 16 (1954), pp. 173-201.

Gal, Z., 'Tel Rekhesh and Tel Qarnei Hittin', *Eretz-Israel* 15 (1981), pp. 213-21.

—'The Settlement of Issachar: Some New Observations', *TA* 9 (1982), pp. 79-86.

Galil, G., 'The Babylonian Calendar and the Chronology of the Last Kings of Judah', *Biblica* 72 (1991), pp. 367-78.

Galil, G., 'A New Look at the "Azekah Inscription"', *RB* 102 (1995), pp. 321-29.

—'The Last Years of the Kingdom of Israel and the Fall of Samaria', *CBQ* 57 (1995), pp. 52-65.

Galpaz-Feller, P., 'The Piye Stela: on "Clean" and "Unclean"', *RB* 102 (1995), pp. 506-21.

Garbini, G., *History and Ideology in Ancient Israel* (New York: Crossroad, 1988).

Garelli, P., 'L'Etat et la légitimité royale sous l'Empire assyrien', in M.G. Larsen (ed.), *Power and Propaganda* (Mesopotamia, 7; Copenhagen: Akademisk Forlag, 1979), pp. 319-28.

Garsiel, M., *Biblical Names: A Literary Study of Midrashic Name Derivation and Puns* (Ramat Gan: Bar-Ilan University Press, 1991).

—'Name Derivations in Judges vi-viii', *VT* 43 (1993), pp. 302-17.

Gaster, T.H., *Myth: Legend and Custom in the Old Testament* (New York: Harper & Row, 1969).

George, A.R., 'Ninurta-Pâqidât's Dog Bite and Other Notes on Comic Tales', *Iraq* 55 (1993), pp. 73-96.

—'The Dogs of Ninkilim', in H. Klengel and J. Renger (eds.), *Landwirtschaft im Alten Orient. Ausgewählte Vorträge der XLI. RAI* (BBVO, 18; Berlin: D. Reimer, 1999), pp. 291-99.

Gerhards, M., 'Die beiden Erzählungen aus 2.Kön.20 und 2.Kön.20, 18 als Ankündigung der Begnadigung Jojachins (2.Kön.25, 27-30)', *BN* 98 (1999), pp. 5-12.

Gertz, J.C., *Die Gerichtorganisation Israels im deuteronomischen Gesetz* (FRLANT, 165; Göttingen: Vandenhoeck & Ruprecht, 1994).

Gese, H., 'Die ältere Simsonüberlieferung (Richter c. 14-15)', in *idem* (ed.), *Alttestamentliche Studien* (Tübingen: J.C.B. Mohr, 1991), pp. 52-71.

Geus, C.H.J. de, 'Richteren 1, 1-2, 5', *Vox Theologica (Assen)* 36 (1966), pp. 32-53.

Geva, S., 'Archeological Evidence for the Trade between Israel and Tyre', *BASOR* 248 (1982), pp. 69-72.

Gibson, J.C.L., *Textbook of Syrian-Semitic Inscriptions* 2 (Oxford: Clarendon Press, 1971).

Gillmayr-Bucher, S., 'Die Richter', in H.M. Schmidinger (ed.), *Die Bibel in der deutschsprachigen Literatur des 20. Jahrhunderts II* (Mainz: Matthias-Grünewald-Verl., 1999), pp. 137-50.

Ginsberg, H.L., 'Judah and the Transjordan States from 734 to 582 B.C.E.', in *Alexander Marx Jubilee Volume* (New York: Jewish Theological Seminary of America, 1950), pp. 349-65.

Ginsberg, H.L., and N.M. Sarna, 'Jephthah', in C. Roth (ed.), *Encyclopaedia Judaica* (9; Jerusalem: Keter, 1971), pp. 1341-44.

Gitin, S., 'The Rise and Fall of Ekron of the Philistines: Recent Excavations at an Urban Border Site', *BA* 50 (1987), pp. 197-222.

—'Tel Miqne-Ekron in the 7th Century B.C.E.: The Impact of Economic Innovation and Foreign Cultural Influences on a Neo-Assyrian Vassal City-State', in *idem* (ed.), *Recent Excavations in Israel: A View to the West* (Dubuque, Iowa: Kendall/Hunt, 1995), pp. 61-80.

—'Assyria and Philistine Ekron', in S. Parpola and R.M. Whiting (eds.), *Assyria 1995* (Helsinki: University of Helsinki, 1997), pp. 77-103.

—'Philistia in Transition: The Tenth Century BCE and Beyond', in S. Gitin, B. Mazar and E.Stern (eds.), *Mediterranean Peoples in Transition* (Jerusalem: Israel Exploration Society, 1998), pp. 162-83.

Gitin, S., and M. Cogan, 'A New Type of Dedicatory Inscription from Ekron', *IEJ* 49 (1999), pp. 193-202.

Gitin, S., T. Dothan and J. Naveh, 'Royal Dedicatory Inscription from Ekron', *IEJ* 47 (1997), pp. 1-16.

Glassner, J.J., *Chroniques mésopotamiennes* (Belles Lettres, Paris: 1993).

Globe, A., 'Enemies Round About', in V.L. Tollers and J. Maier (eds.), *Mapping of the Biblical Terrain: The Bible as Text* (Bucknell Review 33/2, Lewisburg PA: 1974), pp. 233-51.

Glock, A.E., 'Taanach', in E. Stern (ed.), *NEAEHL* (Jerusalem: Israel Exploration Society and Carta, 1993), pp. 1428-33.

Goetze, A., and S. Levy, 'Fragment of the Gilgamesh Epic from Megiddo', *Atiqot (English series)* 2 (1959), pp. 121-28.

Goff, B.L., 'The Lost Jahwist Account of the Conquest of Canaan', *JBL* 53 (1934), pp. 241-49.

Goldberg, J., 'Two Assyrian Campaigns against Hezekiah and later VIIIth Century Biblical Chronology', *Biblica* 80 (1999), pp. 360-90.

Goldziher, I., *Muhammedanische Studien* (Halle: Max Niemeyer, 1888).

Gonçalves, F.J., *L'expédition de Sennachérib en Palestine dans la littérature hébraïque ancienne* (EB, 7; Paris: J. Gabalda & Cie, 1986).

Gooding, D.W., 'The Composition of the Book of Judges', *Eretz-Israel* 16 (1982), pp. 70-79.

Gordis, R., 'Sectional Rivalry in the Kingdom of Judah', *JQR* 25 (1934), pp. 237-59.

Gottwald, N., *The Tribes of Yhwh* (New York: Orbis, 1979).

Görg, M., 'Ein Keilschriftfragment des Berichtes vom dritten Feldzug des Sanherib mit dem Namen des Hiskija', *BN* 24 (1984), pp. 16-17.

—'Zum titel BN HMLK', *BN* 29 (1985), pp. 7-11.

—'Ein Gott Amalek?', *BN* 40 (1987), pp. 14-15.

—*Richter* (NEB, 31; Würzburg: Echter Verlag, 1993).

—'Die Göttin der Ekron-Inschrift', *BN* 93 (1998), pp. 9-10.

Grabbe, L.L., *Judaism from Cyrus to Hadrian* (Minneapolis: Fortress, 1992).

Gras, M., P. Rouillard and J. Teixidor, *L'univers phénicien* (Paris: Arthaud, 1989).

Gray, J., *Joshua, Judges and Ruth* (The Century Bible, London: Nelson, 1967).

Grayson, A.K., *Assyrian and Babylonian Chronicles* (TCS, 5; Locust Valley New York: J.J. Augustin, 1975).

—*Assyrian Rulers of the Early First Millennium (1114-859) I* (RIMA, 2; Toronto: University of Toronto Press, 1975).

—*Assyrian Rulers of the Early First Millennium (858-745) II* (RIMA, 3; Toronto: 1996).

Greenspahn, F.E., 'An Egyptian Parallel to Judges 17, 6 and 21, 25', *JBL* 101 (1982), pp. 129-30.

—'The Theology of the Framework of Judges', *VT* 36 (1986), pp. 385-96.

Greenstein, E.L., 'The Riddle of Samson', *Prooftexts* 1 (1981), pp. 237-60.

Greßmann, H., *Die Anfänge Israels* (Göttingen: 1922).

Grélois, J.P., 'Les annales décennales de Mursili II (CTH 61, 1)', *Hethetica* 9 (1988), pp. 17-155.

Grimal, N., *Les termes de la propagande royale égyptienne de la XIXème dynastie à la conquête d'Alexandre* (Paris: Imprimerie nationale, 1986).

Grimm, D., 'Der Name der Gottesboten in Richter 13', *Biblica* 62 (1981), pp. 92-98.

Grintz, J.M., 'Judges Ch. I', in J.M. Grintz and Liver (eds.), *Studies in the Bible Presented to M. H. Segal* (Jerusalem: 1964), pp. 42-71.

Grootkerk, S.E., *Ancient Sites in Galilee* (Leiden: E.J. Brill, 2000).

Gros-Louis, K.K.R., 'The Book of Judges', in K.R.R. Gros-Louis, J.S. Ackerman and T.S. Warshaw (eds.), *Literary Interpretations of Biblical Narratives* (Nashville: Abingdon Press, 1974), pp. 144-64.

Gross, W., 'Prophet gegen Institution im alten Israel? Warnung vor vermeintlischen Gegensätzen', *TQ* 171 (1991), pp. 15-30.

Grosse, E., *Die Formen der Familie und die Formen der Wirtschaft* (Freiburg, 1896).

Grottanelli, C., 'Motivi escatologici nell'iconografia di un rasoio cartaginese', *RSF* 5 (1977), pp. 18-22.

—'The Enemy king Is a Monster: A Biblical Equation', *SSR* 3 (1979), pp. 5-36.

Guest, P.D., 'Dangerous Liaisons in the Book of Judges', *SJOT* 11 (1997), pp. 241-69.

—'Can Judges Survive without Sources? Challenging the Consensus', *JSOT* 78 (1998), pp. 43-61.

Guillaume, A., 'A Note on הפר השני, Judges VI.25.26.28', *JTS* 50 (1949), pp. 52-53.

Guillaume, P. 'Deborah and the Seven Tribes', *BN* 101 (2000), pp. 18-21.

—'Caution: Rhetorical Questions', *BN* 103 (2000), pp. 11-16.

Gunkel, H., 'Simson', in *idem* (ed.), *Reden und Aufsätze* (Göttingen: 1913), pp. 38-64.

Gunn, D.M., 'Joshua and Judges', in R. Alter and F. Kermode (eds.), *The Literary Guide to the Bible* (Cambridge, MA: Harvard University Press, 1987), pp. 102-21.

—'Samson of Sorrows: An Isaianic Gloss on Judges 13-16', in D.N. Fewell (ed.), *Reading between Texts: Intertextuality and the Hebrew Bible* (Louisville, KY: Westminster / John Knox Press, 1992), pp. 225-53.

Gurewicz, S.B., 'The Bearing of Judges i-ii 5 on the Authorship of the Book of Judges', *ABR* 7 (1959), pp. 37-40.

Gurney, O.R., 'The Myth of Nergal and Ereshkigal', *AnSt* 10 (1960), pp. 105-31.

Guthrie, W.K.C., *Orpheus and Greek Religion* (Princeton: Princeton University Press, 1993).

Güdemann, M., 'Tendenz und Abfassungszeit der letzten Capitel des Buches der Richter', *Monatsschrift für Geschichte und Wissenschaft des Judentums* 18 (1869), pp. 357-68.

Haag, H., 'Gideon-Jerubaal-Abimelek', *ZAW* 79 (1967), pp. 305-14.

Halbe, J., *Das Privilegrecht Jahwes Ex. 34, 10-26: Gestalt und Wesen, Herkunft und Wirken in vordeuteronomischer Zeit* (FRLANT, 114; Göttingen: Vandenhoeck & Ruprecht, 1975).

Halicarnassus, Dionysius of, *Roman Antiquities* (trans. E. Cary; LCL, London: Heinemann, 1960).

Hallo, W.W., 'Jerusalem under Hezekiah: An Assyriological Perspective', in L.I. Levine (ed.), *Jerusalem: Its Sanctity and Centrality to Judaism, Christianity and Islam* (New York: Continuum, 1999), pp. 36-50.

Halpern, B., 'Gibeon: Israelite Diplomacy in the Conquest Era', *CBQ* 37 (1975), pp. 303-16.

—'The Rise of Abimelek Ben-Jerubbaal', *HAR* 2 (1978), pp. 26-32.

—*The Constitution of the Monarchy in Israel* (HSM, 25; Chico, CA: Scholars Press, 1981).

—'The Resourceful Israelite Historian: The Song of Deborah and Israelite Historiography', *HTR* 76 (1983), pp. 379-401.

—'Yaua, Son of Omri, Yet Again', *BASOR* 265 (1987), pp. 81-85.

—*The First Historians: The Bible and History* (San Francisco: Harper and Row, 1988).

—'Jerusalem and the Lineages in the 7th Century', in B. Halpern and D.W. Hobson (eds.), *Law and Ideology in Monarchic Israel* (JSOTSup, 124; Sheffield: JSOT Press, 1991), pp. 71-73.

—'Sociological Comparativism and the Theological Imagination', in M. Fishbane (ed.), *Sha'arei Talmon: Studies in the Bible, Qumran and the Ancient Near East* (Winona Lake: Eisenbrauns, 1992), pp. 53-68.

—'Sybil, or the Two Nations? Archaism, Kinship, Alienation, and the Elite Redefinition of Traditional Culture in Judah in the 8th-7th Centuries B.C.E.', in J.S. Cooper and G.M. Schwartz (eds.), *The Study of the Ancient Near East in the Twenty-First Century: The William Foxwell Albright Centennial Conference* (Winona Lake: Eisenbrauns, 1996), pp. 291-338.

—'Why Manasseh is Blamed for the Babylonian Exile', *VT* 48 (1998), pp. 473-514.

Hamilton, G.J., 'New Evidence for the Authenticity of *bšt* in Hebrew Personnal Names and for its Use as a Divine Epithet in Biblical Texts', *CBQ* 60 (1998), pp. 228-50.

Handy, L.K., 'Hezekiah's Unlikely Reform', *ZAW* 100 (1988), pp. 111-15.

—'Uneasy Laughter: Ehud and Eglon as Ethnic Humor', *SJOT* 6 (1992), pp. 233-46.

Haran, M., 'Book Size and the Device of Catchline', *JJS* 36 (1985), pp. 1-11.

Hardmeier, C., *Prophetie im Streit vor dem Untergang Judas: Erzählkommunikative Studien zur Entstehungssituation der Jesaja- und Jeremiaerzählungen in II Reg 18–20 und Jer 37–40* (BZAW, 187; Berlin: W. de Gruyter, 1990).

Harl, M., G. Dorival and O. Munnich, *La bible grecque des Septante: Du judaïsme hellénistique au christianisme ancien* (Paris: Cerf / CNRS, 1988).

Harlé, P., *La Bible d'Alexandrie: Les Juges* (Paris: Cerf, 1999).

Hart, R. van der, 'The Camp of Dan and the Camp of Yahweh', *VT* 25 (1975), pp. 720-28.

Hartmann, T.A.G., 'נמר in Richter 3, 16 oder die Pygmäen im Dschungel der Längenmaße', *ZAH* 13 (2000), pp. 188-93.

Hasitschka, M., 'Die Führer Israels: Mose, Josua und die Richter', in A. Öhler (ed.), *Alttestamentliche Gestalten im Neuen Testament: Beiträge zur Biblischen Theologie* (Darmstadt: Wissenschaftliche Buchgesellschaft, 1999), pp. 117-40.

Haul, M., *Das Etana-Epos* (GAAL, 1; Göttingen: Seminar für Keilschriftforschung, 2000).

Hauser, A.J., 'The "Minor" Judges—a Re-Evaluation', *JBL* 94 (1975), pp. 190-200.

Hayes, J.H., and P.K. Hooker, *A New Chronology for the Kings of Israel and Judah and its Implications for Biblical History and Literature* (Atlanta: John Knox Press, 1988).

Hayes, J.H., and J.K. Kuan, 'The Final Years of Samaria (730-720 BC)', *Biblica* 72 (1991), pp. 153-81.

Healey, J.F., 'Dagon', in K. Van der Toorn, B. Becking and P.W. van der Horst (eds.), *DDD* (Leiden: E.J. Brill, 1995), pp. 407-13.

Heimpel, W., *Tierbilder in der Sumerischen Literatur* (StPo, 2; Roma: Pontificium Institutum Biblicum, 1968).

Helck, W.H., 'Das Dekret des Königs Haremheb', *ZÄSA* 80 (1955), pp. 109-36.

Held, M., 'The Root ZBL/SBL in Akkadian, Ugaritic and Biblical Hebrew', *JAOS* 88 (1968), pp. 90-96.

Heller, J., 'Die Entmythisierung des ugaritischen Pantheons im AT', in *idem* (ed.), *An der Quelle des Lebens* (Frankfurt am Main: Lang, 1988), pp. 173-83.

Helm, R.W.O., *Die Chronik des Hieronymus* (Eusebius Werke, 7/1; Leipzig: 1913).

Heltzer, M., 'Some Questions Concerning the Economic Policy of Josiah, King of Judah', *IEJ* 50 (2000), pp. 105-108.

Herion, G.A., D.W. Manor and J.K. Lott, 'Devir', in D.N. Freedman (ed.), *ABD* 2 (New York: Doubleday, 1992), pp. 112-13.

Herodotus, *History* (trans. A.D. Godley; LCL, 120; Cambridge, MA: Harvard University Press, 1981).

Herrmann, W., 'Das Aufleben des Mythos unter den Judäern während des babylonischen Zeitalters', *BN* 40 (1987), pp. 97-129.

Herrmann, S., ' "Negatives Besitzverzeichnis", eine mündliche Tradition?', in P. Mommer (ed.), *Gottesrecht als Lebensraum, Festschrift für H.J. Boecker* (Neukirchen-Vluyn: Neukirchener Verlag, 1993), pp. 93-100.

Hertzberg, H.W., *Die Bücher Josua, Richter, Ruth* (ATD, 9; Göttingen: Vandenhoeck & Ruprecht, 1959).

—'Die kleinen Richter', *ThL* 79 (1954), pp. 285-90.

Hesiod, *The Homeric Hymns and Homerica* (trans. H.G. Evelyn-White; LCL, Cambridge, MA: Harvard University Press, 1959).

Hess, R.S., 'Non-Israelite Personal Names in the Book of Joshua', *CBQ* 58 (1996), pp. 205-14.

—'Hezekiah and Sennacherib in 2 Kings 18-20', in R.S. Hess and G.J. Wenham (eds.), *Zion, City of our God* (Grand Rapids: Eerdmans, 1999), pp. 23-41.

Heyns, D., 'A Social Historical Perspective on Amos' Prophecies against Israel', *OTE* 3 (1990), pp. 303-16.

Hill, G.F., *Catalogue of the Greek Coins of Phoenicia* (London: 1910).

Hillers, N.R., 'Note on Judges 5, 8a', *CBQ* 27 (1965), pp. 124-26.

Himbaza, I., 'Retour sur Juges 7, 5-6', *RB* 108/1 (2001), pp. 26-36.

Hinz, V., *Der Kult von Demeter und Kore auf Sizilien und in der Magna Graecia* (Palilia, 4; Wiesbaden: Reichert, 1998).

Hoffman, H.D., *Reform und Reformen: Untersuchungen zu einem Grundthema der deuteronomistischen Geschichtsschreibung* (ATANT, 66; Zürich: 1980).

Hoffman, Y., 'A North Israelite Typological Myth and a Judaean Historical Tradition: The Exodus in Hosea and Amos', *VT* 39 (1989), pp. 169-82.

Hoffner, H.A., 'Histories and Historians of the Ancient Near East: The Hittites', *Orientalia* 49 (1980), pp. 283-332.

—'A Tale of Two Cities: Kanesh and Zalpa', in G.M. Beckman (ed.), *Hittite Myths* (Atlanta: Scholars Press, 1990), pp. 62-63.

—'The Queen of Kanesh and the Tale of Zalpa', in W.W. Hallo (ed.), *CoS* 1 (Leiden: E.J. Brill, 1997), pp. 181-82.

—'Hittite Laws', in W.W. Hallo (ed.), *CoS* 2 (Leiden: E.J. Brill, 2000), pp. 106-19.

Hoftijzer, J., and K. Jongeling, *Dictionary of the North-West Semitic Inscriptions* (HdO, 1.21; Leiden: E.J. Brill, 1995).

Holladay, J.S., 'Religion in Ancient Israel and Judah under the Monarchy', in P.D. Miller, Jr, P.D. Hanson and S.D. McBride (eds.), *Ancient Israelite Religion* (Philadelphia: Fortress, 1987), pp. 249-99.

Holloway, S.W., 'Harran: Cultic Geography in the Neo-Assyrian Empire and its Implications for Sennacherib's "Letter to Hezekiah" in 2 Kings', in S.W. Holloway and L.K. Handy (eds.), *The Pitcher is Broken* (JSOTSup, 190; Sheffield: Sheffield Academic Press, 1995), pp. 276-314.

Homer, *The Odyssey* (trans. A.T. Murray; LCL, 135; London: 1960).

Homère, *Hymnes* (trans. J. Humbert; Belles Lettres, Paris: 1997).

Honigmann, E., 'Sidon', in *PW* II, pp. 2216-29.

Hopkins, D.C., 'The Dynamics of Agriculture in Monarchical Israel', in K.H. Richards (ed.), *Society of Biblical Literature. 1983. Seminar Papers* (SBLSP; 22; Chico, CA: Scholars Press, 1983), pp. 177-202.

—'Life on the Land: Subsistence Struggles of Early Israel', *BA* 50 (1987), pp. 178-91.

Hornung, E., *Aegyptische Unterweltbücher* (Zürich/München: Artemis, 1972).

Houston, W.J., 'Misunderstanding or Midrash? The Prose Appropriation of Poetic Material in the Hebrew Bible (part I)', *ZAW* 109 (1997), pp. 342-55.

Houston, W.J., 'Murder or Midrash? The Prose Appropriation of Poetic Material in the Hebrew Bible (part II)', *ZAW* 109 (1997), pp. 534-48.

Hübner, U., 'Mord auf dem Abort? Überlegungen zu Humor, Gewaltdarstellung und Realien-kunde in Ri 3, 12-30', *BN* 40 (1987), pp. 130-40.

—*Die Ammoniter* (ADPV, 16; Wiesbaden: Otto Harrassowitz, 1992).

Hudson, D.M., 'Living in a Land of Epithets: Anonymity in Judges 19-21', *JSOT* 62 (1994), pp. 49-66.

Hughes, J., *Secrets of the Times* (JSOTSup, 66; Sheffield: JSOT Press, 1990).

Humphreys, W.L., 'The Rise and Fall of King Saul: A Study of an Ancient Narrative Stratum in 1 Samuel.', *JSOT* 18 (1980), pp. 74-90.

Huxley, G.L., *Greek Epic Poetry from Eulemos to Panyassis* (London: 1969).

Hvidberg, F.F., *Weeping and Laughter* (Leiden: E.J. Brill, 1962).

Hylander, I., *Der literarische Samuel-Saul-Komplex (1. Sam. 1-15)* (Uppsala/Leipzig: Almqvist & Wiksell/Harrassowitz, 1932).

Ishida, T., 'The Leaders of the Tribal League 'Israel' in the Pre-Monarchic Period', *RB* 80 (1973), pp. 96-106.

—*The Royal Dynasties in Ancient Israel* (BZAW, 142; Berlin: W. de Gruyter, 1977).

—'The Structure of the Lists of the Pre-Israelite Nations', *Biblica* 60 (1979), pp. 461-90.

—'Royal Succession in the Kingdom of Israel and Judah', in J.A. Emerton (ed.), *Congress Volume, Jerusalem 1986* (VTSup XL, Leiden: E.J. Brill, 1988), pp. 96-106.

—'SOFET: The Leaders of the Tribal League "Israel" in the Pre-Monarchical Period', in T. Ishida (ed.), *History and Historical Writing in Ancient Israel* (SHCANE, 16; Leiden: E.J. Brill, 1999), pp. 36-56.

—'The People of the Land', in *idem* (ed.), *History and Historical Writing in Ancient Israel* (SHCANE, 16; Leiden: E.J. Brill, 1999), pp. 81-96.

Jackson, K.P., 'Ammonite Personal Names in the Context of the West Semitic Onomasticon', in C.L. Meyers and M. O'Connor (eds.), *The Word of the Lord Shall Go Forth* (Winona Lake: Eisenbrauns, 1983), pp. 507-21.

Jacobson, H., 'The Judge Bedan (1 Samuel XII 11)', *VT* 42 (1992), pp. 123-24.

—'Bedan and Barak Reconsidered', *VT* 44 (1994), pp. 108-109.

Jacoby, F., *Die Fragmente der griechischen Historiker I A* (Leiden: E.J. Brill, 1968).

Jans, E., *Abimelech und sein Königtum: Diachrone und synchrone Untersuchungen zu Ri. 9* (ATSAT, 66; St. Ottilien: EOS, 2001).

Janzen, J.G., 'A Certain Woman in the Rhetoric of Judges 9', *JSOT* 38 (1987), pp. 33-37.

Japhet, S., ' "History" and "Literature" in the Persian Period: the Restoration of the Temple', in M. Cogan and I. Eph'al (eds.), *Ah Assyria...* (SH, 33; Jerusalem: Magnes Press, 1991), pp. 174-88.

Jaros, K., *Sichem* (OBO, 11; Fribourg / Göttingen: Universitätsverlag / Vandenhoeck, 1976).

Jeanmaire, H., *Couroi et Courètes* (Lille: Bibliothèque universitaire, 1939).

Jericke, D., 'Josuas Tod und Josuas Grab', *ZAW* 108 (1996), pp. 347-61.

Jobling, D., *The Sense of Biblical Narratives: Three Structural Analyses in the Old Testament* (JSOTSup, 7; Sheffield: 1978).

—'Right-Brained Story of Left-Handed Man: An Antiphon to Yairah Amit', in J.C. Exum (ed.), *Signs and Wonders: Biblical Texts in Literary Focus* (SBLSS, Winona Lake: SBL, 1989), pp. 125-32.

Jones, G.H., 'Holy War or Yahweh's War?', *VT* 25 (1975), pp. 642-58.

Jones-Warsaw, K., 'Towards a Womanist Hermeneutic: A Reading of Judges 19-21', in A. Brenner (ed.), *A Feminist Companion to Judges* (Sheffield: JSOT Press, 1993), pp. 172-86.

Jonker, L.C., 'Samson in Double Vision: Judges 13-16 from Historical-Critical and Narrative Perspectives', *JNSL* 18 (1992), pp. 49-66.

Joosten, J., 'Les Benjaminites au milieu de Jérusalem: Jérémie VI, 1ss et Juges XIX-XX', *VT* 49 (1999), pp. 65-72.

Josephus, F., 'Against Apion', in P. Maier (ed.), *The New Complete Works of Josephus* (Grand Rapids: Kregel, 1999), pp. 937-81.

—'Jewish Antiquities', in P. Maier (ed.), *The New Complete Works of Josephus* (Grand Rapids: Kregel, 1999), pp. 49-661.

Josipovici, G., *The Book of God: A Response to the Bible* (New Haven: Yale University Press, 1988).

Joüon, P., and T. Muraoka, *A Grammar of Biblical Hebrew* (SBib, 14; Rome: Institut Biblique Pontifical, 1996).

Jugel, E., and H.-D. Neef, 'Ehud als Linkshänder: Exegetische und medizinische Anmerkungen zu Ri 3, 15', *BN* 97 (1999), pp. 45-54.

Jull, T.A., 'מקרה in Judges 3: A Scatological Reading', *JSOT* 81 (1998), pp. 63-75.

Junge, E., *Der Wiederaufbau des Heerwesens der Reiches Juda unter Josia* (BWANT, 75; Stuttgart: Kohlhammer, 1937).

Jüngling, H.-W., *Richter 19—Ein Plaidoyer für das Königtum: Stilistische Analyse der Tendenzerzählung Ri 19, 1-30a; 21, 5* (AnBib, 84; Rome: Biblical Institute Press, 1981).

Kaiser, O., *Grundriss der Einleitung in die kanonischen und deuterokanonischen Schriften des Alten Testaments. I. Die Erzählenden Werke* (Gütersloh: Gütersloher Verlagshaus G. Mohn, 1992).

Kaiser, W.C. Jr, *A History of Israel from the Bronze Age through the Jewish Wars* (Nashville: Broadman & Holman, 1998).

Kalimi, I., 'Three Assumptions about the Kenites', *ZAW* 100 (1988), pp. 386-93.

Kallaï, Z., and H. Tadmor, 'On the History of the Kingdom of Jerusalem in the Amarna Period (Ivrit)', *Eretz-Israel* 9 (1969), pp. 138-47.

—'Judah and Israel: A Study in Israelite Historiography', *IEJ* 28 (1978), pp. 251-61.

—'Territorial Patterns, Biblical Historiography and Scribal tradition—a Programmatic Survey', *ZAW* 93 (1981), pp. 427-32.

—'The Southern Border of the Land of Israel-Pattern and Application', *VT* 37 (1987), pp. 438-45.

—'BETH-EL--LUZ and BETH-AVEN', in R. Liwak and S. Wagner (eds.), *Prophetie und geschichtliche Wirklichkeit im alten Israel* (Stuttgart: Kohlhammer, 1991), pp. 171-88.

—'The Twelve Tribe Systems of Israel', *VT* 47 (1997), pp. 53-90.

—' "Dan Why Abides he by Ships"—and the Rules of Historiographical Writing', *JNSL* 23 (1997), pp. 35-45.

Kampen, J., *The Hasideans and the Origin of Pharisaism: A Study in 1 and 2 Maccabees* (SCS, 24; Atlanta: Scholars Press, 1989).

Kapera, Z.J., 'Was YA-MA-NI a Cypriot?', *FO* 14 (1972), pp. 207-18.

—'The Ashdod Stela of Sargon II', *FO* 17 (1976), pp. 87-99.

—'The Oldest Account of Sargon II's Campaign against Ashdod', *FO* 24 (1987), pp. 29-39.

Kaswalder, P., 'Le tribù in Gdc 1, 1-2, 5 e in Gdc 4-5', *SBFLA* 43 (1993), pp. 89-113.

Katzenstein, H.J., *The History of Tyre: From the Beginning of the Second Millennium B.C.E. until the Fall of the Neo-Babylonian Empire in 538 B.C.E.* (Jerusalem: The Schocken Institute for Jewish Research of the Jewish Theological Seminary of America, 1973).

—'Gaza in the Neo-Babylonian Period (626-539 B.C.E.)', *Transeuphratène* 7 (1994), pp. 35-49.

Keel, O., *Studien zu den Stempelsiegeln aus Palästina/Israël* (OBO, 67/88/100/135; Fribourg/Göttingen: Universitätsverlag/Vandenhoeck & Ruprecht, 1985-94).

—*Das Recht der Bilder gesehen zu werden* (OBO, 122; Fribourg: Universitätsverlag, 1992).

Keel, O., and C. Uehlinger, 'Jahwe und die Sonnengottheit von Jerusalem', in W. Dietrich and M.A. Klopfenstein (eds.), *Ein Gott allein?* (OBO, 139; Fribourg: Universitätsverlag, 1994), pp. 269-306.

—*Göttinnen, Götter und Gottessymbole* (QD, 134; Freiburg: Herder, 1998).

Kegler, J., 'Simson—Widerstandskämpfer und Volksheld', in Freund and Stegemann (eds.), *Theologische Brosamen für Lothar Steiger* (BDBAT, 5; Heidelberg: DBAT; Wiss.-Theol. Seminar, 1985), pp. 233-55.

Kellenbach, K., 'Am I a Murderer? Judges 19-21 as a Parable of Meaningless Suffering', in T.A. Linafelt (ed.), *Strange Fire* (BS, 71; Sheffield: Sheffield Academic Press, 2000), pp. 176-91.

Kellermann, D., 'Das Buch Josua und das Buch der Richter', in E. Sitarz (ed.), *Höre, Israel! Jahwe ist einzig* (Biblische Basis Bücher, Stuttgart: KBW, 1987), pp. 69-87.

Kelm, G.L., *Timnah: A Biblical City in the Soreq Valley* (Winona Lake: Eisenbrauns, 1995).

Kelso, J.L., *The Ceramic Vocabulary of the Old Testament* (BASORSup, 5-6; New Haven: ASOR, 1948).

Kempinski, A., and W.-D. Niemeier, 'Tel Kabri 1989-1990', *IEJ* 41 (1991), pp. 188-94.

—'Kabri', in E. Stern (ed.), *NEAEHL* (Jerusalem: Israel Exploration Society and Carta, 1993), pp. 839-41.

Kestemont, G., 'Tyr et les Assyriens', in E. Gubel, E. Lipinsky and B. Servais-Soyez (eds.), *Redt Tyrus/Sauvons Tyr Histoire phénicienne/Fenicische Geschiedenis* (SP, I/II; Leuven: Peeters, 1983), pp. 53-78.

—'Phéniciens en Syrie du Nord', in E. Gubel and E. Lipinsky (eds.), *Phoenicia and its Neighbours* (SP, 3; Leuven: Peeters, 1985), pp. 135-61.

Keukens, K.H., 'Ri 11, 37f: Rite de passage und Übersetzungsprobleme', *BN* 19 (1982), pp. 41-42.

Kilpatrick, P.G., *The Old Testament and Folklore Study* (JSOTSup, 62; Sheffield: JSOT Press, 1988).

Kim, J., *The Structure of the Samson Cycle* (Kampen: Kok Pharos, 1993).

Kirsch, J., *The Harlot by the Side of the Road: Forbidden Tales of the Bible* (London: Century, 1997).

Kitchen, K.A., 'Egypt, the Levant and Assyria in 701', in M. Görg (ed.), *Fontes atque pontes* (AAT, 5; Wiesbaden: Otto Harrassowitz, 1983), pp. 243-53.

Kittel, B.R., *Studien zur hebräischen Archäologie und Religionsgeschichte* (Leipzig: 1908).

Klein, L.R., *The Triumph of Irony in the Book of Judges* (JSOTSup, 68; Sheffield: JSOT Press, 1988).

—'A Spectrum of Female Characters', in A. Brenner (ed.), *A Feminist Companion to Judges* (Sheffield: JSOT Press, 1993), pp. 24-33.

—'The Book of Judges: Paradigm and Deviation in Images of Women', in A. Brenner (ed.), *A Feminist Companion to Judges* (Sheffield: JSOT Press, 1993), pp. 55-71.

Klein, J., 'The Marriage of Martu: The Urbanization of Barbaric Nomads', *Michmanim* 9 (1996), pp. 83-96.

Kloppenborg, J.S., 'Joshua 22: The Priestly Editing of an Ancient Tradition', *Biblica* 62 (1981), pp. 347-71.

Knauf, E.A., 'Zum Text von Ri 5, 14', *Biblica* 64 (1983), pp. 428-29.

—'Beth Aven', *Biblica* 62/2 (1984), pp. 251-53.

—'Besprechung von H.M. Niemann: Die Daniten: Studien zur Geschichte eines altisraelitischen Stammes', *ZDPV* 101 (1985), pp. 183-87.

—'Berg und Tal, Stadt und Stamm—Grundzüge der Geschichte Palästinas in den letzten fünftausend Jahren', in G. Völger, K. von Welck and K. Hackstein (eds.), *Pracht und Geheimnis: Kleidung und Schmuck aus Palästina und Jordanien. Katalog der Sammlung Widad Kawar anlässlich einer Ausstellung des Rautenstrauch—Joest Museums in Zusammenarbeit mit dem Institute of Archaeology and Anthropology der Yarmuk Universität Irbid vom 3. Oktober 1987 bis 27. März 1988* (Ethnologica, 13; Köln: Rautenstrauch—Joest Museums, 1987), pp. 26-35; 417-18.

—*Midian: Untersuchungen zur Geschichte Palästinas und Nordarabians am Ende des 2. Jahrtausends v. Chr* (ADPV, Wiesbaden: Otto Harrassowitz, 1988).

—*Ismael: Untersuchungen zur Geschichte Palästinas und Nordarabiens im 1. Jahrtausend v.chr.* (ADPV, Wiesbaden: Otto Harrassowitz, 2nd edn, 1989).

—'Pireathon—Fer'ata', *BN* 51 (1990), pp. 19-24.

—'Ehud', in M. Görg and B. Lang (eds.), *NBL* (Zürich: Benziger, 1990), p. 487-88.

—'Hesbon, Sihons Stadt', *ZDPV* 106 (1990), pp. 135-44.

—'The Persian Administration in Arabia', *Transeuphratène* 2 (1990), pp. 201-17.

—'Eglon and Ophrah: Two Toponymic Notes on the Book of Judges', *JSOT* 51 (1991), pp. 25-44.

—'King Solomon's Copper Supply', in E. Lipinski (ed.), *Phoenicia and the Bible* (SP, 11; Leuven: Peeters, 1991), pp. 167-86.

—'From History to Interpretation', in D. Edelman (ed.), *The Fabric of History* (JSOTSup, 127; Sheffield: JSOT Press, 1991), pp. 26-64.

—'Dushara and Shai 'al-Qaum: Yhwh und Baal. Dieu', in Th. Römer (ed.), *Lectio difficilior probabilior* (BDBAT 12, Heidelberg: 1991), pp. 19-29.

—'Toponyms and Toponomy', in D.N. Freedman (ed.), *ABD* 6 (New York: Doubleday, 1992), pp. 601-605.

—'The Cultural Impact of Secondary State Formation: The Cases of the Edomites and Moabites', in P. Bienkowsky (ed.), *Early Edom and Moab* (SAM, 7; Sheffield: J.R. Collis Publications, 1992), pp. 47-54.

—'East, People of the', in D.N. Freedman (ed.), *ABD* 2 (New York: Doubleday, 1992), p. 249.

—'Jair', in M. Görg and B. Lang (eds.), *NBL* (Zürich: Benziger, 1992), pp. 271-72.

—'Abel-Keramim', in D.N. Freedman (ed.), *ABD* 1 (New York: Doubleday, 1992), pp. 10-11.

—'Manahath', in D.N. Freedman (ed.), *ABD* 4 (New York: Doubleday, 1992), p. 493.

—'Manahathites', in D.N. Freedman (ed.), *ABD* 4 (New York: Doubleday, 1992), p. 494.

—'Jeremia XLIX 1-5: Ein zweites Moab-Orakel in Jeremia-Buch', *VT* 52 (1992), pp. 124-28.

—'Supplementa Ismaelitica 14: Mount Hor and Kadesh Barnea', *BN* 61 (1992), pp. 22-26.

—'Amoriter', in W. Kasper *et al.* (eds.), *LTK* (Freiburg: Herder, 1993), pp. 537-38.

—'Amalekiter', in W. Kasper *et al.* (eds.), *LTK* (Freiburg: Herder, 1993), p. 483.

—*Die Umwelt des Alten Testaments* (NSKAT, 29; Stuttgart: Verlag Katholishes Bibelwerk, 1994).

—'Stämme Israels', in Fahlbusch (ed.), *Evangelisches Kirchenlexikon* 4 (Göttingen: Vandenhoeck & Ruprecht, 1994), pp. 479-83.

—*Die Umwelt des Alten Testaments* (NSKAT, 29; Stuttgart: Katholisches Bibelwerk, 1994).

—'Midian', in M. Görg and B. Lang (eds.), *NBL* (Zürich/Düsseldorf: Benziger, 1995), pp. 802-804.

—'Aroer', in H.D. Betz (ed.), *Die Religion in Geschichte und Gegenwart* 1 (Tübingen: J.C.B. Mohr, 1998), p. 795.

—'Der Exodus zwischen Mythos und Geschichte: Zur priesterschriftlichen Rezeption der Schilfmeer-Geschichte in Ex 14', in R.G. Kratz, T. Krüger and K. Schmid (eds.), *Schriftauslegung in der Schrift* (BZAW, 300; Berlin: W. de Gruyter, 2000), pp. 73-84.

—'Die Priesterschrift und die Geschichten der Deuteronomisten', in Th. Römer (ed.), *The Future of the Deuteronomistic History* (BETL, 147; Leuven: Peeters, 2000), pp. 101-18.

—'Does "Deuteronomistic History" (DH) Exist?', in A. de Pury and Th. Römer (eds.), *Israel Constructs its History* (JSOTSup, 306; Sheffield: Sheffield Academic Press, 2000), pp. 388-98.

—'Die Priesterschrift und die Geschichten der Deuteronomisten', in Th. Römer (ed.), *The Future of the Deuteronomistic History* (BETL, 147; Leuven: Peeters, 2000), pp. 101-118 (111).

—'Filling in Historical Gaps: How Did Joram Really Die? Or the Invention of Militarism', in J.C. Exum (ed.), *Virtual History and the Bible* (Leiden: E.J. Brill, 2000), pp. 59-69.

—'Jerusalem in the Late Bronze and Early Iron Periods, a Proposal', *TA* 27 (2000), pp. 75-90.

—'Psalm LX und Psalm CVIII', *VT* 50 (2000), pp. 55-65.

—'The Low Chronology and How Not to Deal with It', *BN* 101 (2000), p. 62 n. 30.

—'Vom Prophetinnenwort zum Propheten Buch: Jesaja 8, 3f im Kontext vom Jes 6, 1–8, 16: lectio difficilior', *European Electronic Journal for Feminist Exegesis* 2/2000 (www.lectio.unibe.ch).

—'Wie kann ich singen im fremden Land?', *BK* 55 (2000), pp. 132-39.

—'David, Saul, and the Philistines: From Geography to History', *BN* 109 (2001), pp. 15-18.

—'Who Destroyed Beersheba II?', in U. Hübner (ed.), *FS Manfred Weippert* (OBO, 186, Freiburg, Schweiz: Universitätsverlag, 2002), pp. 181-95.

—'Das Debora-Lied', unpublished.

Knauf, E.A., *et al.*, '*BaytDawid' ou 'BaytDod'? Une relecture de la nouvelle inscription de Tel Dan', *BN* 72 (1994), pp. 60-69.

Knauf, E.A., and S. Maáni, 'On the Phonemes of Fringe Canaanite: The Cases of Zerah-Udruh and "Kamashalta"', *UF* 19 (1987), pp. 91-94.

Knierim, R., 'Exodus 18 und die Neuordnung der mosaischen Gerichtsbarkeit', *ZAW* 73 (1961), pp. 146-70.

Knight, D.A., 'Deuteronomy and the Deuteronomists', in J.L. Mays, D.L. Petersen, and K.H. Richards (eds.), *Old Testament Interpretation: Past, Present and Future* (Nashville: Abingdon Press, 1995), pp. 61-79.

Koenen, K., 'Wem ist Weh? Wem ist Ach?… Wer hat trübe Augen?', *BN* 94 (1998), pp. 79-86.

Konkel, A.H., 'The Sources of Hezekiah in the Book of Isaiah', *VT* 43 (1993), pp. 462-82.

Koopmans, W.T., *Joshua 24 as Poetic Narrative* (JSOTSup, 93; Sheffield: 1990).

Kornfeld, W., 'Onomastica aramaica und das Alte Testament', *ZAW* 88 (1976), pp. 105-12.

Kotter, W.R., 'Beth-Dagon', in D.N. Freedman (ed.), *ABD* 1 (New York: Doubleday, 1992), p. 683.

Kottsieper, I., *Die Sprache der Ahiqarsprüche* (BZAW, 194; Berlin: W. de Gruyter, 1990).

—'"Weisheitstexte" in aramäischer Sprache', in O. Kaiser (ed.), *Weisheitstexte, Mythen und Epen: Weisheitstexte II* (TUAT, 3/2; Gütersloh: Gütersloher Verlagshaus, 1991), pp. 320-47.

—'Die alttestamentliche Weisheit im Licht aramäischer Weisheitstraditionen', in B. Janowski (ed.), *Weisheit ausserhalb der kanonischen Weisheitsschriften* (VWGT, 10; Gütersloh: Gütersloher Verlagshaus, 1996), pp. 128-62.

Kramer, S.N., *The Sumerians* (Chicago: University of Chicago Press, 1964).

—*Sumerian Mythology* (Philadelphia: University of Pennsylvania Press, 1972).

Kratz, R.G., *Die Komposition der erzählenden Bücher des AT* (Uni-Taschenbücher, 2157; Göttingen: Vandenhoeck & Ruprecht, 2000).

Kraus, F.R., 'Die Göttin Nin-Isina', *JCS* 3 (1949), pp. 62-86.

Kruger, H.A., 'Sun and Moon Grinding to a Halt: Exegetical Remarks on Joshua 10, 9-14 and Related Texts in Judges', *HTS* 54 (1999), pp. 1077-97.

Kudat, A., 'Institutional Rigidity and Individual Initiative in Marriages of Turkish Peasants', *AQ* 47 (1974), pp. 288-303.

Kutsch, E., 'Gideon's Berufung and Altarbau Jdc 6, 11-24', *JTS* 81 (1956), pp. 75-86.

—'Berit', in E. Jenni and C. Westermann (eds.), *THAT I* (Munich: Chr. Kaiser Verlag, 1971), pp. 256-66.

Kutscher, R., 'The Cult of Dumuzi/Tammuz', in J. Klein and A. Skaist (eds.), *Bar-Ilan Studies in Assyriology: Dedicated to Pinhas Artzi* (Ramat Gan: Bar-Ilan University Press, 1990), pp. 29-44.

Kübel, P., 'Epiphanie und Altarbau', *ZAW* 83 (1971), pp. 225-31.

Kühne, H., 'The Urbanization of the Assyrian Provinces', in S. Mazzoni (ed.), *Nuove fundazioni nel Vicino Oriente Antico: Realtà e ideologia* (Rome: 1994), pp. 55-84.

Laato, A., 'Assyrian Propaganda and the Falsification of History in the Royal Inscriptions of Sennacherib', *VT* 45 (1995), pp. 198-226.

Lagarce, J. and E. Lagarce, *The Intrusion of the Sea People and their Acculturation: A Parallel between Palestinian and Ras Ibn Hani Data* (SHAP, III; Alep: Aleppo University Press, 1988).

Lagrange, M.J., *Le livre des Juges* (Paris: Lecoffre, 1903).

Laiou, A.E., *Consent and Coercion to Sex* (Washington: 1993).

Lambert, W.G., *Babylonian Wisdom Literature* (Oxford: Oxford University Press, 1960).

—'Ninurta Mythology in the Babylonian Epic of Creation', in K. Hecker and W. Sommerfeld (eds.), *Keilschriftliche Literaturen: Ausgewählte Vorträge der XXXII. RAI* (BBVO, 6; Berlin: Reimer, 1986), pp. 55-60.

—'The Assyrian Recension of Enuma Elish', in H. Waetzoldt and H. Hauptmann (eds.), *Assyrien im Wandel der Zeiten: XXXIXe Rencontre Assyriologique Internationale* (HSAO, 6; Heidelberg: Heidelberger Orientverlag, 1997), pp. 77-79.

Lamprichs, R., *Die Westexpansion des neuassyrischen Reiches: Eine Strukturanalyse* (AOAT, 239; Kevelaer/Neukirchen-Vluyn: Butzon & Bercker/Neukirchener, 1995).

Landy, F., 'Shibboleth: The Password', in *Proceedings of the Tenth World Congress of Jewish Studies* (Jerusalem: World Union of Jewish Studies, 1990), pp. 91-98.

Lanfranchi, G.B., 'Consensus to Empire: Some Aspects of Sargon II's Foreign Policy', in H. Waetzoldt and H. Hauptmann (eds.), *Assyrien im Wandel der Zeiten: XXXIXe RAI* (HSAO, 6; Heidelberg: Heidelberger Orientverlag, 1997), pp. 81-87.

—'Esarhaddon, Assyria and Media', *SAAB* 12/2 (1998), pp. 99-110.

Lang, B., *Monotheism and the Prophetic Minority* (SWBA, 1; Sheffield: Almond Press, 1983).

Langlamet, F., 'Les récits de l'institution de la royauté (I Sam. VII-XII)', *RB* 77 (1970), pp. 161-200.

Lanoir, C., 'Le livre des Juges, l'histoire et les femmes', *Foi et Vie* 96 (1997), pp. 55-71.

Lasine, S., 'Guest and Host in Judges 19: Lot's Hospitality in an Inverted World', *JSOT* 29 (1984), pp. 37-59.

—'Manasseh as Villain and Scapegoat', in J.C. Exum and D.J.A. Clines (eds.), *The New Literary Criticism and the Hebrew Bible* (JSOTSup, 143; Sheffield: JSOT Press, 1993), pp. 163-83.

Lassøe, J., *Studies on the Assyrian Ritual and Series Bit Rimki* (Copenhagen: 1955).

Latvus, K., *God, Anger and Ideology: The Anger of God in Joshua and Judges in Relation to Deuteronomy and the Priestly Writings* (JSOTSup, 279; Sheffield: JSOT Press, 1998).

Layton, S.C., *Archaic Features of Canaanite Personnal Names in the Hebew Bible* (HSM, 47; Atlanta: Scholars Press, 1990).

Le Bonniec, H., *Le culte de Cérès à Rome* (Paris: Klincksieck, 1958).

—'Les renards aux Cerialia', in *idem* (ed.), *Etudes ovidiennes* (Etudes ovidiennes, 43; Frankfurt: Lang, 1989), pp. 27-32.

Le Glay, M., 'Déméter et Koré', in E. Lipinski (ed.), *DCPP* (Louvain: Brepols, 1992), pp. 128-29.

Lefevre, B., *Une version syriaque des fables d'Esope* (Paris: Firmin-Didot, 1941).

Lehmann, G., H.M. Niemann and W. Zwickel, 'Zora und Eschtaol: Ein archäologischer Oberflächensurvey im Gebiet nördlich von Bet Schemesch', *UF* 28 (1996), pp. 343-442.

Lelièvre, A., 'YHWH et la mer dans les Psaumes', *RHPR* 56 (1976), pp. 253-75.

Lemaire, A., *Inscriptions hébraïques*. I. *Les ostraca* (LAPO, 9; Paris: Cerf, 1977).

—'L'incident du Shibbolet (Jg 12, 6): perspective historique', in A. Caquot (ed.), *Mélanges bibliques et orientaux en l'honneur de Mathias Delcor* (Neukirchen: Butzon & Bercker, 1985), pp. 275-81.

—'Populations et territoires de la Palestine à l'époque perse', *Transeuphratène* 3 (1990), pp. 31-74.

—'Asher et le royaume de Tyr', in E. Lipinski (ed.), *Phoenicia and the Bible* (SP, 11; Leuven: Peeters, 1991), pp. 135-52.

Lettinga, J.P., 'A Note on 2 Kings XIX, 37', *VT* 7 (1957), pp. 105-106.

Levin, C., *Der Sturz der Königin Atalja: Ein Kapitel zur Geschichte Judas im 9. Jahrhundert v. Chr* (SBS, 105; Stuttgart: Verlag Katholishes Bibelwerk, 1982).

Levin, C., 'Die Entstehung der Rechabiter', in I. Kottsieper, *et al.* (eds.), *'Wer ist wie du, Herr, unter den Göttern?'* (Göttingen: Vandenhoeck & Ruprecht, 1994), pp. 301-17.

Lévêque, P., and P. Vidal-Naquet, *Clisthène l'athénien* (Belles Lettres, 65; Paris: 1964).

Lévi-Strauss, C., 'Comment meurent les mythes', in *idem* (ed.), *Anthroplogie structurale deux* (Paris: Plon, 1973), pp. 301-15.

Lévy, G.R., 'The Oriental Origin of Herakles', *JHS* 54 (1934), pp. 40-53.

Lewis, B., *The Sargon Legend* (ASOR Dissertations Series, 4; Cambridge MA: ASOR, 1980).

Lidzbarski, M., 'Balsamem', *EsE* 2 (1915), p. 122.

Lie, A.G., *The Inscriptions of Sargon II. Part I, the Annals* (Paris: 1929).

Lincoln, B., 'The Rape of Persephone: A Greek Scenario of Women's Initiation', *HTR* 72 (1979), pp. 223-35.

Lindars, B., 'Some LXX readings in Judges', *JTS* 22 (1971), pp. 1-14.

—'Jotham's Fable—a New Form-critical Analysis', *JTS* 24 (1973), pp. 355-66.

—'A Commentary on the Greek Judges?', in C.E. Cox (ed.), *VI Congress of the International Organization for Septuagint and Cogna* (SBLSCS, 23, Atlanta: Scholars Press, 1987), pp. 167-200.

—*Judges 1-5: A New Translation and Commentary (edited by A. D. H. Mayes)* (Edinburgh: T&T Clark, 1995).

Lindenberger, J.M., *The Aramaic Proverbs of Ahiqar* (Baltimore: The Johns Hopkins University Press, 1983).

Ling-Israel, P., 'The Sennakerib Prism in the Israel Museum—Jerusalem', in J. Klein and A. Skaist (eds.), *Bar-Ilan Studies in Assyriology: Dedicated to Pinhas Artzi* (Ramat Gan: Bar-Ilan University Press, 1990), pp. 213-48.

Lipinski, E., 'Nimrod et Ashur', *RB* 73 (1966), pp. 77-93.

—'Juges 5, 4-5 et Psaume 68, 8-11', *Biblica* 48 (1967), pp. 185-206.

—'Juda et 'tout Israël'', in *idem* (ed.), *The Land of Israel: Cross-Roads of Civilizations* (OLA, 19; Leuven: Peeters, 1985), pp. 93-112.

—'Les racines syro-palestiniennes de la religion carthaginoise', *BCDA* 8 (1987), pp. 28-44.

—'The Territory of Tyre and the Tribe of Asher', in *idem* (ed.), *Phoenicia and the Bible* (SP, 11; Leuven: Peeters, 1991), pp. 153-66.

—'Suffète', in *idem* (ed.), *DCPP* (Turnhout: Brepols, 1992), p. 429.

—'Tanit', in *idem* (ed.), *DCPP* (Turnhout: Brepols, 1992), pp. 438-39.

—'Shemesh', in K. Van der Toorn, B. Becking and P.W. van der Horst (eds.), *DDD* (Leiden: E.J. Brill, 1995), pp. 1445-52.

Lipschits, O., 'Benjamin Region under the Babylonian Rule', *TA* 26 (1999), pp. 155-90.

Liss, H., 'Die Fabel des Yotam in Ri 9, 8-15: Versuch einer strukturellen Deutung', *BN* 89 (1997), pp. 12-21.

Liverani, M., 'The Ideology of the Assyrian Empire', in M.G. Larsen (ed.), *Mesopotamia* (Copenhagen: Akademisk Forlag, 1979), pp. 263-318.

—'The Trade Network of Tyre', in M. Cogan and I. Eph'al (eds.), *Ah Assyria...* (SH, 33; Jerusalem: Magnes Press, 1991), pp. 65-79.

Livingstone, A., 'New Dimensions in the Study of Assyrian Religion', in S. Parpola and R.M. Whiting (eds.), *Assyria 1995* (Helsinki: University of Helsinki, 1997), pp. 165-78.

—*Mystical and Mythological Explanatory Works of Assyrian and Babylonian Scholars* (Oxford: Clarendon Press, 1986).

—*Court Poetry and Literary Miscellanea* (SAA, 3; Helsinki: University of Helsinki Press, 1989).

Livy, *Roman History* (trans. B.O. Foster; LCL; London: Heinemann, 1960).

Lods, A., *Israël: Des origines au milieu du VIIIème siècle* (Paris: 1930).

Lohfink, N., 'Die Ältesten Israels und der Bund: Zum Zusammenhang von Dtn 5, 23; 26, 17-19; 27, 1.9f und 31, 9', *BN* 67 (1993), pp. 26-42.

—'Gab es eine deuteronomische Bewegung?', in W. Gross (ed.), *Jeremia und die "deuteronomistische Bewegung"* (BBB, 98; Weinheim: Belz Athenaüm, 1995), pp. 313-82.

—'Was there a Deuteronomistic Movement?', in L.S. Schearing and S.L. McKenzie (eds.), *Those Elusive Deuteronomists* (JSOTSup, 268; Sheffield: Sheffield Academic Press, 1999), pp. 36-66.

Lorimer, H.L., *Homer and the Monuments* (London: 1950).

Lowery, K.E., 'Sheshai (Person)', in D.N. Freedman (ed.), *ABD* 6 (New York: Doubleday, 1992), p. 1207.

Lubetski, M., 'Lehi', in D.N. Freedman (ed.), *ABD* 4 (New York: Doubleday, 1992), pp. 274-75.

Luckenbill, D.D., *The Annals of Sennacherib* (Chicago: University of Chicago Press, 1924).

—*Ancient Records of Assyria and Babylonia* (Chicago: University of Chicago Press, 1926).

Luqman, *Fables de Lokman* (trans. A. Cherbonneau; Paris: Imprimerie royale, 1846).

MacDonald, B., 'Ammonite Territory and Sites', in B. MacDonald and R.W. Younker (eds.), *Ancient Ammon* (SHCANE, 17; Leiden: E.J. Brill, 1999), pp. 30-66.

Machinist, P., 'Assyria and its Image in the First Isaiah', *JAOS* 103 (1983), pp. 719-37.

Macholz, G., 'Zur Geschichte der Justizorganization in Juda', *ZAW* 84 (1972), pp. 314-40.

Macintosh, A.A., 'The Meaning of *MKLYM* in Judges XVIII 7', *VT* 35 (1985), pp. 68-77.

Mafico, T.J., 'The Term Šapiṭum in Akkadian Documents', *JNSL* 13 (1987), pp. 68-87.

—'Were the "Judges" of Israel like African Spirit Mediums?', in D. Smith-Christopher (ed.), *Text and Experience* (BS, 35; Sheffield: JSOT Press, 1995), pp. 330-43.

Magen, I., 'Shechem', in E. Stern (ed.), *NEAEHL* 4 (Jerusalem: Israel Exploration Society & Carta, 1993), pp. 1345-59.

Malamat, A., 'The Historical Background of the Assassination of Amon, King of Judah', *IEJ* 3 (1953), pp. 26-29.

—'Cushan Rishataim and the Decline of the Near East around 1200 B.C.', *JNES* 13 (1954), pp. 231-42.

—'Doctrines of Causality in Hittite and Biblical Historiography: A Parallel', *VT* 5 (1955), pp. 1-12.

—'The Danite Migration and the Pan-Israelite Exodus-Conquest: A Biblical Narrative Pattern', *Biblica* 51 (1970), pp. 1-16.

—'Syro-Palestinian Destination in a Mari Tin Inventory', *IEJ* 21 (1971), pp. 31-38.

—'Die Wanderung der Daniten und die panisraelitische Exodus-Landnahme: Ein biblisches Erzählmuster', in I. Seybold (ed.), *Meqor Hajjim* (Graz: Dr.-und Verl. Anst., 1983), pp. 249-65.

—'The Kingdom of Judah between Egypt and Babylon: A Small State within a Great Power Confrontation', *ST* 44 (1990), pp. 65-77.

Maly, E.H., 'The Jotham Fable—Antimonarchical?', *CBQ* 22 (1960), pp. 299-305.

Marconi, M., 'Melissa, dea cretese', *Athenaeum* 18 (1940), pp. 164-78.

Marcus , D., *Jephtah and his Vow* (Lubbock, Texas: Texas Tech Pr., 1986).

Marfoe, L., 'The Integrative Transformation: Patterns of Sociopolitical Organisation in Southern Syria', *BASOR* 234 (1979), pp. 21-23.

Margalith, O., 'Samson's Foxes', *VT* 35 (1985), pp. 224-28.

—'More Samson's Legends', *VT* 36 (1986), pp. 397-405.

—'Samson's Riddles and Samson's Magic Locks', *VT* 36 (1986), pp. 225-34.

—'The Legends of Samson/Heracles', *VT* 37 (1987), pp. 63-70.

—'The Meaning and Significance of Ashera', *VT* 40 (1990), pp. 264-97.

Marx, A., 'Forme et fonction de Juges 2, 1-5', *RHPR* 59 (1979), pp. 341-50.

Mathys, H.-P., *Dichter und Beter* (OBO, 132; Freiburg/Göttingen: Universitätsverlag/Vandenhoeck & Ruprecht, 1994).

Matthews, V.H., 'Hospitality and Hostility in Genesis 19 and Judges 19', *BTB* 22 (1992), pp. 3-11.

Maul, S.M., *Zukunftsbewältigung* (BF, 18; Mainz: Ph. von Zabern, 1994).

Mayer, W., *Politik und Kriegskunst des Assyrer* (Münster: Ugarit-Verlag, 1995).

Mayer, D., 'Passages dans le livre des Juges', *SeB* 92 (1998), pp. 35-44.

—'Samson ou l'anamorphose du récit', *SeB* 93 (1999), pp. 3-22.

Mayes, A.D.H., *The Story of Israel between Settlement and Exile: A Redaction Study of the Deuteronomic History* (London: SCM Press, 1983).

—*Judges* (OTG, 98; Sheffield: JSOT Press, 1985).

—'Deuteronomistic Royal Ideology in Judges 17–21', *BibInt* 9 (2001), pp. 243-58.

Mayor Bidai, P., 'The Phoenicians', in W.A. Ward and M.S. Joukowsky (eds.), *The Crisis Years: The 12th Century B.C.* (Dubuque Iowa: Kendall/Hunt, 1992), pp. 132-41.

Mazar, B., 'The Aramean Empire and its Relations with Israel', *BA* 35 (1962), pp. 98-120.

—'The Philistines and the Rise of Israel and Tyre', in *idem* (ed.), *The Early Biblical Period: Historical Studies* (Jerusalem: Israel Exploration Society, 1986), pp. 63-82.

—'Jerusalem: From Isaiah to Jeremiah', in J.A. Emerton (ed.), *Congress Volume, Jerusalem 1986* (VTSup, XL; Leiden: E.J. Brill, 1988), pp. 1-6.

—*Biblical Israel* (Jerusalem: Magnes Press, 1992).

—'The Sanctuary of Arad and the Family of Hobab the Kenite', in S. Ahituv (ed.), *Biblical Israel: State and People* (Jerusalem: Magnes Press, 1992), pp. 67-77.

McCarter, P.K., 'Eshmunasar Inscription', in W.W. Hallo (ed.), *CoS* 2 (Leyden: E.J. Brill, 2000), pp. 182-83.

McClellan, T., 'Towns and Fortresses: The Transformation of Urban Life in Judah from 8th to 7th centuries BC', in P.J. Achtemeier (ed.), *SBL 1979 Seminar Papers* (SBLSP, 16-17; Missoula, MT: Scholars Press, 1979), pp. 277-85.

McGovern, P.E., 'Beth-Shan', in D.N. Freedman (ed.), *ABD* 1 (New-York: Doubleday, 1992), pp. 693-96.

McKay, J.W., *Religion in Judah under the Assyrians: 732-609 B.C.* (London: SCM Press, 1973).

McKenzie, D., 'Judicial Procedure at the Town Gate', *VT* 14 (1974), pp. 100-104.

McKenzie, S.L., 'Why Didn't David Build the Temple? The History of a Biblical Tradition', in M.P. Graham, R.R. Marrs and S.L. McKenzie (eds.), *Worship and the Hebrew Bible* (JSOTSup, 284; Sheffield, Sheffield Academic Press, 1999), pp. 204-24.

McMahon, G., 'History and Legend in Early Hittite Historiography', in A.R. Millard, J. Hoffmeier and D.W. Baker (eds.), *Faith, Tradition and History* (Winona Lake: Eisenbrauns, 1994), pp. 149-58.

McMillion, P., 'Worship in Judges 17-18', in M.P. Graham, R.R. Marrs and S.L. McKenzie (eds.), *Worship and the Hebrew Bible* (JSOTSup, 284; Sheffield: Sheffield Academic Press, 1999), pp. 225-43.

Meier, G., *Die assyrische Beschwörungssammlung Maqlû* (AfO Beiheft, 2; Osnabrück: Biblioverlag, 1967).

Meillier, C., *Callimaque et son temps* (Publications de l'Université, 3; Lille: Université de Lille, 1979).

Meissner, A., 'Alles oder Nichts. Die Tragik des Helden Simson (Richter13-16)', in D. Bauer and A. Meissner (eds.), *Männer weinen heimlich: Geschichten aus dem Alten Testament* (Stuttgart: Katholisches Bibelwerk, 1993), pp. 59-75.

Mendenhall, G.E., 'Amorites', in D.N. Freedman (ed.), *ABD 1* (New York: Doubleday, 1992), pp. 199-202.

Mettinger, T.N.D., *King and Messiah* (ConBOT, 8; Lund: C.W.K. Gleerup, 1976).

Meyer-Opificius, R., 'Simson, der sechslockige Held?', *UF* 14 (1982), pp. 149-51.

Meyers, C., 'An Ethnoarcheological Analysis of Hannah's Sacrifice', in Wright, Freedman and Hurvitz (eds.), *Pomegranates and Golden Bells* (Winona Lake: Eisenbrauns, 1995), pp. 77-91.

Migne, J.P., *Dictionnaire des Apocryphes* (Turnhout: Brepols, 1856).

Milgrom, J., 'The Alleged "Demythologisation and Secularization" in Deuteronomy', *IEJ* 23 (1973), pp. 156-61.

Millard, A.R., 'Large Numbers in the Assyrian Royal Inscriptions', in M. Cogan and I. Eph'al (eds.), *Ah Assyria...* (SH, 33; Jerusalem: Magnes Press, 1991), pp. 213-22.

—'The Question of Distinctiveness in Ancient Israel', in M. Cogan and I. Eph'al (eds.), *Ah Assyria...* (SH, 33; Jerusalem: Magnes Press, 1991), pp. 196-212.

—'The Signs for Numbers in Early Hebrew', in K. van Lerberghe and A. Schoors (eds.), *Immigration and Emigration within the Ancient Near East. Festschrift E. Lipinski* (OLA, 65; Leuven: Peeters, 1995), pp. 189-94.

Miller, G.D., 'A Riposte Form in the Song of Deborah', in V.H. Matthews, B.M. Levinson and T. Frymer-Kensky (eds.), *Gender and Law* (JSOTSup, 262; Sheffield: Sheffield Academic Press, 1998), pp. 117-27.

Miller, G.P., 'Verbal Feud in the Hebrew Bible: Jg 3, 12-30 & 19-21', *JNES* 55 (1996), pp. 105-17.

Miller, J.M., 'Saul's Rise to Power: Some Observations Concerning 1 S 9.1-10.16; 10.26-11.15 and 13.2-14.46', *CBQ* 36 (1974), pp. 157-74.

—'The Israelite Journey through (around) Moab and Moabite Territory', *JBL* 108 (1989), pp. 577-95.

Miller, P.D., 'The Absence of the Goddess in Israelite Religion', *HTR* 10 (1986), pp. 239-48.

—'Animal Names as Designation in Ugaritic and Hebrew', *UF* 2 (1970), pp. 177-86.

Mittmann, S., 'Aroer, Minnith und Abel Keramim (Jdc 11, 33)', *ZDPV* 85 (1969), pp. 63-75.

—'Ri. 1, 16f u.d. Siedlungsgebiet d. Kenitischen Sippe Hobab', *ZDPV* 93 (1977), pp. 213-35.

—'Hiskia und die Philister', *JNSL* 19 (1990), pp. 91-106.

Mobley, G., 'The Wild Man in the Bible and the Ancient Near-East', *JBL* 41 (1997), pp. 217-33.

Moenikes, A., *Die grundsätzliche Ablehnung des Königstums in der hebräischen Bibel* (BBB, 99; Weinheim: Belz Athenäum, 1995).

Momigliano, A., 'Biblical Studies and Classical Studies: Simple Reflections about Historical Method', *BA* 45 (1982), pp. 224-28.

Moore, G.F., *Judges* (Edinburg: T. & T. Clarke, 1966).

Moore Cross, F., 'King Hezekiah's Seal Bears Phoenician Imagery', *BARev* 25 (1999), pp. 42-5.60.

Moorgat-Correns, U., 'Ein Kultbild Ninurtas aus neuassyrischer Zeit', *AfO* 35 (1988), pp. 117-35.

Morag, S., 'Qumran Hebrew: Some Typological Considerations', *VT* 38 (1988), pp. 148-64.

Moran, W.L., *The Tel Amarna Letters* (Baltimore: The Johns Hopkins University Press, 1992).

Mosca, P.G., 'Who Seduced whom? A Note on Joshua 15.18 // Judges 1, 14', *CBQ* 46 (1984), pp. 18-22.

Mottu, H., 'Jeremiah vs. Hananiah: Ideology and Truth in Old Testament Prophecy', in N.K. Gottwald (ed.), *The Bible and Liberation* (New York: Maryknoll, 1984), pp. 235-51.

Mullen, E.T.J., 'The "Minor Judges": Some Literary and Historical Considerations', *CBQ* 44 (1982), pp. 185-201.

—'Judges 1.1-36: The Deuteronomistic Reintroduction of the Book of Judges', *HTR* 77 (1984), pp. 33-54.

Murray, D.F., *Divine Prerogative and Royal Pretention* (JSOTSup, 264; Sheffield, Sheffield Academic Press, 1998).

Murray, G., *Rise of the Greek Epic* (Oxford: 1949).

Murtonen, A., 'Some Thoughts on Judges XVII sq', *VT* 1 (1951), pp. 223-45.

Müller, H.-P., 'Der Aufbau des Deboraliedes', *VT* 16 (1966), pp. 446-59.

—'Die hebräische Wurzel שיח', *VT* 19 (1969), pp. 361-71.

Myers, J.M., *The Book of Judges* (Interpreter's Bible, 2; New York-Nashville: 1953).

Na'aman, N., 'Sennacherib's "Letter to God" on his Campaign to Judah', *BASOR* 214 (1974), pp. 25-39.

—*The Political Disposition and Historical Developments of Eretz-Israel according to the Amarna Letters* (Tel Aviv: Tel Aviv University Press, 1975).

—'Sennacherib's Campaign to Judah and the Date of the LMLK Stamps', *VT* 29 (1977), pp. 61-86.

—'The Inheritance of the Sons of Simeon', *ZDPV* 96 (1980), pp. 136-52.

—*Borders and Districts in Biblical Historiography* (Jerusalem Biblical Studies, 4; Jerusalem: Simor, 1986).

—'The Canaanite City-states in the Late Bronze Age and the Inheritance of the Israelite Tribes (Hebrew)', *Tarbiz* 55 (1986), pp. 463-88.

—'Hezekiah's Fortified Cities and the LMLK Stamps', *BASOR* 261 (1986), pp. 5-21.

—'Canaanites and Perizzites', *BN* 45 (1988), pp. 42-47.

—'Literary and Topographical Notes on the Battle of Kishon (Judges IV-V)', *VT* 40 (1990), pp. 423-36.

—'The Kingdom of Ishbaal', *BN* 54 (1990), pp. 33-37.

—'The Kingdom of Judah under Josiah', *TA* 18 (1991), pp. 3-71.

—'Forced Participation in Alliances in the Course of the Assyrian Campaigns to the West', in M. Cogan and I. Eph'al (eds.), *Ah Assyria...* (SH, 33; Jerusalem: Magnes Press, 1991), pp. 80-98.

—'Chronology and History in the Late Assyrian Empire (631-619 B.C.)', *ZA* 91 (1992), pp. 243-67.

—'Canaanite Jerusalem and its Central Hill Country Neighbours in the Second Millennium B.C.E.', *UF* 24 (1992), pp. 275-91.

—'Israel, Edom and Egypt in the Tenth Century BCE', *TA* 19 (1992), pp. 71-79.

—'The "Conquest of Canaan" in the Book of Joshua and in History', in I. Finkelstein (ed.), *From Nomadism to Monarchy* (Jerusalem: Israel Exploration Society, 1994), pp. 218-81.

—'Tiglath-pileser III's Campaigns against Tyre and Israel', *TA* 22 (1995), pp. 268-81.

—'Rezin of Damascus and the Land of Gilead', *ZDPV* 111 (1995), pp. 105-17.

—'King Mesha and the Foundation of the Moabite Monarchy', *IEJ* 47 (1997), pp. 83-92.

—'The Contribution of Royal Inscriptions for a Re-evaluation of the Book of Kings as Historical Source', *JSOT* 82 (1999), pp. 3-17.

Naveh, J., 'A Hebrew Letter from the 7th C. BC', *IEJ* 10 (1960), pp. 29-130.

Neef, H.D., 'Der Sieg Debora und Baraks über Sisera: Exegetische Beobachtungen zum Aufbau und Werden von Jdc 4, 1-24', *ZAW* 101 (1989), pp. 28-49.

—'Deboraerzählung und Deboralied: Beobachtungen zum Verhältnis von Jdc IV und V', *VT* 44 (1994), pp. 47-59.

—''Ich selber bin in ihm' (Ex 23, 21): Exegetische Beobarchtungen zur Rede vom "Engel des Herrn" in Ex 23, 20-22; 32, 34; 33, 2; Jdc 2, 1-5; 5, 23.', *BZ* 39 (1995), pp. 54-75.

—'Jephta und Seine Tochter (Jdc. xi 29-40)', *VT* 49 (1999), pp. 206-17.

Nel, P., 'The Riddle of Samson', *Biblica* 66 (1985), pp. 534-45.

Nelson, R.D., 'Josiah in the Book of Joshua', *JBL* 100 (1981), pp. 531-40.

—'Realpolitik in Judah (687-609 B.C.E.)', in W.W. Hallo, J.C. Moyer and L.G. Perdue (eds.), *Scripture in Context. II. More Essays on the Comparative Method* (Winona Lake: Eisenbrauns, 1983), pp. 177-89.

—*Raising up a Faithful Priest: Community and Priesthood in Biblical Theology* (Louisville: 1993).

Neufeld, E., *Ancient Hebrew Marriage Laws: With Special References to General Semitic Laws and Customs* (London: Longman Green, 1935).

Nickelsburg, G.W.E., '4Q551: A Vorlage to Susanna or a Text Related to Judges 19?', *JJS* 48 (1997), pp. 349-51.

Niditch, S., 'The "Sodomite" Theme in Judges 19-20: Family, Community and Social Desintegration', *CBQ* 44 (1982), pp. 365-78.

—'Eroticism and Death in the Tale of Jael', in P.L. Day (ed.), *Gender and Difference in Ancient Israel* (Minneapolis: Fortress Press, 1989), pp. 43-57.

—'Samson as Culture Hero, Trickster and Bandit: The Empowerment of the Weak', *CBQ* 52 (1990), pp. 608-24.

—*Folklore and the Hebrew Bible* (Minneapolis: Fortress, 1993).

—'Reading Stories in Judges 1', in F.C. Black, R. Boer and E. Runions (eds.), *The Labour of Reading: Desire, Alienation, and Biblical Interpretation* (SBLSS, 36; Atlanta: SBL, 1999), pp. 193-208.

Niditch, S., and K. Van der Toorn, 'Judges XVI 21 in the Light of Akkadian Sources', *VT* 36 (1986), pp. 248-53.

Niehr, H., *Herrschen und Richten: Die Wurzel špt im Alten Orient und im Alten Testament* (FzB, 54; Würzburg: Echter Verlag, 1986).

—*Rechtsprechung in Israel: Untersuchung zur Gechischte des Gerichtsorganisation im Alten Testament* (SBS, 130; Stuttgart: Verlag Katholisches Bibelwerk, 1987).

—*Der höchste Gott: Alttestamentlischer JHWH-Glaube im Kontext syrisch-kanaanäischer Religion des 1. Jahrtausends v. Chr.* (BZAW, 190; Berlin: W. de Gruyter, 1990).

—'The Rise of YHWH in Judahite and Israelite Religion: Methodological and Religio-Historical Aspects', in D. Edelman (ed.), *The Triumph of Elohim* (Kampen: Pharos, 1995), pp. 45-74.

Nielsen, E., 'Political Conditions and Cultural Development in Israel and Judah during the Reign of Manasseh', in *4th World Congress of Jewish Studies* I (Jerusalem: Magnes Press, 1967), pp. 103-106.

Nielsen, F.A.J., *The Tragedy in History* (JSOTSup, 251; Sheffield: Sheffield Academic Press, 1997).

Nielsson, N.M.P., *The Minoan-Mycenaean Religion and its Survival in Greek Religion* (Lund: Gleerup, 1968).

Nielsson, N.M.P., and M.H. Jameson, 'Thesmophoria', in M. Cary, *et al.* (eds.), *OCD* (Oxford: Oxford University Press, 1996), p. 1509.

Niemann, H.M., *Die Daniten: Studien zur Geschichte e. altisraelitischen Stämmes* (FRLANT, 135; Göttingen: Vandenhoeck & Ruprecht, 1985).

—*Herrschaft, Königtum und Staat* (FAT, 6; Tübingen: J.C.B. Mohr, 1993).

—'Zorah, Eshtaol, Beth-Shemesh and Dan's Migration to the South: A Region and its Traditions in the Late Bronze and Iron Ages', *JSOT* 86 (1999), pp. 25-48.

Nissinen, M., 'Die Relevanz der neuassyrischen Prophetie für die alttestamentliche Forschung', in M. Dietrich and O. Loretz (eds.), *Mesopotamica-Ugaritica-Biblica* (AOAT, 232; Neukirchen-Vluyn: Neukirchener Verlag, 1993), pp. 217-58.

—'Die Liebe von David und Jonatan als Frage der modernen Exegese', *Biblica* 80 (1999), pp. 250-63.

Nöldeke, T., *Untersuchungen zur Kritik des AT* (Hildesheim: 1869).

Noort, E., 'Josua 24, 28-31, Richter 2, 6-9 und das Josuagrab: Gedanken zu einem Strassenschild', in W. Zwickel (ed.), *Biblische Welten* (OBO, 123; Fribourg: Universitätsverlag, 1993), pp. 109-30.

Noth, M., *Das System der zwölf Stämme Israels* (BWANT, 4/1; Stuttgart: Kohlhammer, 1930).

—*Überlieferungsgeschichtliche Studien: Die sammelnden und bearbeitenden Geschichtswerke im Alten Testament* (Darmstadt: Max Niemeyer, 1943).

—'Das Amt des Richters Israels', in W. Baumgartner (ed.), *Festschrift Alfred Bertholet* (Tübingen: J.C.B. Mohr, 1950), pp. 389-412, reprint in *idem, Gesammelte Studien zum A.T.* 2 (ThB, 39; München: Chr. Kaiser Verlag, 1969), pp. 71-85.

—*The History of Israel* (London: 1960).

—'The Background of Judges 17–18', in B. Anderson and W. Harrelson (eds.), *Israel's Prophetic Heritage: Essays in Honor of James Muilenburg* (New York: Harper, 1962), pp. 68-85.

—'Review of Richter's Traditionsgeschichtliche Untersuchungen zum Richterbuch', *VT* 15 (1965), pp. 126-28.

—*Koenige* (BK, IX/1; Neukirchen: Neukirchener, 1968).

Novotny, J.R., *The Standard Babylonian Etana Epic* (SAACT, 2; Helsinki: The Neo-Assyrian Text Corpus Project, 2001).

Nowack, W., *Richter-Ruth* (HKAT, 1.4; Göttingen: Vandenhoeck & Ruprecht, 1900).

O'Brien, M.A., 'Judges and the Deuteronomistic History', in S.L. McKenzie and M.P. Graham (eds.), *The History of Israel's Traditions: The Heritage of Martin Noth* (JSOTSup, 182; Sheffield: Sheffield Academic Press, 1994), pp. 235-59.

O'Connell, R.H., *The Rhetoric of the Book of Judges* (VTSup, 63; Leiden: E.J. Brill, 1995).

O'Doherty, E., 'The Literary Problem of Judges 1, 1-3, 6', *CBQ* 18 (1956), pp. 1-32.

Oded, B., 'The Phoenician Cities and the Assyrian Empire in the Time of Tiglath-pileser III', *ZDPV* 90 (1974), pp. 38-49.

—*Mass Deportations and Deportees in the Neo-Assyrian Empire* (Wiesbaden: L. Reichert, 1979).

—*War, Peace and Empire: Justifications for War in Assyrian Royal Inscriptions* (Wiesbaden: L. Reichert, 1992).

—''Cushan-Rishathaim (Judges 3.8-11): An Implicit Polemic', in M.V. Fox, V.A. Hurowitz and A. Hurvitz (eds.), *Texts, Temples and Traditions* (Winona Lake: Eisenbrauns, 1996), pp. 89*-94*.

Oden, R.A.J., 'Ba'al Shamem and 'El', *CBQ* 39 (1977), pp. 457-73.

Oka, M., 'An Enquiry into the Prehistory of Herakles in the light of the Near Eastern Literature', *JCS* (Kyoto) 7 (1959), pp. 48-64.

Olivier, J.P.J., 'Money Matters: Some Remarks on the Economic Situation in the Kindom of Judah during the Seventh Century B.C.', *BN* 73 (1994), pp. 90-100.

Olmstead, A.T., *History of Assyria* (Chicago: University of Chicago Press, 1923).

Oppenheim, A.L., 'Assyriological Gleanings I', *BASOR* 91 (1943), pp. 36-39.

—'A new Prayer to the Gods of the Night', in *Studia biblica et orientalia* 3 (AnBib, 12; Roma: Pontifico Istituto Biblico, 1959), pp. 282-301.

—*Ancient Mesopotamia* (London/Chicago: University of Chicago Press, 1964).

—'Analysis of an Assyrian Ritual', *HR* 5 (1966), pp. 250-65.

Organ, B., 'Judges 17-21 and the Composition of the Book of Judges' (PhD Dissertation; Toronto: University of St. Michael's College, 1987).

Otten, H., *Eine althethitische Erzählung um die Stadt Zalpa* (SBT, 17; Wiesbaden: Otto Harrassowitz, 1973).

—'Die Königin von Kanish', in P. Garelli (ed.), *Le palais et la royauté* (Paris: Geuthner, 1974), pp. 301-303.

Otten, H.C., and C. Rüster, *Keilschrifttexte aus Boghazköi H. 22, aus dem Bezirk des grossen Tempels* (WVDOG, 90; Berlin: Mann Verl., 1974).

Ottoson, M., *Gilead: Tradition and History* (ConBOT, 3; Lund: C.W.K. Gleerup, 1969).

—'Tradition History, with Emphasis on the Composition of the Book of Joshua', in K. Jeppesen and B. Otzen (eds.), *The Productions of Time* (Sheffield: Almond Press, 1984), pp. 81-106.

Otzen, B., 'Israel under the Assyrians', in M.G. Larsen (ed.), *Power and Propaganda* (Mesopotamia, 7, Copenhagen: Akademisk Forlag, 1979), pp. 251-62.

Ovid, *Fasts* (trans. J.G. Frazer; LCL, London: Heinemann, 1959).

Parker, S.B., 'The Vow in Ugaritic and Israelite Narrative Literature', *UF* 11 (1979), pp. 693-700.

Parker, R., *Athenian Religion: A History* (Oxford: Clarendon Press, 1996).

Parpola, S., 'The Murderer of Sennacherib', in B. Alster (ed.), *Death in Mesopotamia* (Copenhagen: Akademisk Forlag, 1980), pp. 171-82.

—*Letters from Assyrian and Babylonian Scholars* (SAA, X; Helsinki: University of Helsinki Press, 1993).

Parpola, S., and K. Watanabe, *Neo-Assyrian Treaties and Loyalty Oaths* (SAA, II; Helsinki: Helsinki University Press, 1988).

Pausanias, *Description of Greece* (trans. W.H.S. Jones; LCL; London: Heinemann, 1940).

Penchansky, D., 'Staying the Night: Intertextuality in Genesis and Judges', in D.N. Fewell (ed.), *Reading between Texts* (Louisville: 1992), pp. 77-88.

Penna, A., 'L'introduzione al libro dei Giudici (1, 1-3, 6)', in J. Sagües *et al.* (eds.), *Miscelenea Biblica Andres Fernandez* (Madrid: 1961), pp. 521-29.

Perreault, J.Y., 'Céramique et échanges: Les importations attiques au Proche Orient du VIème au milieu du Vème s. av. J.C.', *BCH* 110 (1986), pp. 145-75.

Perry, B.E., *Aesopica* (Urbana: University of Illinois Press, 1952).

Péter, R., 'פר et שור', *VT* 25 (1975), pp. 486-96.

Pfeiffer, H., *Das Heiligtum von Bethel im Spiegel des Hoseabuches* (FRLANT, 183; Göttingen: Vandenhoeck & Ruprecht, 1999).

Pfluger, K., 'The Edict of King Haremhab', *JNES* 5 (1946), pp. 260-76.

Picard, C., 'Tanit courotrophe', in J. Bibauw (ed.), *Hommages à Marcel Renard* (101-103; Bruxelles: Latomus, 1969), pp. 474-84.

Piepkorn, A.C., *Historical Prisms: Inscriptions of Ashurbanipal* (Assyriological Studies, 5/1; Chicago: 1933).

Polliack, M., 'Review of Yairah Amit, The Book of Judges: The Art of Editing.', *VT* 45 (1995), pp. 392-98.

Polyen, P., *Strategemata* (Belles Lettres, Paris: 1949).

Polzin, R., *Moses and the Deuteronomist* (New York: Seabury, 1980).

Pongratz-Leisten, B., 'The Interplay of Military Strategy and Cultic Practice in Assyrian Politics', in S. Parpola and R.M. Whiting (eds.), *Assyria 1995* (Helsinki: The Neo-Assyrian Text Corpus Project, 1995), pp. 241-52.

—*Herrschaftswissen in Mesopotamien* (SAAS, X; Helsinki: New-Assyrian Text Corpus Project, 1999).

Poplutz, U., 'Tel Miqne/Ekron: Geschichte und Kultur einer philistäischen Stadt', *BN* 87 (1997), pp. 69-99.

Porten, B., 'The Identity of King Adon', *BA* 44 (1981), pp. 36-52.

Porten, B., and A. Yardeni, *Textbook of Aramaic Documents from Ancient Egypt* (Jerusalem: 1986).

—'Three Unpublished Aramaic Ostraka', *Maarav* 7 (1991), pp. 207-27.

Posener, G., *Princes et pays d'Asie et de Nubie* (Bruxelles: 1940).

Postgate, J.N., 'Royal Exercice of Justice under the Assyrian Empire', in P. Garelli (ed.), *Le palais et la royauté* (Mesopotamia, 7; Paris: Geuthner, 1974), pp. 417-26.

—'The Bit Akiti in Nabu Temple', *Sumer* 30 (1974), pp. 51-74.

—'The Economic Structure of the Assyrian Empire', in M.G. Larsen (ed.), *Power and Propaganda* (Mesopotamia, 7; Copenhagen: Akademisk Vorlag, 1979), pp. 193-222.

Poucet, J., *Recherches sur la légende des Sabines* (Louvain/Kinshasa: Publications universitaires/Université Lovanium, 1967).

Poursat, J.-C., 'Les découvertes de Tell el-Dab'a et la Crète', in A. Caubet (ed.), *L'acrobate au taureau: Les découvertes de Tell el-Dab'a (Egypte) et l'archéologie de la Méditerranée orientale 1800-1400 av. J.-C.* (Louvre conférences et colloques, Paris: La documentation française, 1999), pp. 181-94.

Préaux, J.G., 'La sacralité du pouvoir royal à Rome', *ACERB* 1 (1962), pp. 108-35.

Price, B.J., 'Secondary State Formation: An Explanatory Model', in R. Cohen and E.R. Service (eds.), *Origins of the State: the Anthropology of Political Evolution* (Philadelphia: Institute for the Study of Human Issues, 1978), pp. 161-86.

Provan, I.W., *Hezekiah and the Books of Kings* (BZAW, 172; Berlin: W. de Gruyter, 1988).

Pury, A. de, *Promesse divine et légende cultuelle dans le cycle de Jacob* (EB, Paris: J. Gabalda, 1975).

—'La ville dans les traditions patriarchales de la Genèse', in F. Brüschweiler *et al.* (eds.), *La ville dans le Proche Orient Ancien* (Cahiers du CEPOA I, Leuven: Peeters, 1983), pp. 219-29.

—'Le raid de Gédéon (Jug 6, 25-32) et l'histoire de l'exclusivisme yahwiste', in Th. Römer (ed.), *Lectio Difficilior Probabilior? FS F. Smyth-Florentin* (DBAT, 12; Heidelberg: Esprint, 1991), pp. 173-205.

—'Erwägungen zu einem vorexilischen Stämmejahwismus', in W. Dietrich and M.A. Klopfenstein (eds.), *Ein Gott allein?* (OBO, 139; Freiburg CH: Universitätsverlag— Vandenhoeck & Ruprecht, 1994), pp. 413-39.

—'Der priesterschriftliche Umgang mit der Jakobsgeschichte', in R.G. Kratz, T. Krüger and K. Schmid (eds.), *Schriftauslegung in der Schrift* (BZAW, 300; Berlin: W. de Gruyter, 2001), pp. 33-60.

—'Situer le cycle de Jacob: Quelques réflexions, vingt-cinq ans plus tard', in A. Wénin (ed.), *Studies in the Book of Genesis: Literature, Redaction and History* (BETL, 155; Leuven: University Press, 2001), pp. 213-41.

Pury, A. de, and Th. Römer, 'Le Pentateuque en question: Position du problème et brève histoire de la recherche', in A. de Pury (ed.), *Le Pentateuque en question* (Genève: Labor et Fides, 1989), pp. 9-80.

Rabin, C., 'Hittite Words in Hebrew', *Orientalia* 32 (1963), pp. 113-39.

Radday, Y.T., and H. Shore, 'An Inquiry into Homogeneity of the Book of Judges by Means of Discriminant Analysis', *Linguistica Biblica* 41/42 (1977), pp. 21-34.

Rainey, A.F., 'Wine from the Royal Vineyards', *BASOR* 245 (1982), pp. 57-62.

—'The Biblical Shephelah of Judah', *BASOR* 251 (1983), pp. 17-23.

Ransome, H., *The Sacred Bee* (London: 1937).

Reade, J., 'Ideology and Propaganda in Assyrian Art', in M.G. Larsen (ed.), *Power and Propaganda* (Mesopotamia, 7; Copenhagen: Akademisk Forlag, 1979), pp. 329-44.

Redditt, P.L., 'Tob', in D.N. Freedman (ed.), *ABD* 6 (New York: Doubleday, 1992), p. 583.

Redford, D.B., *Egypt, Canaan and Israel in Ancient Times* (Princeton: Princeton University Press, 1992).

—'Kush', in D.N. Freedman (ed.), *ABD* 4 (New York: Doubleday, 1992), pp. 109-11.

Reich, R., and B. Brandl, 'Gezer under Assyrian Rule', *PEQ* 117 (1985), pp. 41-54.

Reiner, E., *Šurpu, a Collection of Sumerian and Akkadian Incantations* (AfO Beihefte, 11; Graz: Biblioverlag, 1958).

Reinhartz, A., 'Samson's Mother: An Unnamed Protagonist', in A. Brenner (ed.), *A Feminist Companion to Judges* (Sheffield: JSOT Press, 1993), pp. 157-71.

Rendsburg, G.A., 'The Ammonite Phoneme /T̠/', *BASOR* 269 (1988), pp. 73-79.

—*Diglossa in Ancient Hebrew* (AOS, 72; New Haven, Connecticut: 1990).

—'Confused Language as a Deliberate Literary Device in Biblical Hebrew Narrative', *JHebS* 2 (1999), pp. 1-25.

—'Notes on Israelian Hebrew (II)', *JNSL* 26/1 (2000), pp. 33-45.

Rendtorff, R., *Das überlieferungsgeschichtliche Problem des Pentateuch* (BZAW, 147; Berlin: W. de Gruyter, 1977).

Renger, J., 'Neuassyrische Königsinschriften als Genre der Keilschriftliteratur- Zum Style und zur Kompositionstechnik der Inschriften Sargons II. von Assyrien', in K. Hecker and W. Sommerfeld (eds.), *Keilschriftliche Literaturen: Ausgewählte Vorträge der XXXII. RAI* (BBVO, 6; Berlin: D. Reimer, 1986), pp. 109-28.

Revell, E.J., 'The Battle with Benjamin (Judges XX 29-48) and Hebrew Narrative Techniques', *VT* 35 (1985), pp. 417-33.

Reviv, H., 'The Goverment of Sichem in the El-Amarna Period and in the Days of Abimelech', *IEJ* 16 (1966), pp. 252-57.

—'Elders and Saviors', *OrAnt* 16 (1977), pp. 201-204.

—'The Traditions Concerning the Inception of the Legal System in Israel', *ZAW* 94 (1982), pp. 566-75.

—*The Elders in Ancient Israel* (Jerusalem: Magnes Press, 1989).

Richardson, N.J., *The Homeric Hymn to Demeter* (Oxford: Clarendon Press, 1974).

Richter, W., *Die Bearbeitungen des 'Retterbuches' in der deuteronomischen Epoche* (BBB, 21; Bonn: Peter Hanstein, 1964).

—'Zu den "Richtern Israels" ', *ZAW* 77 (1965), pp. 40-72.

—*Traditionsgeschichtliche Untersuchungen zum Richterbuch* (BBB, 18; Bonn: Peter Hanstein, 1966).

—'Die Überlieferungen um Jephtah: Ri10, 17-12, 6', *Biblica* 47 (1966), pp. 485-556.

Robertson, M., *A History of Greek Art* (Cambridge: Cambridge University Press, 1975).

Rofé, A., 'The Strata of the Law about the Centralisation of Worship and the History of the Deuteronomic Mouvement', in *Congress Volume, Uppsala 1971* (VTSup, 22; Leiden: E.J. Brill, 1972), pp. 221-26.

—'The End of the Book of Joshua According to the Septuagint', *Shnaton* 2 (1977), pp. 217-27.

—'The Acts of Nahash According to 4QSam^a', *IEJ* 32 (1982), pp. 129-33.

—'The History of the Cities of Refuge in Biblical Law', in S. Japhet (ed.), *Studies in the Bible 1986* (SH, 31; Jerusalem: Magnes Press, 1986), pp. 205-39.

—'The Battle of David and Goliath: Folklore, Theology, Eschatology', in J. Neusner, B.A. Levine and E.S. Frerichs (eds.), *Judaic Perspectives on Ancient Israel* (Philadelphia: Fortress Press, 1987), pp. 117-51.

—'Ephraimite versus Deuteronomistic History', in D. Garrone and F. Israel (eds.), *Storia e tradizioni di Israele: Scritti in onore di J. Alberto Soggin* (Brescia: Paideia, 1991), pp. 221-35.

Römer, Th., *Israels Väter* (OBO, 99; Freiburg/Göttingen: Universitätverlag/Vandenhoeck & Ruprecht, 1990).

—'Historiographies et mythes d'origines dans l'Ancien Testament', in M. Detienne (ed.), *Transcrire les mythes* (Paris: Albin Michel, 1994), pp. 142-48.

—'Why Would the Deuteronomists Tell about the Sacrifice of Jephthah's Daughter?', *JSOT* 77 (1998), pp. 27-38.

—'Le livre de Josué: Histoire d'une propagande. Propagande d'une histoire', *FVCb* 37 (1998), pp. 5-20.

—'Pentateuque, Hexateuque et historiographie deutéronomiste: Le problème du début et de la fin du livre de Josué', *Transeuphratène* 16 (1998), pp. 71-86.

Römer, Th., and A. de Pury, 'Deuteronomistic Historiography (DH): History of Research and Debated Issues', in *idem* (eds.), *Israel Constructs its History* (JSOTSup, 306; Sheffield: Sheffield Academic Press, 2000), pp. 24-141.

Römer, W.H., 'Einige Beobachtungen zur Göttin Nininsina', in W. Röllig (ed.), *Lišān miṯḫurti* (AOAT, 1; Neukirchen-Vluyn: Butzon & Bercker Kevelaer, 1969), pp. 279-305.

Römheld, K.F.D., 'Von den Quellen der Kraft (Jdc 13)', *ZAW* 104 (1992), pp. 28-52.

Rose, M., *Deuteronomist und Jahwist: Untersuchungen zu den Berührungspunkten beider Literaturwerke* (ATANT, 67; Zürich: Theologischer Verlag, 1981).

Rose, W.H., *Zemah and Zerubbabel* (JSOTSup, 304; Sheffield: Sheffield Academic Press, 2000).

Rösel, H.N., 'Studien zur Topographie der Kriege in den Büchern Josua und Richter 1', *ZDPV* 91 (1975), pp. 159-91.

—'Studien zur Topographie der Kriege in den Büchern Josua und Richter 2', *ZDPV* 92 (1976), pp. 10-46.

—'Die Überleitungen vom Josua- zum Richterbuch', *VT* 30 (1980), pp. 342-50.

—'Jephthah und das Problem der Richter', *Biblica* 61 (1980), pp. 251-556.

—'Das "Negative Besitzverzeichnis" -Traditiongeschichtliche und historische Überlegungen-', in M. Augustin (ed.), *'Wünschet Jerusalem Frieden'* (Frankfurt: Peter Lang, 1986), pp. 121-34.

—'Ehud und die Ehuderzählung', in M. Weippert and S. Timm (eds.), *Meilenstein* (ÄAT, 30, Wiesbaden: Harrassowitz, 1995), pp. 225-33.

Rosenblatt, N.H., 'Esther and Samson: Portraits in Heroism', *BR* 15 (1999), pp. 20-25, 47.

Rosenthal, F., *Grammaire d'araméen biblique* (Sessions de langues bibliques, 19; Paris: Beauchesne, 1988).

Roth, M.T., *Laws Collections from Mesopotamia and Asia Minor* (Atlanta: Scholars Press, 1994).

—'The Laws of Eshnunna', in W.W. Hallo (ed.), *CoS* 2 (Leiden: E.J. Brill, 2000), pp. 332-35.

—'The Middle Assyrian Laws', in W.W. Hallo (ed.), *CoS* 2 (Leiden: E.J. Brill, 2000), pp. 353-60.

Routledge, B., *Assyrian Imperialism and the Political Economy of Agricultural Change* (Atlanta: SBL, 1992).

—'Learning to Love the King: Urbanism and the State in Iron Age Moab', in W.E. Aufrecht, *et al.* (eds.), *Urbanism in Antiquity* (JSOTSup, 244; Sheffield: JSOT Press, 1997), pp. 130-44.

Rudman, D., 'A Note on the Personal Name Amon', *Biblica* 81 (2000), pp. 403-405.

—'The Second Bull in Judges 6.25-28', *JNSL* 26 (2000), pp. 97-103.

Sader, H., 'Tell Burak: An Unidentified City of Phoenician Sidon', in B. Pongratz-Leisten, H. Kühne and P. Xella (eds.), *Ana šadī Labnāni lū allik: Beiträge zu altorientalischen und mittelmeerischen Kulturen: Festschrift für Wolfgang Röllig* (Kevelaer/Neukirchen-Vluyn: Butzon & Bercker/Neukirchener, 1997), pp. 363-78.

Saggs, H.W.F., 'The Nimrud Letters, 1952 Part II', *Iraq* 17 (1952), pp. 126-60.

—*The Might That Was Assyria* (London: 1984).

—'Additions to Anzû', *AfO* 33 (1986), pp. 1-29.

Salonen, A., *Jagd und Jagdtiere in alten Mesopotamien* (AASF, B 196; Helsinki: Suomalainen tiedeakatemia, 1976).

Sasson, J.M., 'Circumcision in the Ancient Near East', *JBL* 85 (1966), pp. 473-76.

—'Yarim-Lim's Declaration of War', in J.-M. Durand and J.-R. Kupper (eds.), *Miscellanea Babyloniaca: Melanges offerts à Maurice Birot* (Paris: Recherches sur les Civilisations, 1985), pp. 237-55.

—'Yarim-Lim Takes the Grand Tour', *BA* 47 (1986), pp. 246-51.

—'Who Cut Samson's Hair? (And Other Trifling Issues Raised by Judg. 16?)', *Prooftexts* 8 (1988), pp. 330-39.

—'Time... to Begin', in M. Fishbane *et al.* (eds.), *'Sha'arei Talmon': Studies in the Bible, Qumran and the Ancient Near East* (Winona Lake: Eisenbrauns, 1992), pp. 183-94.

—'Origins and Media: Creation Narratives in the Ancient Israel and in Mesopotamia', in L.J. Bord and P. Skubiszewski (eds.), *La création, liberté de dieu et liberté de l'homme dans les récits bibliques* (Paris: Cariscript, 2001).

Sasson, V., 'Murderers, Usurpers, or what? Hazael, Jehu, and the Tell Dan Old Aramaic Inscription', *UF* 28 (1996), pp. 547-54.

Satterthwaite, P.E., 'Narrative Artistry in the Composition of Judges xx 29ff.', *VT* 42 (1992), pp. 80-9.

—' "No King in Israel": Narrative Criticism and Judges 17-21', *TynBul* 44 (1993), pp. 75-88.

Sauer, G. *Jesus ben Sirach* (JSHRZ, 3.5; Gütersloh: G. Mohn, 1981).

Schenker, A., 'Gelübde im Alten Testament: Unbeachtete Aspekte', *VT* 39 (1989), pp. 87-91.

Schiffman, L.H., 'The Laws of Vows and Oaths (Num 30, 3-16) in the Zadokite Fragments and the Temple Scroll', *Revue de Qumran* 15 (1991), pp. 199-214.

Schley, D.G., *Shiloh: A Biblical City in Tradition and History* (JSOTSup, 63; Sheffield: Sheffield Academic Press, 1989).

Schmid, H.H., *Der sogenannte Jahwist: Beobartungen und Fragen zur Pentateuchforschung* (Zürich: Theologischer Verlag, 1976).

Schmid, K., *Erzväter und Exodus: Untersuchungen zur doppelten Begründung der Urspünge Israels innerhalb der Geschichtsbücher des Alten Testaments* (WMANT, 81; Neukirchen-Vluyn: Neukirchener Verlag, 1999).

Schmidt, L., *Studien zu Tradition, Interpretation und Historie in Überlieferungen von Gideon, Saul und David* (WMANT, 38; 1970).

Schmidt, W.H., *Königtum Gottes in Ugarit und Israel: Zur Herkunft der Königsprädikation Jahwes* (BZAW, 80; Berlin: Töpelmann, 1966).

Schmitt, H.-C., 'Das Hesbonlied Num 21, 27ab-30 und die Geschichte der Stadt Hesbon', *ZDPV* 104 (1988), pp. 26-43.

Schneider, T., 'Did Jehu Kill his Own Family?', *BARev* (1995), pp. 26-34.

Schniedewind, W.M., 'The Source Citations of Manasseh: King Manasseh in History and Homely', *VT* 41 (1991), pp. 452-61.

—'History and Interpretation: The Religion of Ahab and Manasseh in the Book of Kings', *CBQ* 55 (1993), pp. 649-61.

Schorch, S., 'Der Name des Gottes von et-Tell/Beth Saida', *BN* 103 (2000), pp. 36-38.

Schulz, A., *Das Buch der Richter und das Buch Ruth* (Bonn: Peter Hanstein, 1926).

Schunck, K.-D., *Benjamin: Untersuchungen zur Entstehung und Geschichte eines israelitischen Stammes* (BZAW, 86; Berlin: Töpelmann, 1963).

—'Wo lag Har Heres?', in *idem* (ed.), *Altes Testament und Heiliges Land,* 1 (BEAT, 17; Frankfurt am Main: Lang, 1989), pp. 177-81.

—'Falsche Richter im Richterbuch', in R. Liwak (ed.), *Prophetie und geschichtliche Wirklichkeit im alten Israel* (Stuttgart: Kohlhammer, 1991), pp. 364-70.

Schüpphaus, J., *Richter—und Prophetengeschichten als Glieder der Geschichtsdarstellung der Richter—und Koenigszeit* (Thesis Bonn: 1967).

Schwegler, H., 'Aufstieg und Fall eines Gewaltmenschen: Abimelech (Richter 9)', in Bauer and Meissner (eds.), *Männer weinen heimlich* (Stuttgart: Katholisches Bibelwerk, 1993), pp. 46-59.

Second, A., *Le Cantique de Débora* (Genève: 1900).

Seebass, H., 'Das Haus Joseph in Jos 17, 14-18', *ZDPV* 98 (1982), pp. 70-76.

Segert, S., 'Paronomasia in the Samson Narrative', *VT* 34 (1984), pp. 254-461.

Servier, J., *Les portes de l'année: Rites et symboles: L'Algérie dans la tradition méditerranéenne* (Les voies de l'homme, Paris: Lafont, 1962).

Seux, M.-J., *Hymnes et prières aux dieux de Babylone et d'Assyrie* (LAPO, 8; Paris: Cerf, 1976).

Shiloh, Y., 'Megiddo', in E. Stern (ed.), *NEAEHL* (Jerusalem: Israel Exploration Society and Carta, 1993), pp. 1003-23.

Shupak, N., 'New Light on Shamgar ben Anath', *Biblica* 70 (1989), pp. 517-25.

Siegert, F., 'L'Héraclès des Juifs', in M.-M. Mactoux and E. Geny (eds.), *Discours religieux dans l'Antiquité: Actes du colloque—Besançon 27-28 janvier 1995* (Paris: Belles Lettres, 1995), pp. 151-76.

Silver, M., *Prophets and Markets: The Political Economy of Ancient Israel* (Boston: Kluwer-Nijhoff, 1983).

Sima, A., 'Nochmals zur Deutung des hebräischen Namens Otniel', *BN* 106 (2001), pp. 47-51.

Simon, U., 'Samson and the Heroic', in M. Wadsworth (ed.), *Ways of Reading the Bible* (London: Sussex, 1981), pp. 154-67.

Simons, J., *Geographical and Topographical Texts of the Old Testament* (SFS, 2; Leiden: E.J. Brill, 1959).

Simpson, C.A., *Composition of the Book of Judges* (Oxford: 1957).

Singer, S.F., 'Is the Cultic Installation at Dan really an Olive Press?', *BaRev* 10.6 (1984), pp. 52-58.

Sladek, W.R., 'Inanna's Descent to the Nether World' (J. Hopkins University Dissertation 1974; Ann Arbor, MI: University Microfilms, 1979).

Smelik, K.A.D., *Converting the Past: Studies in Ancient Israelite and Moabite Historiography* (OTS, 28; Leiden: E.J. Brill, 1992).

—'The Inscription of King Mesha', in W.W. Hallo (ed.), *CoS* 2 (Leiden: E.J. Brill, 2000), pp. 137-38.

Smelik, W.F., *The Targum of Judges* (Leiden: E.J. Brill, 1995).

Smend, R., 'Das Gesetz und die Völker: Ein Beitrag zur deuteronomischen Redaktiongeschichte', in H.W. Wolff (ed.), *Probleme biblischer Theologie* (München: Chr. Kaiser Verlag, 1971), pp. 494-509.

Smith, C., 'Samson and Delilah: A Parable of Power?', *JSOT* 76 (1997), pp. 45-57.

Smith, M., *Palestinian Parties and Politics That Shaped the Old Testament* (London: SCM, 1987).

Smith, M.S., 'The Near Eastern Background of Solar Language for Yahweh', *JBL* 109 (1990), pp. 29-39.

Smyth-Florentin, F., 'When Josiah Has Done his Work or the King Is Properly Buried: A Synchronic Reading of 2 Kings 22.1–23.28', in A. de Pury and Th. Römer (eds.), *Israel Constructs its History* (JSOTSup, 306; Sheffield: Sheffield Academic Press, 2000), pp. 343-58.

—'La Bible, mythe fondateur', in M. Detienne (ed.), *Tracés de fondation* (Bibliothèque de l'école des hautes études, XCIII; Louvain/Paris: Peeters, 1990), pp. 59-66.

Soden, J.M., *Prose and Poetry Compared: Judges 4 and 5 in their Ancient Near Eastern Context* (Ann Abor, MI: University Microfilms, 1990).

Soggin, J.A., *Judges* (London: SCM Press, 1981).

—'Problemi di storia e di storiographia nell'antico Israele', *Henoch* 4 (1982), pp. 1-16.

—'The Migdal Temple, Migdal Sekem Judg 9 and the Artifact of Mount Ebal', in M. Augustin *et al.* (eds.), *"Wünschet Jerusalem Frieden"* (Frankfurt am Main: Lang, 1988), pp. 115-20.

—'Ehud und Eglon: Bemerkungen zu Richter III 11b-31', *VT* 39 (1989), pp. 95-100.

Spalinger, A., 'The Year 712 B.C. and its Implications for Egyptian History', *JARCE* 10 (1973), pp. 95-101.

—'The Foreign Policy of Egypt Preceding the Assyrian Conquest', *CE* 105 (1978), pp. 22-47.

Sparks, K.L., *Ethnicity and Identity in Ancient Israel: Prolegomena to the Study of Ethnic Sentiments and their Expression in the Hebrew Bible* (Winona Lake: Eisenbrauns, 1998).

Spieckermann, H., *Juda unter Assur in der Sargonidenzeit* (FRLANT, 129; Göttingen: Vandenhoeck und Ruprecht, 1982).

Spina, F.A., 'Eli's Seat: The Transition from Priest to Prophet in 1 Samuel 1-4', *JSOT* 62 (1994), pp. 67-75.

Stager, L.E., 'The Finest Olive Oil in Samaria', *JSS* 28 (1983), pp. 241-45.

—'Archeology, Ecology and Social History: Background Themes to the Song of Deborah', in J.A. Emerton (ed.), *Congress Volume, Jerusalem 1986* (VTSup, XL; Leiden: E.J. Brill, 1988), pp. 221-34.

Stähli, H.P., *Solare Elemente im Jahweglauben des Alten Testaments* (OBO, 66; Freiburg/Göttingen: Universitätsverlag/Vandenhoeck & Ruprecht, 1985).

Stahn, H., *Die Simsonsage* (Göttingen: Vandenhoeck & Ruprecht, 1922).

Standaert, B., 'Adonai Shalom (Judges 6-9)', in S.E. Porter and T.H. Olbricht (eds.), *Rhetoric, Scripture and Theology* (JSOTSup, 131; Sheffield: JSOT Press, 1996), pp. 195-202.

Stantley, R.S., and R.T. Alexander, 'The Political Economy of Core-Periphery Systems', in E.M. Schortman and P.A. Urban (eds.), *Resources, Power and Interregional Interaction* (New York: Plenum Press, 1992), pp. 23-49.

Steeger, W.P., 'Sheshan (person)', in D.N. Freedman (ed.), *ABD* 5 (New York: Doubleday, 1992), p. 1207.

Steinberg, N., 'Social Scientific Criticism: Judges 9 and Issues of Kinship', in G.A. Yee (ed.), *Judges and Method: New Approaches in Biblical Studies* (Minneapolis: Fortress, 1995), pp. 45-64.

—'The Problem of Human Sacrifice in War: An Analysis of Judges 11', in S.L. Cook and S.C. Winter (eds.), *On the Way to Nineveh* (Atlanta: Scholars Press, 1999), pp. 114-35.

Stern, E., 'The Dor Province in the Persian Period in the Light of the Recent Excavations at Dor', *Transeuphratène* 2 (1990), pp. 147-55.

—'Mesad Hashavyahu', in D.N. Freedman (ed.), *ABD* 4 (New York: Doubleday, 1992), p. 706.

—'The Many Masters of Dor. I—When Canaanites Became Phoenician Sailors', *BARev* 19 (1993), pp. 22-31.

—'The Babylonian Gap', *BARev* 26/6 (2000), pp. 45-51.

Stipp, H.-J., 'Simson, der Nasiräer', *VT* 45 (1995), pp. 337-69.

Stohlmann, S., 'The Judean Exile after 701 B.C.E.', in W.W. Hallo, J.C. Moyer and L.G. Perdue (eds.), *Scripture in Context. II. More Essays on the Comparative Method* (Winona Lake: Eisenbrauns, 1983), pp. 147-75.

Stolz, F., 'Monotheismus in Israel', in O. Keel (ed.), *Monotheismus im Alten Israel und seiner Umwelt* (BibB, 14; Fribourg: Schweizerisches katholisches Bibelwerk, 1980), pp. 143-84.

Stone, K., *Sex, Honor and Power in the Deuteronomist History* (JSOTSup, 234; Sheffield: Sheffield Academic Press, 1996).

Strange, J., 'The Inheritance of Dan', *ST* 20 (1966), pp. 120-39.

Streck, M.P., and S. Weninger, 'Zur Deutung des hebraïschen Namens Otniel', *BN* 96 (1999), pp. 21-29.

Strong, J.T., 'Tyre's Isolationist Policies in the Early Sixth Century BCE: Evidence from the Prophets', *VT* 47 (1997), pp. 207-19.

Studer, G.L., *Das Buch der Richter* (Bern: 1835).

Suárez de la Torre, E., 'El viaje noctorno del sol y la Nanno de Mimnermo', *EC* 27 (1985), p. 5ff.

Sulzberger, M., *The AM HA-ARETZ: The Ancient Hebrew Parliament* (Philadelphia: 1909).

Sweeney, M.A., 'Davidic Polemics in the Book of Judges', *VT* 47 (1997), pp. 517-29.

Swiggers, P., 'The Word Shibbolet in Jud. XII 6', *JSS* 26 (1981), pp. 205-207.

Taagpera, R., 'Size and Duration of Empires: Growth-Decline Curves, 3000 to 600 B.C.', *SoSR* 7 (1978), pp. 180-96.

Tadmor, H., 'A Note on the Seal of Mannu-ki-Inurta', *IEJ* 15 (1965), pp. 233-34.

—'Philistia under Assyrian Rule', *BA* XXIX (1966), pp. 86-102.

—*The Inscriptions of Tiglath-pileser III King of Assyria* (Jerusalem: 1994).

Tadmor, H., B. Landsberger and S. Parpola, 'The Sin of Sargon and Sennakerib's Last Will', *SAAB* 3 (1989), pp. 3-51.

Talmon, S., 'The New Hebrew Letter from the 7th C. BC in Historical Perspective', *BASOR* 176 (1964), pp. 29-38.

—'The Judean 'am ha'ares in Historical Perspective', in *4th World Congress of Jewish Studies* 1 (Jerusalem: Magnes Press, 1967), pp. 71-76.

— ' "In jenen Tagen gab es keinen mlk in Israel" (Ri 18–21)', in *idem* (ed.), *Gesellschaft und Literatur in der Hebräischen Bibel* 1 (Neukirchen-Vluyn: Neukirchen Verlag, 1988), pp. 44-55.

Taylor, J.G., *Yahweh and the Sun* (JSOTSup, 111; Sheffield: 1993).

—'A Response to Steve A. Wiggins, Yahweh: The God of Sun?', *JSOT* 71 (1996), pp. 107-19.

Täubler, E., *Biblische Studien: Die Epoche der Richter* (Tübingen: J.C.B. Mohr, 1958).

Teixidor, J., 'L'assembée législative en Phénicie d'après les inscriptions', *Syria* 62 (1980), pp. 453-64.

—'La fonction de RAB et de suffète en Phénicie', *Semitica* 29 (1979), pp. 9-17.

Theon, A., *Progymnasmata* (trans. M. Patillon and G. Bolognesi; Budé, Paris: Belles Lettres, 1997).

Thiel, W., 'HEFER BERIT: Zum Bundbrechen im Alten Testament', *VT* 20 (1970), pp. 214-29.

Thiele, E.R., *The Mysterious Numbers of the Hebrew Kings* (Grand Rapids: Eerdman, 1965).

Thompson, H.O., 'Kamon', in D.N. Freedman (ed.), *ABD* 4 (New York: Doubleday, 1992), p. 5.

Thompson, T.L., 'Text, Context and Referent in Israelite Historiography', in D. Edelman (ed.), *The Fabric of History* (JSOTSup, 127; Sheffield: JSOT Press, 1991), pp. 65-92.

Thureau-Dangin, F., *Rituels accadiens* (Paris: E. Leroux, 1921).

Timm, S., *Die Dynastie Omri: Quellen und Untersuchungen zur Geschichte Israels im 9. Jahrhundert vor Christus* (FRLANT, 124; Göttingen: Vandenhoeck & Ruprecht, 1982).

—*Moab zwischen den Mächten: Studien zu historischen Denkmälern und Texten* (ÄAT, 17; Wiesbaden: Otto Harrassowitz, 1989).

Toews, W.I., 'Luz', in D.N. Freedman (ed.), *ABD* 4 (New York: Doubleday, 1992), p. 420.

Tollington, J.E., *Tradition and Innovation in Haggai and Zechariah 1-8* (Sheffield: 1993).

—'The Book of Judges: The Result of Post-Exilic Exegesis?', in J.C. de Moor (ed.),

Intertextuality in Ugarit and Israel (*OTS*, XL, Leiden: E.J. Brill, 1998), pp. 186-96.

Török, L., *The Kingdom of Kush: Handbook of the Napatan-Meroitic Civilisation* (HdO, I.XXXI; Leiden: E.J. Brill, 1997).

Tournay, R.J., 'Polémique antisamaritaine et le feu du *Tofet*', *RB* 104 (1997), pp. 354-67.

—'Les relectures du psaume 110 (109) et l'allusion à Gédéon', *RB* 105 (1998), pp. 321-31.

Tov, E., 'The Growth of the Book of Joshua in the Light of the Evidence of the LXX Translation', in S. Japhet (ed.), *Studies in the Bible 1986* (SH, 31; Jerusalem: Magnes Press, 1986), pp. 321-39.

—'The Septuagint', in M.J. Mulder (ed.), *Mikra: Text, Translation, Reading and Interpretation of the Hebrew Bible in Ancient Judaism and Early Christianity* (CRINT, 2; Assen/Philadelphia: Van Gorcum/Fortress Press, 1988), pp. 159-88.

Treacey-Cole, D.I., 'Perea', in D.N. Freedman (ed.), *ABD* 5 (New York: Doubleday, 1992), pp. 224-25.

Trebolle Barrera, J.C., 'Textual Variants in 4QJudg*a* and the Textual and Editorial History of the Book of Judges', *RQ* 54 (1989), pp. 229-45.

—'Edition préliminaire de 4QJuges*b*: Contribution des manuscrits qumraniens des juges à l'étude textuelle et littéraire du livre', *RQ* 15 (1991), pp. 79-100.

—'Light from 4QJudg*a* and 4QKgs on the Text of Judges and Kings', in D. Dimant and U. Rappaport (eds.), *The Dead Sea Scrolls* (STDJ, 10; Leiden: E.J. Brill, 1992), pp. 315-24.

—'Textual Affiliation of the Old Latin Marginal Readings in the Books of Judges and Kings', in G. Braulik *et al.* (eds.), *Biblische Theologie und gesellschaftlicher Wandel* (Freiburg: Herder, 1993), pp. 315-29.

Tropper, J., 'Die Shibbolet-Falle (Richter 12, 6)', *ZAH* 10 (1997), pp. 198-200.

Tsevat, M., 'Two Old Testament Stories and their Hittite Analogues', *JAOS* 103 (1983), pp. 35-42.

—'Die Namengebung Samuels und die Substitutionstheorie', *ZAW* 99 (1987), pp. 250-54.

Tsumura, D.T., 'Bedan, a Copyist's Error? (1 Samuel XII 11)', *VT* 45 (1995), pp. 122-23.

Tur-Sinai, N.H., *The Book of Job* (Jerusalem: 1967).

Turkowsky, L., 'Peasant Agriculture in the Judean Hills', *PEQ* 101 (1969), pp. 24-46.

Tyrrell, W.B., *Amazons: A Study in Athenian Mythmaking* (Baltimore: The Johns Hopkins University Press, 1984).

Uehlinger, C., 'Nimrod', in K. Van der Toorn, B. Becking and P.W. van der Horst (eds.), *DDD* (Leiden: E.J. Brill, 1995), pp. 1181-86.

—'Gab es eine joschijanische Kultreform? Plädoyer für ein begründetes Minimum', in W. Gross (ed.), *Jeremia und die 'deuteronomistische Bewegung'* (BBB, 98; Weinheim: Beltz Athenäums, 1995), pp. 57-89.

Unger, E., 'Fuchs', in *Reallexikon der Assyriologie* 3 (Berlin: W. de Gruyter, 1957), p. 119.

Ungnad, A., 'Die Zahl der von Sanherib deportierten Judäer', *ZAW* 59 (1941), pp. 199-202.

Unterman, J., 'The Literary Influence of "the Binding of Isaac" (Genesis 22) on "the Outrage at Gibeah" (Judges 19)', *HAR* 4 (1980), pp. 161-66.

Ussishkin, D., 'The Water Systems of Jerusalem during Hezekiah's Reign', in M. Weippert and S. Timm (eds.), *Meilenstein* (ÄAT, 30, Wiesbaden: Harrassowitz, 1995), pp. 289-307.

Utzschneider, H., *Hosea, Prophet vor dem Ende. Zum Verhältnis von Geschichte und Institution in der alttestamentlichen Prophetie* (OBO, 31; Freiburg/Göttingen: Universitätsverlag/Vandenhoeck & Ruprecht, 1980).

Van Daalen, A.G., *Simson: Een onder zoek naar de plaats, de opbouw en de funktie van het Simsonverhaal in het kader van de oudtestamentische geschiedschrijving* (Assen: 1966).

Van der Hart, R., 'The Camp of Dan and the Camp of Yahweh', *VT* 25 (1975), pp. 720-28.

Vanderhooft, D.S., 'Dwelling beneath the Sacred Place: A Proposal for Reading 2 Samuel 7.10', *JBL* 118 (1999), pp. 625-33.

Van der Kooij, A., 'Das assyrische Heer vor den Mauern Jerusalems im Jahr 701 v. Chr', *ZDPV* 102 (1986), pp. 93-109.

— ' "And I also Said": A New Interpretation of Judges II 3', *VT* 45 (1995), pp. 294-306.

Van der Toorn, K., 'Judges XVI 21 in the Light of the Akkadian Sources', *VT* 36 (1986), pp. 248-51.

—'Female Prostitution in Payment for Vows in Ancient Israel', *JBL* 108 (1989), pp. 193-205.

—'Shimige', in K. Van der Toorn, B. Becking and P.W. van der Horst (eds.), *DDD* (Leiden: E.J. Brill, 1995), pp. 1462-64.

Van der Toorn, K., and P.W van der Horst, 'Nimrod before and after the Bible', *HTR* 83 (1990), pp. 1-29.

Van Dijk, P., *Lugal ud me-lám-bi nir-gá : le récit épique et didactique des travaux de Ninurta, du Déluge et de la Nouvelle Création* (Leiden: E.J. Brill, 1983).

Van Dyk, P.J., 'A Folkloristic Approach to the Old Testament', *OTE* 7 (1994), pp. 92-98.

Van Keulen, P.S.F., *Manasseh through the Eyes of the Deuteronomists* (OS, XXXVIII; Leiden: E.J. Brill, 1996).

Van Leeuwen, C., 'Sanchérib devant Jérusalem' (ed. Boer; OTS, 14; Leiden: E.J. Brill, 1965), pp. 245-72.

Van Midden, P., 'Broederschap en Koningschap: Een onderzoek naar de betekenis van Gideon en Abimelek in het boek Richteren' (PhD dissertation; Amsterdam: 1998).

Van Selms, A., 'The Best Man and Bride—From Sumer to St John with a New Interpretation of Judges 14-15', *JNES* 9 (1950), pp. 65-75.

Van Seters, J., *Abraham in History and Tradition* (New Haven/London: 1975).

—*In Search of History: Historiography in the Ancient World and the Origins of Biblical History* (New Haven/London: Yale University Press, 1983).

—'Joshua 24 and the Problem of Tradition in the Old Testament', in W.B. Barrick and J.R. Spencer (eds.), *In the Shelter of Elyon* (JSOTSup, 31; Sheffield: Sheffield Academic Press, 1984), pp. 139-58.

Vanstiphout, H., 'The Importance of "The Tale of the Fox" ', *AS* 10 (1988), pp. 191-228.

Vater Solomon, A.M., 'Fable', in G.W. Coats (ed.), *Saga, Legend, Tale, Novella, Fable* (JSOTSup, 35; Sheffield: JSOT Press, 1985), pp. 114-25.

—'Jehoash's Fable of the Thistle and the Cedar', in G.W. Coats (ed.), *Saga, Legend, Tale, Novella, Fable* (JSOTSup, 35; Sheffield: University Press, 1985), pp. 126-32.

Vattioni, F., 'I sigilli ebraici', *Biblica* 50 (1969), pp. 357-88.

Vaux, R. de, *Les institutions de l'A.T. 1* (Paris: 1958).

—'Le sens de l'expression "peuple du pays" dans l'Ancien Testament et le rôle politique du peuple en Israël', *RA* 58 (1964), pp. 177-73.

—*The Early History of Israel* (Philadelphia: 1978).

Veijola, T., *Das Königstum in der Beurteilung der deuteronomistischen Historiographie: Eine redaktionsgeschichtliche Untersuchung* (AASF, 198; Helsinki: Suomalainen Tiedeakatemia, 1977).

Verbruggen, H., *Le Zeus crétois* (Paris: Belles Lettres, 1981).

Verkinderen, F., 'Les cités phéniciennes dans l'Empire d'Alexandre le Grand', in E. Lipinski (ed.), *Phoenicia and the East Mediterranean in theFirst Millennium B.C.* (SP, 5; Leuven: Peeters, 1987), pp. 287-308.

Vernus, P., 'Inscriptions de la troisième période intermédiaire', *BIFAO* 75 (1975), pp. 1-73.

Vincent, A., *Le livre des Juges: Le livre de Ruth* (Paris: Cerf, 1952).
Vincent, M.A., 'The Song of Deborah: A Structural and Literary Consideration', *JSOT* 91 (2000), pp. 61-82.
Virgil, *Georgics* (trans. R.A.B. Mynors; Oxford: Clarendon Press, 1990).
Vollborn, W., 'Die Chronologie des Richterbuches', in J. Herrmann (ed.), *Festschrift Friedrich Baumgärtel* (EF, A 10; Erlangen: Universitätsbund, 1959), pp. 192-96.
Von Oppenheim, M., *Tell Halaf: A New Culture in Oldest Mesopotamia* (London: Putnam's Sons, 1937).
Von Rad, G., *Theologie des Alten Testaments* (München: Chr. Kaiser Verlag, 1957).
Von Soden, W., 'Gibt es Hinweise auf die Ermordung Sanheribs in Ninurta-Tempel (wohl) in Kalah in Texten aus Assyria?', *NABU* (1990), pp. 16-17.
Von Weiher, E., *Spätebabylonische Texte aus Uruk,* II (ADFU, 10; Berlin: Mann, 1983).
Wallis, G., 'Eine Parallele zu Richter 19, 29ff. und 1 Sam. 11.5ff. aus dem Briefarchiv von Mari', *ZAW* 64 (1952), pp. 57-61.
Walters, S.D., 'Saul of Gibeon', *JSOT* 52 (1991), pp. 61-76.
Waltisberg, M., 'Zum Alter der Sprache des Deboraliedes Ri 5*', *ZAH* 12 (1999), pp. 218-32.
Wapnish, P., 'Lions', in E.M. Meyers (ed.), *The Oxford Encyclopedia of Archeology in the Near East* (New York: Oxford University Press, 1997), pp. 361-62.
Washburn, D.L., 'The Chronology of Judges: Another Look', *BSac* 147 (1990), pp. 414-25.
Wächter, L., 'Zur Lokalisierung des sichemitischen Baumheiligtums', *ZDPV* 103 (1987), pp. 1-12.
Webb, B.G., *The Book of Judges: An Integrated Reading* (JSOTSup, 46; Sheffield: JSOT Press, 1987).
Wehrle, J., 'Josef', in M. Görg and B. Lang (eds.), *NBL* 2 (Zürich: Benziger, 1995), pp. 385-7.
Weidner, E., *Die Inschriften Tukulti-Ninurta I und seiner Nachfolger* (AfO Beihefte, 12; Graz: 1959).
Weiher, E. von, *Spätbabylonische Texte aus Uruk Teil II* (BF, 10; Mainz: Ph. von Zabern, 1983).
Weinfeld, M., 'The Period of the Conquest and of the Judges as Seen by the Earliest and the Later Sources', *VT* 17 (1967), pp. 93-113.
—*Deuteronomy and Deuteronomistic School* (Oxford: Clarendon Press, 1972).
—'Judges and Officer in the Ancient Near East and in Ancient Israel', *IOS* 7 (1977), pp. 65-88.
—'Judges 1.1-2.5: The Conquest under the Leadership of the House of Judah', in A.G. Auld (ed.), *Understanding Poets and Prophets* (JSOTSup, 152; Sheffield: Sheffield Academic Press, 1993), pp. 388-400.
Weippert, M., *The Settlement of the Israelite Tribes in Palestine* (London: SCM Press, 1971).
Weippert, H., 'Das geographische System der Stämme Israels', *VT* 23 (1973), pp. 76-89.
Weiser, A., *Einleitung in das Alte Testament* (Göttingen: Vandenhoeck & Ruprecht, 1949).
Weissert, E., 'Creating a Political Climate: Literary Allusions to Enuma Elish in Sennacherib's Account of the Battle of Halule', in H. Waetzoldt and H. Hauptmann (eds.), *Assyrien im Wandel der Zeiten. XXXIXe RAI* (HSAO, 6; Heidelberg: Heidelberger Orientverlag, 1997), pp. 191-202.
Weitzman, S., 'Reopening the Case of the Suspiciously Suspended Nun in Judges 18.30', *CBQ* 61 (1999), pp. 448-60.
Weldon, F., 'Samson and his Women', in C. Büchmann and C. Spiegel (eds.), *Out of the Garden: Women Writers on the Bible* (London: Pandora, 1995), pp. 72-81.

Wellhausen, J., *Die Composition des Hexateuchs und der historischen Bücher des Alten Testaments* (Berlin: G. Reimer, 1876).

—'Einleitung in das Alte Testament von Friedrich Bleek', in J. Bleek and A. Kamphausen (eds.), *Einleitung in das Alte Testament von Friedrich Bleek* (Berlin: G. Reimer, 1878), pp. 1-5.152-267.547-656.

Welten, P., *Geschichte und Geschichtsdarstellung in der Chronikbüchern* (WMANT, 42; Neukirchen-Vluyn: Neukirchener Verlag, 1973).

Wenning, R., and E. Zenger, 'Der siebenlockige Held Simson: Literarische und ikonographische Beobartungen zu Ri 13-16', *BN* 17 (1982), pp. 43-55.

Wessels, J.P.H., ' "Postmodern" Rhethoric and the Former Prophetic Literature', in S.E. Porter *et al.* (ed.), *Rhetoric, Scripture and Theology* (JSOTSup, 131; Sheffield: Sheffield Academic Press, 1996), pp. 182-94.

—'Persuasions in Judges 2.20-3.6: A Celebration of Differences', in S.E. Porter and T.H. Olbricht (eds.), *The Rhetorical Analysis of Scripture* (JSNTSup, 146; Sheffield: JSOT Press, 1997), pp. 120-36.

West, M.J., *The East Face of Helicon* (Oxford: Clarendon Press, 1997).

Westenholz, J.G., *Legends of the Kings of Akkade* (Mesopotamian Civilizations, 7; Winona Lake: Eisenbrauns, 1997).

Westermann, C., *Die Geschichtsbücher des Alten Testaments: Gab es ein deuteronomistisches Geschichtwerk?* (TBü, 87 [AT]; Güterloh: Chr. Kaiser Verlag, 1994).

Wharton, J.A., 'The Secret of Yahweh: Story and Affirmation in Judges 13-16', *Int* 27 (1973), pp. 48-66.

Whitelam, K.W., *The Just King: Monarchic Judicial Authority in Ancient Israel* (JSOTSup, 12; Sheffield: JSOT Press, 1979).

Whitley, C.F., 'The Sources of the Gideon Stories', *VT* 7 (1957), pp. 157-64.

Whitt, W.D., 'The Divorce of Yhwh and Asherah', *SJOT* 6 (1992), pp. 31-67.

Wiese, K., 'Zur Literarkritik des Buches der Richter', in S. Prank and K. Wiese (eds.), *Studien zu Ezechiel und dem Buch der Richter* (BWANT, 40; Stuttgart: Kohlhammer, 1926), pp. 1-61.

Wilcke, C., 'Philologische Bemerckungen zum Rat des *Shurruppag* und Versuch einer neuen Übersetzung', *ZA* 68 (1978), pp. 231-32.

Williams, J.G., 'The Structure of Judges 2.6-16.31', *JSOT* 49 (1991), pp. 77-85.

Willis, T.M., 'The Nature of Jephthah's Authority', *CBQ* 59 (1997), pp. 33-44.

Wiseman, D.J., 'The Vassal Treaties of Esarhaddon', *Iraq* 20 (1958), pp. 1-99.

—*Chronicles of the Chaldean Kings* (London: British Museum Publications, 1974).

—*Nebuchadrezzar and Babylon* (Oxford: Oxford University Press, 1985).

Wissert, E., 'Royal Hunt and Royal Triumph in a Prism Fragment of Ashurbanipal', in S. Parpola and R.M. Whiting (eds.), *Assyria 1995* (Helsinki: The Neo-Assyrian Text Corpus Project, 1995), pp. 354-55.

Wissowa, G., 'Cerialia', in A.F. von Pauly and G. Wissowa (eds.), *PW III.2* (Stuttgart: A. Druckenmüller, 1899), pp. 1980-81.

Witte, M., 'Wie Samson in den Kanon kam', *ZAW* 112 (2000), pp. 526-49.

Wolff, H.-W., 'Hoseas geistige Heimat', *TZ* 81 (1956), pp. 83-94.

Wonneberger, R., *Redaktion: Studien zur Textfortschreibung im Alten Testament, entwickelt am Beispiel der Samuel-Überlieferung* (FRLANT, 156; Göttingen: Vandenhoeck & Ruprecht, 1992).

Wright, G.E., 'The Literary and Historical Problem of Joshua 10 and Judges 1', *JNES* 5 (1946), pp. 105-14.

Würthwein, E., *Der 'amm ha'aretz im Alten Testament* (BWANT, 17; Stuttgart: 1936).

—'Erwägungen zum sog. deuteronomistischen Geschichtswerk', in E. Würthwein (ed.), *Studien zum deuteronomistischen Geschichtswerk* (BZAW, 227; Berlin: W. de Gruyter, 1994), pp. 1-11.

—'Abimelech und der Untergang Sichems—Studien zu Jdc 9', in E. Würthwein (ed.), *Studien zum deuteronomistischen Geschichtswerk* (BZAW, 227; Berlin: W. de Gruyter, 1994), pp. 12-28.

Wüst, M., 'Die Einschaltung in die Jiftachgeschichte. Ri 11, 13-26', *Biblica* 56 (1975), pp. 464-79.

Wyatt, N., 'The Relationship of the Deities Dagan and Hadad', *UF* 12 (1980), pp. 375-79.

Yamauchi, E., 'Circumcision: Tepe Gawra', in E.M. Blaicklock and R.K. Harrison (eds.), *New International Dictionary of Biblical Archeology* (Grand Rapids: Zondervan, 1983), pp. 446-47.

Yee, G.A., 'By the Hand of a Woman: the Metaphor of the Woman-Warrior in Judges 4', *Semeia* 61 (1993), pp. 99-132.

Yon, M., 'The End of the Kingdom of Ugarit', in M.S. Joukowsky (ed.), *The Crisis Years: The 12th Century B.C.* (Dubuque Iowa: Kendall/Hunt, 1992), pp. 111-22.

Yoo, Y., 'Han-Laden Women: Korean "Comfort Women" and Women in Judges 19-21', *Semeia* 78 (1997), pp. 37-46.

Younger, K.L., 'Judges 1 in its Near Eastern Literary Context', in A.R. Millard, J. Hoffmeier, D.W. Baker (eds.), *Faith, Tradition and History* (Winona Lake: Eisenbrauns, 1994), pp. 207-27.

—'The Configuring of Judicial Preliminaries: Judges 1.1-2.5 and its Dependence on the Book of Joshua', *JSOT* 68 (1995), pp. 75-92.

Zadok, R., 'Historical and Onomastic Notes I: The Date of the Document ADD 1110', *Die Welt des Orient* 9 (1977), pp. 35-39.

Zakovitch, Y., 'bdn = ypth', *VT* 22 (1972), pp. 123-25.

—'The Sacrifice of Gideon (Jud. 6, 11-24) and the Sacrifice of Manoah (Jud. 13)', *Shnaton* 1 (1975), pp. 151-54.

—'Assimilation in Biblical Narratives', in J.H. Tigay (ed.), *Empirical Models for Biblical Criticism* (Philadelphia: University of Pennsylvannia Press, 1985), pp. 175-96.

Zawazki, S., *The Fall of Assyria and Median-Babylonian Relations in Light of the Nabopolassar Chronicle* (Poznan: Adam Mickiewicz University Press, 1988).

Zenger, E., 'Ein Beispiel exegetischer Methoden aus dem Alten Testament', in J. Schreiner (ed.), *Einführung in die Methoden der biblischen Exegese* (Würzburg: Echter Verlag, 1971), pp. 97-148.

—' "Durch Menschen zog ich sie..." (Hos 11, 4)', in L. Ruppert, P. Weimar, E. Zenger (eds.), *Künder des Wortes: Beiträge zur Theologie der Propheten* (Würzburg: Echter, 1982), pp. 183-202.

Zevit, Z., 'Yahweh Worship and Worshippers in the VIIIth Century Syria', *VT* 41 (1991), pp. 363-66.

Zsengellér, J., 'Personal Names in the Wadi ed-Daliyeh Papyri', *ZAH* 9 (1996), pp. 182-89.

INDEXES

INDEX OF REFERENCES

OLD TESTAMENT